ATLAS OF
ASIAN-AMERICAN
HISTORY

ATLAS OF ASIAN-AMERICAN HISTORY

Monique Avakian

Facts On File, Inc.

To Erin

– M.A.

Atlas of Asian-American History

Copyright © 2002 by Media Projects Inc.

Media Projects, Inc. Staff:
Executive Editor: C. Carter Smith Jr.
Project Editor: Carter Smith III
Principal Writer: Monique Avakian
Associate Editor: Karen Covington
Editorial Assistants: Ashley Bradley, James Burmester
Production Editors: Anthony Galante, Aaron Murray
Indexer: Marilyn Flaig

Facts On File, Inc.
132 West 31st Street
New York, NY 10001

Library of Congress Cataloging-in-Publication Data
Avakian, Monique.
 Atlas of Asian-American history / Monique Avakian.
   p. cm.
 Includes bibliographical references (p.) and index.
 ISBN: 0-8160-3699-3 (alk. paper)
  1. Asian Americans—History. 2. Asian Americans—History—Maps. I. Title.

E184.O6 .a89. 2001
973′.0494—dc21   00-049509

Facts On File books are available at special discounts when purchased in bulk quantities for businesses, associations, institutions, or sales promotions. Please call our Special Sales Department in New York at (212) 967-8800 or (800) 322-8755.

You can find Facts On File on the World Wide Web at http://www.factsonfile.com

Cover design by Nora Wertz
Text design by Paul Agresti
Layout by Anthony Galante and Aaron Murray
Maps by Anthony Galante, Aaron Murray, and David Lindroth

Printed in Hong Kong

CREATIVE USA FOF 10 9 8 7 6 5 4 3 2 1

This book is printed on acid-free paper.

CONTENTS

Note on Photos vi

Introduction vii

Acknowledgments ix

Chapter 1   The Asian Heritage: A Short History of a Continent 1

Chapter 2   Gam Saan: The Chinese in 19th-Century America 27

Chapter 3   Closing the Door: Asian Immigration from
Chinese Exclusion 53

Chapter 4   A Question of Citizenship: Asian-American History
from 1910 to 1946 107

Chapter 5   From Red Scare to Yellow Power: Asian-American History
from 1946 to 1972 145

Chapter 6   A New Wave of Americans 168

Chapter 7   Asian America Today 192

Selected Bibliography 206

Index 209

Note on Photos

Some of the illustrations and photographs used in this book are old, historical images. The quality of the prints is not always up to modern standards, as in many cases the originals are from old negatives or the originals are damaged. The content of the illustrations, however, made their inclusion important despite problems in reproduction.

INTRODUCTION

"Detained in this wooden house for several tens of days, it is all because of the exclusion law which implicates me. It's a pity heroes have no way of exercising their prowess. . . ." These bitter words were written by an anonymous Chinese immigrant, detained on the Angel Island Immigration Center in San Francisco Bay in about 1910. The frustration and anger so clear in this lone immigrant's words had ample cause, for as a Chinese, this man was a member of the first group of people explicitly excluded from immigrating to the United States strictly because of his race.

The Chinese Exclusion Act of 1882, which denied immigration rights to "lunatics," "idiots," and Chinese laborers, crystallized a longstanding national debate in a single government action. At that time, when a significant proportion of the U.S. population was either foreign born or just a generation or two removed from the land of their ancestry, the question of who should qualify for citizenship and who should not was one of the central issues in American life.

As this book illustrates, immigration policy is a function of numerous forces. Of those forces, the ebbing and flowing of American industry's demand for cheap—and ideally nonunion—labor played a key role in drawing migrant workers first from China, and then from Japan, India, Korea, and the Philippines to America's shores. It is no accident that this first wave of Asian immigration coincided with the end of the U.S. slavery system and, soon thereafter, with the birth and growth of the American labor movement. Active recruitment of each successive new group of laborers from Asia was a direct result of racially based animosity toward prior groups. For example, after the United States formally annexed the Hawaiian Islands in the 1890s, Korean and Filipino laborers were brought to the islands specifically to break up the growing organizational power of Japanese laborers who had preceded them.

When the backlash against immigration closed the door to most Asian immigrants (and to most immigrants other than northern Europeans) in the 1920s, Asian-American history became not so much the story of the reception that each new group of immigrants received, or even the ways in which each group tried to adapt to their new home, but instead an examination of what qualities make one an American in the first place. If a person is born and raised in the United States, is that person not as much an American as any other—regardless of racial identity or nation of ancestry? If one's parents were born in Japan instead of Britain, France, or Germany, should one be forbidden from owning property in one's adopted home?

Much of Asian-American history in the 20th century dealt directly with questions such as these. World events (such as World War II, the Korean War, the Vietnam War, the cold war, and even economic recessions) have shaped the way in which U.S. society has viewed Japanese Americans, Chinese Americans, Korean Americans, Vietnamese Americans, and all other Asian Americans, whether U.S. or foreign born.

While racially oriented immigration bans are now a thing of the past, Asian Americans continue to confront the burden of constant stereotyping, as the diverse communities that make up Asian America are still viewed by some as a monolithic group. When the media discuss achievements of some Asian Americans and then declare all Asians part of a "model minority," the individual identities of all Americans of Asian descent are called into question, and the very real problems of those individuals who may not fit the simplistic profile go unaddressed. This book attempts to correct the record by pointing out the ways in which such stereotypes have shaped how mainstream America has viewed Asian Americans and, even more important, the ways that individual Americans of Asian descent have challenged those stereotypes.

Because Asian-American history is in truth the overlapping histories of diverse groups of people, the nationalities discussed in this book were included based on volume of immigration to the United States. While people from every nation on earth have migrated to the United States over time, the vast majority of Asian Americans have come from relatively few nations. For that reason, the focus of the *Atlas of Asian-American History* is on Chinese, Japanese, Korean, Asian-Indian, Filipino, and Southeast Asian immigration. In terms of geographic scope the book concentrates on South, Southeast, and East Asia—essentially from India eastward and then northward to the Korean peninsula and Japan.

Consequently some smaller nations, such as Nepal, Bhutan, and Mongolia, are not emphasized, based on the relatively small number of immigrants in the United States from those countries. Likewise, Russia and the other nations of the former Soviet Union, which together encompass a vast portion of the Eurasian continent and are home to significant populations that can clearly be considered Asian, are also not included because migration from the central Asian republics, Siberia, and elsewhere in these regions has also been relatively small. Additionally, most immigrants from the former Soviet Union have come from the European territory west of the Urals, and hence fall outside the scope of this work.

Similarly, Pacific Islanders, though sometimes included in discussion of Asian and Asian-American history, are not Asian, properly speaking. While the book includes a brief review of precolonial Hawaiian history, that discussion is included to give context to the larger discussion of Hawaii's transformation into a plantation economy operated by white Americans and worked by Chinese, Japanese, Filipino, Korean, and other Asian laborers.

Also, a note on language. In recent years, standard practice for the translation of Chinese words has shifted away from the use of Wade-Giles style to favor pinyin. In general, this book follows that trend, exept in rare cases, where an individual is so commonly known in a nonpinyin form that a translation to pinyin would hinder clarity.

As an illustrated history of the immigration, migration, and acculturation of diverse groups to American society, this book addresses the theme of movement in several ways. In one sense, the struggle of Asian Americans to achieve acceptance and full civil rights is referred to as a movement. On a more basic level, the migration of people from place to place is another form of movement. Beginning with the early Chinese miners who arrived in California's Gold Mountains in search of riches and stretching all the way to modern-day professionals from the Philippines or India arriving to work in U.S. hospitals or high-tech laboratories, movement has defined the Asian-American experience. For that reason, the form of this book—an atlas—is especially appropriate. It is our hope that the maps included in these pages will help give concrete life to the story of how geographic as well as cultural and political borders have been crossed over the century and a half of Asian-American history. Likewise, we hope readers come away with an understanding of the consequences of those crossings and of the barriers that remain in the in the road toward full equality for all.

ACKNOWLEDGMENTS

The author and editors wish to thank the many people who have contributed greatly to this project. It was first conceived by Facts On File's Eleanora von Dehsen. Although the road to this book's completion has had its stops and starts, and bumps and turns, Eleanora and her noble team of successors Nicole Bowen, Terence Maikels, Dorothy Cummings, Gene Springs, and Cathy Rincon have together exhibited, not only an unerring editorial and design sense of what the project demands, but also perseverance, patience, and expertise. It was a pleasure working with them all.

The cartography work was also a collaborative effort. Many maps were prepared by David Lindroth, a very skilled independent illustrative map maker. Anthony Galante and Aaron Murray of Media Projects Incorporated contributed maps also, as well as handling production and layout work.

On the editorial side, an enormous amount of research went into this project, and we are grateful for all the hard work on that front performed by Carter Smith, Melissa Hale, Karen Covington, Kenneth West, Ashley Bradley, and Kimberly Horstman.

THE ASIAN HERITAGE
A Short History of a Continent

Asia, the world's largest continent, is home to three out of every five people on Earth. The combined populations of two of its countries—India and the People's Republic of China—make up more than a third of the world's population. Today, Americans of Asian descent are one of the fastest-growing population groups in the United States.

Because the number of civilizations in Asia is so large, Asian history is far more than one story. Instead, it is the story of many peoples, the unique civilizations they built, and the way that those civilizations have interacted with one another.

THE CROSSROADS OF ASIA

Throughout history, the continent of Asia has served as a crossroads of civilization. To Europeans, the promise of Asian trade led not only to exploratory excursions around the southern tip of Africa into the Indian

Geographically, the Ural Mountains east of Moscow divide Asia in the east from Europe in the west. Because this book focuses on those immigrants that have come to the United States in the largest numbers—from India, China, Japan, Korea, the Philippines, and Southeast Asia—the map below focuses on south and east Asia where those nations are located.

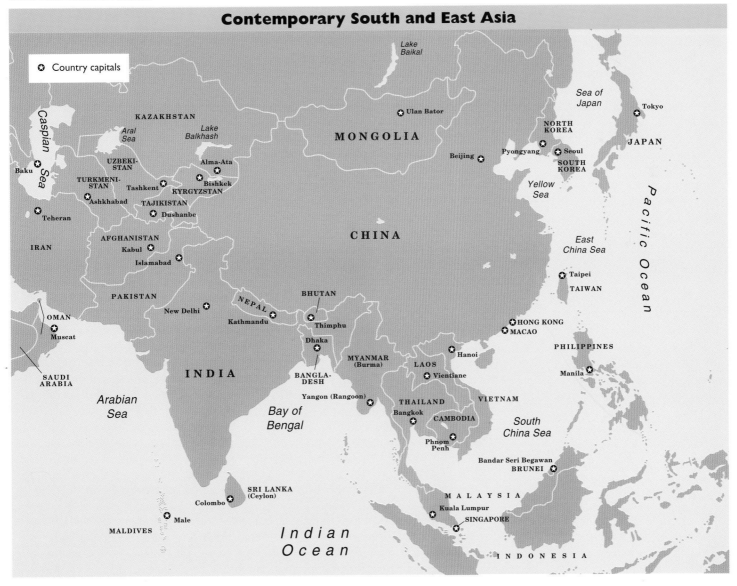

Contemporary South and East Asia

Hinduism

Hinduism is one of the oldest major religions in the world, dating from about 1500 B.C. Hindu beliefs are codified in two sacred books, the Vedas and the Upanishads. The Hindu caste system ranks people from the time they are born into four different groups, or *varna*:

1. brahmans, or priests;
2. *kshatria*, or rulers and warriors;
3. *vaisia*, landowners and merchants;
4. *sundra*, or peasants and laborers

The hierarchy ends with these four castes. Below these castes are outcasts known as untouchables because members of the four castes are forbidden from touching them. Untouchables work in jobs at the lowest end of the economic spectrum—cleaning, sewage maintenance, and similar fields.

The Hindu goal in life is to reach a state of enlightenment through which one can avoid the continual cycle of birth, death, and reincarnation. Enlightenment is achieved through the practice of yoga, compliance with scriptures, and devotion to a guru. The cyclical nature of life is symbolized by the chief Hindu gods, including Brahma (the Creator), Vishnu (the Preserver), and Shiva (the Destroyer).

Ocean and beyond to the shores of Southeast Asia, but also—however accidentally—to the discovery of North and South America.

Asia's status as a crossroads did not develop as a result of European contact. Because the continent is home to many of the world's oldest as well as economically and culturally rich civilizations, Asia has witnessed a complex pattern of cultural interplay. Buddhism, for example, emerged from India, and though it largely died out there, it spread to much of East and Southeast Asia, becoming the dominant religion in Southeast Asia, China, Japan, and Korea.

However, most individual Asian nations also have a long history of armed invasion by outside forces—from the Aryan occupation of the Indus valley of present-day India in about 1500 B.C. to the Mongol invasion of China in the 13th century A.D. to the repeated attacks on Korea, first by the Chinese and then by the Japanese. These invasions, while spurring the transport of culture from one region to another, have also contributed to a great wariness among many Asian civilizations toward outsiders. Ironically, this same pattern of condemning the influence of foreigners while simultaneously borrowing from and adapting some of their cultural practices and traditions has been a key element in Asian-American history. Likewise, this pattern has affected the way different Asian peoples viewed and adapted to each other, the way Asians viewed European outsiders beginning in the 16th century, and the way Asian immigrants to the United States have been viewed by white Americans since the first Chinese immigrants began arriving in California in the 19th century. The paradox of hostility toward outsiders on the one hand and eventual acceptance of some of their cultural traditions on the other is a theme that has infused the history of not only Asia but also the United States.

INDIA

In India, as elsewhere, geography influenced the emergence of early civilization. Natural barriers such as the towering Hindu Kush and Himalaya Mountains limited contact between the Indian subcontinent and the rest of Asia. However, the mountains did not completely protect India. On many occasions, invaders forced their way through steep passes in the Hindu Kush to descend onto the fertile plains of northern India.

The first Indian civilization is thought to have risen about 2500 B.C. in the Indus River valley. Little is known about the Indus valley

civilization, in part because scholars have not yet deciphered its form of writing. However, the remains of two well-planned cities—Harappa and Mohenjo-Daro—have revealed that a powerful government ruled the Indus valley for more than 1,000 years.

ANCIENT INDIA

In about 1500 B.C., the Aryans, a tribe of nomadic herders, crossed the Hindu Kush and conquered a dark-skinned people of northern India known as Dravidians, the descendants of the Indus valley civilization. The Aryans brought their own traditions and beliefs to India, gradually creating a new culture whose patterns continue to shape India to the present day.

The Aryans developed a written language, called Sanskrit, but maintained a rich oral tradition. During their conquest of India, a social structure emerged that gradually evolved into a rigid caste system. The system limited contact between the lighter-skinned Aryans and the dark-skinned Dravidians, who as a conquered people were now at the bottom of the social ladder. The main castes, or social groups, were the priests, the warriors, the landowners and merchants, and the peasants. Lowest of all were the outcasts, mainly Dravidians, who also became known as the untouchables. Untouchables were forced to work the dirtiest jobs, such as handling dead animals or sweeping the streets. Because they worked with dirt and blood, they were thought to be impure and they were forbidden to touch caste members.

The caste system included strict rules about every part of daily life. Each person's job was determined by his or her caste. A person's caste was determined by birth alone. Members of one caste could not marry, eat with, or work with members of another caste.

The caste system is one of the central tenets of Hinduism, one of the world's oldest religions. Although Hindus worship many gods, the three main gods in their pantheon are Brahma, the Creator; Vishnu, the Preserver; and Shiva, the Destroyer. Together, the three gods could be thought of as one god, called Brahman, the supreme force that unites everything in the universe. To Hindus, the ultimate goal of life is to free the soul from its individual existence and achieve reunion with a larger universal-soul. Hindus believe this process takes more than one lifetime.

Hindus of all castes were able to follow these strict rules because of their belief in reincarnation, or rebirth of the soul into a new body. They believed that each person would be reborn again and again until that

Aryan Invasion of Ancient India

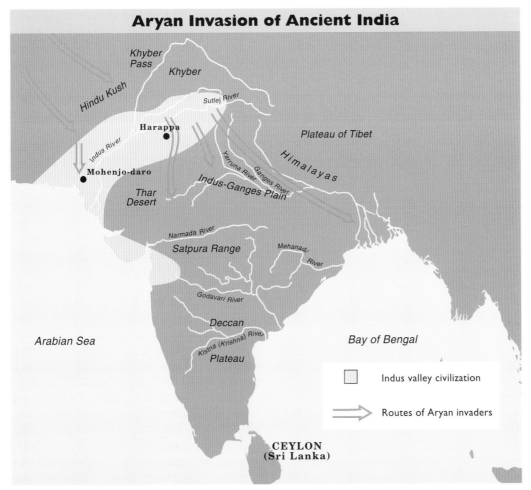

In around 1500 B.C. a nomadic people from central Asia, calling themselves Aryans, crossed the Khyber and Bolan passes into the Indus valley. As they did so, they conquered Indus valley cities and then left them abandoned, as they settled throughout northern India. Unlike the peoples of the Indus valley civilizations, the Aryans had no system of writing. Instead their priests preserved their culture by memorizing long hymns and poems in the Aryan language, an early version of the Sanskrit, which remains a sacred language in India.

Buddhism

Buddhism was founded in the 5th and 6th centuries B.C. by followers of Siddharta Gautama, later known as Buddha, or the Enlightened One. Like Hindus, Buddha taught that life is cyclical and that one is continually reincarnated before reaching a state of enlightenment. For Buddhists, this state is called nirvana. At the center of Buddhism are the Four Noble Truths:

1. Life is suffering.
2. The cause of suffering is desire.
3. The cure for suffering is to remove desire.
4. To remove desire, follow the Eightfold Path.

The Eightfold Path consists of:
1. Right knowledge.
2. Right thinking.
3. Right speech.
4. Right conduct.
5. Right livelihood.
6. Right effort.
7. Right mindfulness.
8. Right concentration.

person reached spiritual perfection. The Hindus thought that a person's caste was a reward or punishment for the way he or she lived in a past life. Those who led a good, dutiful life might be reborn into a higher caste. Those who lived a bad life might be reborn into a lower caste, or even into the body of an animal.

By the 6th century B.C., some Hindus were critical of the power of priests, the highest caste. One critic was Siddhartha Gautama, born a Hindu in 563 B.C. He set out to reform Hinduism, but his teachings became the basis for a new religion—Buddhism.

Although little more is known of the historic life of Gautama, legends of his life have been passed down through the ages. According to tradition, he was the son of a rich nobleman and as such was shielded inside palace walls throughout his young life, attended by servants. At about age 30, he left the palace and came across three men—one old, one sick, and one who had died. For the first time, he learned about aging, illness, and

death. On another trip he met a holy man, who carried nothing but a begging bowl, yet still appeared happy. Gautama realized that there was more to life than possessions. Leaving behind his wife and young child, Gautama set out on a spiritual quest. After a long search for the meaning of life, he discovered certain basic truths. He later taught that the only way to salvation was to overcome desire. Desire was the cause of pain and suffering. Buddhism offered guidelines to achieve nirvana, the condition of wanting nothing. From India, Buddhism spread to China, Korea, Japan, and Southeast Asia.

Throughout India's long history, the northern plain was a battleground for rival rulers. Some built strong empires. Among these, the Maurya Empire (321 B.C.–183 B.C.) and the Gupta Empire (A.D. 320–A.D. 467) left their mark on India. Asoka, the best-known Maurya ruler, extended his rule over much of India. After he converted to Buddhism, he set out to establish a government based on nonviolence and religious tolerance.

By the time of the Gupta Empire, Buddhism in India had been reabsorbed into Hinduism, although its influence remained strong in other parts of Asia. The caste system became more restrictive, and new subcastes emerged. Strict rules forbade people of different castes from speaking to one another. At the same time, the arts flourished. Artists and writers produced some of India's finest works during the Gupta period. In science and technology, Indians made important advances. They devised a decimal system and developed the concept of zero, ideas that would later be carried from India to western Europe.

By the 6th century A.D., Hindu traditions were deeply rooted in Indian society. The caste system and the power of the Brahmans, or priestly caste, helped ensure a stable social order at a time when warfare among Hindu princes prevented political unity.

These conditions were challenged in the 10th century, when the forces of Islam advanced into northern India. During the next 300 years, Muslim rulers, known as sultans, extended their control over much of the subcontinent. From their capital at Delhi, the sultans set up a strong government.

Unlike earlier conquerors of India, the Muslims were not absorbed into Hindu society. They would remain a powerful separate force strongly hostile to Hindu beliefs. To Muslims, who believed in one god, called Allah, the Hindu worship of many gods was a terrible evil.

Among the many points of conflict between Muslims and Hindus was the Muslim belief in the equality of all believers and the Hindu belief in the caste system. Muslims also insisted on strict obedience to the Koran, while Hindus were tolerant of many religious beliefs. Despite the frequent clashes, some blending occurred between Hindu and Muslim cultures, especially in the artistic and intellectual fields.

THE MUGHAL DYNASTY

In the 16th century, Babur, a chieftain of the Mongol people (a nomadic group from the steppes or grasslands of Mongolia) led Muslim Turks from central Asia into India. Babur, an ancestor of the great warrior Genghis Khan (whose exploits are discussed later in this chapter), founded an empire known as the Mogul or Mughal dynasty, which lasted more than 300 years.

Akbar, Babur's grandson, became the greatest of Mughal rajahs. Just 13 years of age when he came to the throne in 1556, he ruled for 50 years. Within the first few years of his reign, he conquered most of India and part of central Asia. He then turned his attention to strengthening his empire.

To improve the government, Akbar set up a civil service. Each job was given to qualified persons only, ensuring that many able people entered government service.

Construction of the Taj Mahal in the Indian city of Agra was begun in 1631 by the Muslim Shah Jahan of India. Built as a tomb in memory of Jahan's deceased wife, Mumtaz Mahal, it took 22 years to complete. The shah died, imprisoned by his son, before construction of an identical black tomb could be built for him. (Library of Congress)

To improve the lot of farmers, Akbar reformed the tax code. At the time, the major tax was on agricultural products, and each farmer was subject to the same tax. Under the new system, land was classified according to its ability to bear crops. Thus, taxes were lowered for those with less productive land.

Akbar proved a compassionate leader in other ways as well. There were fewer executions under his rule, and he ordered his officials to treat people kindly. He helped avert famine when regions suffered poor farming years by sending wheat from other, more fertile areas.

Although he was a Muslim, he followed a policy of religious tolerance, not only in words but also in deeds and in his private life—marrying women of different faiths. Two wives were Hindu, one was Christian, and one was Muslim. Akbar then did away with taxes that had been levied on non-Muslims and protected their temples. He also welcomed scholars of different faiths to his court.

Under Akbar, the Mughal court became a center of culture. The influence of Persia (modern-day Iran) was clear, as many wealthy Indians learned to speak Persian. Persian art, literature, and architecture were popular. Over time, Persian and Indian elements joined to form a separate Mughal style.

Akbar's grandson, Shah Jahan (1628–1658), was one of India's greatest builders. His major achievement was the Taj Mahal, a memorial to his wife. It is made of white marble with semiprecious stones set in flowerlike patterns and in sayings from the Koran.

The Taj Mahal was Shah Jahan's greatest achievement. Like other successors of his grandfather, Jahan reversed Akbar's policy of religious tolerance. As a result, he and other successors to Akbar faced a constant threat of rebellion from Hindu princes, which led to a looser rein on power. As Mughal power weakened in the late 17th century, the vacuum created opened new opportunities, first for Portuguese, and then for other European traders.

CHINA

Like India, China was also surrounded by imposing geographic barriers that limited contact with outsiders. High mountain ranges, rugged plateaus, deserts, and the Pacific Ocean protected China. As a result, the Chinese came to see their land as the Middle Kingdom—the center of the universe.

The first Chinese civilization developed in the Yellow River valley. There, fertile soil, called loess, was easily worked. However, this region of China suffered from droughts and floods, and the Yellow River earned the title "River of Sorrows" for the death and destruction brought by its flooding.

ANCIENT CHINA

During ancient times, powerful rulers extended control over the farming villages of the Yellow River valley. The Shang dynasty (1523 B.C.–1027 B.C.) was the first of many families to rule China. Many traditions and beliefs that emerged in Shang times shaped Chinese civilization for thousands of years.

The ancient Chinese believed that the gods controlled the forces of nature. They also believed that their ancestors could influence the gods. Shang kings acted as priests, performing daily ceremonies to ask their ancestors for the favor of the gods. The Shang invented a system of writing that used pictograms, or pictures of objects, and ideograms, symbols that expressed ideas or actions. The Shang also developed skills in bronze working and silk weaving and invented an accurate calendar that was adopted by later civilizations.

The Zhou dynasty (1027 B.C.–221 B.C.), which followed the Shang, built on these early achievements. The Zhou claimed to have won the "Mandate of Heaven," or divine right to rule. According to this belief only a just ruler who provided good government was entitled to rule.

The Zhou ruler established a system of feudalism, dividing his land among powerful nobles who then owed loyalty, military service, and tribute to the king. These feudal lords expanded the borders of China, often setting up their own independent states. As their states expanded, they developed complex bureaucracies, organizing the government into departments with appointed officials. In Zhou China, government officials gained an important place in society. Despite frequent warfare among rival feudal states, the Zhou era was a time of economic growth.

It was also a time that saw the flowering of three schools of thought that would shape Chinese history: Confucianism, Taoism, and Legalism. Confucius, who was born in about 551 B.C., was China's most influential philosopher. He was concerned with how to establish a stable, orderly society. Confucius taught that each person had a place in society, and each individual had responsibilities and duties toward others. He urged the ruler to set a good example.

Confucius (Hulton Getty Archives)

Confucius emphasized filial piety, or respect for one's parents and elders, and loyalty, courtesy, and hard work.

Taoism was both a religion and a philosophy. Taoists were most concerned with contemplation and achieving harmony with nature. The third school of thought, Legalism, claimed that the only way to achieve a stable society was through strict government control and rigid obedience to authority.

Legalist principles dominated the government of Shih Huang Ti, a powerful leader of the feudal state of Qin, who united China in 221 B.C. After years of civil war that ended the Zhou dynasty, Shih Huang Ti was determined to build a strong central government. He appointed officials loyal to him and improved the transportation system to ensure his control of the empire. His most spectacular achievement was the building of the Great Wall to protect northern China from invaders.

Although the Qin Empire was short lived (221 B.C.–202 B.C.), the subsequent Han Empire (202 B.C.–A.D. 220) was one of the most brilliant periods in Chinese history. Han rulers extended the border of China and established efficient government based on a civil service open to men of talent. During Han rule, the arts, sciences, and learning advanced. As trade increased, new ideas, including Buddhism from India, entered China.

As Europe was experiencing the Middle Ages (ca. 5th to 15th centuries A.D.) China entered two long periods of peace and good government. Under the Tang dynasty (A.D. 618–917) and Song dynasty (A.D. 960–1279), Chinese civilization spread. Its far-reaching influence ranged from Korea and Japan in the east to Southeast Asia and the borders of India.

The Chinese produced remarkable works of art and technology. They invented paper and a process for printing, developed the magnetic compass, and began to use gunpowder. As the economy expanded, the Chinese came in contact with ideas and new products from other parts of the world.

Despite these advances, Chinese society remained largely unchanged. Confucian ideals remained the basis of government and family life. The Chinese also continued to accept the idea that each person had his or her place in society and that an inferior owed loyalty and respect to a superior.

THE MONGOL EMPIRE

In the 13th century, the Mongols overran China and set up their own government. The Mongol threat to China began in about A.D. 1200 when a warlord named Genghis Khan united all of Asia's Mongol peoples. He gathered together an enormous army that traveled on horseback, lived off the land, and conquered all whom they came in contact with. In 1279, Genghis Khan's successors forced the Song rulers of China to abandon their rule.

Among Genghis Khan's successors was the emperor Kublai Khan (1260–1294). During his reign, traders who received his permission were allowed to travel across Asia to the cities of China. Among the traders who visited his court was the Venetian traveler Marco Polo. Polo lived in China from 1275 to 1292, during which time he became trusted enough by Kublai Khan to hold office for a time. When Polo finally returned home to Venice, carrying with him items such as noodles (which Italians had never seen before), he published a book describing the advanced civilization he had encountered. But Europeans refused to believe his reports.

In the 14th century, the Chinese drove out the Mongols and established the Ming dynasty. The Ming ruled China from 1368 to 1644 and created one of the greatest eras of orderly government and social stability in human history. Besides the dynasty's founder, the Hung Wu emperor (1368–1398), the Ming dynasty's strongest ruler was the Yung Lo emperor known as "The Consolidator" (1403–1424). One of Yung Lo's major achievements was to incorporate the states of South and Southeast Asia into China's tribute system. This tribute system was based on a global form of feudalism between the emperor of China and the rulers of other countries. Inherent in this relationship was the implication that China was the largest and oldest state in the world, and that as such, it was the source of civilization in general. The Son of Heaven (China's emperor) fulfilled his "fatherly" role by ensuring orderly government in the tributary "children" states by confirming the succession of new rulers, sometimes offering military protection against attack, and usually offering the opportunity for some trade with China.

Although this system was backed by China's military strength, the Ming rulers usually did not enforce this order of things through military means. Instead, they simply demanded that any foreign rulers who wished contact with the Middle Kingdom (China) accept its terms and acknowledge the universal supremacy of the Son of Heaven. Trade with China was incredibly valuable, and the formalities of the performance of the kowtow (the "three kneelings and nine prostrations"), the exchange of envoys, tribute, and conduct of diplomatic relations were the price to be paid.

Yung Lo's planned expansion of China's tribute system was marked by seven great maritime expeditions that began in 1405 and continued until 1433. These expeditions were led for the most part by a Muslim eunuch named Zheng He, whom the Chinese emperor considered well-suited by his faith to the job of extracting tribute from the Islamic rulers of South Asia. The first fleet sailed from 1405–1407 with 62 vessels carrying 28,000 men, and reached India, as did the second and third. The fourth voyage (1413–1415) reached Aden, and Hormuz on the Persian Gulf. A fifth voyage also went as far as Aden, and during the sixth, the fleet visited Southeast Asia, India, the Persian Gulf, and Africa. The seventh voyage started out with 27,500 men and reached Hormuz again in 1431–1433. Chinese vessels visited far down the east coast of Africa,

and seven Chinese reached Mecca, the Muslim holy city.

The development of Chinese shipbuilding and navigation techniques made Zheng He's voyages possible. His seagoing vessels, known as junks, were enormous—with four decks and up to a dozen watertight compartments. They navigated by compass and by using detailed sailing directions that brought them to the coasts of China's neighbors such as Siam (Thailand) and Vietnam, as well as to some 50 far-off places that were also enrolled as vassal states. Missions from Hormuz and the African coast came to China four times, from Bengal 11 times. Rulers in Sumatra and Ceylon (Sri Lanka) were brought back into the tribute system by force. The leaders of these expeditions gained adventure, fame, and profit. Commercially, these expeditions provided a line of communication with overseas Chinese communities in Southeast Asian ports. Politically, the tribute system was expanded from

Genghis Khan orders a caning. (Library of Congress)

In about the year 1200, the Mongol people of Asia's vast eastern steppe, or grassland, united under the command of Temujin, or Genghis Khan, which means "ruler of all between the oceans." Even after the empire divided into four territories, or khanates, in the the mid-13th century, it remained strong, as rulers of the three western khanates pledged loyalty to the China-based Great Empire of the Khan, in Turkistan, Russia. Between 1275 and 1292, the Venetian traveler Marco Polo traveled across Asia to the court of Kublai Khan, returning to Europe via the South China Sea and Indian Ocean.

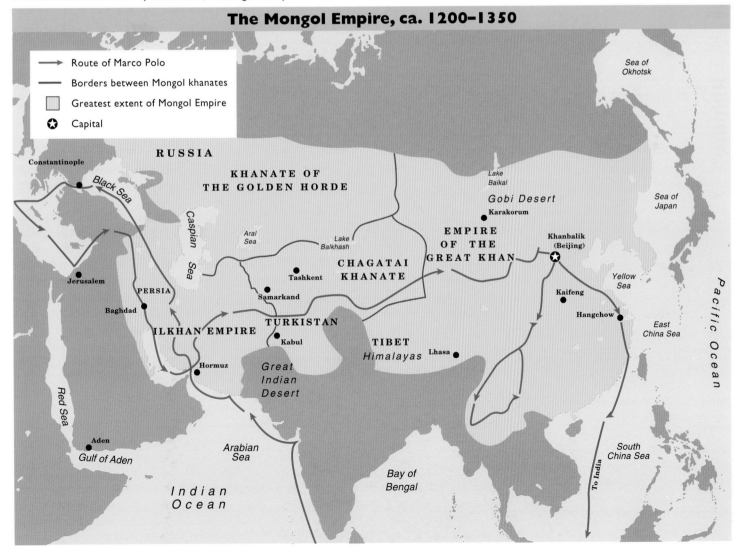

The Mongol Empire, ca. 1200–1350

→ Route of Marco Polo
— Borders between Mongol khanates
☐ Greatest extent of Mongol Empire
✪ Capital

The drawing above depicts Marco Polo on the Silk Road to China. As far back as Roman times, this trade route connected Europe and China allowing for the trade of silk, spices, and precious metals. (Library of Congress)

Manchu women's clothing was very simply cut, with material used for them varying with the seasons. In summer, wealthy women often wore an extremely light fabric known as ko-pu, while wearing siao-kien, a heavier material, in spring and fall, and touan-tse in winter. (from The Historical Encyclopedia of Costumes by Albert Charles Auguste Racinet)

land-based trading partners to sea-trading partners, thus incorporating much of the known world into the Chinese concept of the universal rule of the Son of Heaven.

After early 1433, China's days as a naval power were suddenly over, never to resume. One reason for this abrupt end was their great cost: At a time when the Ming were paying for military campaigns against the Mongols and financing the building of Peking (Beijing), the expeditions were criticized as expensive adventures. Rivals of the court eunuchs who promoted the expeditions, the scholar-officials, opposed the ventures so much that Zheng He's accomplishments were practically erased from the historical record.

Zheng He was an organizer, a commander, a diplomat, and a valued member of the court, but he was not a trader. Unlike traders in India, Arabia, or Europe, he was not interested in establishing commercial ventures overseas. This was partially due to the fact that the Ming government's major source of revenue came from land tax and not from trade tax. Thus, Ming China failed to become a maritime power. Through this default, the eastern seas and eventually China's own coast would be dominated by a succession of non-Chinese seafaring peoples—the Japanese; the Portuguese and Spanish; the Dutch; and finally the British, French, Russians, and Americans. First however, another group of invaders would

arrive out of the north of China, from a region known as Manchuria. These invaders, knonw as the Manchu, would dominate overthrow the Ming Empire to rule China from 1644 to 1910, when China would be transformed into a republic.

THE MANCHU PERIOD

North of China lies an enormous plain, historically populated by a variety of people. In the 16th century, these many tribal peoples united to form a powerful force known as the Manchu. In time, the Manchu became sufficiently strong to expand southward toward Ming China. By the turn of the 17th century, the Ming Empire had grown weak. High taxes had led many of its subjects into rebellion. Seeing an opportunity for expansion, in 1644, the Manchu swept into China and overthrew the Ming dynasty.

During the Manchu period, known as the Qing dynasty (1644–1910), the government kept a strong hand on power by using Chinese officials in the government and continuing the Chinese practice of civil service examinations. The Manchu also honored scholars and set about collecting great writings of China's past.

They also backed these accomodating measures with force by installing armies in major cities and moving Chinese officials from place to place so that the officials would never become too powerful in any region. They also ordered the destruction of books that cast them in an unfavorable light. And finally, they ordered that all Chinese men wear their hair as Manchu men did—by shaving most of their heads and wearing a long braid, known as a queue, down the back.

KOREA

The ancient land of Korea has been known as both the Land of the Morning Calm and the Hermit Kingdom. Both names are somewhat inaccurate, for the country's history has been anything but calm. Although Korea is geographically isolated from the world at large, it has been the scene of bloody wars between its three powerful neighbors—China, Japan, and Russia—for centuries.

The Korean peninsula stretches about 600 miles south from the eastern rim of Asia. Manchuria in present-day China borders it to the north. To Korea's west across the Yellow Sea is China, and to the east across the Sea of Japan lies Japan. The country is a land of rocky hills and mountains, with only 25 percent of the land suitable for farming. Korea's total land area is roughly 85,000 square miles, about half the size of California.

According to Korean mythology, the country began when a god turned bear into a woman. This woman had a son named Tangun. He began the country called Chosun in 2333 B.C.

Outside of mythology, little is known for certain of the peoples of the Korean peninsula prior to the establishment of the Han dynasty in China in 202 B.C. since no written records exist describing Korea before that time. Korean historians believe that the peninsula was first settled thousands of years prior to that date by tribes that came from the Altai Mountains in central Asia. These people migrated eastward toward Mongolia, Siberia, Manchuria, and Korea. Based on archeological remains found throughout the peninsula, it appears that these peoples had arrived via the northwestern coastal lowlands by the third millennium B.C. Initially fishermen and hunters, by around the 1st century B.C., the people of had developed a farming-based society, governed by three kingdoms. One of these kingdoms, Silla, unified the Korean peninsula in A.D. 668. In 918, Silla was overthrown and the Koroyo dynasty was established. In 1392, the Yi dynasty was inaugurated. It lasted until 1910.

THE "LITTLE BROTHER"

The Yi kings ruled Korea for more than six centuries, but they were troubled by frequent invasions and revolts sparked by their Japanese, Russian, and Chinese neighbors.

In the 15th and 16th centuries, the country was prosperous. It came to accept a close alliance with China, with whom it shared a common religion, Buddhism. Although China did not consider Korea its colony, Korea was a "little brother" state to China, the "parent" state. In time, however, other nations would seek to influence the Hermit Kingdom.

In the 15th and 16th centuries, Russia, under Czar Ivan IV (better known as Ivan the Terrible) began to expand eastward to Siberia to the Pacific Ocean. Eventually, Russia reached the frontiers of Manchuria, Korea, and the Siberian coast opposite the islands of Japan.

Russia's expansion was worrisome to Japan, particularly since the Japanese also had designs on Korea. Both Japan and Russia knew that if either country were to challenge China for regional power, control of the Korean peninsula was critical since it made an ideal invasion route in and out of the Asian mainland.

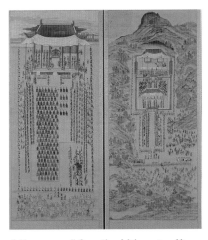

A Korean scroll from the 16th century Yi dynasty (Korean Information Service)

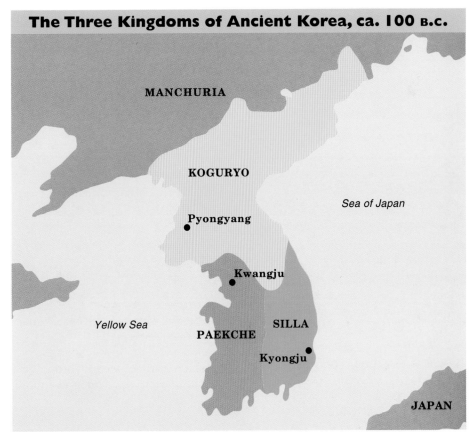

In the 1st century B.C. three kingdoms—Koguryo, Paekche, and Silla—formed on the Korean peninsula. The three fought for control on the peninsula for 500 years before Silla triumphed, uniting Korea under one government in 688 B.C.

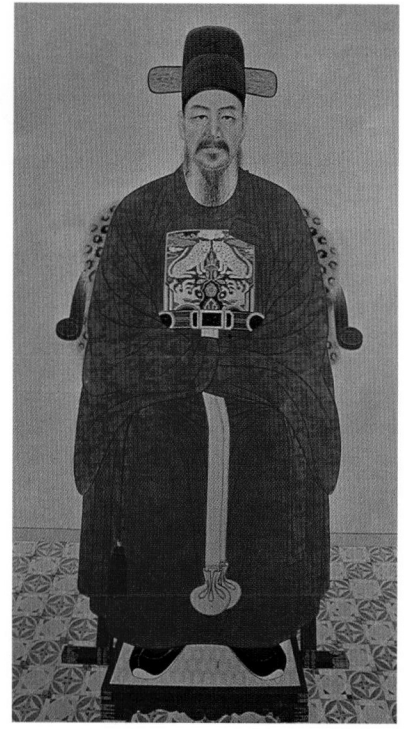

A Korean nobleman of the 16th century
(Korean Information Service)

The first attack on Korea was made by Japan in 1592, when it invaded the peninsula with a force of 200,000 men and captured the capital city of Pusan. When Korea appealed to China for help, the Chinese sent troops to fight alongside the Korean army. Rather than face two armies, the Japanese withdrew. In 1597, Japan made a second attempt to take Korea, but failed once again.

Korea's independence was not to last long. In 1627, 17 years before they overthrew the Ming dynasty in China, Manchu invaders seized control of Korea. For the next 250 years, Korea closed itself off from the outside world, with no contact with any foreign nation—with the exception of Manchu China.

JAPAN

To the east of both China and Korea lies the Japanese archipelago. Four main islands—Hokkaido, Honshu, Kyushu, and Shikoku—plus thousands of smaller islands make up the nation. Because of Japan's mountainous geography most of its inhabitants lived along the coastline.

Modern historians believe that the first distinct Japanese society dates back to 8000 B.C. These early people were a community of hunters, gatherers, and fishing people now called Jomon. By the 3rd century B.C., the Jomon were absorbed into a more advanced society—a farming society called Yayoi.

The sea strongly influenced Japan, providing a source of food and a barrier to invaders. Even today, young Japanese schoolchildren learn that their country's history began when the god Izanagi stood above the sea with his wife Izanami, atop "the floating bridge of heaven." After lowering his tightly held jeweled spear into the dark waters, he withdrew it, salt drops falling from the tip of the spear. As they fell, they hardened into a group of islands.

Izanagi then brought to life other gods. One, a sun goddess, sent her grandson Ningi to Earth to rule the new land. He arrived on the island of Kyushu carrying gifts from his grandmother—a huge jewel, a sacred sword, and a bronze mirror. These three objects remain today the symbols of the Japanese emperor's authority in Japan.

According to tradition, the year 660 B.C. is the date of the founding of Japan as a nation under the mythological Emperor Jimmu. According to the legend, Jimmu was a mortal descendent of the sun goddess Amaterasu, who sent him to Earth to establish order. Jimmu, Amaterasu, and other deities are still worshiped as part of Japan's Shinto religion.

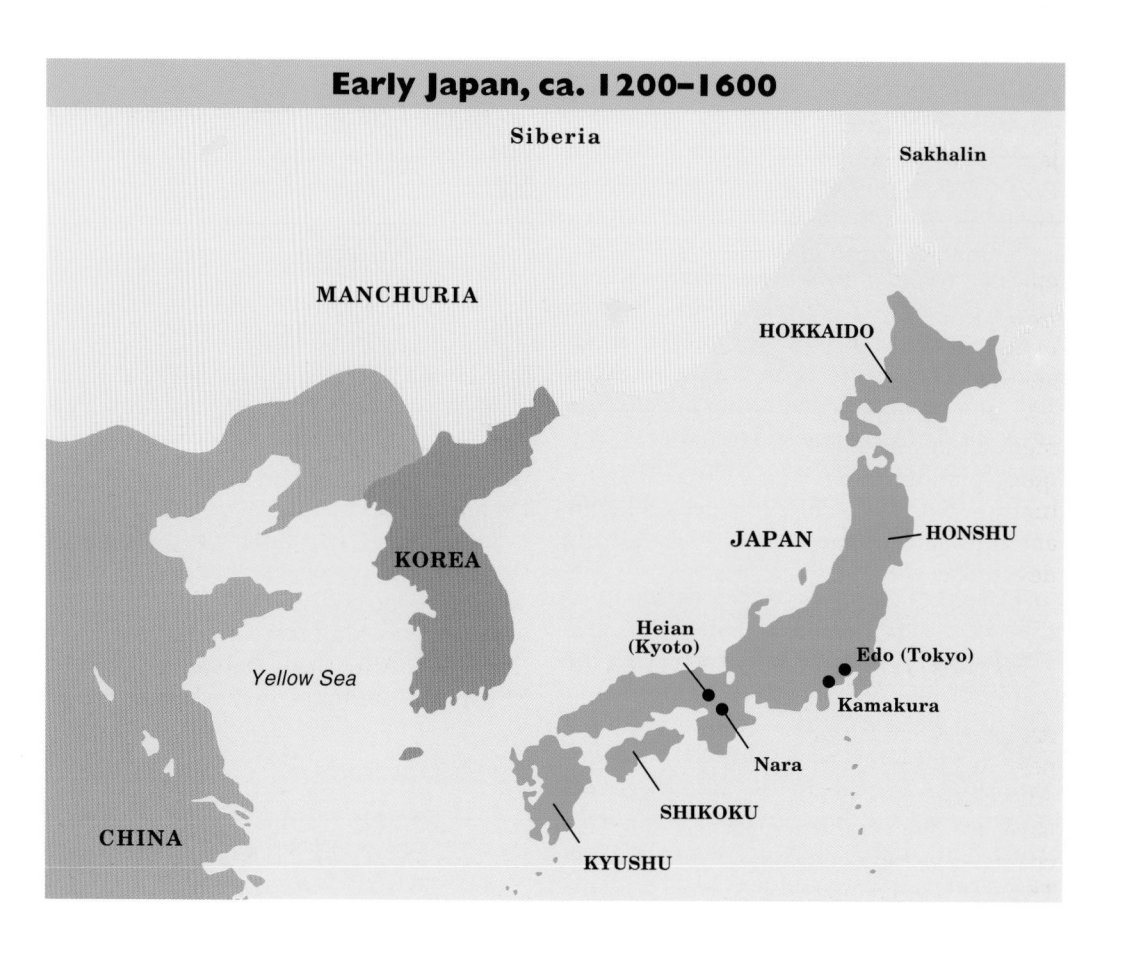

Shinto emphasizes both traditional Japanese deities and the forces of nature. Shinto developed out of the beliefs of Japan's early inhabitants. Nature played a central role in the religious worship of these early people, and all natural objects—including trees, mountains, rivers, the sun, or the moon—were imbued with living spirit, or *kami*. Thus early the early people of Japan viewed nature with great reverence and respect. In time, ancestor worship developed as another key tenet of traditional Japanese belief. Reverence for nature and ancestor worship fused together as the two key principles of Shinto, the only indigenous religion of Japan.

Because Shinto reflects Japan's history and traditions, it has become known as Japan's national religion. Many modern Japanese (and Japanese Americans), even those of other religions, continue to practice Shinto, and many mix elements of other religions with Shinto practices.

EARLY JAPAN

The Japanese title *mikado* means "ruler by divine right." Because of this idea, the emperor has always been held in high honor by the Japanese. Throughout Japan's history, both male and female rulers have been highly revered, even though their political power was usually in name only.

In A.D. 400, the Yamato family came to power, establishing the first and only Japanese dynasty. Under the leadership of Prince Shotuku (572–622), the Yamato family unified the Japanese islands under a single central government. During Shotuku's reign, Buddhism came to Japan from Korea and China. The Buddhist view—that life is a cycle of endless death and rebirth, which can only be escaped by reaching enlightened nirvana through meditation and other practices—was quickly adopted by Japan's rulers. Eventually, a Buddhist culture arose in Japan, and uniquely Japanese forms of Buddhism developed.

BORROWING FROM CHINA

Another practice borrowed from the Chinese was the Chinese form of writing. Although Japanese is a distinctly different language from those spoken in China, the character method of writing is quite similar. The first written Japanese history and poetry appeared during the reign of Empress Gemmyo (703–724).

The Japanese also took from China the idea of establishing a permanent capital. The Empress Gemmyo founded the first imperial capital in Nara in 710. When the capital moved to Heian-kyo (Kyoto) in 794, the Heian period (794–1185) began. The Japanese began to develop customs imported from China. Women took the lead in the development of Japanese literature, and Lady Shikubu Murasaki's novel *The Tale of the Genji*, written in about 1000, is a magnificent literary achievement.

Other Chinese influence was less welcome. In 1179, and again in 1281, Japan was threatened by China. Mongol warriors, led by Kublai Khan, tried to invade Japan. In the first attack, the Mongols were driven off by a strong wind and the courage and skill of Japanese samurai warriors. The second attack was halted by a typhoon, which destroyed the entire invading fleet. A Japanese chronicle described the typhoon of 1281:

The wind blew fiercely. The billows surged up to heaven, the thunder and the lightening dashed against the ground so that it seemed as if the mountains were crumbling down and high heaven falling to earth.

To the Japanese, the typhoon was not a coincidence, but a kamikaze, or divine wind, that had saved their country from invasion. This confirmed the ancient Japanese belief in the nation's divine origin and purpose in the world.

THE RISE OF FEUDALISM

Within Japanese society, an aristocracy emerged, led by the Fujiwara family. Members of the Fujiwara family became representatives of the emperors and thus held the real political power, but the imperial court continued to exist. Japanese respect for the imperial family and the highly religious nature of the emperor's role were still strong forces in Japanese culture.

In the late 12th century, the Taira clan vied with the Minamoto clan for control of the nation. After many battles, a victorious Minamoto Yoritomo took charge in 1192 and based his military headquarters in Kamakura. He took the title of shogun and built a system of feudal government that lasted 150 years. Known as the Kamakura period (1185–1333), it was a time of complicated relationships between puppet

---

The Way of the Warrior

During the Tokugawa era (1603–1868), Chinese Confucianism became very influential in Japan, particularly among samurai warriors. Samurai lived by a code known as Bushido, or "the way of the warrior." Bushido combined samurai loyalty and tradition with Confucian beliefs. The samurai's first duty was always to his lord and superior, for whom he would fight to the death. The code supported the samurai's unwavering responsibility to his lord, the nation, and the emperor.

According to the code, death was always better than surrender. If ever faced with capture, the samurai usually chose to commit seppuku (hara-kiri). This form of ritual suicide usually involved slitting open the stomach. Often a second samurai would complete the process by beheading his friend. Seppuku was considered especially well done if the samurai composed a poem while dying. Adherents believed that this form of suicide allowed the warrior to die with honor.

For the samurai warrior, the act of dressing for battle was a complex ritual. In the sequence of illustrations above, an archer prepares for battle, first by washing ritually and shaving the front and crown of his head, then donning layers of traditional clothing from a silk loin cloth to a full suit of armor. (from The Historical Encyclopedia of Costumes by Albert Charles Auguste Racinet)

rulers—those who appeared to have political power—and those who really ruled the country. In 1199, the Hojo family held the reins of government.

The Askikaga period, also called the Muromachi period, followed the fall of the Hojo government in 1333. This era lasted until 1568 and saw civil wars and a struggle for power between the various shoguns. The Onin War of 1467–1477 resulted in the collapse of the shogunate and all central power.

The century that followed is called the "Era of Warring States." This period was also known by the term *gekokojo*, "the lower defeats the upper," because vassals overthrew their lords. The new feudal lords were called daimyos. Though their domains were small, each daimyo controlled all the people in his territory—warriors, peasants, and merchants.

The Askikaga court was dominated by Zen (a sect of Buddhism) philosophy and tastes, which prize natural and simple ways. Followers of Zen put their beliefs into practice through rituals such as the tea ceremony, flower arrangement, and garden cultivation. These ordinary activities have great significance in Zen, for if performed correctly, they are thought to reflect the order and harmony of the universe. Another important art form that grew out of Zen was the Japanese No drama. Exemplifying the simplicity of Zen, with its bare stage and limited number of actors, No plays usually used Shinto or Buddhist beliefs or historical incidents for their themes.

During the Askikaga period, the Japanese began to look outward. The first Europeans—Portuguese traders—arrived in 1543. Six years later, St. Francis Xavier brought Roman Catholicism to Japan. In 1570, the port of Nagasaki opened to world trade.

Only a few centuries before, Japan had been an undeveloped and isolated nation. By the mid-16th century, the Japanese were able to compete on equal terms with the Chinese and Europeans. Merchants, both foreign and domestic, became prominent in Japanese society. Kyoto became the economic and political heart of the country. Technical advances, such as better farming methods that increased rice harvests, spurred economic growth.

The years between 1568 and 1600 are called the Azuchi-Momoyama period. During this time, Japan was again united under the efforts of leaders Oda Nobunaga and, after Nobunaga's assassination, Hideyoshi Toyotomi.

In an effort to stabilize Japan and control rebellious peasants, Hideyoshi enacted harsh measures. He introduced heavy taxes on the peasants and used the revenues to build great castles and palaces. Hideyoshi also forbade peasants to own or carry weapons, thus ending their ability to revolt. Finally, he prohibited any change in profession; this meant that warriors had to remain warriors, peasants had to remain peasants, and merchants had to remain merchants. Hideyoshi himself had risen to power from common roots, but he did not want his subjects to do the same.

As the presence of Christian missionaries grew in Japan, many Japanese leaders feared a religious and political takeover by outsiders. Hideyoshi officially banned Christianity in 1587. He declared that all missionaries must leave the country and demanded that Japanese Christians convert to Zen Buddhism. In 1597, he enforced these degrees by crucifying nine missionaries and 17 Japanese Christians.

Hideyoshi had great plans to "conquer the world"—which to him meant China and Korea. He invaded Korea in 1592, but Chinese forces repulsed his troops. He renewed the attack in 1597, but the invasion was abandoned after his death the following year.

After Hideyoshi's death, several shoguns competed for power. These conflicts set the stage for Japan's return to isolationism. Japan eventually became a world unto itself—an isolated nation of people who believed the Pacific Ocean would protect them from the outside world.

THE TOKUGAWA ERA

The course of Japanese history took a dramatic turn in the Tokugawa era, which lasted from 1603 to 1868. For 265 years, the Tokugawa family ruled Japan, strengthening and unifying the country from within while isolating the people from the outside world. Tokugawa Iyeyasu took power through military conquest during the Battle of Sekigahara in 1600. He founded his family's military government three years later.

The country was divided among more than 200 feudal lords. Those who had supported Tokugawa Iyeyasu's rise to power received the best land. The Tokugawa government enforced its power with a system of "alternate attendance," which required the lords to spend a part of the year at the Tokugawa capital of Edo (present-day Tokyo). Their families were held hostage there year-round to reduce the possibility of revolt. Guards along the roads to and from Edo checked for illegal weapons or for wives attempting to sneak out of the city. Though strictly bound to the shogun, loyal lords were free to govern their own lands without interference.

The Tokugawa family never sought the imperial throne, but the emperor's role became one of ceremonial and religious leadership. No one could approach the emperor without receiving permission from a Tokugawa representative.

Although Zen Buddhism remained influential, Chinese Confucianism began to play an important role in Japan. Because Confucianism stresses the importance of loyalty to rulers and respect for tradition, the philosophy served to solidify Tokugawa rule. Tokugawa Iyeyasu himself was a Buddhist, but his religious beliefs also included Shinto elements. Like the samurai warriors of the time, he adopted a strict code of ethics. This code supported his desire for an orderly country ruled by a strong government. Confucian philosophy also supported the class structure firmly established by the Tokugawa shogunate. The top class consisted of the warrior-rulers. Peasant farmers were next in line, followed by artisans. Merchants, or *chonin*, held in low regard by Confucius and his followers, occupied the lowest rung on the ladder.

Notwithstanding the low status of merchants, Tokugawa Iyeyasu saw the practical value of foreign trade and was reluctant to isolate his country from the world. In the earliest years of the Tokugawa shogunate, Japanese ships continued to travel abroad, and Japan welcomed traders from Korea, China, Portugal, England, and Spain. He was more tolerant of Christians living in Japan than his predecessor Hideyoshi had been. But as Christians entered Japan illegally and more Japanese began to practice the religion, his son Hidetada and other Japanese leaders feared domination by the Spanish and Portuguese. This fear led to the widespread persecution of Japanese Christians.

Between 1613 and 1626 more than 3,000 Japanese Christians died at the hands of the government. It was not unusual for Christians to be crucified or beheaded. In 1637, more than 20,000 Christian-led peasants rebelled in Shimabara and were subsequently massacred by the shogun's warriors.

The suppression of Christianity led to more restrictions for the Japanese people. Tokugawa Iemitsu (1623–1651) issued a series of proclamations known as the Exclusion Decrees. Japanese faced death if

ART OF THE GENROKU PERIOD

Despite Japan's isolation from the outside world, the nation's own culture flourished during this period. Near the end of the 17th century, a renaissance in the arts took place. This period, known as the Genroku period (1688–1704), saw the flowering of Kabuki theater, which evolved from simple dance performances to dramatic plays. Kabuki was a realistic and dramatic form of theater, a sharp departure from the calm and religious No dramas of earlier times.

Haiku, poetry written in 17-syllable form (a line of five syllables followed by one of seven, finished by another five-syllable line), was written by poets such as Basho. One of Basho's most famous poems is "A Crow on a Bare Branch":

> *On a withered bough*
> *A crow alone is perching:*
> *Autumn evening now.*

The most popular visual art of the period is known as *ukiyo-e*, or "pictures of a floating world." Artists produced ukiyo-e pictures by carving and coloring wooden blocks and then pressing them against paper. Master artists like Huksai and Hiroshige raised ukiyo-e to a high art. Colored copies of ukiyo-e pictures could be made easily and sold to people at reasonable prices, thus creating an art for the common people. Because this work was created with commerce in mind, it tended to express the tastes of merchants more than any other class.

DUTCH TRADERS IN JAPAN

During the early 17th century, Japan's rulers severely limited Japan's contact with the outside world. Books were banned, Christians persecuted, and almost all foreigners forced to leave Japan. While a few Dutch traders were allowed to stay, their movement was limited to the island of Deshima in Nagasaki Bay. This tiny colony became Japan's only link to the outside world.

Though Deshima was designed to limit contact between the Dutch and the Japanese citizenry, contact between the two cultures was unavoidable. The Dutch lived as they did in Holland. They imported furniture, clothes, and books. Officials appointed to deal with the Dutch learned Western customs and outside news. Japanese interpreter-students began to seek out methods and knowledge that they lacked, even though such learning was against the law.

In time, restrictions on contact were gradually relaxed. Some Japanese became convinced of the importance of contact with other nations. Students who engaged in "Dutch learning" helped to spread this idea, stressing that Japan could not continue to progress without learning about new scientific discoveries from the West. Although critics still demanded that Japan stay away from Western "barbarians," by the mid-19th century, these students called for a return to the world, using the slogan "Eastern ethics and Western science." The students felt that Japan had fallen behind and was in danger because of its ignorance.

After the Meiji Restoration of 1868, when the new emperor opened Japan to the outside world, these students became revered teachers and translators. Because they could read, write, and speak Dutch, they were familiar with European advances in geography, astronomy, navigation, and mathematics. Also, they translated many Western books into Japanese. Though these "Dutch learners" had not succeeded in convincing their leaders to open up Japan to the world, once the door was reopened, they helped their country adapt quickly.

caught trying to leave the country. Japanese already visiting or living overseas were forbidden to return, under threat of execution. Foreign books were banned. The building of oceangoing ships was prohibited, and crews of foreign vessels were to be executed if their ships landed in Japan. The shogunate allowed only a few Dutch traders to stay in Japan, and they were confined to the small island of Deshima in Nagasaki Bay.

JAPANESE ISOLATIONISM

By 1639, Japan had closed its doors to the rest of the world, beginning the most extreme period of isolation in Japan's history. Despite this isolation, the period witnessed a revolution in the arts, particularly during the years 1688 to 1704, known as the Genroku period. New forms of poetry, drama, and art were developed. Cities were the focus of Tokugawa culture. Edo, now Tokyo, was at the enter of this cultural revolution.

When Iyeyasu moved his capital to Edo in 1600, it was little more than a village, but it evolved rapidly. The shogunate and the families of the daimyos needed merchants, artists, craftspeople, and servants to supply their needs. Merchants who sold their wares in Edo flourished and the city soon became the commercial center of all Japan. By 1790, Edo had become one of the world's largest cities, with a population of more than 1 million.

As the cities and population of feudal Japan grew, the nation's economy began to change. Conflict broke out between the agricultural economy of the countryside and the trade-based economy of urban Japan. In keeping with Confucian ethics, the shogunate considered urban merchants the lowest social class and taxed them heavily. Nevertheless, they prospered.

The samurai, on the other hand, struggled during the Tokugawa period. Trained only in war and paid little in peace, many samurai had difficulty finding other work. Some became civil servants, but many spent their days in idle boredom. Although they received some income from land taxes, these were paid in rice, while everything they needed to buy had to be paid for in cash. The shogunate forgave much of the samurai debt, but many samurai still became deeply indebted to urban moneylenders.

Despite heavy taxation, a group of peasant entrepreneurs emerged that had adapted to the money-driven economy of trade. Newly formed crafts guilds also supported the efforts of artisans. However, the peasants left behind in the wake of change suffered greatly. With no land of their own, many became tenant farmers who worked the lands of wealthier nobles in return for a place to live. This arrangement, similar to the sharecropping system of the American South and the peonage system of colonial Latin America, created a cycle that locked tenant farmers into poverty.

During the second half of the Tokugawa rule, uprisings broke out both in cities and the countryside. Between 1783 and 1787, opposition to the shogunate grew among the poor. Widespread famines in 1838 threatened the national economy but there was no rebellion broad-based enough to overthrow the feudal system.

Although the Tokugawa shogunate was rarely in danger of overthrow during its 265-year reign, by the second half of the 19th century, many Japanese had become restless. Students were tired of censorship. Merchants and craftspeople were tired of heavy taxes. A few young intellectuals wished to seize upon the economic and political developments of the West, particularly in the area of science. Intellectuals also launched a movement called *kokugaku* (national learning) to develop self-respect and revive interest in ancient Japanese literature. The *kokugaku* movement also supported the right of the emperor to rule the country directly.

While the government relaxed some of the restrictions it had initially imposed in the 17th century (the ban on non-Christian Western books was lifted in 1720, for instance), the Tokugawa still refused to open Japan's borders to outsiders. Despite attempted visits by the French, the British, Russians, and Americans, the isolation policy remained in force well into the 19th century. It would take a menacing threat from the outside, combined with growing internal unrest, for Japan to consider rejoining the world.

SOUTHEAST ASIA

East of India, across the Bay of Bengal, lies Southeast Asia. It includes the present-day countries of Myanmar (Burma), Thailand, Laos, Cambodia, Vietnam, Malaysia, Indonesia, Singapore, and Brunei. The Philippine Islands, which lie to the northwest of Indonesia, are sometimes considered part of Southeast Asia as well since the people of the Philippines share a common ancestry with those in other regions of Southeast Asia. (For most of its history, the Union of Myanmar was known as Burma. In 1989, Burma's dictatorial military government changed the country's name. For purposes of description of events prior to 1989, the historical name of Burma is used.)

EARLY CIVILIZATIONS IN SOUTHEAST ASIA

In 1891, on the banks of the Solo River in Java, Indonesia, part of a human skull believed to be a million years old was found. Little else is known of Southeast Asia before about 8000 B.C., when waves of people began to move into the region, chiefly from the north, moving down the Malay Peninsula. While this may have been one of the earliest incursions by northern people into Southeast Asia, it was far from the last. For much of its history, the region has been one of the world's most culturally diverse. Burma alone includes more than 100 different language groups.

Most of the population of Southeast Asia are descendants of the Malay, settlers who arrived in two waves, between about 2000 B.C. and 1000 B.C. The earliest group settled in central Sumatra and the Sunda Islands. The second wave settled along the coastal regions.

The Malay developed the method of cultivating rice in irrigated paddies. They raised cattle, pigs, and chickens, and trained water buffalo to work as labor animals. The Malay were also seafarers who carried trade to the coasts of India, East Africa, and Madagascar.

In addition to the Malay, other peoples inhabiting Southeast Asia are the Negrito, who populate the inland regions of Malaysia and the Philippines and until recent decades were still a preindustrial seminomadic society; the Mon, who arrived from China and followed the Mekong River southward, or traveled the rivers of Burma, and then settled there; the Khmer, who also traveled the Mekong south, before heading east into Laos; and the Vietnamese, who are believed to have originated in China as well.

Much of the great ethnic diversity of Southeast Asia is rooted in geography and trade. Southeast Asia lies on the most direct sea route between India and China. Throughout Asian history, the key to political power has often been control of trade routes and harbors. Pirates frequently terrorized trade ships, and powerful local kings used their fleets to protect merchants from those pirates. In return, the kings charged merchants high fees to use their ports or pass through their waters.

TRADERS FROM INDIA

Even before the rise of the Gupta Empire (A.D. 320–A.D. 467) in India, traders from South Asia were plying the seas of Southeast Asia, attracted by gold from the Malay Peninsula, precious jewels, spices, and fragrant woods such as sandalwood.

During the Gupta era, Buddhist missionaries were active in Southeast Asia. Hinduism, too, spread widely in the region. The people of Southeast Asia adopted many Hindu beliefs and worshiped Hindu gods—particularly Shiva and Vishnu. However, key tenets of Hinduism—the caste system, in particular—were not adopted.

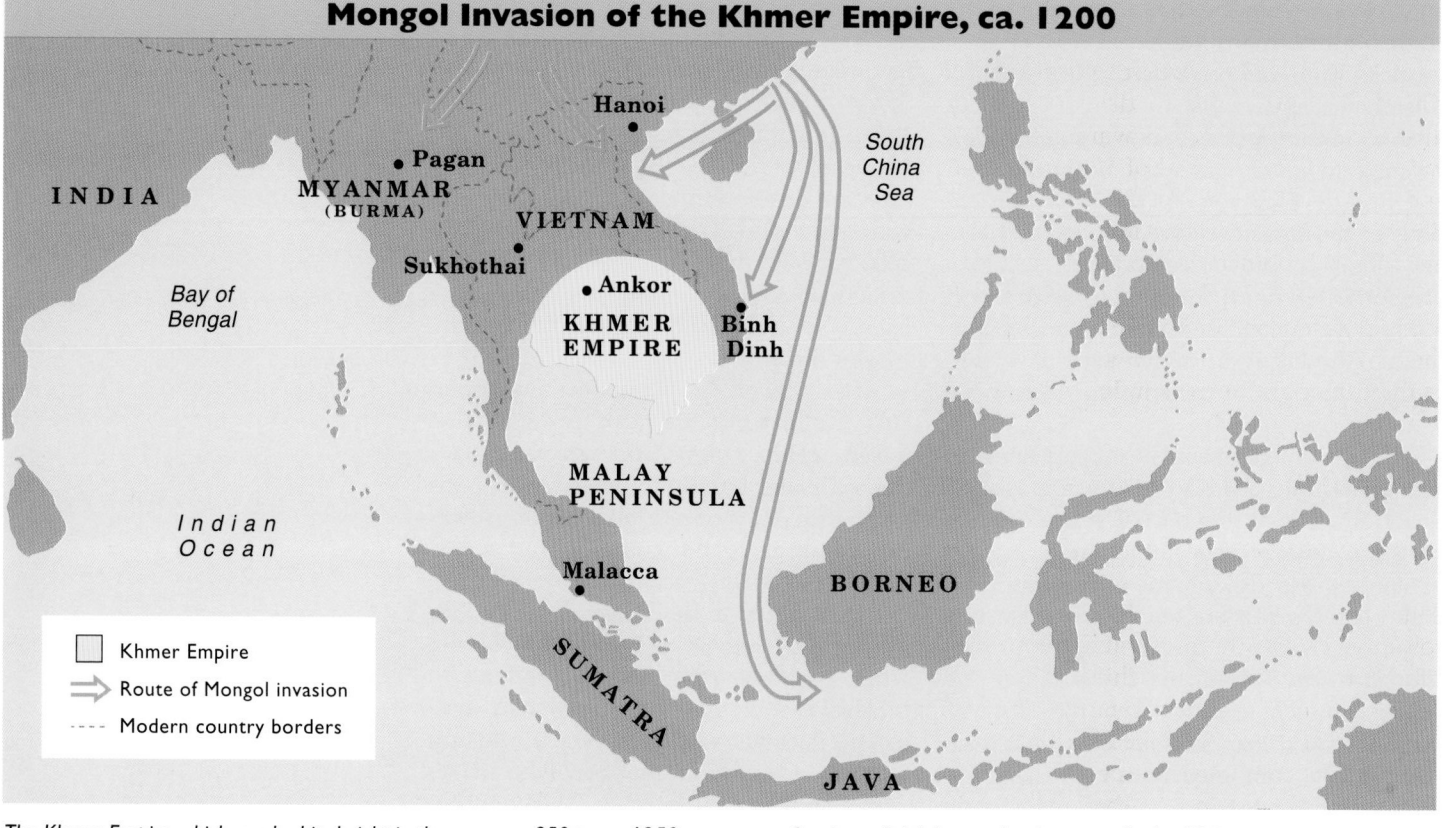

Mongol Invasion of the Khmer Empire, ca. 1200

The Khmer Empire, which reached its height in the years A.D. 850 to A.D. 1250, was among Southeast Asia's longest-lived empires. In the 13th century, Mongol invaders, who managed to capture neighboring Vietnam and Burma, weakened the Khmer Empire, but did not defeat it. The Khmer capital of Ankor Wat finally fell to Thai invaders in 1430.

In time Indian culture spread into many secular aspects of Southeast Asian societies. Poets wrote long, elegant poems in Sanskrit, featuring Hindu gods and warriors. Southeast Asian rulers adapted Indian architectural styles in building their palaces and temples and enjoyed Indian music and dance. Some kings even recruited Indian Brahmans to serve as royal officials in their courts. In addition, Indian traders and merchants often settled permanently in Southeast Asia with their families.

THE KHMER EMPIRE

Many kingdoms rose and fell in Southeast Asia's river valleys and deltas and on its islands. None was ever able to unite the region, but many of these kingdoms had periods of glory and left monuments of lasting beauty.

Among the most long-lived empires of the region was the Khmer. The Khmer came from the northern part of present-day Cambodia and moved southward along the Mekong River before establishing a small kingdom in the late 6th century. They then gradually expanded at the expense of neighboring kingdoms. The greatest Khmer

king was Jayavarman II, who came to the throne in A.D. 802. In his 50-year reign, he greatly enlarged the Khmer, reaching the border of Burma.

Each of the major religions in the region was brought by outsiders. From India came both Hinduism and Buddhism. By the 14th century, Muslim traders carried their religion with them to the region, and more recently Christian missionaries have affected Southeast Asia as well. Because of the heavy influence of China in the region, Confucianism has also had a major impact.

The Khmer's greatest period is known as the Ankor period (850–1250), after the capital city of Ankor. The most famous building in Ankor is Ankor Wat, a temple to the Hindu god Vishnu. Built in the early 12th century, the temple is more than half a mile long. Although now in ruins, during its use the temple had a surrounding moat reflected its nine golden-roofed towers, each in the shape of a lotus blossom, symbolizing the beauty, fragrance, and power of life. Ankor Wat included a library, as well as living quarters for priests.

Khmer aristocrats lived in fine houses with tile roofs, as opposed to the thatched-roof homes of commoners. They rode in

Women in Khmer Society

Women in 6th and 7th century Khmer society in present-day Cambodia, as in many Southeast Asian societies, had high status. Women in the lower classes ran market stalls, selling ivory, feathers, oils and perfumes, and pearls. Upper-class women were often well educated and frequently served as royal judges. All the king's guards and servants were women, for only women were allowed in the palace.

gold and silver sedan chairs, carried on the shoulders of their servants.

Following the Ankor period, the Khmer Empire began to decline. It was threatened by Mongol warriors, who sacked Vietnam's capital of Hanoi in 1257 and conquered Burma in 1287. The Khmer Empire never fell to the Mongols, but it eventually did succumb to another group of people—the Thai—who followed the Mongols from China. The Thai established their own kingdom, which grew stronger as the Khmer grew weaker. In 1430, a Thai army captured Ankor.

CHINA'S IMPACT ON SOUTHEAST ASIA

Although China saw Southeast Asia as a collection of "little brother states" that owed tribute to the emperor, Chinese cultural influence on the region was far less significant than might be imagined. Certainly, to the Chinese, the various peoples on its southern frontier were "barbarians" much in the same way that Koreans and any other outsiders were. As such, virtually every leader in Southeast Asia was forced at one time or another to pay tribute to the emperor. Some even showered China with gifts in exchange for protection. Only Vietnam fell under direct Chinese rule, however. Around 100 B.C., during the Han dynasty, China took much of Vietnam, and Vietnam remained under Chinese influence for 1,000 years.

Even with China's political domination of Vietnam, its influence on Southeast Asia, was strictly political, as opposed to cultural. Although the Vietnamese accepted many Chinese ways, including Chinese literature, political concepts, and Confucian and Buddhist ethics, they never thought of themselves as Chinese. The Vietnamese kept their own language and customs and frequently rebelled against Chinese leaders. When the Tang dynasty grew weaker in the early 10th century, Vietnam broke away and became an independent kingdom.

In the 12th century, Kublai Khan's Mongol warriors swept into Southeast Asia, devastating local villages to such a degree that 100 years later Marco Polo would comment that they "cannot be reoccupied and barely traveled through." Nonetheless, Mongol China's impact was strictly military. Nor did Chinese influence grow after the Ming expelled the Mongols from China. Even during the brief period (discussed earlier) in which Zheng He's fleet sailed the Indian Ocean as far as East Africa, thus emphasizing Middle Kingdom's place at the center of the political universe, China never set out to colonize far-flung—or even most nearby—territories. Nor did it seek to establish formal trading partners. Instead, the most active trading continued to come from the region's west—from India. Consequently, it was Indian culture that remained the most influential in Southeast Asia.

MUSLIM TRADERS

During the last years of the Khmer Empire in Burma, Muslim traders from Arabia and India began to reach Southeast Asia. Between the 13th and 15th centuries, these traders brought with them their religious beliefs, much as the Hindu and Buddhist traders before them had done.

By the 13th century, the north Indian port of Cambay had become a thriving hub of trade between Europe, the Middle East, and East Asia. Persians, Arabs, Armenians, and Turks carried pearls, perfumes, dyes, and Venetian glass into Cambay to exchange them for timber, spices, silk, tin, and gold brought from Java, Borneo, Sumatra, and the Malay Peninsula by Muslim merchants. Indian Muslims recognized the advantage of establishing themselves closer to the sources of their raw materials. Hence many moved to Indonesia and eventually concentrated much of their business in the Malayan coastal town of Malacca.

By 1500, Malacca had become a booming city-state, nominally under the rule of a Malay, but in practice dominated by Indian merchants. Malacca's streets were soon crowded with people from around the world, trading in goods from across Eurasia. "Men cannot estimate the wealth of Malacca," one Portuguese visitor wrote.

In time, Islam spread to local kings, who became Muslims while holding on to some of their Hindu practices. In addition, Islam filtered down to many of the common people in the region who were attracted to Islam's message that all believers are equal in the eyes of Allah.

THE COMING OF THE EUROPEANS

As Ming dynasty junks sailed the waters of the Indian Ocean to proclaim China's preeminent position in Asia and Muslim merchants began moving eastward into Southeast Asia, European vessels still seldom left the waters of the Mediterranean.

Prince Henry the Navigator (Library of Congress)

By the mid-15th century, just a few years after the Chinese emperor outlawed overseas voyages, this situation began to change. Two nations in particular, Portugal and Spain, began searching for new trade routes. As a result, they sponsored many voyages of discovery.

EXPANDING HORIZONS IN EUROPE

Advances in technology helped make the European voyages of exploration possible. Using travelers' reports such as those of Marco Polo and information from Arab geographers, mapmakers drew more accurate land and sea maps. On charts of the oceans, they began to include lines of latitude, which showed distance north and south of the equator. Mapmakers also showed the direction of ocean currents. Navigators developed better ways to chart courses at sea. Sailors could calculate a ship's latitude using the astrolabe, an instrument that measured the positions of stars. They had no instruments to measure longitude, the distance east and west of a certain point, but they could estimate it. Europeans also adopted the magnetic compass, a Chinese invention that had reached them via Arab traders in the 13th century. With it, sailors could determine their location even when they were out of sight of land. Shipbuilders designed sailing vessels that were well suited to ocean voyages. For example, the Portuguese developed a three-masted ship called a caravel that could carry more sail than earlier European ships, while also having more room for cargo and food supplies. Europeans also used the lateen, or triangular sail, an innovation borrowed from the Arabs. The lateen and another improvement, the stern rudder, gave ships greater speed.

PORTUGUESE EXPLORATION

Portugal led the way in voyages of exploration. Initially the Portuguese were at a disadvantage in trade with Asia because Portugal faced the Atlantic Ocean rather than the Mediterranean Sea. Most spices were brought overland by Arab merchants to ports in the eastern Mediterranean. From there, Italian ships carried goods across the Mediterranean to Europe.

During the 1400s, Portugal was ruled by several practical, ambitious monarchs who wanted to increase their nation's wealth. They supported voyages in search of gold. They also concluded that the only way to gain a share of the rich spice trade was to bypass the Italian and Muslim traders who controlled the Mediterranean markets.

Prince Henry, commonly known as Prince Henry the Navigator, encouraged the early Portuguese explorations. He established an informal school for sailors at Sagres on the southern tip of Portugal. There he brought together astronomers, geographers, and mathematicians to share their learning with Portuguese sea captains and pilots.

At first, the Portuguese tried to open new trade routes by conquering coastal cities in North Africa. But the Sahara caravans that had once brought gold to North Africa from the West African kingdoms no longer operated. The Portuguese then decided to seek the source of gold itself, and they began to explore the west coast of Africa. Historically, the sea route along the African coast had been unpopular because ocean currents and winds off Cape Bojador often drove ships onto the rocky coast and wrecked them. To avoid this, the Portuguese charted a new route. They sailed west, where they discovered two groups of islands in the Atlantic—Madeira and the Azores. From these islands, they picked up favorable winds and currents that carried them south safely along the African coast.

As the Portuguese moved south, they searched for gold wherever African rivers ran into the Atlantic. However, they could not travel far inland along the rivers because of waterfalls and rapids. Instead the Portuguese established trading stations along the coast of Africa where Portuguese traders bought gold and ivory from people living nearby. In fact, the area became known to Europeans as the Gold Coast. In 1441 traders also began purchasing slaves, paving the way for the transatlantic slave trade to the Americas that would begin in earnest in the 16th century.

After Prince Henry's death in 1460, Portuguese exploration lagged. But in 1481, King John II launched new efforts. John II dreamed of a rich trading empire in Asia. He knew that to do so, he had to find an all-water route around Africa that would allow Portugal to trade directly with India and China. The king urged Portuguese sea captains to explore farther and farther south along the African coast.

In 1488, Bartholomeu Dias rounded the southern tip of Africa. Dias named it the Cape of Storms because his ship had been buffeted so violently there. But King John II renamed it the Cape of Good Hope because he realized Dias had found the passage around Africa to India. King John II then decided to send an expedition to India. In 1497, after much preparation, Vasco da Gama set out from Portugal with four ships. Da Gama quickly rounded the Cape of Good Hope and visited cities along the East African coast. At one port, he picked up an Arab pilot who helped the Portuguese sail on to India. Da Gama reached the Indian port of Calicut in May 1498. His voyage took Portugal one step closer to realizing King John II's vision of a trading empire in Asia.

After da Gama's voyage established a water route, the Portuguese moved quickly to build trade with Asia. They could now avoid Arab and Italian middlemen and buy spices directly. Therefore, they could sell spices at a quarter of the earlier price and still make a good profit. Soon, Portugal dominated the spice trade in Europe.

THE PORTUGUESE TRADING EMPIRE

When Vasco da Gama reached India, local rulers asked him why he had come. His reply: "Christians and spices." Christian missionaries accompanied Portuguese traders wherever they established trading posts, but the traders were mainly interested in spices, which Europeans used to preserve meat. Portuguese ships carried cargo from Ceylon (modern-day Sri Lanka), and cloves and nutmeg from the East Indies.

Arab merchants, who had traded in India for centuries, resisted the Portuguese efforts to win trading privileges from local Hindu and Muslim princes. Because the Arab traders were Muslims, the Portuguese saw the competition for control of the spice trade as a Christian crusade. They burned Arab ships and wharves, ransacked Muslim cities of East Africa, and tortured prisoners.

In 1509, the Portuguese appointed Afonso de Albuquerque governor of their trading posts. Over the next six years, Albuquerque pursued a ruthless policy that created the basis of a Portuguese trading empire. From his headquarters at Goa on the west coast of India, he seized key points along the trade routes. For example, he captured Hormuz at the entrance of the Persian Gulf, which gave Portugal control of the Indian Ocean. Most important, Albuquerque seized the narrow Strait of Malacca, the gateway to the Moluccas, which Europeans called the Spice Islands. By controlling the Strait of Malacca, Portugal hoped to prevent other

Europeans from getting a foothold in the East Indies.

FIERCE COMPETITION

Portuguese control over the Strait of Malacca made that nation the preeminent European power in Southeast Asia at the turn of the 16th century, but it did not prevent other European nations from challenging Portugal's position. Foremost among Portugal's rivals was Spain.

While Christopher Columbus's famous voyage in 1492 led to the "discovery" of the New World, the Italian mariner who sailed under a Spanish flag was not interested in discovering uncharted lands. Instead, his mission was simply to find a shortcut to Asia that would allow Spanish ships to reach China and the Spice Islands more quickly. Even upon his death, that is what Columbus believed he had done.

Whether or not Columbus had landed directly in Malacca, he could still lay claim to the lands that he did set shore upon. Therefore, shortly after Columbus's landing, Spain and Portugal asked Pope Alexander VI, as head of the Catholic world, to determine which newly discovered lands could be claimed as Spain's and which could be claimed as Portugal's. Specifically, Spain petitioned the pope for full control of the lands that lay on the west shores of the Atlantic. In 1493, Alexander VI granted to Spain all lands west of a line running 100 leagues west of the Cape Verde Islands in the eastern Atlantic. Under this demarcation, Spain received possession of most of the Americas, while Portugal gained the rights to non-European territory east of that line, from land in South America that would become Brazil, eastward all the way to Southeast Asia, thereby confirming Portuguese rights to the spice trade. The pope's original line of demarcation was later shifted westward to give Portugal a slightly larger claim in Brazil. Meanwhile, Spanish and other European powers challenged Portugal's claim on the Spice Islands of Asia.

By the early 1500s Europeans clearly recognized that Columbus had not achieved his mission but had in fact found a "New World." While that realization ushered in a new age of exploration and colonization in the Americas, it did not eliminate the goal of finding a faster route to the Indies. In 1519, a Portuguese nobleman named Ferdinand Magellan decided to sail around the southernmost reaches of the New World in hope of finding that route. Ironically, he sailed under a Spanish flag.

Vasco da Gama (Library of Congress)

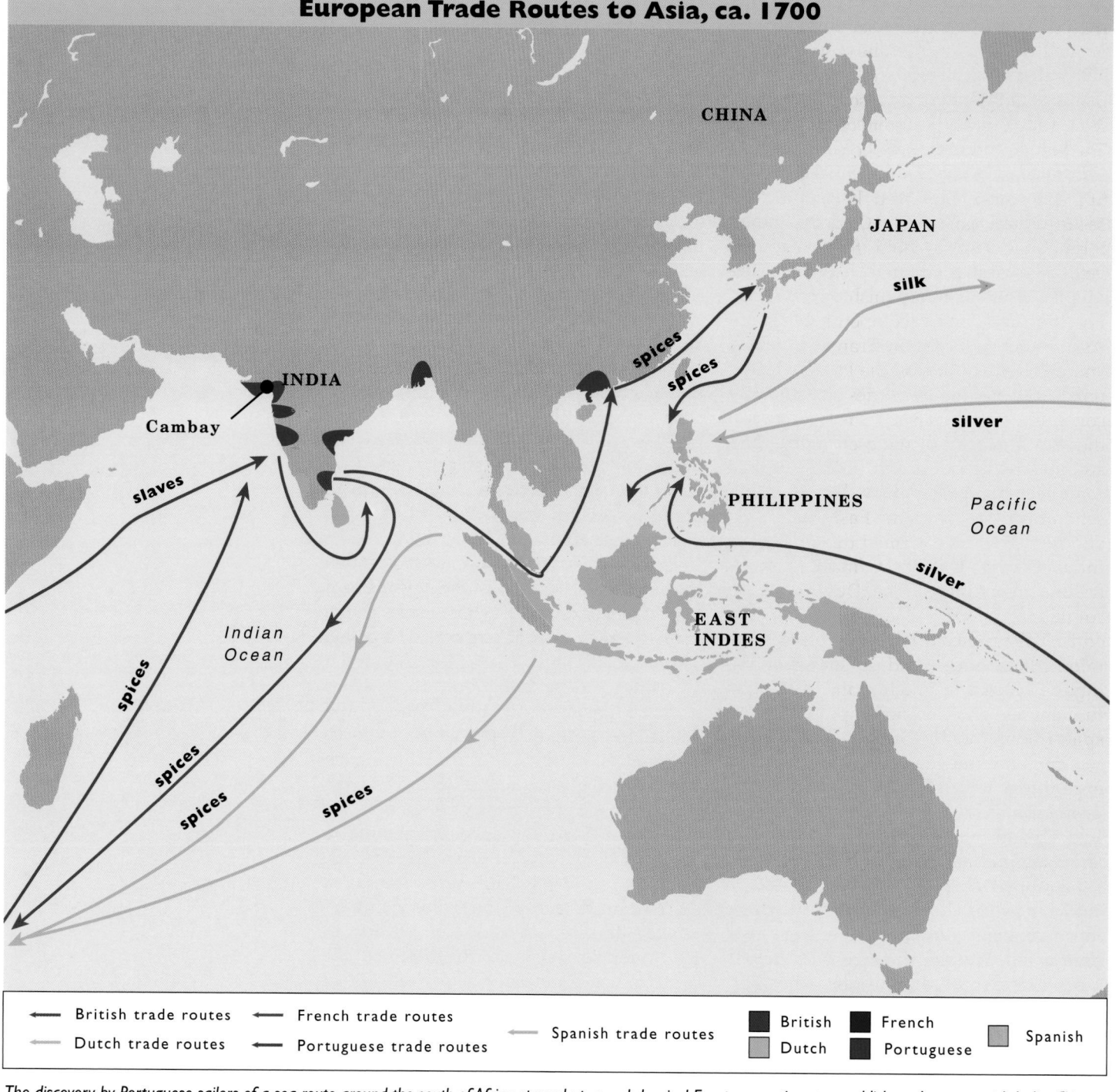

European Trade Routes to Asia, ca. 1700

British trade routes — French trade routes — Spanish trade routes — Dutch trade routes — Portuguese trade routes

British French Dutch Portuguese Spanish

The discovery by Portuguese sailors of a sea route around the south of Africa opened up a rush by rival European nations to establish trade routes with India, China, and the East Indies, which were so rich in exotic spices that they were long known to Europeans as the Spice Islands. The map above shows the major European nations involved in the trade, and the primary goods they traded along their respective routes.

Setting out in September 1519 with a crew of 230, Magellan and his men crossed the Atlantic and moved southward along the Atlantic coast of South America. As the arduous journey progressed, however, disaster dogged the crew. One ship capsized and the crew of another mutinied. Eventually, Magellan's ships passed through a strait at South America's southern tip and passed into the Pacific Ocean. That strait is now known as the Strait of Magellan.

After exploring part of South America's west coast, Magellan and his remaining crew set out across the vast Pacific. Enduring three months of hunger, disease, and malnutrition during the crossing, the crew arrived on a chain of Asian islands that the king of Spain christened the Philippines in honor of his son, Philip II.

Although Spain made its claim to the Philippines in 1522, it was not until 1565 that the Spanish established a real foothold there. In 1561, the Spanish founded the colonial capital of Manila and, from that base, began sending missionaries and soldiers throughout the islands to convert the populace.

Along with these efforts, Spain also managed to unify the diverse tribal peoples together into a single system of government. The task, however, did not go unresisted. As early as 1621, Filipinos rose up against the Spanish system of forced labor and land seizure in the name of the Catholic Church. Further rebellions would follow in later years at an increasing rate.

In addition to Spanish competition, Portugal faced stiff competition for the Asian spice trade from France, England, and the Netherlands by the late 1500s. The northern European countries knew that by conquering or bypassing a few key ports, they could break Portuguese control of the spice trade.

The Dutch acted first. In 1595, they sent a fleet to explore the East Indies. Seven years later, they formed the Dutch East India Company, which financed many trading expeditions. The Dutch were as ruthless as the Portuguese in gaining their ends. They attacked Portuguese ships and raided Portuguese trading stations. During the 1600s, the Dutch replaced the Portuguese as the dominant power in the spice trade.

England and France also sent trading expeditions to Asia. Because the Dutch position was so strong in the East Indies, English and French merchants concentrated on India. The English and French established small outposts along the southern coasts of India. They were able to win trading privileges in these areas in part because the Mughal Empire in India was weak in the south. In addition, some Hindu princes made alliances with Europeans against their Muslim rulers.

TRADE WITH CHINA AND JAPAN

The first Portuguese traders met Chinese merchants in Malacca. Tempted by Chinese silks, satins, and porcelain, the Portuguese sailed east into Chinese waters and, with permission from the Ming Chinese, established a trading port on the island of Macao. In an effort to limit foreign influence, the Chinese confined other European traders who arrived later to the port of Canton.

In 1542, a storm blew a Portuguese ship off course. The battered vessel found refuge in the Japanese islands, and a new source of trade was opened. At first, the Japanese welcomed trade with Portugal. Soon, Spanish vessels also visited Japan from across the Pacific, carrying potatoes, watermelons, and pumpkins from their colonies in the Americas.

Despite the growing trade, both the Chinese and Japanese continued to regard Europeans as barbarians. Aside from guns, Europeans had few goods they wanted. Furthermore, the Chinese and Japanese distrusted Europeans, having heard stories about the Portuguese and Dutch seizing land in the East Indies.

The activities of Jesuit missionaries also strained relations. At first, Japanese tolerated Christians. Later, however, Chinese and Japanese rulers suspected that the Christian missionaries were allies of the foreign traders who were taking land at gunpoint.

In Japan, Protestant merchants from England and the Netherlands encouraged the shoguns' suspicions of Portuguese and Spanish Catholics. However, their interference did them little good. By 1639, the Japanese had expelled all foreigners except the Dutch, who were allowed to sail one trade ship annually into the port of Nagasaki.

BRITISH IMPERIALISM IN INDIA AND SOUTHEAST ASIA

For almost 200 years, from 1526 to about 1712, able Mughal emperors ruled a powerful empire. During the 18th century, however, the empire suffered from a lack of strong rulers. Government efficiency declined and provincial governors became increasingly independent.

In the early days of the Mughal Empire, both Hindus and Muslims had rallied behind the emperor. As the emperor's prestige faded, however, war broke out between the two religious groups. In addition, a number of people saw the Mughal government as extravagant and oppressive. In the mid-18th century, rival Indian princes competed for power. Europeans took advantage of these internal struggles to advance into India.

As the Mughal Empire collapsed, French and British trading companies battled for control of trade with India. During the 18th century, the British East India Company successfully promoted its interests on the subcontinent. The East India Company had been founded in 1600 to make money by selling Indian products such as cotton cloth, silk, sugar, and jute in world markets.

As rivalry with France threatened its profits, the British East India Company became increasingly involved in Indian

A Mughal emperor wearing a cloth turban that ends in a point over the forehead; the turban also features a golden band set with pearls and precious stones. (from The Historical Encyclopedia of Costumes by Albert Charles Auguste Racinet)

political and military affairs. In 1756, at the outbreak of the Seven Years War in Europe, Robert Clive, an employee of the British East India Company, raised an army and ousted the French. He then used his army to ensure that a government favorable to the British East India Company ruled the Indian state of Bengal. Clive and his successors continued to interfere in local Indian affairs until the British East India Company became the most powerful authority in India.

The British East India Company practiced commercial colonialism; that is, it controlled India's foreign trade and used its army to keep friendly local rulers in power. To protect its interests, the company built forts and maintained an army of sepoys, Indian soldiers who served in European armies. During the late 1700s and early 1800s, the British East India Company gained direct control over some parts of India.

Though regulated by the British government, the British East India Company had a fairly free hand in India until the mid-19th century. By this time, many members of Parliament felt that the British government should assume responsibility for India. In 1857, an uprising known as the Sepoy Rebellion gave Parliament the excuse it needed to end the rule of the British East India Company and administer Indian affairs directly.

The immediate cause of the Sepoy Rebellion was rumors that bullet cartridges used by sepoys were greased with beef and pork fat. These rumors angered both Hindu and Muslim soldiers: Hindus were forbidden to

During the late 19th century, Great Britain stood as the most powerful colonial force in Europe. By 1900, the Indian subcontinent was a patchwork of lands ruled directly by Britain's Queen Victoria and numerous principalities ruled by local Indian princes in name only, with all real power resting in British hands.

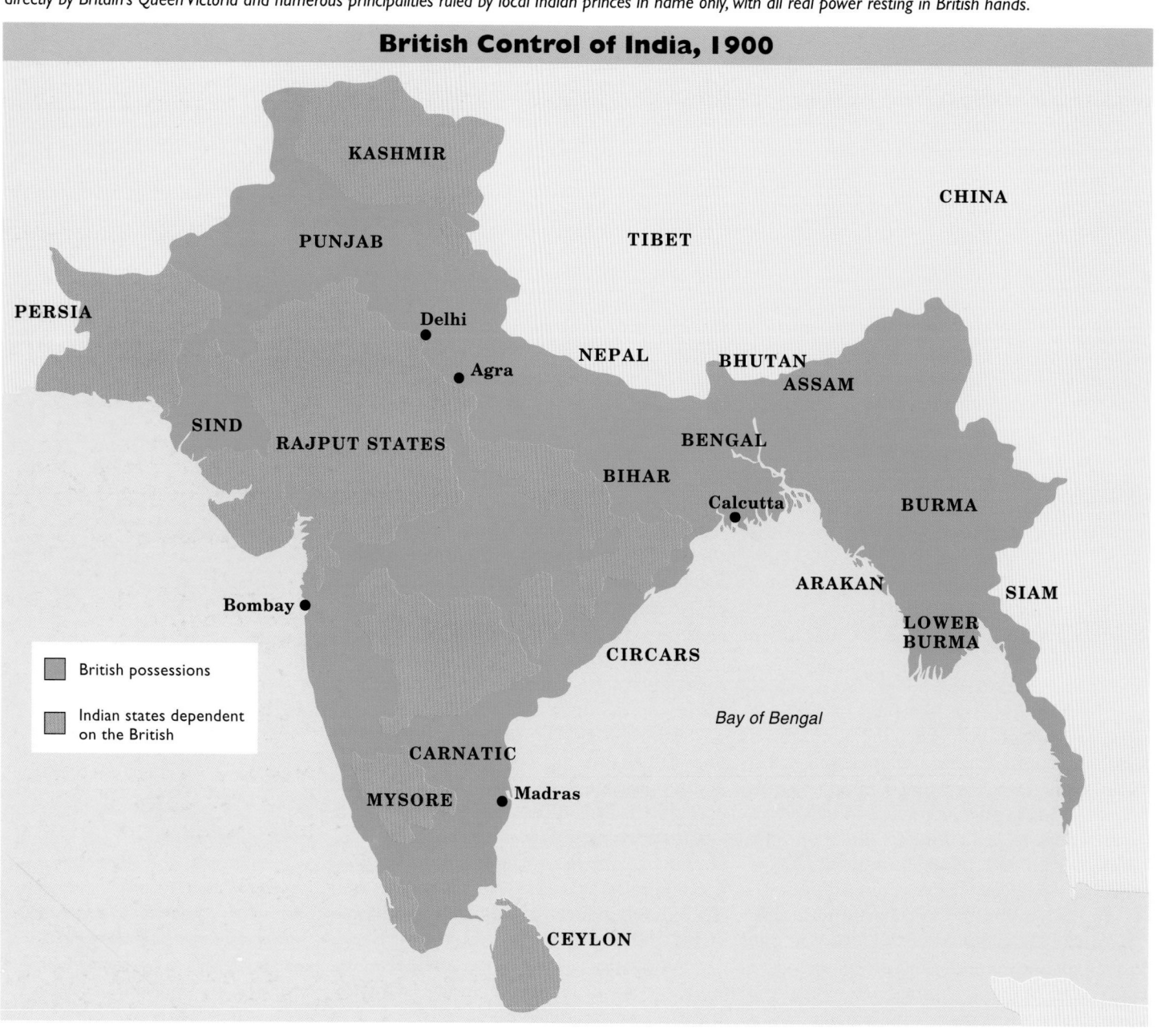

British Control of India, 1900

KASHMIR

CHINA

PUNJAB

TIBET

PERSIA

Delhi

NEPAL

BHUTAN

Agra

ASSAM

SIND

RAJPUT STATES

BENGAL

BIHAR

Calcutta

BURMA

ARAKAN

SIAM

Bombay

LOWER BURMA

CIRCARS

Bay of Bengal

■ British possessions

▨ Indian states dependent on the British

CARNATIC

MYSORE Madras

CEYLON

Colonial Asia in 1900

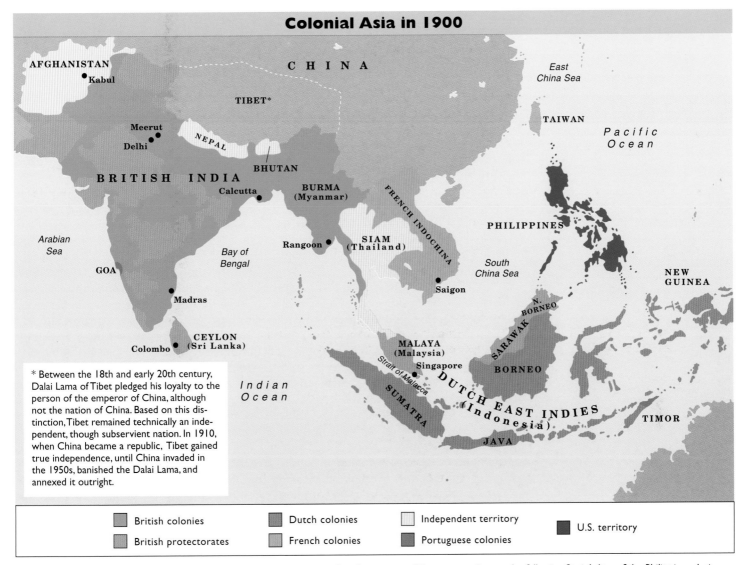

* Between the 18th and early 20th century, Dalai Lama of Tibet pledged his loyalty to the person of the emperor of China, although not the nation of China. Based on this distinction, Tibet remained technically an independent, though subservient nation. In 1910, when China became a republic, Tibet gained true independence, until China invaded in the 1950s, banished the Dalai Lama, and annexed it outright.

Legend:
- British colonies
- British protectorates
- Dutch colonies
- French colonies
- Independent territory
- Portuguese colonies
- U.S. territory

By the end of the 19th century, much of Asia had been divided up into colonial territories of European nations and—following Spain's loss of the Philippines during the Spanish-American War of 1898—the United States.

touch beef, and Muslims were forbidden to touch pork. The sepoys also resented British efforts to make them adopt Christian and European customs.

The rebellion among the sepoys spread across India. Hindu and Muslim princes supported the Sepoy Rebellion because they saw the British as a threat to their power. Peasants joined the uprising in protest against the severe hardships of their lives. British troops suppressed the rebellion, and in 1858 the British Parliament took governing control of India from the British East India Company.

After 1858, the British government established full colonial rule in India. A cabinet minister in London was made responsible for Indian affairs, while a British viceroy in India carried out government policy. British governors ruled about two-thirds of India, including the parts that the East India Company had controlled directly. Local Indian princes stayed on as rulers in the rest of the country, but British officials called residents closely supervised these Indian rulers. In 1877, British prime minister Benjamin Disraeli had Parliament officially grant Queen Victoria the title of Empress of India.

In 1890 about 1,000 British officials ran a colonial government that ruled some 280 million Indians. During the Age of Imperialism, the British had a clear idea of what they thought India should become. Unlike the British East India Company, which had encouraged its officers to learn Indian languages and observe local customs, the British colonial government tried to impose British culture on India. British officials believed that by adopting European ways, Indians would improve their lives. Consquently, they encouraged the Indian people to abandon their traditions and learn to speak, dress, and live like Europeans.

British rule affected Indian life in various ways. In countless Indian villages, the coming of the British had little direct impact:

A Mughal emperor (from The Historical Encyclopedia of Costumes by Albert Charles Auguste Racinet)

Farmers tilled their fields as they had for centuries, the caste system dominated village life, and the people observed traditional religious practices. However, British colonial policies opened the door to major economic and social changes.

The Industrial Revolution in Britain influenced British economic policy in India. The British East India Company had sold Indian-made luxury items abroad, but the British government saw India as a source of cheap raw materials for British factories. It also felt that India, which had a large population, would serve as a market for British manufactured goods. Britain, therefore, tied the Indian economy closely to its own.

The British discouraged local Indian industries. They encouraged Indian farmers to stop growing food and start growing cotton. Factories in Britain then used the Indian cotton to produce finished goods, which were sent back to India to be sold. Although this policy benefited British manufacturers, it hurt local industries in India. Village artisans could not compete with the cheaper, mass-produced British imports. Moreover, British efforts to encourage the production of export crops, such as cotton, reduced the amount of food that was grown. As a result of reduced food supplies, famines killed millions of Indians during the 1800s.

On the other hand, British rule in India led to better communication and increased trade. By building new canals, roads, and railways, the British opened up India's vast interior to trade. The opening of the Suez Canal in 1869 made trade faster and easier between Europe and the rest of Asia. Telegraph lines also made communications easier between Britain and India. These developments resulted in a tremendous increase in exports from India.

CHINA IN TURMOIL

In 1800, China was the leading power in Asia. Ever since Marco Polo brought tales of riches back from his 13th century journey to the court of Kublai Khan, Europeans had dreamed of tapping the China trade. For the Chinese, however, opening trade with Europe had little value. The Chinese viewed their civilization as the greatest on Earth and all foreigners as inferiors. Some trade with Europe did take place, first in 1535 with the Portuguese, who established a trading outpost on the island of Macao, and then in 1564 with Spaniards crossing the Pacific for the Philippines from their colonies in the Americas. For the most part , though, trade was intermittent.

By the late 18th century, British merchants began shipping large amounts of opium from India into the Chinese port of Canton, reaping enormous profits in the process. From then on, the Manchu government found its empire slipping into chaos. The 19th century was filled with war, famine, and disease, all of which acted to drive thousands overseas in search of a better life.

Although Emperor Jia Qing banned such imports, by the 1830s, the traffic in opi-

A British ship bombards Canton in 1839 during the First Opium War. (Library of Congress)

This three-paneled silk screen illustrates 15-year-old Mutsuhito traveling to Edo for his coronation as emperor in 1868. (Library of Congress)

um had reached some 18,000 chests a year—a lucrative trade that Great Britain had little interest in losing. In 1839, after commissioner Lin Tse-hsu forced foreign delegations to surrender $11 million worth of opium, the British navy bombarded Canton, overwhelming Chinese defenses and forcing the drug trade to reopen. In the aftermath of the attack, which became known as the First Opium War, China was forced to pay Great Britain $21 million in damages.

An even greater consequence of the First Opium War was the forcing open of ports along the Chinese coast by the British. Ports such as Canton, Amoy, Foochow, Ningpo, and Shanghai were now open to European trade. The port of Hong Kong was not only opened to trade but ceded to Great Britain outright. China was now compelled to allow foreigners to live in all of these port cities and prohibited from exercising legal jurisdiction over them.

The Chinese humiliation did not go unheeded by other Western powers. In the aftermath of the war, American, French, Russian, Portuguese, and other merchants all demanded favorable trade agreements of their own, and the Chinese were powerless to refuse. In 1856, diplomats from Great Britain, France, the United States, and Russia, armed with 30 gunboats and about 3,000 troops, forced the Chinese to grant even greater concessions. When Manchu officials tried to delay implementation of the new trade terms, foreigners destroyed the ancient Summer Palace in Peking (present-day Beijing). This attack became known as the Second Opium War. Upon the palace's destruction, the emperor ordered 11 more ports opened and agreed for the first time to allow foreigners into the interior of China. The new treaty also permitted diplomats to live in Peking and formally legalized the import of opium. China's ability to control its relations with the outside world had been annihilated.

Not all of China's ill fortune during the 19th century came from the outside world, however. The Manchu government was widely regarded as corrupt and, as such, faced a steady stream of internal revolt. The bloodiest of these revolts, known as the Taiping Rebellion, began six years before the Second Opium War.

Hung Hsiu-chuan, a Cantonese Christian who believed that he had been chosen to establish China as a "Heavenly Kingdom of Peace," attracted thousands of followers to a movement called Taiping (from the Chinese words for "great peace") by mixing elements of Christianity with Confucianism. Over the course of a bloody 16-year struggle that lasted from 1850 to 1866, the Taipings captured the city of Nanking and held it as their capital from 1853 to 1860. Although the Chinese army retook Nanking in 1866, the war wreaked havoc on China, bringing epidemics, starvation, and death to as many as 20 million Chinese, and spurred a tide of refugees fleeing the country for destinations worldwide, including the United States.

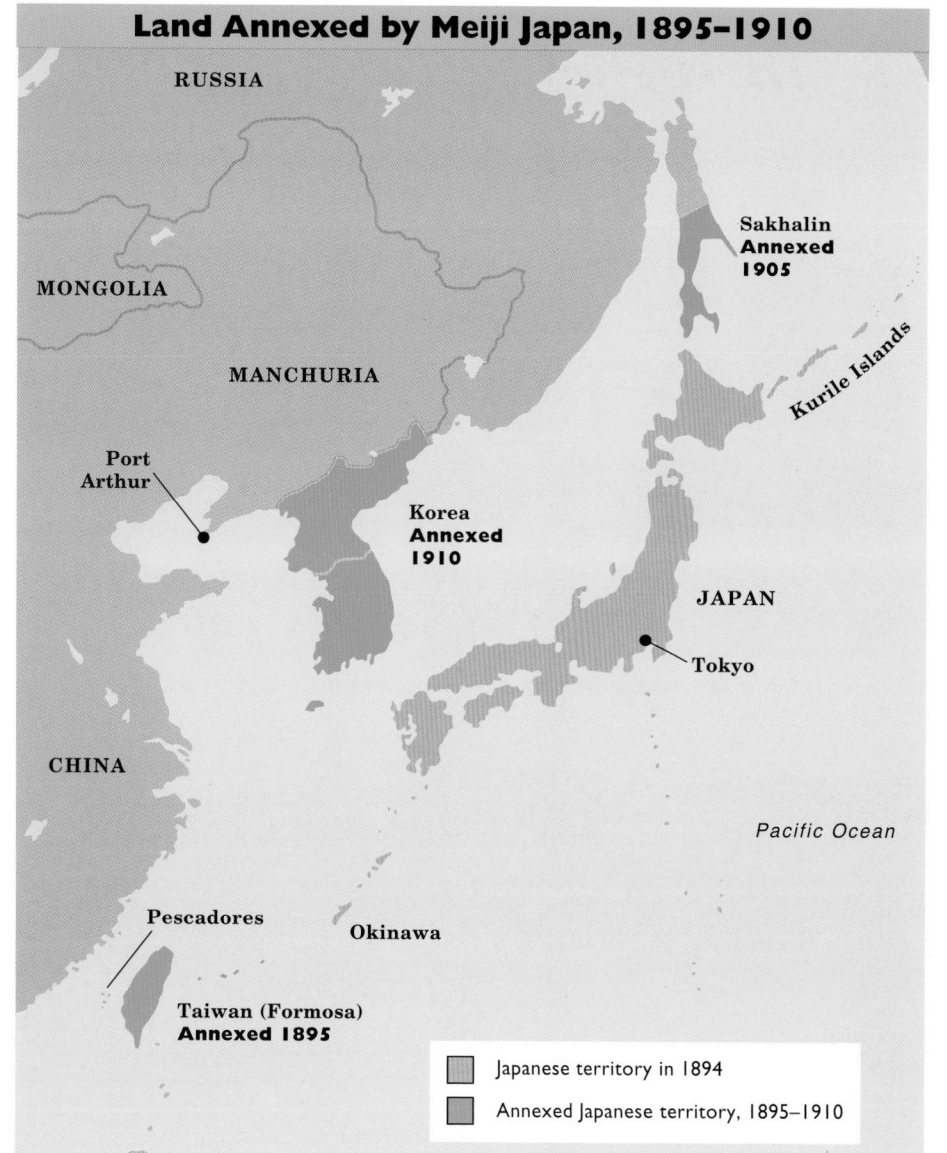

Land Annexed by Meiji Japan, 1895-1910

RUSSIA

MONGOLIA

MANCHURIA

Sakhalin
Annexed
1905

Kurile Islands

Port
Arthur

Korea
Annexed
1910

JAPAN

Tokyo

CHINA

Pacific Ocean

Pescadores

Okinawa

Taiwan (Formosa)
Annexed 1895

Japanese territory in 1894

Annexed Japanese territory, 1895–1910

THE MEIJI RESTORATION
IN JAPAN

In 1853, U.S. commodore Matthew Perry arrived in Edo Bay, Japan, with a fleet of four heavily armed warships and asked that Japanese ports be opened to U.S. trade. With the exception of the Dutch colony in Nagasaki Bay, trade—or any sort of contact with the West—was strictly forbidden under Japanese law. Hence Japan had been completely shut off from the outside world since 1603. Upon seeing Perry's armed display, however, the Japanese felt they had no choice but to accede to the American's demands. The Treaty of Kanagawa was signed, becoming the first of many with Western powers that the government would sign over the next few years. By 1860, Japan had granted trading rights to numerous foreign nations.

The opening of trade relations with outsiders led to dramatic changes within the Japanese government, largely because

Japanese leaders worried that without reforms their nation would be overrun by foreign influence. In 1866, the Tokugawa shogunate, or ruling family of Japan, was overthrown by reform-minded samurai. Two years later, 15-year-old Mutsuhito became Emperor Meiji (1852–1912).

Under the rule of Emperor Meiji, Japan was modernized. Instead of attempting to cling to tradition as China had when faced with pressure from the outside, Japan underwent a dramatic period of rapid change known as the Meiji Restoration. The three main aspects of the government's reform program were land reform, industrial modernization, and militarization.

Prior to the Meiji Restoration, wealth had been concentrated in the hands of the ruling Tokugawa family and a group of territorial lords known as daimyo. Following the restoration, the daimyo lost their lands to the small farmers who lived on them. Land ownership was at best a mixed blessing for Japanese peasants, however. Instead of providing assistance to these new small landowners, the government subjected them to heavy annual taxes. Because the taxes were based on land held rather than crops produced, farmers who suffered poor harvests had difficulty, not only in growing enough to eat, but also in paying their debts. By the 1880s, famine was widespread. In response, the government began allowing limited numbers of citizens to emigrate. Most of these emigrants became contract laborers in Hawaii.

Unlike the Chinese Qing rulers, Japan's Meiji government decided to combat Western influence by acquiring a knowledge of Western technology and weaponry. Japan sent delegations of dignitaries to the United States and Europe to learn about Western methods. Western-style factories were built, and the first Japanese railroad opened in 1872. In addition, the country developed a new legal and political system in 1889 to help it gain recognition in the West.

Most of the income derived from land taxation and factory modernization was poured into the military. By 1910, Japan had defeated both China and Russia in battle and had annexed Korea. This aggressive military stance would help fuel the anti-Japanese sentiment of non-Asian Americans in Hawaii and on the mainland United States and would set the stage for an international power struggle that would last a half century and play itself out across a wide spectrum of venues—from school board meetings in early 20th-century San Francisco to far-flung Pacific island battles during World War II.

The Chinese in 19th-Century America

According to Chinese legend, "the wonderful Land of Fusang," possibly near present-day Acapulco, Mexico, was visited during the latter half of the 5th century by a Buddhist missionary from China named Hwui Shan. *Fusang,* translated as "super" or "colossal," had existed for centuries in Chinese mythology as an earthly paradise located somewhere across the Pacific. According to Hwui Shan's journals, this legendary land lay 20,000 *li* (or about 6,500 miles) east of the Kamchatka Peninsula in Siberia. Hwui Shan supposedly crossed the Pacific to the Aleutian Islands and Alaska. He then sailed down the west coast of North America, finally arriving in Mexico. Describing what he found there, he wrote,

That region has many Fusang trees and these give it its name....The people of the country eat [its sprouts]....They spin thread from the bark and make coarse cloth ...The wood is used to build houses and they use Fusang bark to make paper.

Some historians speculate that Hwui Shan may have been describing the maguey, or century plant. Archeologists say that Indians of Mexico used it in all of the ways Hwui Shan described. Often reaching a height of 30 feet, the plants could easily have been mistaken for trees.

Hwui Shan is thought to have stayed in Fusang for 40 years, during which time he may have made a number of religious conversions. Historians of pre-Columbian civilizations in Mexico have found traces of Buddhism in the Mayan religion. While Hwui's story cannot be viewed as uncontestable fact—for at the very least he surely embellished the truth—it seems quite possible that he did reach the Americas nearly 500 years before Leif Erickson saw Vinland on the Atlantic coast.

Although Hwui Shan may have sailed down the West Coast on his way to Mexico, no record exists of his setting foot on the mainland of what is now the United States. Even as recently as the late 18th century, Chinese seamen were just an occasional sight in the seaport towns along the Atlantic coast. According to the U.S. census, there were just three Chinese in the United States in 1820, the first year a census report was issued.

Chinese migration did not begin in earnest until the mid-19th century. As discussed in chapter 1, thousands of migrants were driven from China both by international and civil wars, and by hunger, poverty, and the high taxes levied by the government as a result of these wars. For many poor Chinese, life at home held little hope for a better future.

It was in this climate of economic hardship that news of great wealth—real and exaggerated—to be earned in California began spreading in China's coastal cities and villages. The source of this wealth was gold—gold so abundant that the Chinese would begin calling California by a new name: Gam Saan, or Gold Mountain.

THE GOLD RUSH

In 1848 James Marshall discovered gold at Sutter's Mill in California quite by accident, and had no idea that the few tiny sparkling flakes held in his hand foretold of a gold rush that would change tens of thousands of lives, as well as the development of a state and nation.

People from all over the world poured in to California to strike it rich. In one year, tiny San Francisco (population 812 in 1848) grew into a boomtown with a population of 25,000. The initial group of prospectors with "gold fever" became known as "Forty-Niners" and their shouts of "Eureka!" (I've found it!) echoed through the foothills between California's Yuba and Mariposa Rivers. Between 1848 and 1850 an estimated 80,000 people, mostly men, arrived in California. By 1854 as many as 24,000 Chinese were working in and around the gold fields. By 1870, 63,000 Chinese had migrated to the United States, 77 percent of whom lived in California.

LEAVING CHINA

More than 2 million people left China between 1840 and 1900, traveling not only to the United States but also to Canada, Africa, South America, Australia, and elsewhere in

LILY FEET

In 10th century China, a unknown prince began the practice of foot binding because he loved the small feet of his concubine, Yao Niang. Thus began a 1,000-year practice of binding the feet of young girls in order to keep them small. "Lily feet," as they were called, were considered beautiful and a symbol of gentility.

Although the term sounds harmless, the practice was really very cruel. The process would begin when a girl was between three and 11 years old. After her foot was washed in hot water and massaged, the girl's toes were turned under and pressed against the bottom of her foot. The arches were broken as the foot was pulled straight with the leg, and then the toes were wrapped tightly with a bandage to hold them in place. Over several years, a girl's feet would shrink until they could fit into special three-inch-long "lotus shoes." The process left girls with deformities that made walking incredibly painful. Bindings severely resticted blood circulation to the toes, sometimes requiring amputation of infected toes. Other times gangrene set in and toes would fall off.

In addition to symbolizing status, bound feet also ensured adherence to the Confucian ideal of family loyalty because women who could barely walk could not wander off. Among China's elite, families were unable to arrange marriages for their daughters if they had unbound feet.

The practice of foot binding continued in China until the Qing Dynasty was overthrown in 1911. Of the relatively few Chinese women who came to the United States before then, most were from peasant families and did not have bound feet, since they needed to be able to work in the home and in the fields. Some women and girls, however, did arrive in America with "lily feet." In general, they lived in San Francisco and other cities where men from wealthy Chinese families had launched businesses.

Asia. Beginning in the late 1840s and early 1850s, Chinese by the tens of thousands set off for America as *wah gung*, or laborers. They bid farewell to their families, homeland, and the only way of life they had known to make their fortunes in a land they had never seen.

Almost all of these migrants were men, in part because cultural taboos discouraged women from venturing anywhere alone. Furthermore, the roles and obligations of Chinese women as family-centered daughters, wives, and widows were well defined by Confucian ethics. Women of all social classes were considered inferior to men. The crippling practice of foot binding among both the gentility and peasants aspiring to marry into the upper classes symbolized not only this dominant sexist attitude but Confucian restraints against travel as well. Most significantly, the women stayed behind during this period because they, like everyone around them, firmly believed their husbands and sons would be returning home in a few short years.

During the mid-1850s, a few adventurers did return to China from America, and tales of their wealth and success in the land of "American wizards" spread like wildfire across the countryside. Thousands of male migrants, also fully expecting to return home wealthy in two to five years, quickly prepared to earn similar success. They said their good-byes and set out by foot or boat to port cities such as Hong Kong and Canton. There, they packed aboard ships bound for either Gold Mountain or the Hawaiian Islands, which the Chinese called Tan Heung Shan, or "Fragrant Sandalwood Hills."

FROM GUANGDONG AND FUJIAN

In the latter half of the 19th century, most of the sojourners to the United States and to what was then the Kingdom of Hawaii were from the Guangdong and Fujian provinces in southeast China. Chinese laborers and businessmen were lured not only by the true success stories of the first fledgling migrants to return, but also by exaggerated tales of the wealth to be had in the United States. The port city of Canton (modern-day Guangzhou), an international trading post located in the Guangdong province, served as a conduit for information as well as goods. There, American and European merchants and sailors shared news of the outside world,

especially news of the California gold rush of 1849.

As discussed in the previous chapter, internal strife also encouraged many Chinese to leave their homeland and cross the Pacific to America. Many migrants from Guangdong sought refuge from violent conflicts at home, whether they were small-scale fights between family groups within villages or large-scale peasant uprisings such as the Taiping Rebellion of 1854–1864 or the British Opium Wars (1839–1842; 1856–1860), which had proved massively disruptive to China on economical, cultural, and psychological levels.

The economic chaos and societal upheaval that came with war routinely took the heaviest toll on the poorest groups. Following the British victories in the Opium Wars, China's Qing government forced rural farmers to pay high taxes in order to paying the enormous reparations demanded by the British. Chinese peasants unable to pay such large taxes lost their land, which was their only secure employment as well as their source of food. Though industries such as textile production existed in China, jobs were scarce, particularly after the Opium Wars forced China into the competitive world markets. In Guangdong province, this stressful economic situation was further intensified by a population explosion. In the 63 years before 1850, China's population had increased by 76 percent. Raging floods ruined crops, making widespread hunger and poverty even worse.

Unlike the first wave of Guangdong-based free laborers, most of the Chinese leaving Fujian were contract laborers. Foreign merchants, passing through Fujian's major port of Quanzhou, attracted Chinese laborers to work as servants overseas. Though contracted to work for years at low wages, the system did offer the men, many of them homeless, hope for a better life, something that seemed unlikely if not impossible in economically depressed Fujian. Many laborers, often illiterate as well as displaced by the chaos that followed the Taiping Rebellion, were easily fooled into believing that they were actually traveling as free men employed by labor companies. Instead, they had become ensnared in the virtual slavery that was the "coolies trade." Despite the common use of the term *coolie* to describe Chinese immigrants in the United States, few true coolies actually were bound for U.S. shores. Instead many wound up toiling in the European colonies of the Caribbean, Africa, and elsewhere.

PACIFIC VOYAGE

Thanks to the development of the steamship, by the mid-1860s the journey from China to San Francisco shortened into one month instead of two. The Pacific Mail Steamship Company, which began round-trip operations between China and the United States in 1866, was the first company to take advantage of the new technology.

Since steamships were less dependent on wind and weather than the clipper sailing ships of the previous era, they were a more reliable form of transportation. Steamships were also larger than the clippers, holding twice as many people.

The more efficient steamships and rising competition from rivals of Pacific Mail led to lower fares for passage, which encouraged more Chinese (and later, Filipinos, Koreans,

GUANGDONG AND FUJIAN PROVINCES:
The Sources of Chinese Immigration

Guangdong: Most early Chinese immigrants to the United States were independent laborers seeking their fortunes in America. Most came from Kwangtung (modern Guangdong) and the island of Hainan. Many had exposure to the West through Canton (present-day Guangzhou), a major port city and international trading post. The Chinese from this region had access to information on foreign events such as the 1849 gold rush through contact with Americans and Europeans, whose presence in China increased after the Second Opium War (1856–1860).

Fujian: The Chinese "coolies," or contract laborers, who went to Cuba and Latin America during the 19th century came from the depressed province of Fujian, north of Guangdong. Europeans and Americans passed through Quanzhou, a major Fujian port in the silk trade. These foreign merchants offered Chinese laborers work as overseas servants—an offer that seemed attractive following the turmoil caused by the Taiping Rebellion. Many laborers were either homeless or deceived by promises that they were emigrating as free workers recruited by labor companies.

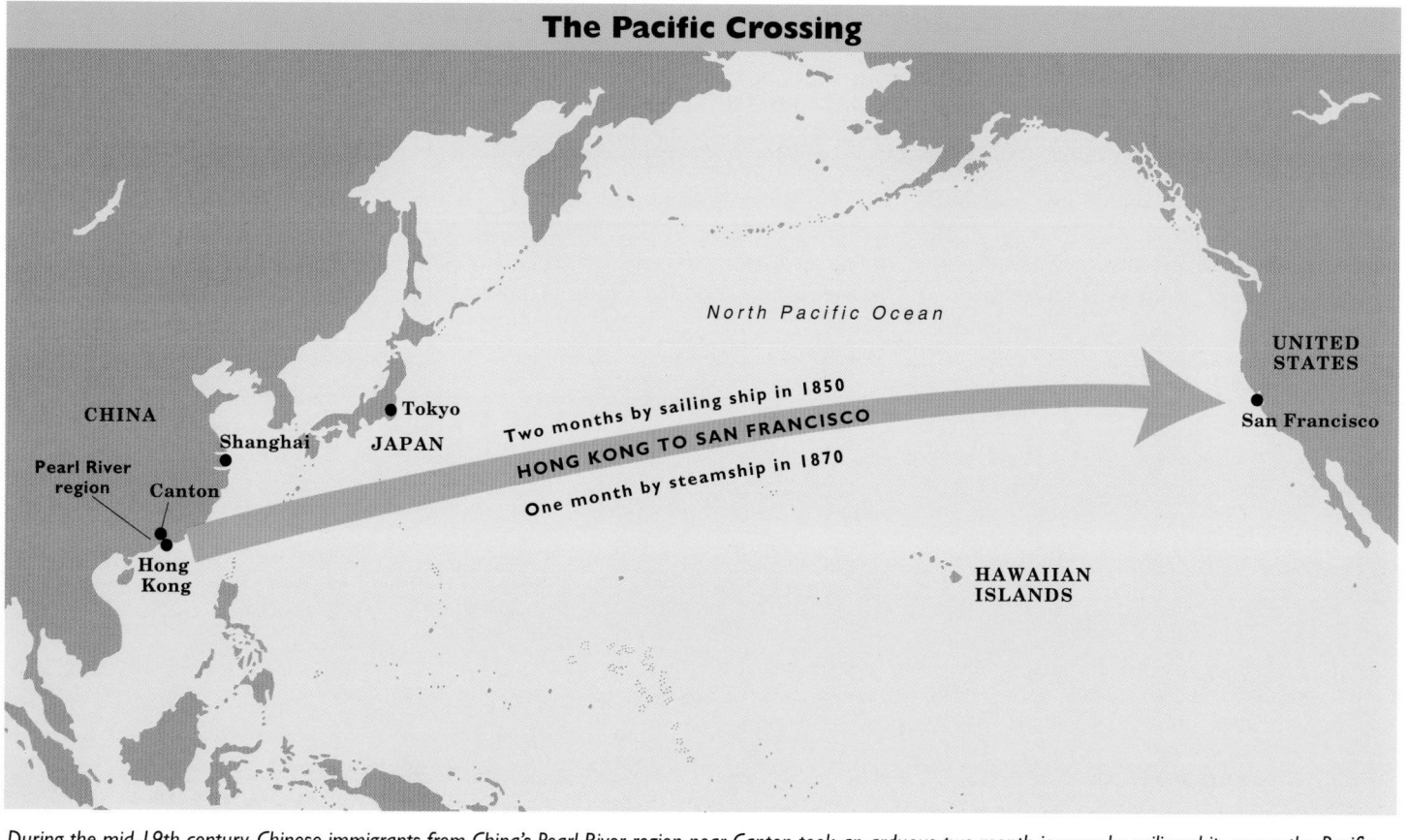

The Pacific Crossing

Two months by sailing ship in 1850
HONG KONG TO SAN FRANCISCO
One month by steamship in 1870

During the mid-19th century, Chinese immigrants from China's Pearl River region near Canton took an arduous two-month journey by sailing ship across the Pacific from Hong Kong to the United States. The coming of oceanfaring steamships in the late 19th century cut the duration of the voyage in half.

Indians, and Japanese) to voyage to America. By 1870 the fare had dropped from its 1855 peak of $280 per person to just $13.

Still, the vast majority of Chinese migrants had a difficult time raising money for the great journey. A lucky few were able to borrow money from immediate family members, but most families did not have such financial resources readily available. To ease the burden, family and district associations served as community loan banks to lend money to individuals. Since family honor was (and remains) a central concept in traditional Chinese culture, loans were always repaid. Thus, the association system succeeded and played an important historical role in China. (Later on in the United States, such organizations aided new immigrants in a variety of ways.)

The majority of Chinese laborers, though, secured their ocean passage through the credit-ticket system. Under this arrangement, employers paid for the trip and promised a salary (always lower than that of white American workers) in exchange for a labor contract detailing a certain number of hours to be worked per day in the United States over a period of three to seven years. When this contract expired, Chinese workers were free to seek

other opportunities, though many would argue that their opportunities were limited because of the subsistence-level existence they had suffered in the United States for so long.

Though the development of the steamship improved travel somewhat, the journey itself remained arduous and onboard conditions improved little. Overcrowding, poor food, and widespread disease were common since companies such as Pacific Mail placed monetary profit above human welfare.

"I ate wind and tasted waves for more than twenty days," a Chinese traveler said of the journey in a poem carved upon the walls of San Francisco's Angel Island immigration station. Hard and lumpy rice, tiny pieces of dried tofu, and watery soup often composed the daily gruel. Nausea caused by the constant rocking of the ship to and fro exacerbated stomach discomfort. Hundreds of people crammed together tightly with no way to bathe or clean up vomit caused by seasickness added to an inevitable and horrible odor. Anxiety about an uncertain future in a strange land contributed to sleeplessness. Many died along the way since such conditions made it easy for disease to spread quickly. Dreams of elaborate wealth and grand

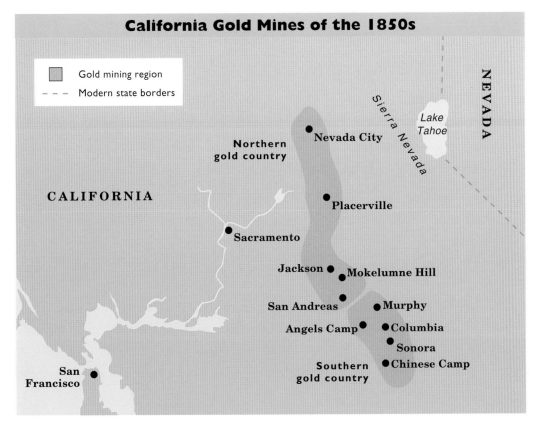

California Gold Mines of the 1850s

Gold mining region
- - - Modern state borders

NEVADA

CALIFORNIA

Sierra Nevada

Lake Tahoe

Nevada City

Northern gold country

Placerville

Sacramento

Jackson • • Mokelumne Hill

San Andreas • • Murphy

Angels Camp • • Columbia

Sonora

Southern gold country • Chinese Camp

San Francisco

California's gold country was concentrated west of Sacramento. During the 1850s, many small mining camps boasted Chinese communities, as the name of one of them—Chinese Camp—makes clear. While cities such as San Francisco would continue to support significant Chinese-American communities after the gold rush ended in the 1860s, most of the small mining camps were abandoned.

returns to loving families in China helped sustain those who finished the treacherous journey.

CHINESE MINERS

Once arrived in Gold Mountain, Chinese migrants found life little easier than it had been en route. In fact, daily life for all miners was difficult. After an arduous journey by land or sea, weakened and lonely miners arrived to discover crowded mining camps, a pervasive aura of greed and lawlessness, and grossly inflated prices for basic goods such as bread and potatoes. Miners frequently wrote home complaining about exhorbitant prices. One wrote that he had paid $11 for a jar of pickles and two sweet potatoes, and $7.50 for two spools of thread and a needle. The price of flour reached as much as $800 a barrel, and eggs cost $3 each. Greedy storekeepers called their practice of inflating prices for fortune seekers "mining the miners."

Though the Chinese later improved the placer method to work the claims, at the onset of the gold rush, most miners panned for gold with a hand-held kitchen skillet or flat pan. Prospectors filled the pan with gravel, dipped it into a stream, and swirled the mixture around to wash the dirt away from any gold that would settle to the bottom. This process involved squatting for long hours in the hot sun with hands submerged in icy stream water.

Most miners worked alone or in small groups in the gold fields, whereas the Chinese labored in skillful teams in a more organized fashion. As soon as the take from panning became poor, whites moved on to other sites. Using water skills learned in China's Pearl River delta, Chinese miners built dams and other blockages to change the course of streams. This left long beds of sand to be dug and sifted through. Their patience, inventiveness, and ingenuity did not yield fortunes, but Chinese miners generally retrieved enough gold this way to earn $2 to $3 per day. Most white miners of the 1850s, it should be noted, earned $6 to $10 per day—though that higher amount stemmed from their ability to lay claim first to the best fields.

By 1854 nearly 24,000 Chinese worked in and around California's gold fields. Most Chinese worked as independent prospectors grouped into small, organized companies such as the Ah Louie and Sham

CHINESE MINING METHODS

The gold rush of 1848 brought many fortune seekers to California. By 1854, as many as 25,000 Chinese were working in or around the goldfields. They brought with them mining methods far more efficient than the simple gold panning method initially used by white miners. Chinese methods included:

The Placer Method

The placer method was the most popular mining technique used by the Chinese. Gold-bearing earth was placed in a pan of water. While earth was slopped out of the pan with the water, gold dust was left at the bottom. This method was improved by building troughs leading to cradles or rockers, which handled larger amounts of water. The Chinese introduced other technology to mine placer gold, including water-wheels to lift water from streams into troughs. The Chinese also built wing-dams to divert stream water to troughs.

Hydraulic Mining and Deep Shaft Mining

Deep shaft mining, which involved drilling underground mine shafts to access silver and gold, and hydraulic mining, involving the use of high-pressure hoses to blast away rock and sediment in order to separate precious metals form the earth, required too much capital for most Chinese. Even those who had the money were usually unwilling to invest because white mobs might destroy or steal the hoses, drills, or other equipment. Many less fortunate Chinese miners were forced to work for companies that employed hydraulic or deep shaft techniques once the placer gold had all been mined.

Mining Fashions

Chinese miners in the California mine country dressed as they did in Manchu China. They wore wooden shoes, wide-brimmed hats, blue cotton blouses, wide-legged trousers, and their hair cut very short up front with a long, long braid (called a queue) hanging down their backs. The whites usually wore tall boots, suspenders, thick beards, various types of hats, and the newly invented Levi's jeans.

While Chinese usually worked independantly of white miners, some, like these at Auburn Ravine in California in 1852, found work as laborers. (California State Library)

Because Chinese miners were often forced to work claims only after they had been abandoned by white miners, they found less gold than whites. However, they were able to find gold where whites had found none using techniques they imported from China.

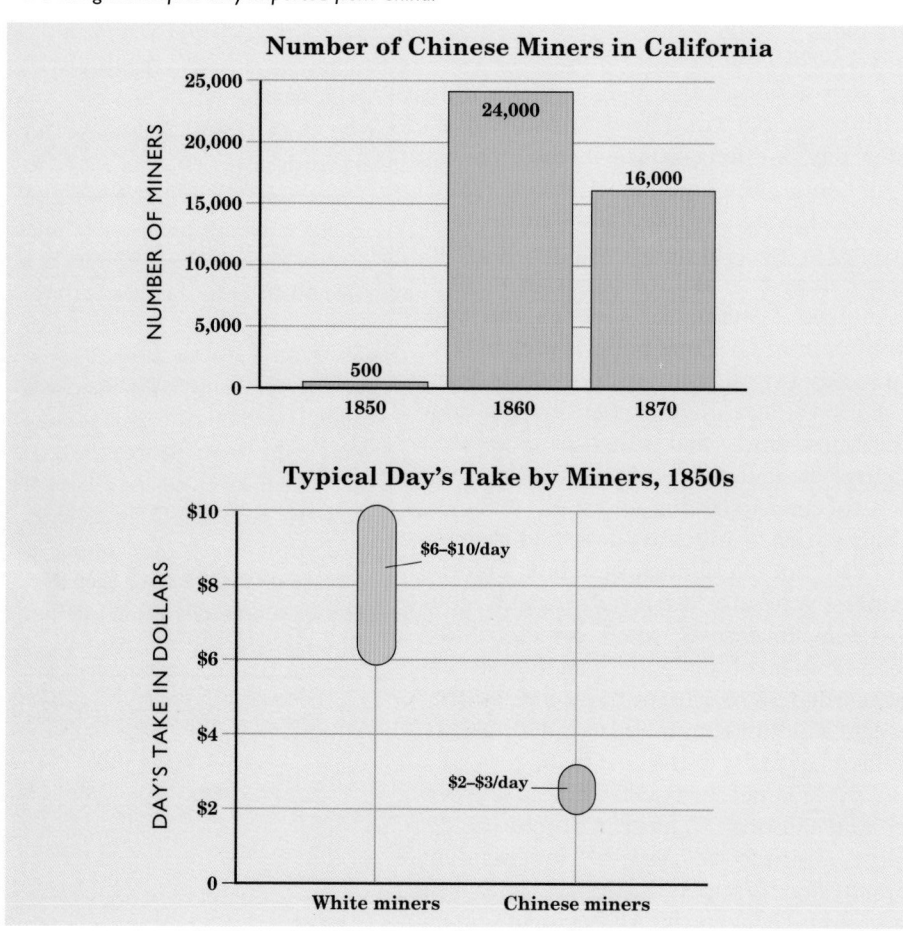

Number of Chinese Miners in California

Typical Day's Take by Miners, 1850s

Kee Companies. Rather than purchase mining claims outright, many of these companies obtained "preemptive claims," by which the miner filed a required application with the county record office and marked boundaries along the claim. Then, after a few years of renewing these preemption claims, the most successful companies purchased the land outright.

However, very few miners of any race found the elaborate fortunes they had dreamed of. Even James Marshall, the gold panner who had made the gold discovery at Sutter's Mill, and John Sutter himself met with financial ruin and disillusionment in the end. As for the Chinese, as surface gold became harder to find and the competition for worthy claims increased, they found themselves increasingly subject to prejudice from the majority white community.

Though Chinese immigrants were invited by the governor of California to stand side-by-side with whites in 1850 to celebrate California's admission to the union, just two short years later Chinese immigrants felt the sting of the new state's first piece of discriminatory legislation. The foreign miners' license tax, initially intended to drive Spanish and Mexican miners out of competition, forced all those classified as "ineligible for citizenship," including Chinese, to pay the state a fee of $2 to $3 per month. The racist intent of the bill was obvious, as a 1790 federal law already prohibited nonwhites from becoming naturalized citizens. By the time the tax was declared unconstitutional and finally repealed in 1870, California had collected some $5 million from Chinese laborers.

The next tax, also motivated by racism, passed in 1855. This law taxed the owner of a ship $50 for each passenger ineligible for U.S. citizenship, constituting the first step toward shutting out Chinese migrants. Three years later, California law forbade Chinese passengers from disembarking from ships except in an emergency.

Socially as well as legally, the climate grew hostile toward the Chinese (and other minorities), especially after the gold rush peaked and thousands competed for claims that were quickly running dry. Mining company bosses often favored hiring the hardworking Chinese, who would do the work whites shunned and for less than half the pay. And the Chinese, already earning so little, were less likely than whites to go on strike. This situation fed festering feelings of jealousy and resentment toward the Chinese as a labor group.

General lawlessness, drunkenness, and nervousness over money also pervaded the crowded mining camps and surrounding towns, adding fuel to the fire of hatred. Furthermore, violent solutions to conflict, racist attitudes, and gun-toting renegades had always been part of the pioneer West. Mob violence against the Chinese remained unchecked and was even supported by court rulings such as the California state Supreme Court decision in *People v. Hall*.

PEOPLE V. HALL

The *People v. Hall* decision set convicted murderer George W. Hall free because three of the four witnesses to the crime happened to be Chinese. Hall and two others had been convicted in 1853 for the murder of Ling Sing, and Hall was sentenced to death by hanging. When the state reviewed the case, the verdict was reversed. Without the testimony of the three Chinese witnesses, there was too little evidence to convict the white murderer, who was soon released.

The discriminatory ruling of *People v. Hall,* aimed not only at the Chinese but African Americans, Hispanic Americans, and Native Americans as well, underscored the legislative effects of such blatant

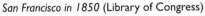

San Francisco in 1850 (Library of Congress)

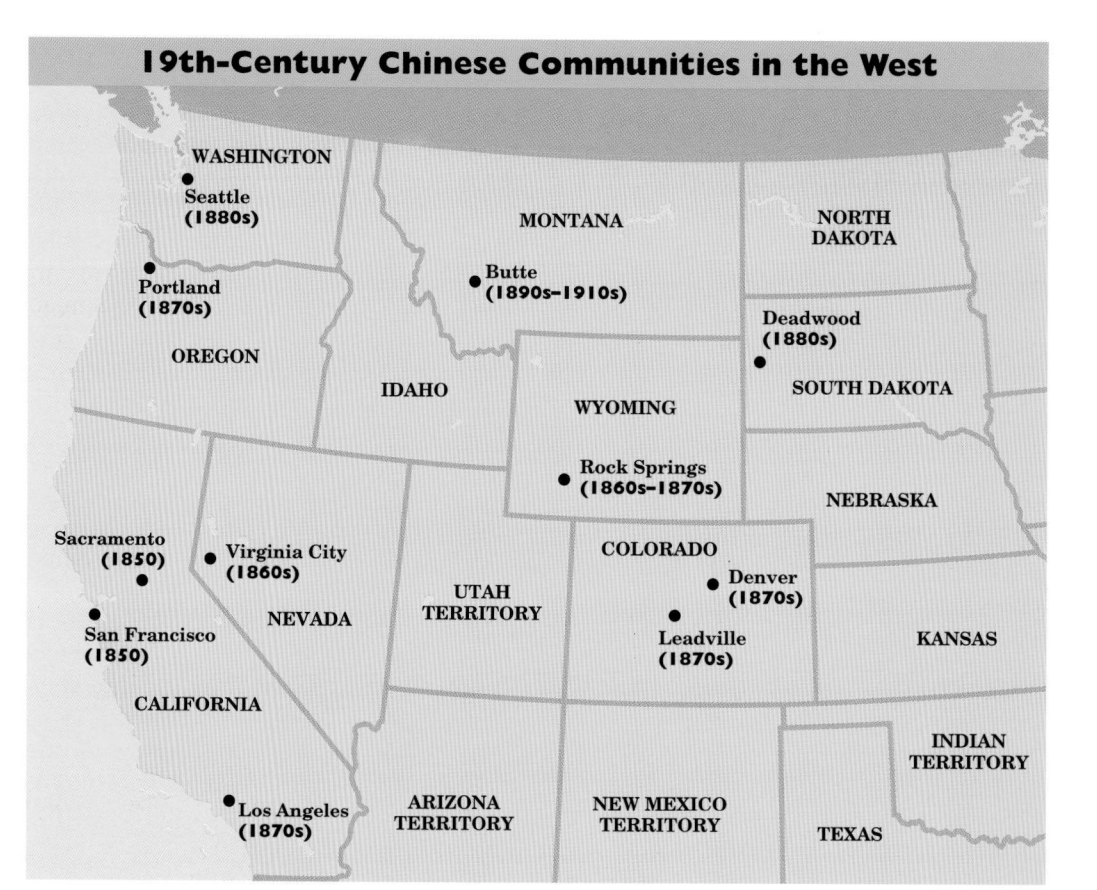

19th-Century Chinese Communities in the West

San Francisco's Chinatown in the 1860s
(Library of Congress)

prejudice. The ruling, passed by the California Supreme Court in 1854, stated that only whites could give testimony in courts of law. This essentially ensured that those who committed crimes against nonwhites would go unpunished if the only witnesses happened to be "colored," meaning "black," "red," or "yellow-skinned."

Many 19th century writers, cartoonists, and politicians, not to mention the public at large, applied degrading adjectives such as "savage," "childlike," "lustful," and "heathen," first to Native Americans, then to African Americans, then to Chinese immigrants. People with darker skin, different hair, eyes, customs, and dress, became lumped together as one enemy—a stereotypical, threatening, nonwhite "other."

CHINESE COMMUNITIES IN THE 19TH CENTURY

Across the western and, later, the eastern portions of the United States, Chinese neighborhoods or "Chinatowns" within the growing cities provided community for immigrants. A feeling of belonging became especially important to those who perennially felt like strangers in a land grown increasingly hostile to their presence.

Bustling streets filled with newly opened stores and restaurants, merchants and vegetable peddlers, and signs painted in Chinese characters put residents at ease. Characteristically poetic names for stores such as Wa Yung ("The Flowery Fountain") and Man Li ("Ten Thousand Profits") echoed the hopes and dreams of immigrant merchants—many still intending to make a grand return to China carrying a nest egg for their families.

Job opportunities within the growing business communities offered alternatives to new immigrants not interested in mining the gold fields. Early ventures included restaurants, retail stores, tailor shops, and laundries.

Laundry as a business did not exist in China, and traditionally, Chinese men did not do the family's laundry. American women taught Chinese immigrant men how to use washboards and flat irons, appliances that were unheard of in China at that time. Chinese-American laundries became a common and relatively successful business beginning in the early 1850s.

It was an easy business to start, for a new immigrant could open a laundry with as little as $75. A sign, a stove, a trough, a drying room, and a place to sleep composed the basic necessities. Poor English skills did not hold a laundryman back from success—"yes," "no," finger-pointing, and a few drawings got the job done.

Laundry jobs proved plentiful. In addition, white workers bent on keeping the Chinese out of the mines, farms, factories, and railroads did not seem to care about the laundry business—after all, it was considered women's work. The squeeze from other job sectors proved severe: by 1900 one of every four employed Chinese in California worked in a laundry.

While laundries and a few other businesses provided a degree of financial stability, traditional cultural celebrations helped Chinese immigrants and their communities thrive. Altars built to honor Chinese gods such as Kwan Yin, goddess of mercy, and Kwan Kung, god of literature and war, carried forth the immigrants' religious faith. The "Pure Brightness Festival" of Qing Ming honored ancestors, and the raucous Chinese New Year, with cheers of *"Gung hay fat choy!"*, wished good luck and prosperity for all. Chinese theater served, not only as entertainment, but also as a means of continuing cultural traditions in the new land. Hundreds of men, smoking cigars and sitting upon rows of benches, regularly attended weekly performances, some lasting up to six hours. Familiar food, native languages, and shared experiences helped ease the struggle and pain experienced by many immigrants so far from home.

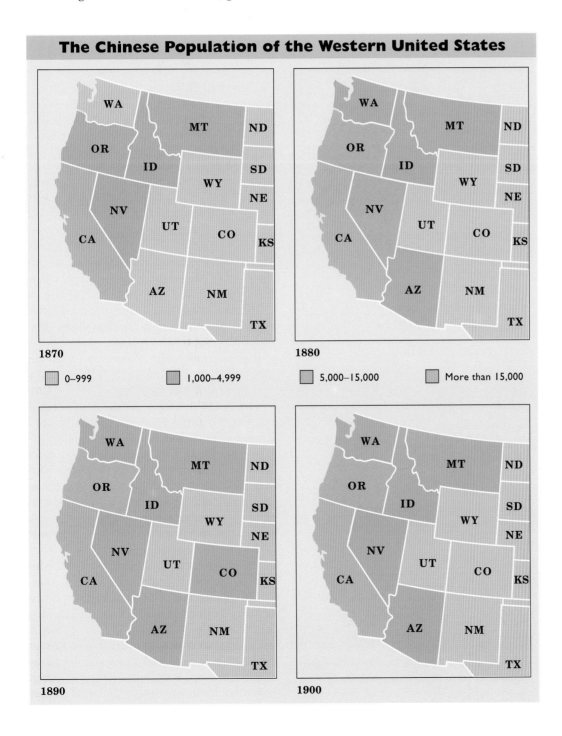

The Chinese Population of the Western United States

1870

1880

☐ 0–999   ☐ 1,000–4,999   ☐ 5,000–15,000   ☐ More than 15,000

1890

1900

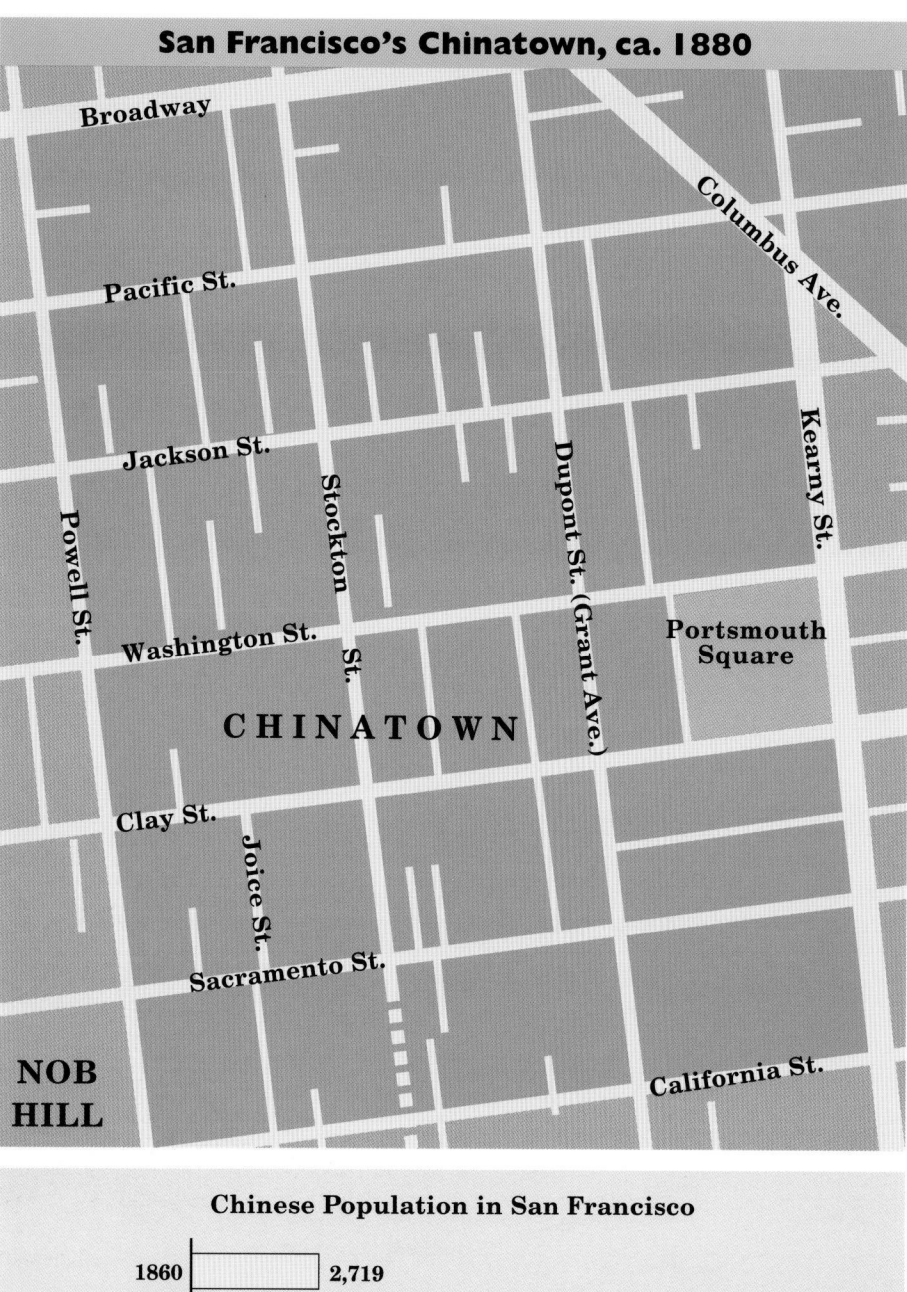

San Francisco's Chinatown, ca. 1880

Broadway
Pacific St.
Jackson St.
Washington St.
Clay St.
Sacramento St.
California St.
Columbus Ave.
Kearny St.
Dupont St. (Grant Ave.)
Stockton St.
Powell St.
Joice St.
Portsmouth Square
CHINATOWN
NOB HILL

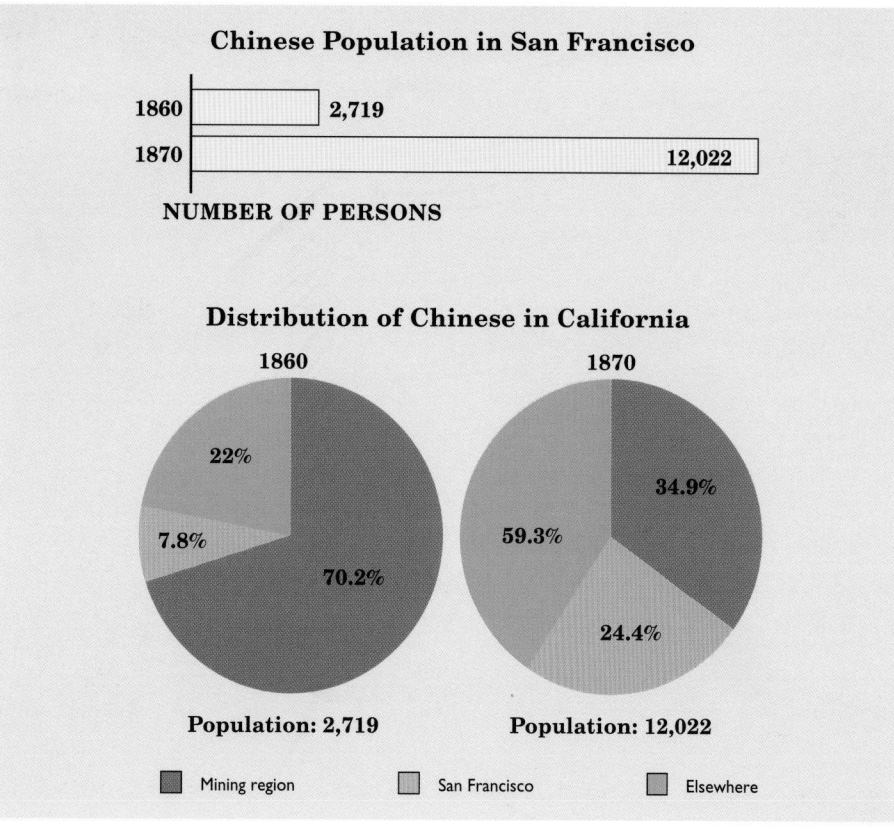

Chinese Population in San Francisco

1860 — 2,719
1870 — 12,022

NUMBER OF PERSONS

Distribution of Chinese in California

1860
22%
7.8%
70.2%
Population: 2,719

1870
34.9%
59.3%
24.4%
Population: 12,022

Mining region   San Francisco   Elsewhere

THE BIRTH OF SAN FRANCISCO'S CHINATOWN

During the 1850s a number of early immigrants opened shops, restaurants, and other establishments in and around San Francisco's Portsmouth Square. These first businesses catered to the needs of miners, but even before the end of the peak years of the gold rush, San Francisco's Chinatown had become a vibrant, self-sufficient community. By 1877 Chinatown's businesses catered primarily to the Chinese population and covered 12 square blocks. Among the businesses in that era's Chinatown were 33 retail stores, five restaurants, three tailors, and five butcher shops.

As the gold rush slowed, immigrant miners traded rural life for the city. San Francisco and Chinatown changed along with the times. San Francisco's population grew from 2,700 in 1860 to more than 12,000 in 1870. The nature of businesses had also changed by 1870, but even more important, a new pattern had been set in motion. Workers with an entrepreneurial spirit had become factory laborers dominated by white bosses. The same scenario took place across the West as mining operations ceased.

OTHER CHINESE COMMUNITIES

The small Chinatowns that grew around the mining camps often disappeared when the mines played out. However, many of California's fledgling Chinese communities thrived. In addition to San Francisco (Dai Fou, "Big City"), Chinese communities grew in Sacramento (Yee Fou, "Second City"), Stockton (Sam Fou, "Third City"), and the smaller Marysville.

In 1870 California still retained a large portion (77 percent) of the United States's Chinese immigrants. Others roamed the West, searching for mining jobs in states such as Colorado, Montana, and Nevada. The 1880 copper boom in Butte, Montana, proved attractive and followed the state's silver boom and earlier gold rush. In that year Chinese laborers constituted 21 percent of Butte's population.

San Francisco's pattern of boom and squeeze repeated itself for the Chinese miners in Butte. After 1883, when the state supreme court declared mining claims filed by noncitizens to be void, Chinese laborers opened tailor shops, laundries, and restaurants. They also hired themselves out as domestic servants—all occupations considered by American men to be women's

Chinese factory workers make shoes in Lowell, Massachusetts. (Library of Congress)

work. Since few American women ventured out to live in or near mining camps, such jobs were plentiful.

Eventually, Chinese began to trickle to the East Coast in search of work, increasing their numbers during the 1880s. They joined small groups of their countrymen already established on the Atlantic coast and grew strong Chinatowns in places such as New York City and Boston. By 1890 New York's Chinese population had grown to 3,000 with a community planted around Mott Street.

NEW CHINESE BUSINESSES

During the mid-1860s, most miners left California's waning gold fields for other

work. Many Chinese immigrants found employment building the transcontinental railroad. Others went to work on farms, and many returned to San Francisco, which had become an important manufacturing center when the American Civil War had disrupted production in the eastern United States. Those who did not open restaurants, stores, or laundries often found jobs in San Francisco factories making cigars, textiles, or footwear. No one tried to drive the Chinese away from these jobs, which were tedious and low paying.

The rapid expansion of San Fracisoco's manufacturing sector demanded a steady supply of inexpensive labor. Chinese workers increasingly found themselves in

Scenes from Virginia City, Nevada (Library of Congress)

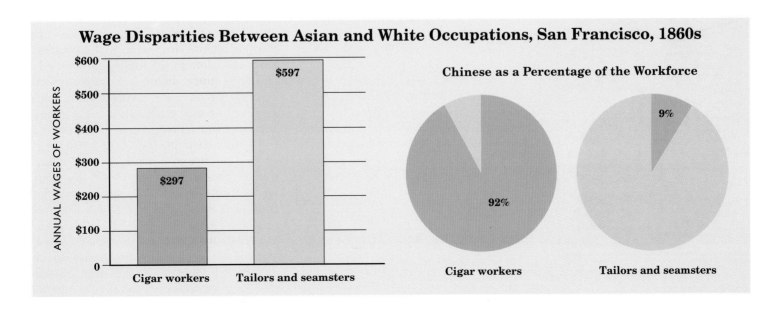

Wage Disparities Between Asian and White Occupations, San Francisco, 1860s

A Chinese family in Washington State (Library of Congress)

The seal of the Chinese Six Companies
(MPI Archives)

the low-wage industries. By the mid-1860s, 92 percent of cigar workers in San Francisco were Chinese. They usually earned around $300 per year. In contrast, tailors earned nearly $600 per year, but only 9 percent of that workforce was Chinese.

Over time, competition from the East Coast's larger and more efficient factories proved hard to beat. By the turn of the century almost all of the West's light industries had ceased production. Once again, immigrants were forced to seek other work.

Chinese restaurants, laundries, domestic occupations, and merchants inside the Chinese neighborhoods continued to grow and provide sustenance for the community, but other, less honorable occupations involving drugs, gambling, and prostitution also prospered within the boundaries of Chinatown.

THE CHINESE SIX COMPANIES

Chinese merchants played a key role in the growth of the Chinese-American commu-

nities in the cities of the United States. San Francisco's Chinatown formed its first merchants' association in 1849. The association welcomed new arrivals and helped them negotiate the new language and find housing and work. The original organization gradually grew into a network of six district associations, which collectively became known as the Chinese Six Companies. Each district association, patterned after its root district back in Guangdong province, umbrellaed over a number of family groups or clan associations. This link to the Chinese homeland kept the same strong relationships alive in the United States.

The activities of the Chinese Six Companies fell into five categories. The first focused on helping new arrivals with health care, jobs, housing, and money. The communications and burial segment helped arrange for the shipment of the dead back to China for traditional burial and communicated messages to living relatives in China. The security and community mediation arm took on the task of

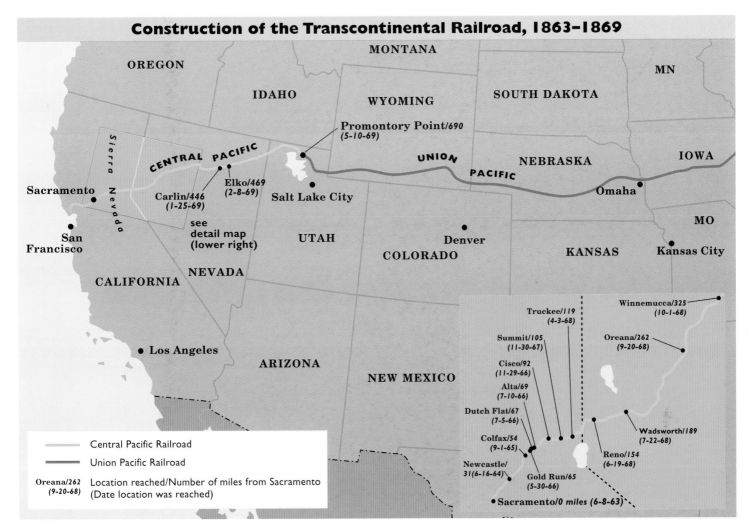

Construction of the Transcontinental Railroad, 1863–1869

In 1863, construction began on the nation's first transcontinental railroad system. The system actually consisted of two different railroads—the Union Pacific, constructing track westward from Omaha, Nebraska, and the Central Pacific, responsible for the construction of track eastward from Sacramento, California, which involved cutting across the high Sierra Nevada. Because so few white workers were willing to take on the treacherous assignment, Central Pacific recruited Chinese workers, who from 1865 to 1869 performed all aspects of construction, including dynamiting tunnels though snowy mountains. As can be seen from the map above, progress on the Central Pacific's construction was quite painstaking.

settling internal disputes among Chinese Americans and operated its own police force. Community representatives worked with the white business community to further Chinese business interests. And in the area of legal defense, the Six Companies hired white lawyers to challenge unjust laws and negotiate better treatment for Chinese in the courts.

In return for these services, the Six Companies collected membership fees, imposed taxes to support programs, and installed systematic checks at docks to make sure departing Chinese paid their debts before leaving.

Such networks of association held together all the major Chinese communities in the United States. During the 1880s, a national group collected the state associations into a national organization called the Chinese Consolidated Benevolent Association (CCBA). Other ethnic benevolent associations helped immigrants with loans, housing, jobs, and assimilation. The CCBA, however, went a step beyond to become a well-organized national defense against hate crimes, racist legislation, and bigotry.

THE TRANSCONTINENTAL RAILROAD

In 1848 Aaron H. Palmer, an American policy maker, put forth his vision for the role of Chinese laborers in the development of western America. Stressing the importance of steam transportation in the Pacific, he submitted a plan to Congress that would establish San Francisco as the center of trade between the United States and China. He claimed a railroad connecting the West Coast with the East would bolster economic success, and he specifically

Chinese laborers in the Sierra Nevada (Library of Congress)

called for Chinese laborers to build it. Palmer went on to recommend that the Chinese be brought to the United States to cultivate the farmland of California as well. In keeping with the concept of America's "manifest destiny"—a term coined in 1845 by a New Yorker named John L. O'Sullivan, editor of *United States and Democratic Review* magazine to signify the United States's inevitable supremacy over all the lands of North America—Palmer

urged the importation of labor as the fastest way to ensure America's economic and ideological expansion.

Congress authorized construction of the United States's transcontinental railroad to begin in 1863. This significant route of transport was to be built from both directions simultaneously. The eastward track was laid from Sacramento through the Sierra Nevada and eventually into Utah. The westward track, built mainly by

Irish immigrants working for Union Pacific Railroad, started in Omaha, Nebraska.

Chinese laborers did indeed become the core of the workforce on the eastward Central Pacific Railroad portion of the railroad and performed all aspects of construction: clearing trees, laying track, damming rivers, and digging ditches. At Central Pacific's request, the Chinese Six Companies helped recruit laborers from China and the Chinese-American communities. Between 1865 and 1869, the total number of Chinese railroad workers grew from 50 to nearly 12,000. As with mining, the jobs were readily available: Whites refused to work certain sections of the track's construction, citing high levels of danger and risk.

LIVING AND WORKING CONDITIONS

One of the most dangerous tasks was blasting tunnels through the peaks of the Sierra Nevada. Lowered in round, waist-high baskets that had their origins in Han dynasty China (206–208 B.C.), workers drilled holes and laid nitroglycerine in cliff sides. After lighting each fuse, they had to shout to be hauled back up before the explosion. Because many Chinese died performing this work, the expression "not a Chinaman's chance" was born.

Living and working conditions differed for the workers of the two railroads. The Irish working for Union Pacific worked eight-hour days for a monthly wage of $31, plus money for room and board. Working in the plains states, the Irish faced the threat of attack from Native Americans, a danger the Chinese, working in the mountains, usually did not have. The Chinese working for Central Pacific earned the same monthly wage as the Irish, but worked longer days, from sunrise to sunset. Chinese laborers received no money for room and board—they lived in tents by the side of the railroad instead.

The worst working conditions for the Chinese occurred during the forced camp winter of 1866. According to the rules imposed by Congress, the sooner the railroad companies completed the track, the more land grants and government subsidies they earned. This time pressure heavily influenced Central Pacific's decision to force the laborers to work throughout the winter. Despite knowledge of such gruesome tragedies as the 1846 Donner Party expedition, in which members of a group of pioneers stranded in the High Sierras took to cannibalism in order to survive,

Central Pacific's greedy managers still sent the Chinese into the vicious mountain winter of the Sierra Nevada.

That winter, the entire construction site was covered by roofs and walls of snow. The workers lived, laid track, and slept in the deep tunnels they dug under the 40-foot snowdrifts. At times, snow slides buried entire work crews and camps. Replacement crews would arrive in the spring to find horrific frozen corpses of miners still clutching their shovels and picks.

THE STRIKE OF 1867

Approximately 5,000 Chinese workers demanded improved conditions during a walk-out strike in June 1867. The workers asked for an eight-hour day and a raise to $45 per month. The Central Pacific's chairman, Charles Crocker, ordered the workers' food supply lines cut. Starving and lonely in the far-away mountains, the laborers gave up within a week and returned to finish the railroad.

The eastward and westward tracks of the transcontinental railroad finally met in the middle on May 10, 1869, at Promontory Summit, Utah. However, the very men who so heavily labored along the track lines were completely excluded from the celebratory publicity at the job's conclusion. As a white man's hammer drove down the final golden spike into the rail, white company bosses smiled for the crowd and press. No one rewarded or even thanked the Chinese laborers, many of whom had died in the process of uniting the eastern and western halves of the United States. Instead, Central Pacific laid off the Chinese workers, leaving nearly 12,000 unemployed in one fell swoop.

THE BURLINGAME TREATY OF 1868

In 1868, one year before the transcontinental railroad was completed, American representative Anson Burlingame met with the Manchu government of China to negotiate an important treaty regarding fair play between the two nations. Hoping to maintain a steady supply of labor to complete the railroad, the United States agreed to end limits on Chinese immigration. The Chinese Six Companies, at the forefront of the fight for civil rights protection, took advantage of the negotiations to press for protections for Chinese immigrants in the United States.

Their initiative met with success. In exchange for the right to import Chinese laborers without limit. the U.S. government promised not to interfere in China's internal problems. And members of the Chinese-American community received the title of "permanent residents" with "the same privileges, immunities and exemptions with respect to travel or residence" as may be enjoyed by citizens of a most favored nation.

CHINESE FARMERS

Chinese-American labor made the expansion of California agriculture possible. As railroad labor had been, farm labor in the Golden State was in short supply from the beginning, and California relied heavily on Chinese former miners to harvest the state's wheat. When the transcontinental railroad was finished, the demand for farmworkers skyrocketed as the new transport route spurred the growth of new agricultural markets. Farmers planted fruits, vegetables, and flowers alongside wheat and shipped the products across the nation by rail.

Chinese farmhands not only labored in the fields—some went into business for themselves. Though discriminatory laws forbade Chinese immigrants from owning the land they worked, a few Chinese entrepreneurs struck up cooperative relation-

Thanks in large part to Chinese irrigation techniques, the San Joaquin and Sacramento River deltas became some of the world's most fertile farmland during the 19th century.

The San Joaquin and Sacramento River Deltas

ships for profit-sharing with their white bosses. Some rented as well as worked the land as tenant farmers, and others operated "truck" gardens, meaning that they would produce vegetables which would then be trucked to market for sale. Chinese farmworkers also developed innovative fruit cultivation and irrigation techniques.

INNOVATIONS IN AMERICAN AGRICULTURE

In addition to manual labor, Chinese farmworkers significantly contributed to California's agricultural success with the use of their considerable skill and expertise. Beginning in the 1860s Chinese workers applied traditional irrigation techniques on U.S. soil. They met with tremendous success, for Guangdong's Pearl River delta and California's San Joaquin and Sacramento River deltas share similar environmental conditions. In a little less than two decades, the Chinese reclaimed nearly 5 million acres of historically flooded and useless land and created some of the world's most fertile farmland.

Chinese farmworkers transformed the swamps and marshes of northern and central California by constructing networks of irrigation channels, levees, dikes, and ditches. Chinese reclamation workers used shovels, pitchforks, spades, and hooks to dig out the muddy earth. Standing in the blistering sun, waist-high in water, the workers made miles of dams and drainage devices by hand. Many of contemporary California's machine-made levees and drainage pathways still have the original Chinese walls and canals strongly intact at their core.

Chinese laborers used their knowledge and skill in the area of fruit cultivation as well. Oregon's Ah Bing used his horticultural skills to breed today's popular Bing cherry. Florida's Lue Gim Gong developed the first frost-resistant orange, sparking a huge industry in that state.

Despite such significant contributions to American agriculture, the Chinese once again met with the dual-wage system, earning $10 to $20 per month less than white farmhands. And in an increasingly familiar pattern, Chinese farm laborers experienced prejudice and hatred just as the miners and rail workers had.

RESENTMENT OF CHINESE AGRICULTURAL WORKERS

For all of the important improvements that Chinese Americans brought to the agricultural industry in 19th century central California, their growing population and presence in the labor force angered the white farmhands. In Sacramento County alone, the percentage of Chinese farmworkers shot up from 45 percent in 1870 to nearly double that just 10 years later. Farm owners made bigger profits from the Chinese workers by paying them less than whites. From the bosses' point of view it made sense to hire Chinese laborers instead of whites. As in other economic sectors, this dual-wage system fueled ethnic conflict between the two groups of workers. The movement against the Chinese intensified as increasing numbers of white workers suffered economically in the 1870s and 1880s.

THE ANTI-CHINESE MOVEMENT

Economic hardship coupled with suspicion of a perceived enemy are the two principal ingredients used to unite any smattering of desperate and disgruntled people into hate movements. Both conditions existed during the late 19th century. White workers distrusted the Chinese because they perceived them as an ethnic group who were stealing jobs away from the "true Americans."

Hostility, resentment, and discriminatory legislation toward the Chinese mounted steadily, from the 1854 California Supreme Court case of *People v. Hall* to the Nationality Act of 1870 to the Page Act of 1875 to the growth of California's influential Workingman's Party. The movement reached its peak in 1882 when, amid the hysteria and violence of the anti-Chinese movement that raged across the West, Congress passed the Chinese Exclusion Act, expressly forbidding immigration of Chinese laborers altogether.

KNOW NOTHINGS, THE WORKINGMAN'S PARTY, AND ANTI-CHINESE SENTIMENT

As the economy turned sour in the latter part of the 19th century, cresting in a national economic depression in 1893, racist movements against all foreigners became more organized. Across California angry, unemployed white workers burned homes and stuffed Chinese workers onto railroad cars in a violent effort to literally

A Workingman's Party anti-Chinese rally in San Francisco in 1870 (Library of Congress)

The economic downturn of the 1870s and 1880s, followed by the national depres-

In 1878, the Workingman's Party of California (WPC) ran a slate of candidates for office in California under the slogan "The Chinese Must Go!" Flyers made by WPC members showed a large, black-booted leg labeled "WPC" kicking a Chinese man across the Pacific Ocean toward China.

As several WPC candidates won seats in the California legislature, a wave of Chinese immigrants left the state's hostile environment. Many made the long journey back to China, while others crossed the Rocky Mountains to settle in cities such as Chicago, Boston, and New York. New Chinatowns quickly developed as significant numbers of Chinese joined those already living in urban areas. Fewer than 50 Chinese lived near New York City's Mott Street in 1870, but by 1890 the population had ballooned to nearly 3,000. As became the trend in western cities, the "new" urban Chinese rarely ventured outside of their neighborhood areas, transforming U.S. Chinatowns into "cities within cities," whole and complete unto themselves.

The political expression of America's antiforeigner strain initially reared its head in the mid-19th century with the formation of the American Party. The many Americans who disagreed with their racist viewpoint referred to American Party members as "Know-Nothings." Founded in 1852 when several secret, anti-Catholic organizations united, the group stood for the continued enslavement of black Americans and against the immigration of anyone other than white Anglo-Saxon Protestants. Know-Nothings, who gained their nickname from the vow that members took, to answer "I know nothing" whenever asked about the organization, engaged in mob violence on both coasts and succeeded in winning six governorships in U.S. elections.

In 1878, the Workingman's Party of Cal-

—From the Workingman's Party of California manifesto, drafted in 1877

"We have made no secret of our intentions.... Before ... the world we declare that the Chinaman must leave our shores.... We declare that we cannot hope to drive the Chinaman away by working cheaper than he does. None but an enemy would expect it of us; none but an idiot could hope for success; none but a degraded coward and slave would make the effort. To an American, death is preferable to life on a par with a Chinaman."

force them off the land. From the San Joaquin valley to the southern orange-growing counties, white mobs attacked and killed the Chinese, who record this time in their history as "the driving out."

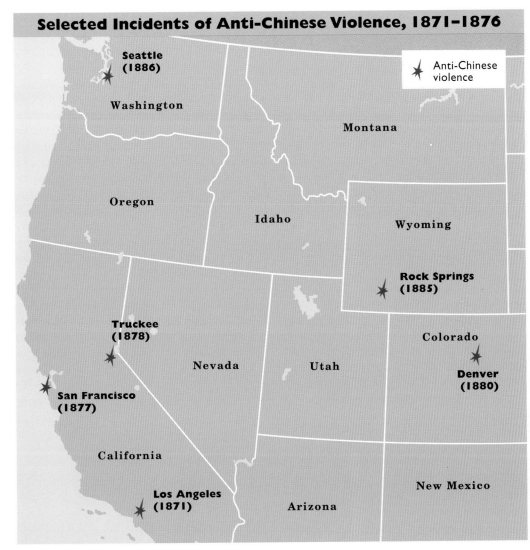

Selected Incidents of Anti-Chinese Violence, 1871–1876

Seattle (1886)

Washington

Anti-Chinese violence

Montana

Oregon

Idaho

Wyoming

Rock Springs (1885)

Truckee (1878)

Colorado

Nevada

Utah

Denver (1880)

San Francisco (1877)

California

New Mexico

Los Angeles (1871)

Arizona

Beginning in the 1870s, incidents of violence against Chinese-American communities in the West increased. Shown above are selected incidents and their locations.

sion of 1893, contributed to the workers' view of the Chinese as an evil enemy. The high cost of the Civil War, inflated credit, and large-scale failed commercial ventures formed the basis of America's economic woes, but white workers looked for a more tangible scapegoat to blame for their troubles. Though high numbers of other immigrants abounded, the Chinese made an easy target for racists because they "stood out" as physically and socially different.

As the rural Chinese flooded into the segregated urban Chinatowns, the Chinese became even more physically separated from the larger white population, which in turn bred more fear and suspicion on both sides. The existence of the vice trade (drugs, organized crime groups known as tongs, gambling, and prostitution) in Chinatown further escalated anti-Chinese sentiment as it reinforced the notion of the Chinese as lustful and immoral non-Christian heathens.

"THE HEATHEN CHINEE"

The latter half of the 19th century abounds with examples of anti-Chinese sentiment. The 14th Amendment pointedly did not grant Asians citizenship alongside African Americans. The Queue Ordinance of 1873 forced Chinese prisoners to abandon their traditional Manchu hairstyle of the long braid worn down the back, known as a queue.

Discriminatory legislative and political actions were bolstered by the prejudice running throughout the wider culture: The public distrusted the Chinese. Lyrics from a popular song of the 1870s, for instance, reflect white workers' fear of being overrun by the "Yellow Peril":

> O, California's coming down, as you can plainly see.
> They are hiring all the Chinamen and discharging you and me;

*But strife will be in every town throughout the
Pacific shore,
And the cry of old and young shall be, "O, damn,
twelve hundred more."*

The mass popularity of Bret Harte's poem, "The Heathen Chinee," first published by the *Overland Monthly* in 1870, also reflected and contributed to the growing perception of the Chinese as uncivilized, inferior, and evil. Though the poem's principal message is ambiguous, lines such as these carry clear racist overtones:

*That for ways that are dark
And for tricks that are vain
The heathen Chinee is peculiar.*

The poem appeared in newspaper after newspaper across the nation. Eventually the phrase "heathen Chinee" became a common part of everyday speech, conjuring up a cartoonish stereotype with each utterance.

Even elected officials contributed to the growing racist hysteria. In 1874, President Ulysses S. Grant declared that the majority of Chinese immigrants were brought to the United States against their will, feeding the previously discredited rumor of a U.S. "coolie trade," or forced indentured servitude by Chinese laborers—a practice common in other countries during the 19th century but not in the United States. Three years later, a California senate committee drafted the "Address to the People of the United States upon the Evils of Chinese Immigration." This report concluded that the Chinese would never assimilate into the larger society:

*[The Chinese] have never discovered the difference
between right and wrong, never ceased the worship
of their idol gods, or advanced a step beyond the tradition of their native hive.*

The document went on to proclaim that their very existence in America threatened Christian values, asserting that "where no Chinese soul has been saved . . . a hundred white [souls] have been lost by the contamination of their presence."

It is true that prostitution, gambling, drug use, and tong organizations existed in America's Chinatowns. Tongs, often referred to as the Chinese mafia, are influ-

The "heathen Chinee," as depicted in a 19th-century cartoon (Library of Congress)

This illustration appeared in Frank Leslie's Illustrated Newspaper *in the late 19th century. It depicts a group of white tourists visiting an opium den in San Francisco. Such sensationalistic scenes were common features in the press, and they served to feed popular notions of the "heathen Chinee." (Library of Congress)*

ential and secretive Chinese criminal organizations involved in the underground vice trades. While most Chinese belonged to an above-board district group related to the Six Companies, some did have membership in tongs.

THE TONGS

In 1880 more than 3,000 tongs operated illegal brothels, gambling joints, and opium dens in U.S. Chinatowns. By the turn of the century rival tongs waged wars in almost every Chinatown in the nation. In New York City, the Hip Sing tong took control of Pell and Doyer Streets while the On Leongs claimed Mott Street.

The tongs patterned themselves after the Guangdong-based Triad Society, an anti-Qing dynasty political group. Tongs in the United States focused on economics, not politics, and operated initially as rivals to the Six Companies. Then the tongs went underground in search of higher profits, and they soon controlled a network of illegal businesses. As with any organized crime ring, tong power was achieved and maintained via physical intimidation and the procurement of protection money from aboveboard merchants.

By 1860 nearly 10 percent of San Francisco's male Chinese worked for tong bosses in either the opium or gambling trades. Curious and drug-addicted whites, both male and female, ventured into these establishments alongside Chinese immigrant men. Even so, the existence of tongs, gambling, drug use, and prostitution in Chinatowns fed into the stereotype of the lustful, immoral, "heathen Chinee."

Opium is an addictive drug containing morphine and derived from the poppy flower. It can be smoked or eaten. Crude opium from India was imported into China, where it was made into black, gummy, pill-shaped balls that were imported into San Francisco. Tin boxes containing up to four ounces of the substance were then sold for about $8 per can in Chinatowns across the United States.

Many Chinese had become opium addicts largely due to aggressive marketing of the product in China by British merchants. As discussed in chapter 1, when the Manchu government of China attempted to shut down the opium trade in their country because of the damaging impact the drug

FAN-TAN AND PAI GOW

Traditionally, the Chinese did not look upon gambling as an immoral vice. In 19th-century America, the most popular gambling games were the traditional mahjong, fan-tan, and *pai gow*. Any number of people can play fan-tan, which involves a random number of buttons or chips placed in a bowl. The buttons are removed four at a time. Players bet on the final number that will be left at the end. Lucky fan-tan gamblers can fatten their winnings nearly tenfold in less than an hour. *Pai gow* is a heavy betting game played with 32 dominoes that are thrown like dice. Today, *pai gow* is so popular that the game appears in legal American establishments such as Las Vegas's Caesar's Palace. Contemporary illegal game rooms still operated by tongs in San Francisco and New York Chinatowns feature blackjack and poker as well as the traditional gambling games.

A Chinese prostitute in San Francisco
(Library of Congress)

Donaldina Cameron

While the Page Law cut the percentage of Chinese women working as prostitutes by limiting the number of female immigrants allowed in the United States, it did little for women and girls already in the country who had been tricked or stolen into lives in the trade. Donaldina Cameron, administrator of the Occidental Board of Foreign Missions in San Francisco, made helping these women and girls her life's work. Between 1895 and 1938 Cameron, known as Lo Mo, or "the mother," to those she helped, and Fahn Quai, or "the white devil," to the tong leaders she challenged, rescued more than 3,000 women and girls. Cameron and her allies would often travel underground tunnels, scale fences, and climb along rooftops to rescue waiting women. She would then take the women in at her mission house; give them money to travel back to China if they chose; or teach them English, reading, and homemaking skills. Cameron House, named in her honor, still operates in San Francisco, providing services to families and the community.

was having on its populace, Great Britain acted with force, waging and winning the two Opium Wars against China. In the United States, opium remained legal until 1914.

In New York City's Chinatown, most of the opium dens sprang up around Mott, Pell, and Park Streets. Users entered small, dark basement rooms to smoke the drug. After removing their shoes and coats, the addicts, both white and Chinese, reclined on broad wooden plank benches to smoke the drug. They used pipes known as *yen tsiang*. The stems of these "opium pistols" were often two feet long and usually made of ivory-tipped bamboo; the bowls were fashioned from hard, red clay. Visits to the smoke houses often lasted 24 hours and addicts usually paid $1 for the *li yuen* type of opium and 25 cents for the less potent *pen yen*. The Americanized expression "to have a yen (desire)" for something can be traced back to the use of this drug.

In Chicago and cities farther west, some of the dens, also called "joints," were elaborately decorated in a traditional Chinese style. The opium rooms often housed or were situated near tong-run gambling rooms.

The third area of large-scale profit for the tongs was prostitution. The buying and selling of women as sexual objects fell under an organized criminal import-export network set up between operatives in China and the United States. It is estimated that law enforcement officials in America were paid up to $500 each by the tongs to ignore the existence of female slaves and prostitutes. According to estimates, between 1852 and 1873, San Francisco's Hip Yee Tong garnered more than $200,000 from the illegal and lucrative trade.

PROSTITUTION

As mentioned earlier, very few women accompanied their husbands on the journey from China. From the start of the gold rush, most women living in the mining camps and urban areas worked as prostitutes. Some of them were white; most were Chinese.

The white prostitutes worked for themselves or for wages paid by brothel owners. The Chinese prostitutes, many of them no older than 15 or 16, were sold into this kind of bondage by their peasant fathers for as little as $70. Exporters in China sometimes kidnapped the girls or tricked their families into believing they would work as domestic servants on Gold Mountain. Once on U.S. soil, the girls were resold by Chinese importers for $1,000 or more.

Life in America's urban Chinatowns and rural work camps was grim for these Chinese peasant girls. Upon arrival, the girls were taken to the barracoon or "Queen's Room," forced to strip off their clothes, and made to stand naked with hundreds of others to be sold at auction. The "lucky ones" became the indentured concubines of the well-to-do or worked in establishments serving these wealthier Chinese men. The others—a majority of whom were urban prostitutes—lived short, miserable lives trapped in tiny rooms called cribs, servicing vast numbers of Chinese laborers who would pay as little as 25 cents each for the prostitute's sexual services. Untreated sexually transmitted diseases and constant physical abuse ensured that the girls died young, most before the expiration of the four- or five-year "employment contracts" they had been forced to sign with their thumbprint as new arrivals fresh off the boats.

In the remote, rural mining camps, Chinese prostitutes served white as well as Chinese men. The white men looked down on the girls as the lowest of the low, calling them calling them names and often abusing them.

Resistance to life as a "singsong girl" or "a hundred men's wife" usually proved futile, as those refusing to work were severely beaten or physically tortured. Runaways, rarely successful, had a difficult time procuring other work, for the vast majority of Chinese prostitutes were unskilled and illiterate, even in their native language.

Sometimes, whites from the larger community aided the young women, as in the case of China Annie, who had run away from the Yeong Wo Company in Idaho City. During the trial following her arrest, a sympathetic judge allowed her to return to the man she had recently married. Another former prostitute, originally sold to Chinese exporters for two bags of seed, married the man who won her in a poker game. The woman, Polly Bemis, eventually became so well respected by her Idaho neighbors that Grangeville's Polly Creek bears her name.

The Chinese Six Companies tried unsuccessfully to work with local law enforcement officials to stop the tong-controlled prostitution trade. Later on, exceptionally brave Chinese Americans and religious missionaries such as Donaldina Cameron rescued thousands of Chinese prostitutes from their painful, dead-end existence.

The U.S. Congress tried to solve the problem with the passage of the Page Law of 1875. This law prohibited the immigration of Chinese women for "immoral purposes" and did dramatically cut the percentage of Chinese women to be imported as prostitutes. By 1880 only 24 percent of the 3,171 Chinese women living in America worked as prostitutes. Forty-six percent of female Chinese migrants, many of them former prostitutes, had secured jobs as housekeepers by that time.

The enforcement of the Page Law, however, once again reflected white America's racist outlook, for all female migrants had to prove that they were not coming to America to work as prostitutes. To be considered guilty until proven innocent is in direct opposition to the U.S. democratic criminal justice code. The Page Law ultimately restricted the immigration of all Chi-

nese women to the United States, once again making it difficult for Chinese families to stay together and make America their home.

THE NATIONALITY ACT OF 1870

The Chinese struggle for civil rights protection began early. In 1855 Chan Yong applied for citizenship; though reporters described Yong as more "white" in physical appearance than most Chinese, San Francisco's federal court denied his request, based on the 1798 Naturalization Law that allowed citizenship to "whites" only. The 1862 case of *Ling Sing v. Washburn*

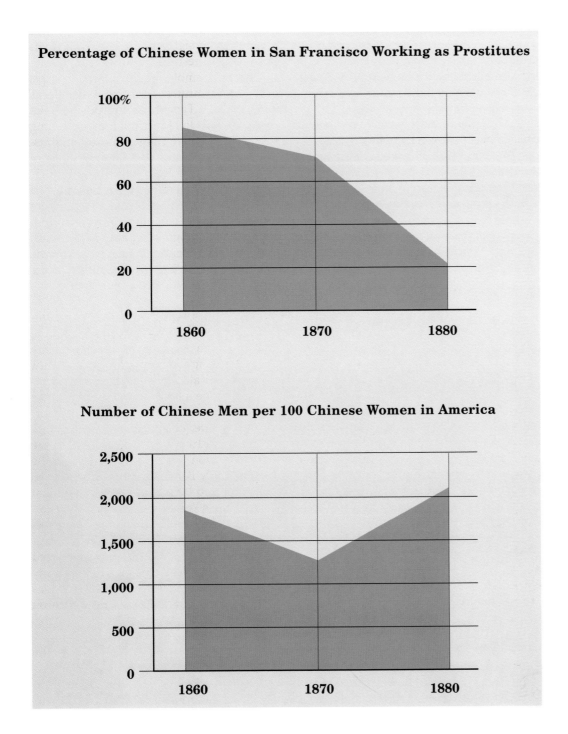

Percentage of Chinese Women in San Francisco Working as Prostitutes

Number of Chinese Men per 100 Chinese Women in America

brought a temporary victory to the Chinese civil rights movement when courts declared a state law invalid because it violated the federal constitution. The key Burlingame Treaty followed in 1868, further strengthening the push for civil rights protection. However, the passage of the Nationality Act in 1870 proved to be a major setback for the movement. The federal law specifically denied Chinese Americans the right to naturalized citizenship.

By this time many Chinese immigrants had become settled enough to consider making the United States home, yet obstacles to this goal grew in number. Chinese families seeking permanence in California faced a newly segregated school system, set up in 1870, whose superintendent flatly declared all nonwhite races inferior. The Chinese seemed forever destined to be strangers in America; there seemed to be little hope of setting down permanent roots in the United States when federal and state governments joined the public in making it clear that Chinese were unwelcome.

The federal Nationality Act helped cement the "us versus them" mentality that had been festering for so long across the United States. As if a red flag of attack had been waved, growing numbers of hysterical white workers burst into an anti-Chinese reactive stance, thronging into city streets and rural areas to shout: "Get out! Get out!" Pockets of such mob violence erupted across the West during the 1870s

and 1880s. Writer Mark Twain reported one such act in his article "Roughing It":

As I write, news comes that in broad daylight in San Francisco, some boys have stoned an inoffensive Chinaman to death, and that although a large crowd witnessed the shameful deed, no one interfered.

Incidents only increased in intensity. In 1877 U.S. Army and U.S. Navy forces joined San Francisco's Committee of Vigilance to restore order during an anti-Chinese riot that began on July 23 and lasted three days. (The committee had formed May 4, 1851, with bylaws authorizing it to arrest, try, and punish men for murder, robbery, or arson; to order that every person known to be a criminal "leave this port within five days of [June 9, 1851]"; and to look over all immigrants arriving in San Francisco and to reject those who were not judged likely to become good citizens.) Rioters numbering in the thousands fought police, burned buildings, and attacked Chinese Americans across the city. The following year saw the entire Chinese population of Truckee, California, driven out of town by angry mobs. Denver experienced anti-Chinese violence in 1880, and five years later Rock Springs, Wyoming, saw 28 Chinese murdered during a violent riot.

Leadership at the federal level continued to discriminate against the Chinese, keeping the unfounded fear of a "Yellow Peril takeover" fresh in the minds of the

Anti-Chinese violence in Rock Springs, Wyoming, in 1885 (Library of Congress)

THE MAIN PROVISIONS OF THE CHINESE EXCLUSION ACT OF 1882

1. Entry of Chinese laborers (skilled and unskilled laborers and miners) to the United States is suspended for 10 years.
2. Any shipmaster who knowingly aids the immigration of Chinese laborers into U.S. ports shall be punished by a fine of up to $500 for each Chinese laborer brought, with possible imprisonment of up to one year.
3. Those laborers who are exempt shall be provided and registered with a certificate from the collector of customs, stating his name, age, occupation, last place of residence, physical marks or peculiarites, and other facts necessary for identification. The certificate shall permit the return and reentry into the United States.
4. Any Chinese other than laborers (students, professors, and other professionals) shall produce a certificate issued by China, in English, stating the right to enter into the United States, name, title, age, height, physical peculiarities, former and present occupation or profession, and place of residence in China.
5. False impersonation, certificate forgeries, and name substitutions shall be punished by a fine of up to $1,000 and imprisonment of up to five years.
6. The master of all vessels arriving in the United States shall issue a full report on the Chinese passengers taken on board at all ports or face punishment.
7. The collector shall examine all aforementioned passengers, comparing the certificates with the list before any passenger shall land in the United States.
8. Every vessel whose master knowingly violates these procedures shall be liable to seizure and condemnation.
9. Any person who knowingly helps a Chinese enter the United States who is not eligible for entry shall be fined up to $1,000 and imprisoned for up to one year.
10. No Chinese person shall be allowed to enter without the certificate required to land from a vessel and shall be deported immediately if found on U.S. land without such certificate.
11. Diplomatic and other officers of the Chinese government shall be permitted entry with a certificate, with their household servants.
12. No state court or court of the United States shall issue Chinese citizenship. All existing laws to the contrary are repealed.

This cartoon commentary on the Chinese Exclusion Act, by Thomas Nast, shows the Republican Party elephant and a Democratic Party tiger pulling a Chinese immigrant—causing the tree of liberty to be pulled from its roots. (Library of Congress)

public. Declared President Rutherford Hayes in 1879: "The present Chinese invasion . . . [is] pernicious and should be discouraged. Our experience in dealing with the weaker races—the Negroes and Indians . . . —is not encouraging."

Aspiring state and local politicians and third-tier political parties increasingly took up the banner of hatred to win political office. Dennis Kearney's antiforeigner Workingmen's Party grew strong in California and took on a particularly anti-Chinese bent.

THE CHINESE EXCLUSION ACT OF 1882

China and the United States agreed in 1881 that the U.S. federal government could unilaterally "regulate, limit or suspend" the entrance of Chinese laborers into the United States. Powerful labor unions across the nation pressured Congress to go a step further and pass the Chinese Exclusion Act of 1882. The vote in the House approved the act overwhelmingly: 201 to 37, with 51 abstaining.

This act barred the immigration of all Chinese laborers, "lunatics," and "idiots" into the United States for a 10-year period. Chinese merchants, students, and diplomats were exempt as long as they secured special papers, known as Section 6 certificates. The act was the first and only law in U.S. immigration history that ordered that a group of people of a specific nationality be banned from U.S. shores.

The Exclusion Act made it difficult for Chinese bachelors already living in the United States to imagine ever getting married. In 1880, fewer than 4,000 Chinese women lived in California, where the Chinese male population exceeded 70,000. Worse still, Chinese men now had no hope of ever bringing wives, fiancées, and families over from China. The men had to leave the United States in order to be reunited with loved ones.

The original international treaty of 1881 had allowed Chinese men already living in the United States to travel back to China and

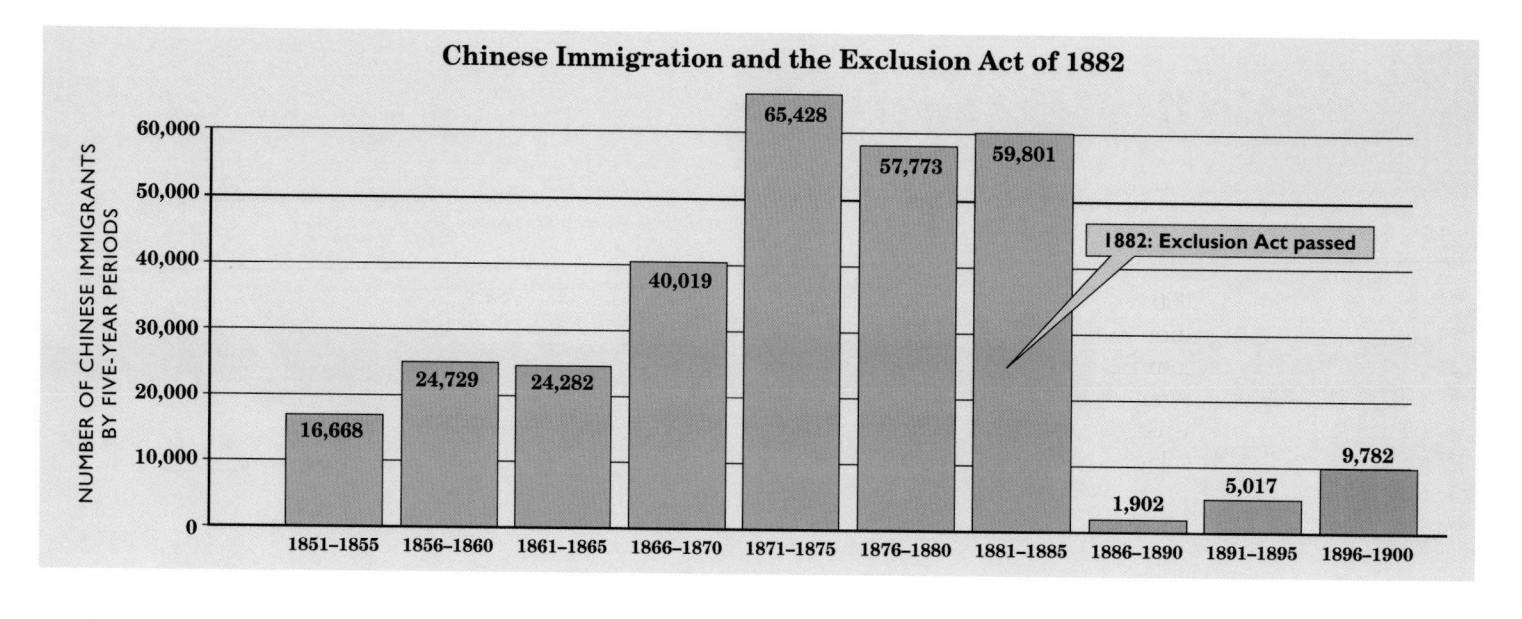

Chinese Immigration and the Exclusion Act of 1882

reenter the United States. That changed, however, in 1888 with the passage of the Scott Act. The 20,000 immigrant laborers visiting China at the time were now forced to stay. Though several U.S. senators and the Chinese government challenged the ruling many times, the Scott Act remained in effect until the mid-20th century.

The 1882 Exclusion Act was renewed in 1888 and again in 1892 with the passage of the Geary Act. This measure took anti-Chinese discrimination to an unprecedented level, requiring every Chinese person in America to register with the government. The Geary Act required that every Chinese immigrant carry a photo I.D. bearing a physical description. Congress deemed this necessary because so many Americans claimed to be unable to tell Chinese individuals apart since "they all looked and sounded alike."

Many individuals and groups, including the ever-present but ineffectual Six Companies, stood against the Geary Act. Kentucky congressman James Bennet McCreary stated in 1893: "There is no good reason for our Government to still further violate the treaty between the United States and China by requiring [Chinese resident aliens] to be tagged, marked and photographed." The Geary Act also allowed for arrests without warrants, denied bail, and stipulated that white witnesses testify in any case involving Chinese immigrants.

Renewal of the Exclusion Act came once more in 1902, this time with the date of expiration left blank. The Exclusion Act remained in effect until its repeal in 1943, when China and the United States allied together during World War II against a new enemy: Japan.

CLOSING THE DOOR
Asian Immigration from Chinese Exclusion

Sometime around 2000 B.C. an enormous wave of migration took place, as some of the most accomplished seafaring peoples in history began crossing the Pacific Ocean from Southeast Asia, settling at last in the small archipelago in the mid-Pacific known today as the Hawaiian Islands.

SETTLEMENT OF HAWAII

The Polynesians who first settled in Hawaii came originally from Southeast Asia. Between 4000 and 2000 B.C. a maritime culture based on seagoing canoes emerged in the islands of Indonesia. These first Melanesian peoples became skilled navigators and traders, plying their canoes throughout the Indonesian archipelago. By 2000 B.C. Melanesians from the central Moluccas islands had colonized the eastern coast of New Guinea. Over the next 1,000 years, these Lapita colonists, named after their distictive red-slipped pottery, continued to spread east to the islands of present-day Melanesia. The reasons for this migration are uncertain, but population expansion was a likely cause. Lapita colonists reached Fiji, the eastern boundary of present-day Melanesia, by 1300 B.C. and made their way eastward to the islands of Tonga and Samoa by 1000 B.C.

Over 1,000 years of geographical isolation, the Lapita settlements on Tonga and Samoa evolved into a new and distinctive Polynesian culture. Both the Melanesians and Polynesians were advanced Stone Age peoples. Each made skillful use of stone, bone, and shell tools, cultivated tubers and fruit trees, and kept domesticated pigs, chickens, and dogs. While the Polynesians did not retain the pottery skills of their Lapita ancestors, their double-hulled and outrigger canoes were technological marvels.

The transoceanic migration of Indonesian seafarers to Micronesia, Polynesia, and eventually Hawaii, beginning at least 4,000 years ago, has been called one of the most dramatic voyages in history. Traveling across the vast Pacific in double-hulled canoes, these migrants used wave patterns as well as the stars as navigation tools. The map below shows their route of migration.

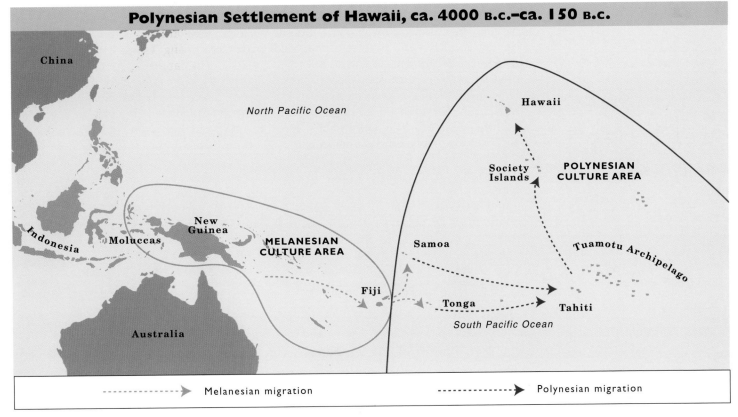

Polynesian Settlement of Hawaii, ca. 4000 B.C.–ca. 150 B.C.

China

North Pacific Ocean

Hawaii

Society Islands

POLYNESIAN CULTURE AREA

New Guinea

Indonesia   Moluccas

MELANESIAN CULTURE AREA

Samoa

Tuamotu Archipelago

Fiji

Tonga

Tahiti

South Pacific Ocean

Australia

- - - - → Melanesian migration   - - - - → Polynesian migration

> "The traders brought labor and fancy diseases—in other words, long, deliberate, infallible destruction—and the missionaries brought the means of grace and got them ready. So the two forces are working together harmoniously, and anybody that knows anything about figures can tell you exactly when the last Kanaka will be in Abraham's bosom and his islands in the hands of the whites."
>
> —Mark Twain,
> Letter from the Sandwich Islands

The Hawaiian Islands

European voyagers of the 18th century reported seeing double-hulled canoes at Tahiti more than 90 feet long. Matted leaf sails let the Polynesians harness the wind by tacking, or setting a zig-zag forward course by shifting the direction of the sails.

Beginning in about 150 B.C., Polynesian colonists from Tonga and Samoa launched a remarkable new seaborne migration to the east. Over the next millenium, their descendants spread throughout the vast ocean expanse of present-day Polynesia. Once again, the most likely explanation for this dispersal was population growth. The Polynesians first sailed their open double canoes, loaded with livestock and seed plants, as well as men, women, and children, to Tahiti and the Society Islands. From there, further generations continued north to Hawaii, east to Easter Island, and south to New Zealand. The Polynesians were arguably the greatest navigators in history. Without aid of navigational tools or devices, they made journeys of up to 2,400 miles across a vast ocean from isolated island to isolated island. They relied on observations of star and sun positions, prevailing winds and swell directions, cloud patterns, and homing birds. During their long voyages, they could sustain themselves by fishing and collecting rainwater.

POLYNESIAN SETTLEMENT OF HAWAII

The first Polynesian settlers reached Hawaii in about A.D. 400. Because the Polynesians had no written language, there is no record of this amazing migration. Anthropologists believe that Polynesian migration to the islands may have continued intermittantly as late as the 1300s but that mutual contact between Hawaii and Tahiti had ceased by 1400. The more fertile high volcanic islands of Hawaii permitted the Polynesians to move beyond their subsistence-level social organization characteristic of Melanesia and to develop a richly ceremonial religious, social, and political life. During centuries of isolation, a separate Polynesian culture emerged on Hawaii. The name Hawaii itself derives from the word for homeland. The Hawaiians were highly skilled fishers and farmers. Taro plants, in particular, were cultivated on irrigated terraces. Their largely wooden villages, with earthen and stone religious sites, were governed by a strict system of laws and taboos, administered by local rulers and chiefs. In the late 18th century, the isolation that Hawaiian settlers had lived in for over a millenium came to a sudden end. The impact of contact with *haoles* (foreigners) was to be devastating.

EUROPEANS ARRIVE IN HAWAII

In January 1778, British naval officer Captain James Cook, in search of the elusive Northwest Passage to Asia, stumbled upon the Hawaiian island of Kauai. Shortly thereafter, he named the Hawaiian archipelago the Sandwich Islands after the fourth earl of

Sandwich, John Montagu, Britain's chief naval minister.

The Hawaiians greeted Cook and his crew with favor, offering food, water, and celebration. Having never seen sailing ships such as Cook's *Resolution* and *Discovery*, nor light-skinned men dressed in the European fashion of the time, the islanders thought Cook to be Lono, their god of agriculture. They entertained the explorers for two weeks during that season's harvest festival, which was already under way. The following winter, Cook's crew sought shelter on the Big Island of Hawaii. Once again hailed as Lono and his entourage, Cook and his men enjoyed yet another favorable greeting, rich with feasts. Two weeks later, they sailed away—only to return again shortly afterward to repair a mast on the *Resolution*. This time, the weary Hawaiians became annoyed with the Englishmen, as the foreigners had already seriously depleted their food supply. A misunderstanding over a small boat taken from Cook by some islanders quickly erupted into a major conflict. Cook attempted to take a tribal chief

James Cook (Library of Congress)

The map above illustrates the route that British captain James Cook followed during two voyages to the Hawaiian Islands and the events immediately following this early contact with Europeans.

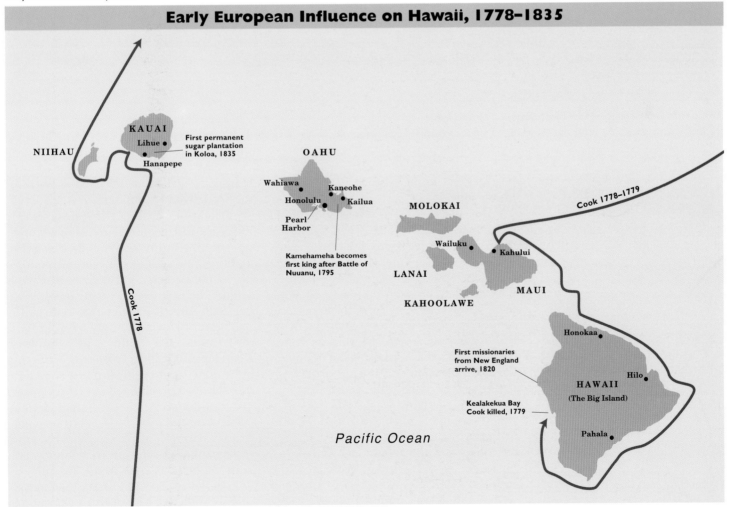

Early European Influence on Hawaii, 1778–1835

years the Chinese continued to refer to the Hawaiian Islands as Tan Heung Shan, or the Sandalwood Mountains.

In addition to impacting the economic life of Hawaii, contact with Cook's expedition and the Europeans that followed dramatically influenced the internal political life of the islands. At the time of Cook's arrival, the islands had no central governing authority. Kamehameha, one of the strongest of Hawaii's many tribal leaders, recognized the value of European weapons and sailing vessels in furthering his military and political plans of uniting the islands. Kamehameha even revamped his traditional Polynesian style double-hulled canoe to mimic a Western schooner. Armed with two cannons procured from Europeans, he set out to conquer and unite all eight islands under his rule. By 1795 he succeeded in joining together six islands into the Kingdom of Hawaii. In

The islanders saw few visitors until eight years later, in 1786, when increasing numbers of ships from England, Spain, Russia, France, and the United States began dropping anchor offshore. Hawaii's location, midway between the East and West, made the islands a logical place to rest and restock supplies. Americans involved in the whaling industry and the thriving trade between Asia and North America figured in the transformation of Oahu's Pearl Harbor into a major deep-water port. Fragrant Hawaiian sandalwood became a huge export to Canton, often exchanged for silks and tea to be brought back to the West. The sandalwood trade would be short-lived, however, as over-cutting decimated the supply by the 1820s. Nonetheless, for many

hostage, and in the ensuing battle, he lost his own life.

After a Hawaiian commandeered a boat belonging to Captain James Cook's expedition, Cook's men retaliated by attempting to take a Hawaiian chief hostage until the boat was returned. As a result, the dispute turned violent, and when a battle broke out, Cook was killed. (Bishop Museum)

CHRONOLOGY OF HAWAIIAN HISTORY, 1778–1852

1778	British explorer James Cook arrives in Hawaii. One year later he is killed after he attempts to take the Hawaiian chief hostage.
1804	A major epidemic, either bubonic plague or cholera, sweeps through the Hawaiian Islands, killing half the population. The disease was brought by Westerners who were resistant to its effects.
1810	King Kamehameha I unifies the Hawaiian Islands into a single kingdom.
1820	Missionaries from the New England Congregationalist Church arrive in Hawaii to convert the population to Christianity. King Kamehameha II agrees to forbid the practice of native religion.
1835	William Hooper of Boston establishes the first sugar plantation on the islands. Within a year, he begins urging his employers to ship him "a colony of Chinese."
1839	Queen Kaahumanu, a convert to Christianity, bans the public performance of hula dancing.
1843	Although the United States had recognized Hawaii's independence the previous year, it installs George Brown as commissioner of Hawaii.
1848	Under pressure from white advisers, King Kamehameha III introduces the concept of land ownership to Hawaii when he launches the Great Mahele, a reallocation of land rights. Under the new system, white foreigners quickly buy a third of all land.
1852	The first 293 Chinese contract laborers arrive in Hawaii.

1810, after 15 more years of war, the last two islands, Kaua'i and Ni'ihau, joined the kingdom.

In addition to military weapons and trade deals, foreign visitors also brought new germs to Hawaii, which led to the deaths of an alarming number of islanders. The Hawaiian people had no natural resistance to European diseases such as smallpox, measles, cholera, leprosy, or bubonic plague. Sicknesses that only weakened Europeans killed many thousands of Hawaiians. In 1804 alone, nearly half the Hawaiian population died during a major epidemic, believed to have been either bubonic plague or cholera. When Captain Cook first discovered the island chain, the Hawaiian population numbered nearly 300,000. A century later, the population had dwindled to fewer than 60,000.

The presence of foreigners also presented a radical challenge to traditional Hawaiian culture. Prior to European contact, Hawaiians believed that gods lived and acted through the forces of nature. The people believed that their Polynesian ancestors had been led over 2,000 miles of ocean to the Hawaiian islands by Laamaomao, the god of the winds. Hawaiians worshiped other gods such as Ku, the god of war, Kanaloa, ruler of the ocean, and Pele, goddess of volcanoes. Prayer and food offerings accompanied almost every aspect of daily life, and reverence was given to every living thing, for all beings possessed divine power, or mana.

High priests shared with tribal priests the top positions in Hawaiian society in a rigid caste system similar to that of feudal Europe or Hindu India. Ancestral lines determined three levels of social status: chiefs and nobles (*ali'i*); priests, teachers, and healers (kahuna); and commoners (*maka'ainana*). All people lived by a body of elaborate rules called *kapu*, a word derived from the Polynesian word *taboo*, or "forbidden." Some rules focused on agricultural practices and the protection of natural resources. Other *kapu* specified rules of behavior. One such rule stated that men and women had to eat separately; another forbade a commoner's shadow to cross the path of a high chief. Hawaiians believed the gods would punish those who broke *kapu* with violent death.

By 1820, Kamehameha's eldest son Liholiho became King Kamehameha II and shared rule with his father's wife, Ka'ahumanu. She and other high-ranking females wanted to change the *kapu* system in order to advance the status of women. Kamehameha II allied himself with the cause by making a radical move—he ate with high-ranking women at a public feast. When he went unpunished by the gods, he ordered the cessation of other *kapu* laws.

Commoners, too, began to question the old ways and beliefs as they pondered the new ideas and customs brought to

Hawaii by the foreigners. When 14 Protestant missionaries from the New England Congregationalist Church arrived on the Kona coast on April 4, 1820, the king readily allowed them to preach their religion.

The missionaries quickly set out to replace all Hawaiian customs with Christian practices—establishing schools, hospitals, and churches. They printed Bibles and created the first written alphabet for the Hawaiian language. Typical Hawaiian clothing also changed radically as the Protestants taught the Hawaiian women how to sew garments in the European fashion. Royal women who had been able to acquire silks and other fabrics through trade with Asia embraced the new styles and dispensed with traditional layered skirts made of tapa cloth.

Eventually, the missionaries gained trust to such a degree that they began advising the ruling class in political matters. Protestantism became the official religion of Hawaii less than a decade after the Protestants arrived. The ruling class accepted Protestantism so deeply that in 1831 they drove out all Catholic missionaries and imprisoned Hawaiians openly practicing Catholicism. However, when the French government responded by sending a warship to blockade the port of Honolulu in 1839, the Hawaiian government agreed to grant religious freedom to Catholics.

American missionaries influenced the government to make other moves toward democracy. In 1839 King Kamehameha III recognized the rights of all Hawaiians to "life, limb, the labor of his hands and productions of his mind," in a declaration of rights. An official constitution followed in 1840, establishing a supreme court and a two-house legislature, with the upper house controlled by royalty and the lower house elected by the commoners. Two years later, the United States recognized the Kingdom of Hawaii's status as an independent nation. In 1843 France and Great Britain did the same.

THE HAWAIIAN PLANTATION SYSTEM

Ultimately, the sweeping economic development that characterized Hawaii during the first half of the 19th century would transform a homogeneous agricultural society into a regimented, hierarchical farming machine controlled by white American plantation owners and worked by a racially diverse group of laborers.

Hawaii became a major whaling port during the mid-19th century. (Library of Congress)

Depletion of Pacific Whaling Grounds

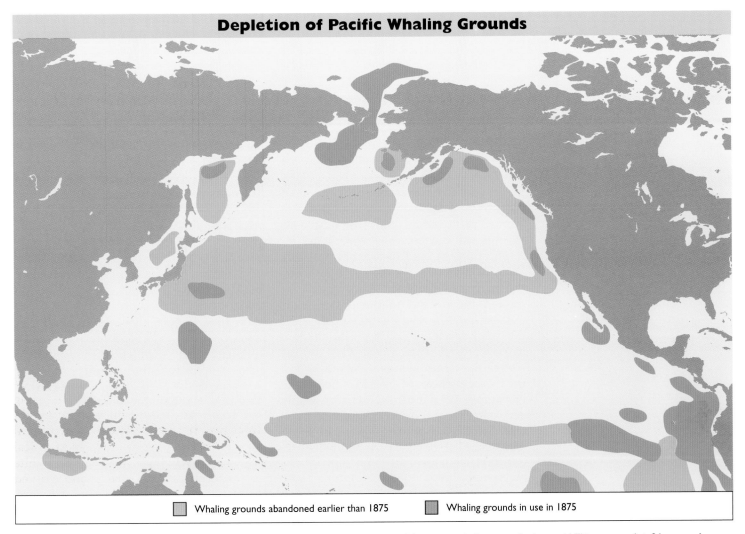

Whaling grounds abandoned earlier than 1875 ■ Whaling grounds in use in 1875

For a brief period during the late 19th century, white settlers turned Hawaii into one of the major whaling ports in the world. This era was brief, however, because whaling grounds disappeared rapidly, as the map illustrates.

Political and social changes came about as well, also because of the influence of white American businessmen and missionaries.

After Hawaii's sandalwood industry collapsed in 1820, Hawaii's next major source of income emerged—the whaling industry. Consumers around the world desired whale oil for fuel, and a tremendous number of whales populated the Pacific Ocean. The ports of Honolulu and Lahaina in particular became popular byways for whaling ships. By the 1860s, however, whaling declined sharply for several reasons: overhunting, a worldwide fuel-source switch to petroleum and coal, and the loss of whaling ships converted or abandoned during the U.S. Civil War. At the Civil War's end, whaling was supplanted by a new industry whose inexhaustible harvest prompted white planters to actively import thousands of newcomers to Hawaii to labor in the fields—sugar.

THE GREAT MAHELE

To understand the manner in which the sugar industry helped transform Hawaii, one must start with the land. To harvest large crops of sugar requires vast tracts of land. However, for the white businessmen who arrived in Hawaii, procuring the land necessary for sugar planting was no simple task. It was not so much that the *haoles* did not own enough land, but that private property itself was not a concept Hawaiians understood since all land was held by the king. However, the rules soon changed.

In 1848 King Kamehameha III initiated a dramatic restructuring program called the Great Mahele. Under the program, Kamehameha III divided Hawaii's land into three parts. He kept one-third for himself, gave one-third of the land to chiefs he held in favor, and put the remainder up for sale. By the mid-19th century, white American planters, who had pushed for the Great

Mahele, had gained control of a third of all land in Hawaii. (Plantation dominance of land continues today: In 2000, Castle & Cooke, the parent company of the Dole Corporation, owned 98 percent of the land on the island of Lanai.)

The Mahele, a Hawaiian word that means "division," ended up dividing most ethnic Hawaiians from the land and benefiting foreign buyers. In 1850 the Hawaiian legislature passed a law that allowed commoners to claim ownership of the small plots of land known as *kuleanas* that they worked and lived on. However, most commoners still did not fully understand the implications of land ownership and sale. What is more, many were not able to buy the many new imported goods circulating around them. Finding themselves landholders, but low on cash, they made quick decisions to sell their plots of land, in most cases for very little money. Most did not realize the consequences involved in selling the very means of their livelihood; others simply did not file their claims legally, and some were refused claims that rightfully belonged to them. Even today, only a small number of *kuleana* lands belong to native Hawaiians.

Most of the lands ended up in American hands. American investors combined the various acres of *kuleana* lands they bought into large sugar and—after horticulturist John Kidwell imported the fruit from Jamaica in around 1885—pineapple plantations. Once white businessmen set up their plantations, however, they found themselves in a dilemma: They had too few workers to plant and harvest the sugarcane crops. The rapid decrease in Hawaii's population caused by continuing epidemics of disease had helped create a massive labor shortage. What is more, planters found that many of the remaining Hawaiians resisted the regimented labor and meager wages of plantation labor. Because native Hawaiians had plenty of good fishing opportunities to supplement their food supply, they were not in dire need of employment as laborers. Ironically, this Hawaiian disinterest in plantation labor helped fuel the prejudice of many white investors, who came to view Hawaiians as lazy and undependable.

American planters thus decided to import workers from afar. Taking the advice of Hawaii's first sugar planter, Boston's William Hooper, they sought to procure "a

Plantation workers quarters at the Hilo Plantation in Hawaii. The poor living conditions in plantation villages fueled discontent. (Hawaii State Archives)

colony of Chinese." The Chinese had earned a reputation on the mainland United States as hardworking, skilled, and cooperative. The planters, mainly American businessmen and sons of American missionaries, formed the Royal Hawaiian Agricultural Society in 1850 to bring in workers from China. The first group of 293 contract laborers, or "coolies," from China arrived in 1852. Two years later, the president of the society declared, "We shall find Coolie labor to be far more certain, systematic, and economic than that of the native. They are prompt at the call of the bell, steady in their work, quick to learn, and will accomplish more [than Hawaiian laborers]."

than accomodate their ethnic rivals by learning to speak in their tongue, both groups preferred to learn Hawaiian in order to speak to each other on the Hawaiian plantations.

Not all Chinese immigrants to the Hawaiian Islands remained laborers. Some migrant workers were able to establish farms of their own, sometimes even importing their own laborers from China to help tend them. They also grew sugarcane, as well as other crops such as coffee, potatoes, taro, and bananas, but Chinese farmers in Hawaii really made their mark in rice cultivation. In fact, rice cultivation in Hawaii came to be dominated by Chinese planters, who brought with them great skill and technical knowledge.

CHINESE LABORERS

During the second half of the 19th century, more than 50,000 Chinese came to Hawaii. As had been the case with the Chinese sojourners to the "gold mountains" of California, almost all of them came from Kwangtung and were known as Punti, or "local people." However, the first few hundred came from Fukien (present-day Fujian), north of Kwangtung on the coast of China. These immigrants were ethnic Chinese minorities that the Punti called Hakkas, or "guest people," and, not only did they speak in dialects that were incomprehensible to Punti, but they had competed with their countrypeople from Kwangtung (sometimes violently) for control of fertile Pearl River delta lands in China. Rather

THE RISE OF KING CANE

Despite the successful introduction of rice farming, it was sugar production that transformed Hawaii, not rice. Sugar production grew so rapidly in the second half of the 19th century that the industry came to be called "King Cane." Demand for sugar had been growing steadily in the United States, and white U.S.-born growers sought to secure the market through diplomatic means. The means was found when the United States and the Kingdom of Hawaii both signed the Reciprocity Treaty of 1875. The trade agreement stipulated that the United States would end import taxes on Hawaiian sugar. The agreement lowered sugar prices on the mainland and increased the demand for

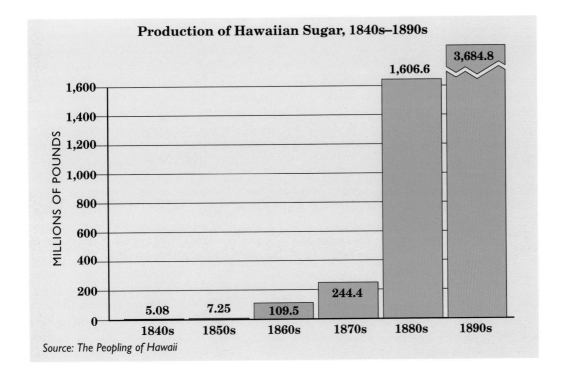

Production of Hawaiian Sugar, 1840s–1890s

Source: *The Peopling of Hawaii*

Women on a sugar plantation attend to their washing in around 1900. (Hawaii State Archives)

Hawaiian sugar over other, more expensive imported sugar. In return, Hawaii promised that its ports and harbors would open only to American ships—thus shutting the rest of the world out of lucrative Hawaiian trade and dramatically increasing the Kingdom of Hawaii's reliance on the United States. By the late 1880s most of Hawaii's sugarcane crop was shipped to the United States.

Prior to the signing of the Reciprocity Treaty, native Hawaiians still composed the majority of plantation workers. However, that changed quickly once the treaty was signed. A bigger market required more production in less time. In the years 1852 to 1875, only about 100 Chinese laborers per year had arrived in Hawaii. From 1876 to 1899, that figure rose to more than 2,000 workers annually.

Most Chinese workers signed contracts requiring their labor for three to five years. Nearly two-thirds of Chinese immigrants to Hawaii during the second half of the century worked on sugar or rice plantations.

Most left plantation life, however, when their contracts expired, or in some cases, when they borrowed enough money to buy their way out. In contrast to the Chinese experience on the mainland, many Chinese succeeded in moving quickly to a more independent life in Hawaii. In addition to those who achieved success in farming, some Chinese of the 1880s also entered the fishing industry, and some moved into better-paying trades such as retail, jewelry, money-lending, and skilled construction. As early as 1882, the expiration of Chinese labor contracts was taking its toll on the plantation labor force. That year, only about 5,000 out of a total Chinese population in Hawaii of 15,000 worked on plantations. By 1902 just 4,000 Chinese still worked on the plantations.

As on the mainland, Chinese immigrants in Hawaii faced discrimination, both from white citizens' groups like the anti-Chinese Workingmen's Union, which formed in 1883, and from individuals. But the fevered anti-Chinese hysteria of the western United States did not develop in the Pacific. Nonetheless, white planters had a strong interest in preventing Chinese and other imported laborers from establishing too much independence. In 1887 the Hawaiian legislature passed a law that took away the vote from Chinese born outside of Hawaii. When the Kingdom of Hawaii was annexed by the United States in 1893, U.S. laws—including the Chinese Exclusion Act of 1882, which banned further immigration from China to the United States—became Hawaiian law as well. In 1899 and 1900, when an epidemic of bubonic plague struck Honolulu's Chinatown, the territorial government burned down the neighborhood to keep the disease from spreading—a response the Chinese community criticized as racially motivated.

As on the mainland, Chinese organizations in Hawaii formed to protect the interests of the local Chinese community. One of the most important of these organizations was the United Chinese Society, which functioned in much the same way as San Francisco's Chinese Six Companies. The group, founded in the 1890s, helped immigrants in crisis and combated social and legal prejudice. Chinese in Hawaii also developed district associations and fraternal societies, although on a much smaller scale than on the mainland.

Though criminal activity did exist in the Chinese community in Hawaii, life for Chinese in Hawaii was more stable than in the largely isolated, heavily male Chinese communities on the mainland. Insular Chinatowns did form, but the all-encompassing isolation that characterized Chinatowns of the mainland did not develop.

Hawaii's greater opportunity for entrepreneurial activity by immigrants both fed and was nourished by the community's stable social structure. The greatest reason for this stability was the presence of wives and children. While San Francisco's Chinatown was a largely male society, Chinese communities in Honolulu and other Hawaiian towns were also home to families. Not only did more Chinese women and children immigrate to Hawaii, but many Chinese men married Hawaiian women, started families, and committed their lives to their new land.

JAPANESE LABOR IN HAWAII

During the reigns of King Kamehameha IV (1854–1863) and King Kamehameha V (1863–1872), many laborers from different countries came to work in Hawaii. Beginning in 1859, immigrants from Polynesia began arriving, just as their ancestors had centuries before. Then in 1868, the first Japanese arrived, followed by the Portuguese during the 1870s. Hawaiian plantation owners began importing Korean,

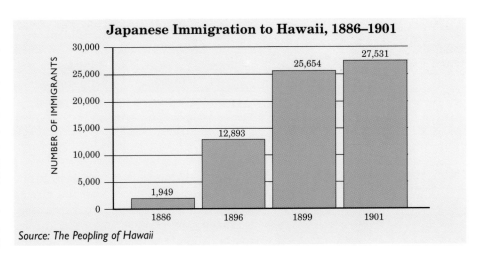

Japanese Immigration to Hawaii, 1886–1901

Source: The Peopling of Hawaii

Japanese immigrants arrive in Hawaii in about 1900. (Hawaii State Archives)

A Japanese baby and child in Hawaii at the start of the 20th century (Hawaii State Archives)

Commodore Matthew Perry (Library of Congress)

Kumamoto districts hit hardest by poverty. Most early Japanese immigrants to Hawaii came from these areas.

Hawaii beckoned to the struggling peasants with its stable political climate and attractive financial opportunities. Word passed quickly that in three years, contract laborers could earn enough money in Hawaii to return to Japan, and then buy and farm the land again. To save the same amount of money in Meiji Japan, it seemed, would take at least three times as long. (This estimate later proved to be wrong, due to Japan's high inflation rate and because of the immense difficulty contract laborers in Hawaii would encounter trying to save money.)

A small number of students, sailors, adventurers, and even samurai, along with various other laborers, sojourned to Hawaii and the mainland. Since the tradition of *dekasegi* (leaving home to supplement income) had long been common in Japan, the concept of "sojourner" was not a new one to the immigrants.

In time, Emperor Meiji actively encouraged travel and promoted the migration of Japanese labor to Hawaii and the mainland, as these arrangements helped expand contact with the West. Unlike the crumbling imperial government of China during the same period, the Japanese government took special interest in its sojourners. This interest had a direct impact on U.S.-Japanese diplomatic relations.

Racial discrimination toward Japanese immigrants proved to be intense in the mainland United States and became the focus of most of the dialogue between the two nations. Japanese diplomatic involvement with Hawaii, however, primarily revolved around labor action, the unionization of Japanese, and the strikes and demands of interethnic labor groups.

The first group of immigrants to leave Japan did so in 1868, the year the Meiji Restoration began. This group, though, did not emigrate with the offical sanction of the new government. Hawaii's Bureau of Immigration paid Japan-based American businessman Eugene M. Van Reed $1,925 to secure a group of Japanese laborers to work on Hawaii's sugar plantations. On June 19, 1868, 141 men and six women and children, all recruited from the Japanese city of Yokohama, landed in Honolulu's harbor. They came to be known as the Gannen Mono ("first year men").

The Gannen Mono experiment was not a successful one. Most members of the group came from the cities and had little agricultural experience. None of them

Filipino, and Puerto Rican workers to the multinational labor forces after the turn of the 20th century.

The Japanese began migrating during Japan's period of rapid modernization known as the Meiji Restoration. When American commander Matthew Perry's gunships arrived in Edo Bay in 1853, Japan had been closed to foreign contact for centuries. Once the Emperor Meiji (1852–1912) ascended to the throne, however, his government determined that the best way to protect the nation from foreign intrusion was to learn as much as possible from the West and then undertake a rapid program of industrialization and militarization. To pay for his sweeping reform programs, Emperor Meiji raised taxes. Japan's peasant farmers, unable to pay the stiff increases, soon suffered from economic hardship and food shortages. More than 300,000 of Japan's farmers lost their land, with southern Japan's Yamaguchi, Hiroshima, and

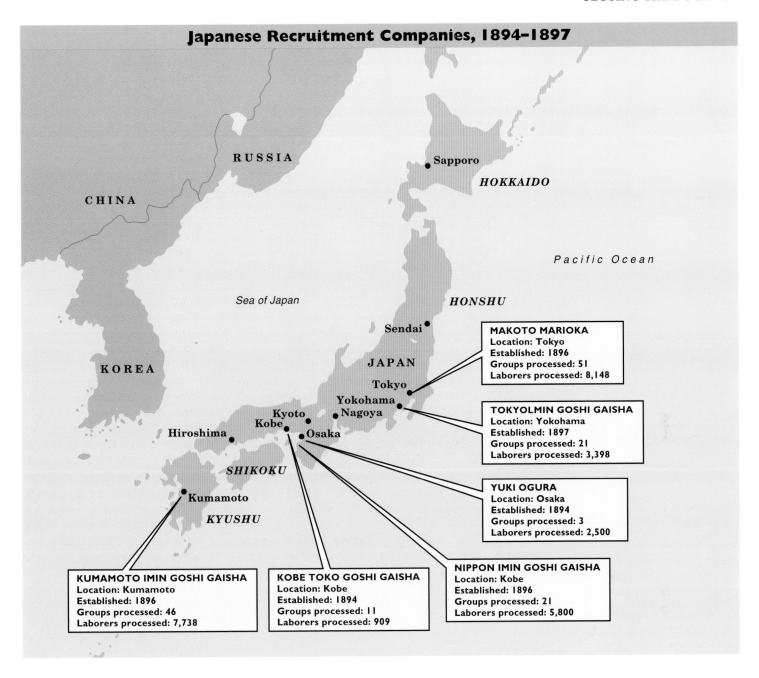

Japanese Recruitment Companies, 1894–1897

MAKOTO MARIOKA
Location: Tokyo
Established: 1896
Groups processed: 51
Laborers processed: 8,148

TOKYOLMIN GOSHI GAISHA
Location: Yokohama
Established: 1897
Groups processed: 21
Laborers processed: 3,398

YUKI OGURA
Location: Osaka
Established: 1894
Groups processed: 3
Laborers processed: 2,500

KUMAMOTO IMIN GOSHI GAISHA
Location: Kumamoto
Established: 1896
Groups processed: 46
Laborers processed: 7,738

KOBE TOKO GOSHI GAISHA
Location: Kobe
Established: 1894
Groups processed: 11
Laborers processed: 909

NIPPON IMIN GOSHI GAISHA
Location: Kobe
Established: 1896
Groups processed: 21
Laborers processed: 5,800

were prepared for the authoritarian attitudes of their employers. Before long, both laborers and planters complained to the Bureau of Immigration. The Japanese government sent emissaries to Hawaii to investigate charges of mistreatment. Forty workers returned to Japan immediately while the rest of them remained to finish their contracts.

Despite the negative experience of the Gannen Mono, Japan and the Kingdom of Hawaii remained on good terms, signing a treaty of friendship and trade on August 19, 1871. However, no other group of immigrants ventured out of Japan to sail to Hawaii until 1885.

In 1883 and 1884, a series of natural disasters severely weakened Japan's economy, providing another push toward emigration for Japanese seeking brighter

prospects. A "pull" effect also drew Japanese laborers after the United States annexed Hawaii in 1893. Because U.S. statehood brought the Chinese Exclusion Act into effect in the islands, Hawaiian planters found themselves increasingly short-handed without the steady stream of new Chinese labor they had come to rely on for decades. In 1885, the Meiji government officially reversed the long-standing policy of banning emigration and officially sanctioned migration to Hawaii. Thus began a period of enormous change for Hawaii that would reshape the ethnic makeup of the islands. Between 1885 and 1925, 200,000 Japanese left for Hawaii and another 180,000 headed for the mainland United States. By 1899, more than 70 percent of Hawaii's plantation labor came from Japan.

During the years immediately after 1885, the Meiji government carefully monitored the contract labor system, for the treatment of its sojourners was a matter of national honor. The sojourners themselves were also expected to uphold that strong sense of national identity, and only healthy, physically strong, and literate workers were allowed to emigrate.

After 1894, the Japanese government regulated emigration companies through legislation such as Imperial Ordinance number 42, Law to Protect Emigrants (1894). Similar laws were passed in 1896 and 1907. Passports continued to be restricted by the government, and applicants requesting emigration had to meet specific character requirements.

Though the Japanese emperor remained involved in the lives of his subjects overseas, Hawaiian plantation owners were not subject to Meiji control. Japanese migrants, like the Chinese before them, endured grueling conditions on sugar and pineapple plantations, working long hours under three- to five-year contracts for low wages. The status of plantation workers as contract laborers tied them to the land and prevented them from taking work elsewhere. Under these circumstances, Chinese and Japanese laborers had little leverage with which to organize for better treatment.

American planters maintained a viselike hold not only on their laborers but on the Kingdom of Hawaii itself. No episode illustrates that hold better than the overthrow of the Kingdom of Hawaii.

THE END OF HAWAIIAN MONARCHY

King David Kalakaua reigned as king of Hawaii from 1874 to 1891. A controversial monarch, he fashioned himself as a European-style ruler, dressing in Western clothing and surrounding himself with American and European advisers. Although many people felt that he helped breathe life back into Hawaii's fading cultural traditions, such as Hawaiian music and hula dancing, even his supporters criticized his selection of advisers. Others thought he was too loose with his money, especially when he built himself a lavish palace. Many agreed, however, that his grand tours of the world added to the islands' prestige.

By any measure, Kalakaua's reign did much to cement the bonds between Hawaii and the United States. His 1874 visit to meet U.S. president Ulysses S. Grant (the first made to the United States by a reigning monarch from any nation) came at a key moment in the negotiations that led to the Reciprocity Treaty of 1875. This treaty ended taxes on Hawaiian sugar imports to the

This chart, which shows the number of laborers by nationality on Hawaii's sugar plantations in selected years for which statistics were available, illustrates that by 1899, Japanese labor had become the largest single segment of the workforce.

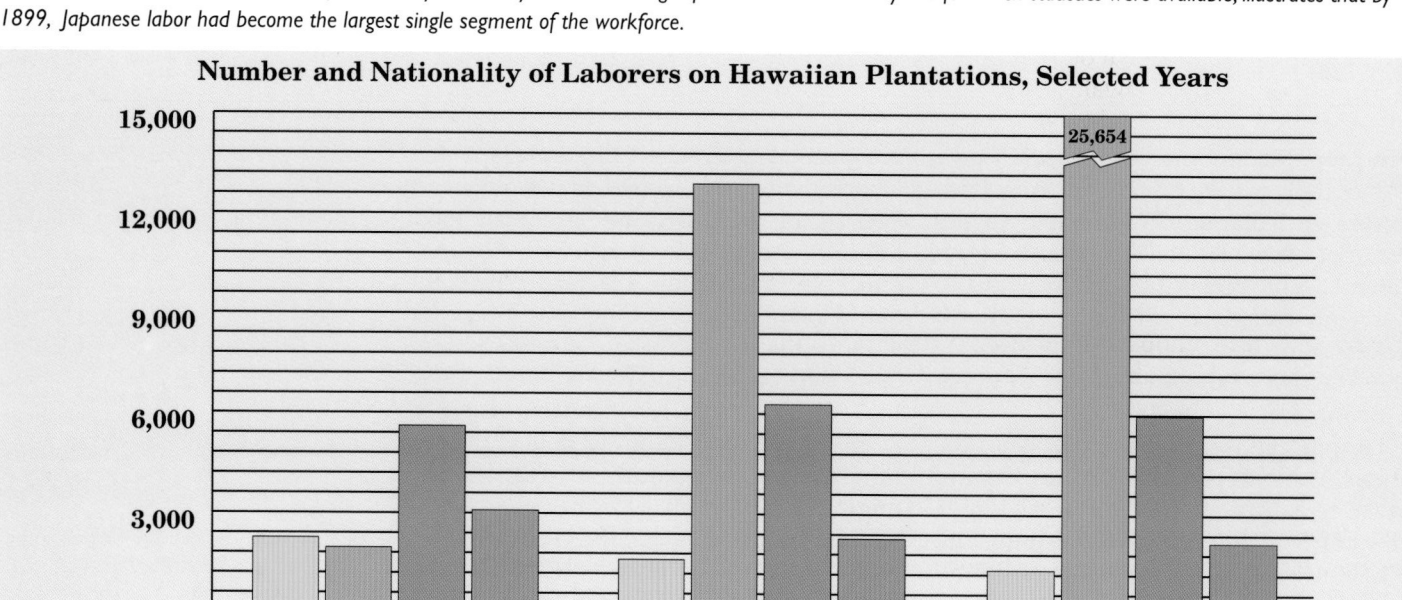

Source: The Peopling of Hawaii

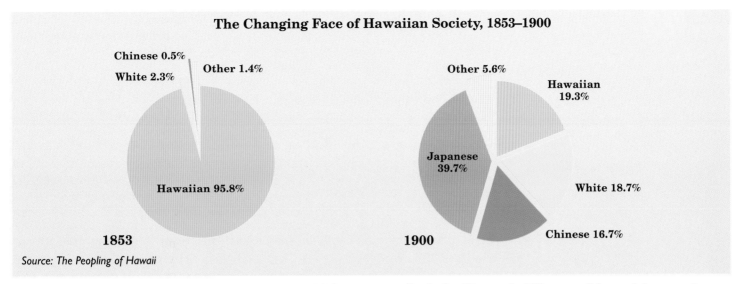

The Changing Face of Hawaiian Society, 1853–1900

1853

Chinese 0.5%
White 2.3%
Other 1.4%
Hawaiian 95.8%

1900

Other 5.6%
Hawaiian 19.3%
Japanese 39.7%
White 18.7%
Chinese 16.7%

Source: The Peopling of Hawaii

These pie charts illustrate the changing ethnic makeup of Hawaii. In 1853, just one year after the first Chinese arrived, 96 percent of the population was native Hawaiian. By 1900, when the Organic Act made Hawaii a U.S. territory, less than 20 percent of Hawaii's population was native Hawaiian.

United States and made the United States Hawaii's sole trading partner.

By 1887 King Kalakaua's lavish ways had placed the kingdom deeply in debt and had earned him the nickname the Merry Monarch. That year, the king was stripped of much of his power following an armed rebellion by a coalition of a few of native Hawaiian revolutionaries and a larger group of white planters who had grown tired of his rule.

In the aftermath of the revolt, the planters pushed through a new constitution that brought them even more political power. The new constitution stipulated that voting rights be granted only to men with $3,000 in property or an income of $600 per year—a specification that cut out most non-whites. The same year, Hawaii granted the United States exclusive rights to use the deep water port of Pearl Harbor as a naval base.

At his death in 1891, Kalakaua was succeeded by his sister, Lydia Liliuokalani, who became Hawaii's first and last ruling queen. Liliuokalani pressed for the return of indigenous power through the restoration of Hawaii's 1864 constitution. By this time, however, native Hawaiians had become a minority in their own homeland and had lost control of both the land and the nation's economy. At the same time, American businessmen in Hawaii were actively trying to convince the United States to annex Hawaii as a territory. In fact, when U.S. president Benjamin Harrison left office, a treaty of annexation was before the U.S. Senate. That same year, a small, armed group of revolutionaries (including nine Ameri-

cans, two Britons, and two Germans), deposed the queen with the help of a U.S. cruiser anchored offshore and the tacit support of the U.S. State Department. Grover Cleveland, the new U.S. president, suspected that his State Department had had a direct role in supporting the rebellion without his authorization, and he urged the American planters to restore the queen to her throne and refused to authorize Hawaii's annexation without an investigation. Nonetheless, when the rebels placed the queen under house arrest and formed a new government in 1894 with Sanford B. Dole, a Honolulu-born American lawyer and a leading advocate of Hawaii's annexation, as president, Cleveland reluctantly recognized the new Republic of Hawaii. Four years later, on August 12, 1898, Cleveland's successor, William McKinley, signed a Joint Resolution of Annexation, making the islands offically a territory of the United States. Many Hawaiians opposed the move, but it was too late for protest. Annexation meant U.S. citizenship rights for all Hawaiians—except, in accordance with American law, for all foreign-born Asians ineligible for U.S. citizenship.

On June 14, 1900, U.S. Congress voted for the creation of the Territory of Hawaii with the Organic Act. The legislation provided that a governor and top officials be appointed by the U.S. lawmakers. Hawaii's whites, though accounting for only 18 percent of the population in 1900, had complete control of the government. In sum, the white planting class of Hawaii had replaced the ancestral line of native monarchs as the new ruling class of the islands. Meanwhile,

Japanese and Chinese Hawaiians, who together represented more than half the population, did not even have the right to vote. This sociopolitical disparity erupted in labor strife and, occasionally, violence in Hawaii during the first decade of the 20th century.

At the same time, labor gained more clout. Ironically, the impetus that gave laborers more leverage to fight for rights was the Organic Act itself. Upon the act's passage, Hawaii became subject to U.S. laws. The anti-Chinese Exclusion Acts stopped all new immigration from China to Hawaii. U.S. jurisdiction also nullified the contracts of plantation laborers, since the use of contract labor violated U.S. law. Thus, the Organic Act of 1900, which offically established Hawaii as a U.S. territory, reshaped labor relations in Hawaii. Laborers who previously had no choice but to accept their situation suddenly had the opportunity to organize for better conditions at the turn of the century, using as leverage the possibility that they would leave the plantation for other work. After the act was passed, the Japanese emerged at the forefront of the labor movement in Hawaii, and their growing strength posed an enormous threat to the interests of the Hawaiian Sugar Planters Association (HSPA) and other management groups.

Queen Liliuokalani of the Kingdom of Hawaii (Library of Congress)

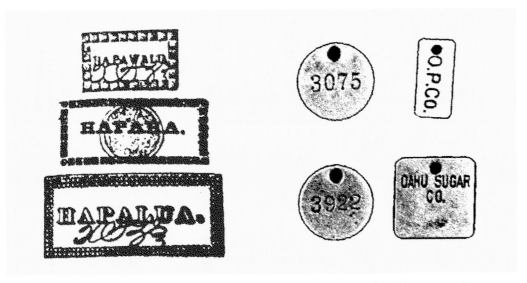

Plantation owners paid laborers in script (left), currency that could only be redeemed at plantation-owned stores. Bangos (right) were identification tags worn by laborers. Each featured a four-digit number that overseers used instead of the workers' names. (MPI Archives)

LIFE ON THE PLANTATION

In some ways, life on the Hawaiian plantations was easier for the Chinese and Japanese than it had been for the early Chinese miners and merchants in the mainland United States. For one thing, women and children moved to Hawaii as laborers along with the men. In fact, as early as the 1860s, women and children had specifically been recruited by planters for the express purpose of creating stability on the plantations. By 1894 female laborers composed about 7 percent of the workforce; 30 years later, that number had doubled. Women and children did cooking, sewing, and laundry to earn money inside the work camps as well as working in the fields alongside men—cutting, carrying, and loading sugarcane. As is often the case, women and children earned less money than men for the same type and amount of work.

To a certain extent, work on the sugar plantation resembled that of the cotton plantations of America's rural sharecropping South. Harvesting, in particular, proved to be exhausting labor. Field workers labored in clouds of dust, surrounded by miles of stalks growing 10 to 12 feet high in the hot and humid island environment. Though workers wore heavy clothing for protection, the stinging needles of the cane leaves cut hands, arms, and legs badly as dead leaves were stripped from the stalks in what the workers called *hole, hole* work. After stripping, the stalks had to be cut down manually with machete, cane by cane. The canes were then tied into bundles and loaded onto railway cars headed for the sugar mills. In the mills, workers crowded into swelteringly hot and noisy rooms, where they operated huge machines such as boilers, furnaces, centrifugal drums, and presses, to boil the cane juices into molasses and sugar.

In addition to recruiting women and children, the planters made certain other concessions to workers for the sake of preserving stability. For Chinese New Year, plantation bosses often gave workers three days off with pay and a bonus of $2. Japanese immigrant laborers celebrated the Japanese emperor's birthday each third of November. After Filipino workers arrived in Hawaii, they were permitted to celebrate the annual outdoor festival of Rizal Day, in honor of José Rizal, a hero in the fight for Filipino freedom. To promote religious expression, some plantation owners handed out free Bibles, while others built Christian churches—and sometimes even Buddhist temples.

Workers earned wages, however small, and ate fairly decently at the camps. A typical male laborer earned $6 every 26 days; a typical female earned $5 in the same period. Instead of cash, though, some camps such as those on William Hopper's Koloa Plantation used paper coupons called script. The script could only be used at the company store located on and operated by the plantation. The

THE DOCKING SYSTEM

The docking system, an elaborate system of fines for a range of behaviors that might threaten the control of the plantation managers, was a major factor in keeping Hawaiian plantation laborers in a state of perpetual debt, which in turn made it easier to keep laborers working, even after their initial labor contracts had expired. Some typical fines are listed below:

Breaking a wagon through negligence	$ 5.00
Refusal to do work as ordered	$ .25
Trespassing	$ .50
Cutting a harness	$ 2.00
Insubordination	$ 1.00
Neglect of duty	$ .50
Drunkenness	$ .50
Drunken brawling	$ 5.00
Gambling	$ 5.00
Inefficient work	$ .50
10–15 minutes late for work	a fourth of a day's wage
Unexplained absence from work	two days' wages for each day absent

Source: The Chinese-American Heritage

script system made it almost impossible for workers to save money for the future and further tied them to the plantation.

Housing for plantation laborers varied somewhat, depending on the owner, but workers were always crowded together, and living conditions were often unsanitary. Many houses in the camps were far from weatherproof, and poor drainage ensured flooding. Some cottages and barracks, however, sported good roofs and, after the turn of the century, gardens for flowers and vegetables.

For the most part, daily life for plantation laborers was grueling. A piercing siren blasted workers awake at 5 A.M. as plantation policemen ran through the barracks shouting, "*Hana-hana*—work, work!" White foremen called *lunas* grouped the workers into crews of about 25. The *luna* usually rode above the workers on a galloping horse, shouting insults and curt directions while snapping his whip. Though the Hawaiian government outlawed whipping as punishment, the law did not prevent it from happening. Other physical punishments occurred, although they were not the norm, as they had been on slave plantations in the American South. On the Olowalu Plantation, *lunas* kicked Chinese workers who were slow to return from their 10-minute lunch break; *lunas* at other locations beat workers for offenses such as standing up to stretch. The docking system, a system of fines for a range of transgressions ranging from brawling to "inefficient work," constituted the major form of nonphysical punishment for rule breakers.

The prisonlike conditions of the plantation weighed heavily on workers who were used to a more independent lifestyle. Though the labor was as tedious and physically demanding as the farming and fishing that many of the workers had done at home, laborers in Hawaii did not have the advantage of independent decision-making, frequent breaks, and regular socializing.

Many planters viewed their workers as pieces of property, often listing them in sales receipts alongside goods ordered from the clearinghouse. A list from the Laupahoehoe Plantation (1890) reads: ". . . bonemeal, canvas, Japanese laborers, macaroni, a Chinaman." A ticket found in the receipt box of Grove Farm Plantation on Kauai, dated 1908, includes "Filipinos" underneath "fertilizer." In most cases, laborers in Hawaii were not even given the respect of being called by name by their employers. Instead, each worker was assigned a four-digit number stamped onto a metal badge called a *bango*. *Bangos* hung from a chain worn around the neck or from a belt loop.

"We worked like machines," reported one Korean worker. "We were watched constantly." Bosses banished even the most casual conversation between workers, who spent a minimum of 10 hours each day, six days a week, bent over in tedious field work. One Japanese work crew made up a song that expressed their feelings about the conditions they faced while working: "Hawaii, Hawaii/But when I came/What I saw/Was hell/The boss was Satan/The *lunas*/His helpers."

Thousands of immigrant laborers chose to run away from their contractual obligations, and many were arrested for desertion. Most stayed on the plantations, however, some opting to escape their pain through the use of drugs and alcohol. Fermented molasses mixed with water and yeast yielded a potent "swipe wine" popular with the workers. Some Chinese cooks even packed opium into workers' lunch pails so addicts could smoke in the middle of the workday. Other workers' resisted the harsh, demoralizing conditions of plantation life more creatively, by feigning sickness repeatedly or by hiding within the recesses of the tall cane stalks in order to avoid the barking *lunas*. Card playing and gambling also provided a diversion for workers, though they were fined if caught doing so.

During the Kingdom of Hawaii period, contract laborers sporadically resisted poor treatment, but as discussed previously, no large-scale, organized union activity took hold in Hawaii until the Organic Act of 1900 made Hawaii a U.S. territory subject to American law. In fact, contract laborers signed specific legal work agreements with planters that forbid strikes. In addition to delineating a set period of service and a wage scale, contract labor agreements typically made that the worker promise to be "industrious, docile, and obedient," and "work faithfully and cheerfully according to the laws of the country." Though U.S. federal law ended the contract labor system in 1900, the HSPA maintained control of the Asian workforce with the creation of a centralized labor office, set wage levels, and coordinated methods of employment across the islands.

Thus, when workers did try to mount any sort of labor action prior to the turn of

A plantation overseer, or luna, *watches over Chinese laborers in the field in about 1900.* (Hawaii State Archives)

the century, they met with failure. In 1891, for example, when 200 Chinese workers marched to Kapaau to protest low wages, they were not even able to arrange a meeting with the planters. They returned to work when ordered, though a violent riot erupted between the laborers and plantation police.

After the passage of the Organic Act of 1900, strikes became more frequent, as did violence. In 1903, a group of Chinese workers attacked a *luna* and then buried the injured man under a 10-foot pile of cane stalks. The following year, a number of Korean work groups set fire to their fields.

To planters, the profit motive was not the only reason to try to prevent workers from organizing. Many owners saw themselves in a brotherly or fatherly light—helping to civilize "backward" local people and immigrants and to develop the world's lands in a manner not only personally profitable, but befitting the extension of America's "manifest destiny," a term coined in 1845 by a New Yorker named John L. O'Sullivan, editor of *United States and Democratic Review* magazine to signify the United States's inevitable supremacy over all the lands of North America.

A common method of control used by plantation owners was "divide and rule," establishing hierarchical divisions of people to maintain order. High-ranking white superiors oversaw and arranged for the basic housing needs of the lowly workers. The workers were further stratified by ethnicity, with each new immigrant group ranked below the group preceding. In 1882, whites made up 88 percent of foreman and clerk positions. Nearly 50 percent of laborers were Chinese at that time, but not one held the rank of *luna*. By the turn of the century, at which time Japanese laborers outnumbered Chinese, nothing had changed. "Where there is a drop of the Anglo-Saxon blood, it is sure to rule," summed up a high-ranking official of Theo H. Davies and Company in 1904.

Many foremen went out of their way to pit one immigrant group against another in order to maintain control. As early as the 1850s, *lunas* publicly praised Chinese workers as examples for native Hawaiians to emulate. Bosses fed competitive urges, ordering the Chinese to periodically ridicule the Hawaiian men by calling them "*wahine! wahine!*"—implying that the natives' work was substandard because they worked like "women! women!" After 30 years of relying on the speed and skill

of the Chinese, in 1878 plantation owners began to import Portuguese workers because they did not want to become too dependent on one ethnic group of workers, for that would give labor too much potential power. After the arrival of Japanese workers, bosses continued to foster competition between ethnic groups. In 1898, 300 Japanese workers chased 100 Chinese from the Spreckelsville Plantation on Maui. The following year, four Chinese were killed during a Chinese-Japanese riot on Oahu's Kahuku Plantation.

To encourage animosity between the groups, planters often paid workers of different ethnicities different wages. For example, when Filipinos began arriving after the turn of the century, planters paid them to compete in productivity tests with Japanese cane cutters, who earned 30 cents more per day than the Filipinos.

Even plantation housing reflected racial divisions and plantation hierarchy, with the owners living in large well-maintained homes similar to the "big houses" of America's slave-powered plantations. Some owners mixed the races within the barracks of the work camps in an effort to generate stability. Most, however, kept the workers divided, thereby keeping the different races from banding together to air grievances or organizing multiethnic actions.

Many languages were spoken on the plantations, a condition that proved to be both a barrier and a bridge to understanding. Native Hawaiians, Chinese, Portuguese, Japanese, and in time Koreans and Filipinos, had difficulty communicating on the job because each group spoke a different language. Although early Chinese immigrants of differing ethnicities had picked up Hawaiian in order to communicate, with each new nationality arriving on the islands (and a lower and lower percentage of native Hawaiians), an easier method of communication became necessary. *Lunas* needed to communicate with workers without learning several different languages. Thus, plantation bosses used English as the language of command and eventually a simplified language called pidgin English developed on the plantations. This language not only enabled bosses to give directions to workers, but it also became a key tool used by workers to build a community among themselves.

Words from different languages combined into pidgin: "Will you pick coffee?" translated into "You like *hemo* (a Hawaiian word) *coppe ke* (a Japanese phrase)?" and "I have no work, therefore I cannot eat," became "No more *hana-hana* (Hawaiian), no can *kaukau* (Hawaiian)." Newspaper advertisements, too, used the cobbled vernacular. An ad for a new Chinese restaurant read: "Disee new Lau Yee Chai chop sui place no so hard to find, Chinee red and Chinee jade paint all oveh. . . . You come looksee, eh?" Pidgin English became so common on the isolated plantations that when workers left at their contracts' expiration, they were surprised to discover that they had to learn an entirely new language—standard English!

Workers from different regions of the world also ate differently and behaved according to varied traditional customs. Gradually, however, plantation workers began to eat, sing, and play games together as well as labor together, and similarities between people came to light as human relationships inevitably developed. The growing family-base on Hawaiian plantations encouraged and supported such positive and nurturing community interaction. Strong bonds between people helped encourage immigrants to settle in Hawaii, rather than automatically return to their home countries when their contracts expired.

KOREAN IMMIGRATION TO HAWAII

Not all nationalities of laborers came to interact peacefully in Hawaii, as the story of Korean labor recruitment at the start of the 20th century illustrates. Like the Japanese, Korean immigrants, both in Hawaii and in the mainland United States, were fiercely nationalistic. And like Japan,

In 1904, Japan and Russia went to war over control of the Korean peninsula. Although Russia initially controlled much of northeast China, Japan won a decisive victory, taking control not only of Russia's holdings in China but also the Korean peninsula, which became a protectorate of Japan before being annexed outright in 1910.

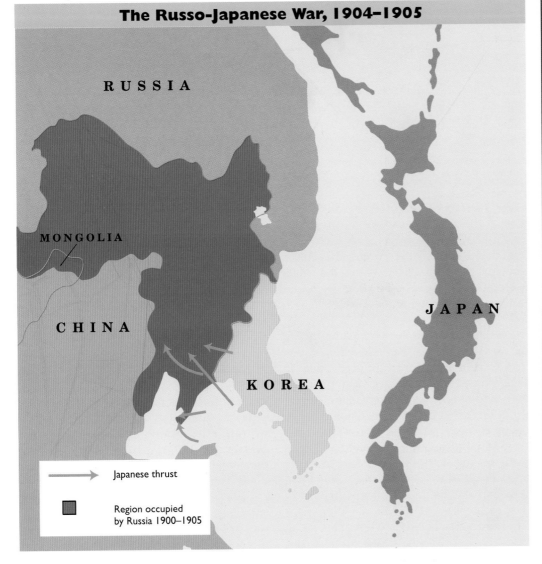

The Russo-Japanese War, 1904–1905

RUSSIA

MONGOLIA

CHINA

JAPAN

KOREA

→ Japanese thrust

▨ Region occupied by Russia 1900–1905

Ever since the start of the 17th century, China had dominiated the affairs of the Kingdom of Korea. During the reign of the Japanese emperor Meiji (1852–1912), however, Japanese isolationism came to a sudden end. In 1876 Japan forced Korea to sign a "treaty of friendship and commerce."

With this treaty, Japan immediately challenged China's supremacy in Korea, backing anti-Chinese movements in Korea and successfully arranging the assassination of Korea's pro-Chinese Queen Min. Following Japan's defeat of China in the 1894 Sino-Japanese War, China turned over its control of Korea to the Japanese, initiating what would be a harsh 40-year occupation in which the Japanese government attempted to systematically dismantle all vestiges of independent Korean culture.

Over the years, the Japanese occupational government in Korea took away civil rights protections, banned books and magazines, jailed dissenters, and prohibited free public political meetings. By the 1930s, Koreans were forced to convert to Shintoism, and by 1938 the teaching of the Korean language had become illegal. Soon after that ban, all Koreans had to give up their Korean names and use Japanese names instead.

This oppression at the hands of the Japanese, whom Koreans viewed as barbaric and parasitic, only served to strengthen the Koreans' anti-Japanese feelings. Resistance erupted sporadically in Korea throughout the early part of the century, including the armed rebellions of 1907–1909 that resulted in the deaths of nearly 15,000 Koreans. Protests for independence began peacefully and in earnest again in 1919, as thousands marched in Korea chanting, "*Mansei! Mansei!*" (May Korea live ten thousand years!) Seven thousand Koreans lost their lives in that protest. Villages were destroyed and many Koreans were imprisoned by the Japanese government in its violent crackdown.

Korean men on board a ship in Seoul (Library of Congress)

Korea had spent centuries isolated from most of the world.

Unlike Japan, however, Korea had been dominated by China from the 1600s through the mid-1800s. After the Meiji Restoration in Japan, however, Korea began feeling Japan's growing presence as well. In 1876 Japan forced Korea to sign a "treaty of friendship and commerce," thus becoming the only trading partner other than China that Korea had had for centuries. Then, in 1882, Korea became the last Asian nation in the world to open its markets to the West.

After 1876, Japanese merchants began raking in huge profits at Korea's expense. Politically, the Japanese interfered at pivotal moments throughout the years, backing reformist Koreans against the Chinese in 1884 and conducting the assassination of the pro-Chinese Queen Min.

The rivalry between China and Japan came to a head in 1894, when Japan defeated China in the Sino-Japanese War. As a result, China relinquished all control of Korea. However, instead of gaining freedom from foreign domination, Korea remained at the center of regional power struggles.

In 1904, Japan and Russia went to war over control of the Korean peninsula. Japan won a decisive victory, and in a peace settlement brokered by U.S. president Theodore Roosevelt (for which the he would win the Nobel Peace Prize in 1905), Japan was granted status as the protector of Korea, in order to "guarantee" Korean independence. Korean independence was a mirage, however, and in 1910, Japan's domination over the peninsula was made official when it formally annexed the nation.

For the next 35 years, Japan would ruthlessly rule over the Korean people, seeking to wipe out Korean culture completely with totalitarian tactics. Japan stationed two divisions of its army along the peninsula, and Japanese nationals installed themselves in key Korean government positions, from which they parceled out government land to Japanese immigrants at prices well below their real value.

When the HPSA first began to heavily recruit Korean laborers to work in Hawaii between 1901 and 1905, Koreans were an oppressed people whose homeland was being stolen from them. At home, Koreans faced droughts that worsened the economic upheaval and famine caused in the wake of the political and military turmoil of the Russo-Japanese War. Therefore, like the Chinese and Japanese immigrants to Hawaii and the mainland United States before them, early Korean laborers were also "pushed" from their home. With private fishing banned and millions of farmers left landless, the hardship seemed insurmountable. "We left Korea because we were too poor," remembered one Korean immigrant to Hawaii. "We had nothing to eat. There was absolutely no way we could survive."

KOREAN RECRUITMENT
TO HAWAII

To white planters in Hawaii at the turn of the century, Korean hatred for the Japanese provided an ideal opportunity to divide plantation labor against itself. Beginning in 1900, the HPSA erected recruiting stations along Korea's coastline. Host cities for the planters' profitable enterprise included Kimchaek (formerly Songjin), Wonsan, Inchon (formerly Chemulpo), Seoul, and Pusan.

Labor recruiters and Christian missionaries visiting Korea near the turn of the century played a significant role in encouraging families to leave for Hawaii. Recruiters displayed newspaper advertisements and signs informing readers that plantation laborers in Hawaii received free housing, medical care, and $16 per month for a 60-hour work week. That monetary figure, translated into Korean dollars, equaled what was then the very large sum of 64 *won*.

Recruiters described Hawaii as a "paradise" where "clothing grew on trees, free to be picked," and where "gold dollars were blossoming on every bush." Hawaiian sugar planters loaned money to Korean laborers desperate to leave the country through a bank they set up in Korea, with loans to be repaid according to the terms of their three-year contracts.

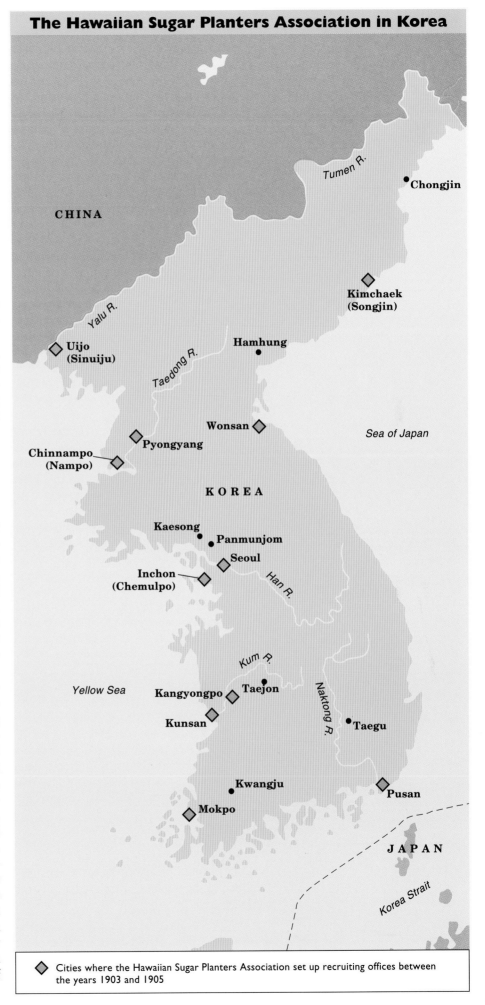

The Hawaiian Sugar Planters Association in Korea

Cities where the Hawaiian Sugar Planters Association set up recruiting offices between the years 1903 and 1905

Christian missionaries visiting Korea bolstered the claims of the recruiters, describing Hawaii as a "haven of peace and plenty." They encouraged new converts to go to the new land where they would be around others of a like mind. As migrants boarded the boats they greeted one another with the hopeful phrase *Kaeguk chinch wi* ("The country is open; go forward").

Forty percent of all early Korean immigrants to the United States were Christians. Hopeful for their future in such a calm and beautiful land, many men took their wives and children along. Between 1903 and 1906 nearly 10 percent of the 6,685 migrating Korean adults were women.

Once in Hawaii, many Korean Christians founded churches on Hawaiian plantations, and Christianity spread quickly among Korean laborers living in the camps. Many plantation owners were happy to help pay for church construction in order to keep workers content and to discourage the gambling and drunkenness so prevalent in the work camps.

Religion helped many immigrant laborers cope with the harsh realities of plantation life. At the mercy of plantation bosses and and without a union or—after the Russo-Japanese War—a government back home to turn to for help, Korean immigrants devised a hierarchical form of self-government to protect themselves from abuse.

Every plantation village made up of at least 10 Korean families created a governing council called a *donghoe*. The *donghoe* held judicial power and could prosecute wrongdoers. Each year the adult males of the Korean workers' community elected a village chief (*dongjang*), a police chief (*sach'al*), a police force (*Kyongch'al*), and a group of men known as the Sworn Brotherhoods. The Sworn Brotherhoods, made up of about 50 members identified by specific tattoos, protected Korean workers against outsiders. Eventually, this quasi-legal group focused on resolving conflicts that erupted within the Korean community itself.

KOREAN LABOR IN HAWAII

Japan's domination of Korea ensured that the migration of Koreans to Hawaii and then to the mainland United States during the early 1900s would be short-lived and characterized by relatively small numbers. In 1903, around 500 Korean laborers migrated to Hawaii. In 1905, at the height of the Russo-Japanese War, the number jumped to 11,000, but following Japan's victory that year, the number fell back down to fewer than 100 the following year. By 1940, the Korean-American population in the mainland United States had reached a total of only 1,711. Mass migration of Koreans to the United States would not occur until the 1970s.

Most early Korean immigrants, like the Chinese and Japanese before them, were young adults between the ages of 16 and 44. They were recruited from urban as well as rural areas; thus, while some came from farming backgrounds, the remainder were a more diverse group made up of students, city laborers, police officers, government clerks, miners, and Buddhist monks. Like the Japanese, the Korean immigrants as a group were mainly literate.

The first small groups of Korean laborers were recruited to work on Hawaii's sugar and pineapple plantations in 1903. Planters relying on the "divide and rule" strategy to control their workers imported Korean labor to replace Japanese workers and thereby break up the growing strength of fledgling Japanese-led unions. Japanese workers had formed such unions to demand higher wages and better conditions after the Organic Act of 1900 ended the contract labor system in Hawaii. Korean workers were only too happy to comply with any effort they deemed anti-Japanese.

The flow of immigration from Korea to Hawaii halted suddenly in 1905—the year Korea became a Japanese protectorate—when the Japanese government barred Korean laborers from leaving for Hawaii. Japan instituted the ban in order to curtail competition from Korea in Hawaii's labor market and also to thwart the fledgling Korean independence movement growing in Hawaii, in the U.S. mainland, and in Korea. Many more Koreans would have come to the United States had the 1905 ban not been imposed.

The year 1905 also marked the start of Korean remigration, as those already in Hawaii began to set sail for the mainland West Coast. Their numbers totaled nearly 1,000 by 1907. The vast majority of Koreans migrating from Hawaii moved to California.

For early Korean immigrants, the choice to be a settler or a sojourner was irrelevant. All issues of personal choice and definition revolved around Korea's ongoing fight for independence from Japan. Korean immigrants felt that they could not return from a land of relative freedom to live under the Japanese flag, but they also

LABOR UNREST IN HAWAII

KAUAI

NIIHAU

● Lihue

⑨ ● Hanapepe

OAHU

Waialua ③

⑤ ② Aiea

Waipahu ⑦

⑥ Honolulu

MOLOKAI

Kaanapali ④ ⑧

Lanai City ● ① ● Pa'ia

Lahaina

LANAI MAUI

KAHOOLAWE

Hilo ●

⑩

HAWAII

Pacific Ocean

① In one of 20 strikes in Hawaii that year, Japanese workers at the Pioneer Mill in Lahaina, Maui, strike in April 1900 over the deaths of three mill hands, gaining control of the plantation and town. Major concessions result. Among the other plantations seeing strikes that year are Olowalu, Spreckelsville, and Kilauea.

② In May 1904, 1,000 Japanese laborers strike the Oahu Sugar Company in Waipahu after they are forced by a *luna* (plantation overseer) to participate in mandatory lotteries.

③ In December 1904, 2,000 men demonstrate at Waialua in protest against their failure to receive a wage increase, despite an increase in the price of sugar.

④ On May 22, 1905, after a laborer loses an eye while being beaten by a *luna*, at the Kaanapali Camp on Maui, 1,400 Japanese demonstrate for the *luna's* dismissal. When national guardsmen arrive, a riot breaks out, and a worker is killed and two others wounded. The strike ends when the *luna* is fired.

⑤ In 1906, 1,700 Japanese strike on Waipahu Plantation, demanding higher wages. Although police are called in to intimidate strikers, the workers win concessions before resuming work.

⑥ In 1909 the Japanese Federation of Labor and Filipino Laborers' Association strike, demanding higher wages, an eight-hour day, paid maternity leave, and an insurance fund for retired employees. Eight thousand workers—77 percent of the workforce on Oahu—are joined by Spanish, Portuguese, and Chinese, generating the first major interethnic strike. The strike lasts six months and incurs losses of $11.5 million. In April the "77 Cents Parade," organized by strike leaders, is staged by 3,000 Japanese and Filipino strikers and their families, who march through the streets of Honolulu protesting their daily wage of 77 cents. Planters evict strikers, and many die from unsanitary conditions in "tent cities." In the end strikers gain a 50 percent wage increase.

⑦ In May 1909 more than 7,000 Japanese workers strike on Aiea Plantation in Oahu, demanding pay equal to other ethnic workers. Thousands of workers are evicted, jailed, and and even killed before the strike ends in August.

⑧ In March 1912, 400 Okinawan workers strike in Pa'ia, Maui. They demand the dismissal of a *luna* and plantation police who tried to disband a wedding party.

⑨ In 1924 the Filipino Laborers' Association demands better wages and housing, culminating in the bloody strike at Hanapepe, Kauai, with 20 deaths and numerous injuries.

⑩ In 1938, Japanese dock workers at Hilo, Hawaii, strike and are attacked with tear gas, fire hoses, and bird shot.

could not divorce themselves from the struggle of their people. "How we Koreans in America dare to forget prison-like Korea! and try to return to that place! We must struggle in exile. Yes, we shall return when we have a freedom bell and a national flag," declared the San Francisco–based *New Korea* magazine (*Sinhan Minbo*). Particularly after 1910, when Japan formally annexed Korea, the spirit of patriotism (*aeguk chongsin*) and the dream of Korean sovereignty (*kwangbok*) became the supreme guiding forces behind all choices and decisions of Koreans in America. They would fuel a highly organized immigrant group that gathered strength in exile in the United States.

GROWING LABOR STRIFE

Plantation laborers of every ethnicity had always been dissatisfied with working conditions on Hawaii's plantations. Workers' physical labor helped create Hawaii's profitable agriculture industry and contributed greatly to the development of Hawaii's entire economy, yet the workers shared none of the benefits of this success.

Prior to the start of the 20th century, worker resistance took varied forms—negotiation attempts, sporadic violence, physical escape, false illness, drug abuse, and drunkenness. None of these resulted in permanent change for the workers. After 1900, workers consolidated their power by organizing themselves into large groups. Hawaii's immigrant laborers, especially Japanese and, later, Filipino laborers, began to use the strike as a method to force the owners to sit down at the bargaining table.

Owners did not easily relinquish control. When 1,700 Japanese workers put down their hoes and machetes in unison to demand higher wages at Waipahu Plantation in 1906, the manager, E. K. Bull, responded with a call for police assistance. The Hawaiian government sent 47 officers armed with rifles to patrol the plantation. The officers roamed the camps day and night, questioning any workers who passed by them. Bull planned to intimidate the workers into submission, even threatening at one point to use the police squad to evict strikers from their homes and force them off the plantation. The Japanese, however, refused to bend under the pressure, forcing Bull to negotiate with them in order to end the strike.

The success of the 1906 strike spelled the beginning of a working-class consciousness among plantation laborers. At first, however, the unions structured themselves around ethnicity, such that Japanese joined Japanese unions and Filipinos joined Filipino unions. These "blood unions" continued to divide labor's power and pit ethnic groups against one another—exactly as owners had always intended.

Planters had long paid workers different wages according to race as a means of fostering ethnic rivalry. In the early 1900s, Japanese workers earned $18 per month while Portuguese workers earned $22.50 per month. Both groups performed the same jobs using the same methods, yet owners paid them differently according to their ethnic background.

In May 1909, 7,000 Japanese belonging to the Higher Wage Association (Zokyu Kisei Kai) on Oahu's Aiea Plantation went on strike for four months to protest the wage differential system. Thousands of other Japanese workers on Oahu and other Hawaiian Islands sent food and money to the strikers, so that they could continue the action. Japanese doctors provided free medical care to strikers and their families. The broad base of support from nonunion members helped the strikers win—eventually. In November 1909, three months after the strike ended, Aiea owners raised the Japanese workers' wages and ended the differential system.

But the victory was not complete, for a new thrust of owner control had been set in motion. Though the Japanese workers' demands were addressed in Oahu, the strike had been broken first by the importation of Korean, Hawaiian, Chinese, and Portuguese strikebreakers. Filipinos proved to be the next ethnic group the owners imported en masse, for the specific purpose of breaking the power of striking laborers.

THE FILIPINOS

The Philippines' history as a Spanish colony from 1571 to 1898 greatly influenced Filipino culture. It was the Spanish who introduced Roman Catholicism, which remains the dominant religion in the Philippines. In addition, centuries of of intermarriage between Filipinos and Spaniards has given many Filipinos Spanish blood and surnames.

Nonetheless, life under Spanish rule was difficult for most ethnic Filipinos. Under Spanish law, only *illustrados*, or those with mostly Spanish blood, could own land, hold an important government office, or receive an education. Many Filipinos were forced to labor as slaves or work along the sea-based trade routes that connected Spain's far-flung empire of New Spain. (Most of New Spain was in the Americas, with the capital at Mexico City, but the Philippines were also considered part of New Spain. Silks, spices, and other items from Asia arrived once a year in Acapulco, Mexico, aboard Spanish galleons. In fact, a small number of ethnic Filipinos during the mid-1700s jumped ship at Acapulco and traveled to the then-Spanish settlement of New Orleans to become the very first Filipinos to settle on American soil.)

THE U.S.-PHILIPPINE WAR

In the late 19th century, resistance to harsh Spanish rule gave birth to an active Filipino liberation movement. Among the most prominent voices speaking up for the rights of Filipinos was Dr. José Protasio Rizal, a young Filipino doctor, novelist, and poet. In 1886, Rizal published the book, *Noli Me Tangere* (Touch Me Not), a work that harshly criticized Spanish rule. In response, the Spanish colonial government forced Rizal into exile.

Not content to be silenced, Rizal responded by organizing a political party called the *Liga Filipina* from exile in Hong Kong. In 1892, Rizal returned to the Philippines, where he was promptly arrested and sent again into exile—this time to the Philippine island of Mindanao.

Four years later, and one year after rebels in Spanish-controlled Cuba began their own military campaign against Spanish rule, a young military officer named Emilio Aguinaldo led a group of Filipino patriots in a revolt on the island of Luzon. After Aguinaldo's appeal to the United States for arms failed, however, Aguinaldo was obliged to accept a peace treaty with the Spanish colonial government. Aguinaldo himself was forced into exile. In the aftermath of the settlement, the Spanish arrested José Rizal and executed him—despite Rizal's pledge of nonviolence and complete lack of involvement in the revolt. Today, Rizal is a martyred hero among the Filipino people. December 30, the day of his death, remains a national holiday when people recount his heroic deeds. The tales that constitute his legacy take on a supernatural glow as he is often portrayed as a man who caught bullets with his bare hands and, in the end, rose from the grave.

In 1898, the campaign for liberation from Spain came to a turning point—both

Dr. José Protasio Rizal (National Archives)

Emilio Aguinaldo (National Archives)

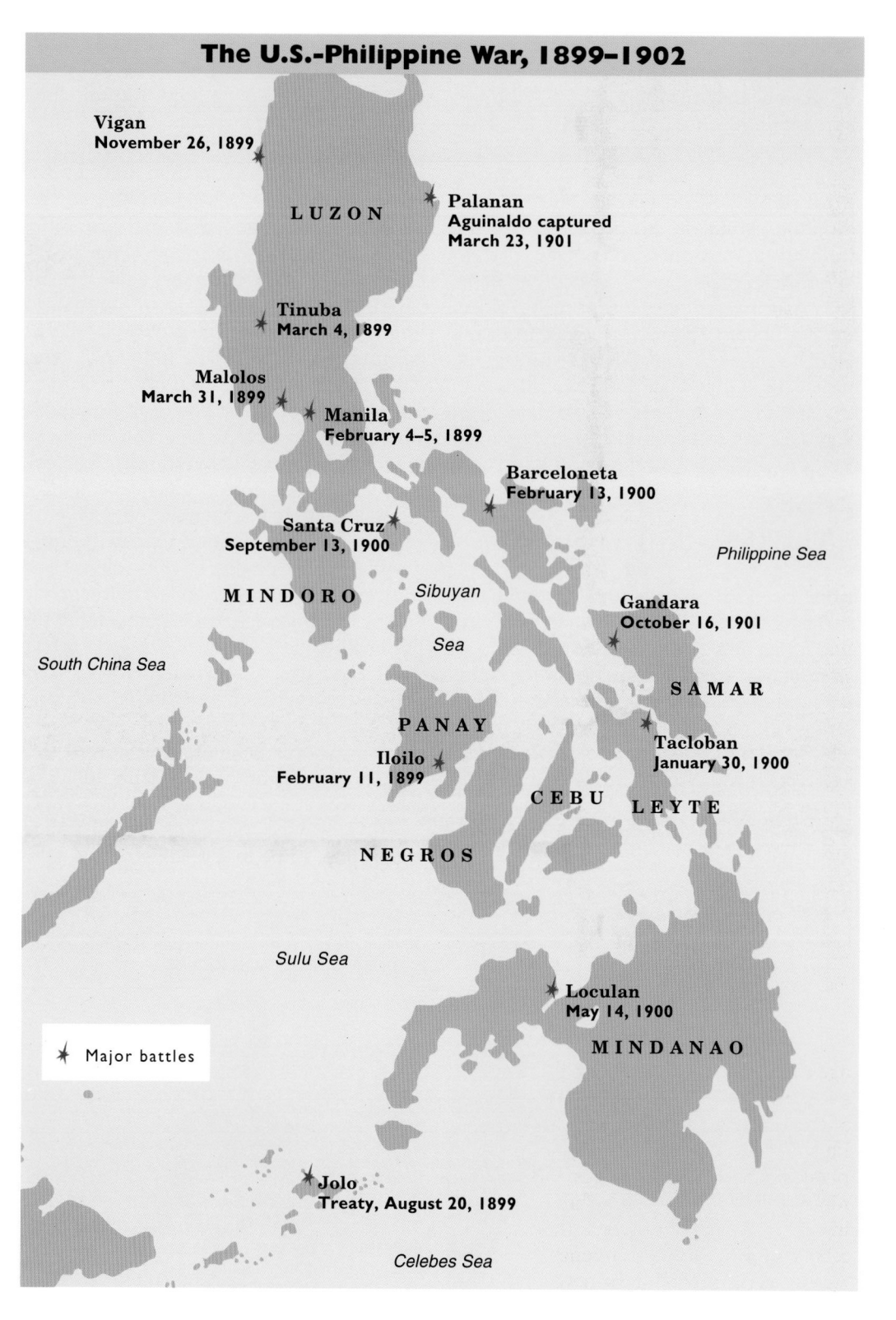

The U.S.-Philippine War, 1899–1902

Vigan
November 26, 1899

LUZON

Palanan
Aguinaldo captured
March 23, 1901

Tinuba
March 4, 1899

Malolos
March 31, 1899

Manila
February 4–5, 1899

Barceloneta
February 13, 1900

Santa Cruz
September 13, 1900

Philippine Sea

MINDORO

Sibuyan

Sea

Gandara
October 16, 1901

South China Sea

SAMAR

PANAY

Iloilo
February 11, 1899

Tacloban
January 30, 1900

CEBU LEYTE

NEGROS

Sulu Sea

Loculan
May 14, 1900

MINDANAO

✶ Major battles

Jolo
Treaty, August 20, 1899

Celebes Sea

in the Philippines and in Cuba. In February, an American battleship, the USS *Maine*, which had been sent to Cuba to protect American citizens during the Cuban revolt, exploded mysteriously in Havana harbor. The explosion forced the hand of President William McKinley, who had previously expressed caution about intervening in Cuba, despite vocal calls for American intervention in the U.S. press.

Moving quickly to develop a strategy of attack against Spanish Cuba, the McKinley administration came up with a novel approach—to attempt to capture Manila, and then use that capture as leverage in later negotiations over Cuba. On August 13, 1898, Manila fell to U.S. forces.

After the easy victory in Manila, American strategy began to shift away from merely using the Philippines as a bargaining chip and toward annexing the islands outright. Despite the shift, the McKinley administration encouraged Emilio Aguinaldo to come out of exile and renew his battle

Filipino freedom fighters pose during the U.S.-Philippine War. Emilio Aguinaldo is seated in the front row, second from right. (National Archives)

against Spain for the rest of the islands—even promising Aguinaldo that the United States would support an independent Philippines. With the help of weapons supplied by the United States, Aguinaldo's forces gained control of the Philippines within two weeks. Immediately thereafter, the rebels proclaimed independence and named Aguinaldo president of the new republic.

Independence was short-lived. Without notifying Aguinaldo's government, American and Spanish diplomats convened peace negotiations. As a result of the meetings, Spain agreed not to grant the Philippines independence but instead to cede control of the islands to the United States. Officially, the Philippines were given the status of a protectorate of the United States—much in the same way that Korea would become a protectorate of Japan following the Russo-Japanese War of 1904–1905.

The United States took its role of "protector" very literally. President McKinley said he decided to annex the Philippines after he had been told by God while praying that it was America's duty to "uplift" and "educate" the Filipinos. In keeping with this policy, McKinley established a policy of "benevolent assimilation," by which the U.S. Army would oversee the installation of U.S.-style municipal governments, so that Filipinos could learn American principles of justice and abandon thoughts of rebellion.

To the Filipinos, however, there could be no justice without freedom, and the fight for freedom was not over. In March 1899, fighting broke out between U.S. and Filipino forces. Although the Filipinos far outnumbered the U.S. forces, by the end of March more than 3,000 Filipino rebels lay dead.

Over the next three years, the United States and the Filipino rebels under Aguinaldo fought a bloody struggle for control of the Philippines. Often refered to

WELL, I HARDLY KNOW WHICH TO TAKE FIRST!

A cartoon commentary on the U.S. overseas empire: President William McKinley is shown as a waiter, while Uncle Sam mulls over his options. (Library of Congress)

as the U.S.-Philippine War, the conflict is one of the lesser-known episodes in U.S. history, and when it is discussed, it is often referred to as an "insurrection" that concluded the more geopolitically prominent conflict between the United States and Spain. However, if the fierceness of a war is any indication of its significance, then this latter conflict between the Filipino rebels and the United States rates as more important than the Spanish-American War.

In 1900, Aguinaldo's forces began a campaign of guerilla warfare, initiating hit-and-run ambushes on American forces. In response, the United States abandoned the policy of "benevolent assimilation" in favor of a more forceful policy. As rebel ambushes continued, U.S. commanders declared martial law and, as Spain had done in Cuba, began confining insurgents and those suspected of aiding them in internment camps.

The following year, the Americans captured Aguinaldo and forced him to publicly pledge his loyalty to the United States. It became clear that hostilities were not over, however, when on September 28, Filipino insurgents in the village of Balangiga launched a surprise attack on American troops, killing 48 soldiers. In a brutal retaliation, U.S. general Jacob Smith ordered that Balangiga be destroyed, specifically telling his men to "kill everyone over ten." Ameri-

can troops then massacred 5,000 civilians and burned the village to the ground. Such scorched-earth tactics essentially ended hostilities. Though rebel guerrillas fought sporadically until 1913, the largely forgotten U.S.-Philippine War was over by 1902.

William Howard Taft, who later became president of the United States, became the first civilian governor general of the Philippines in 1903. Many Americans subscribed to the popular opinion that the Filipino "savages" needed American help to become "civilized." Taft echoed this paternalistic attitude when he referred to the Filipino people as "our little brown brothers." Some Americans, however, criticized the relationship between the United States and the Philippines as imperialist and economically motivated.

Officially, the mission of the United States was to educate and prepare the Filipino people to run their own democracy. In addition to restructuring Philippine schools on the American model, Taft's Philippine education program paid for a small group of immigrants known as the *pensionados* to gain a college education in the United States. After earning their degrees, most returned to the Philippines and secured jobs of high rank, often within the government. The *pensionados* program began in 1903 and ended in 1910.

Though the United States helped modernize the Philippines, revamp its educational system, and reshape its government, the economy remained heavily skewed toward the wealthy few. Most Filipinos remained poor and landless. Thus, when recruiters from the HPSA arrived in the islands with their rags-to-riches tales and contract offers, they found a receptive audience.

FILIPINO LABOR IN HAWAII

Three events coincided to usher in the first wave of Filipino immigration into Hawaii. The first, the annexation of the Philippines by the United States in 1903, allowed Filipinos to emigrate under the status of "American nationals." The second, the Gentlemen's Agreement of 1908 between the United States and Japan (discussed later in this chapter), limited the importation of Japanese labor to Hawaii, driving up the demand for another wave of cheap labor. The third, the strike of 1909, pushed the HSPA to recruit a new group—the Filipinos—to break the growing power of the Japanese-led labor movement in Hawaii.

The HSPA began recruitment of Filipinos during the strike of 1909. On August 7 of that year, a plantation owner requested a shipment of Filipino workers from C. Brewer and Company, an import and recruitment company, "to put into our day gang. . . . In this way perhaps we can stir the Japs a bit." This was one of many requests for Filipino strikebreakers the importers received over the course of what was to be a long work stoppage.

Filipino laborers recruited by the HSPA called themselves *sakadas*, meaning agricultural worker, a name used only by Filipinos in Hawaii. (Peasant farmers in the Philippines are referred to as *tao*.) Like the Chinese and Japanese farmers who had come to Hawaii before them, the *sakadas* felt pressed to leave their troubled homeland primarily for economic reasons. Ethnic Tagalogs, Visayans, and Ilocanos, recruited from rural northern Luzon because of their experience with agricultural work, all signed on for three-year contracts.

HSPA recruiters, called "drummers" in the Philippines, helped spread "Hawaiian fever" among potential prospects. The recruiters showed enticing movies in public squares and told exaggerated tales of opportunities in the "land of glory." HSPA agents convinced the desperate and strug-gling farmers that they could earn $2 a day in Hawaii (an enormous amount for a Filipino *tao*). The immigrants signed on believing that they would return home wealthy enough to pay off their debts, recover their family homes, and regain respectable standing in the community.

Like the other immigrants before them, the early Filipino immigrants were

Recruited by Hawaiian labor organizations that needed workers after the influx of Japanese was restricted by the Gentlemen's Agreement of 1907–1908, early Filipino immigrants came from the Ilocano provinces in northwest Luzon and the Cebuanao provinces. In Luzon, the narrow coastal plains were unsuitable for cultivating export crops. Emigration to Hawaii therefore provided an opportunity for profitable work. The inhabitants of Cebu were also familiar with working on plantations, which facilitated their choice to emigrate.

Origins of Early Filipino Immigration to the United States, 1898–1910

primarily male. Unlike the Chinese and the Japanese, most were not married. Of the Filipino women who did come to the United States in the early 20th century, most went with their husbands or fathers to Hawaii, where the plantations offered a more settled life than could be found in the mainland United States. Of the 61,649 Filipinos recruited by the HSPA between 1909 and 1924, 7,322 were women and 4,651 were children.

Between 1909 and 1920, the Japanese plantation workforce had been reduced from nearly 70 percent to only 44 percent. During the same period, Filipino workers had risen to make up 30 percent of the plantation workforce. By 1920, 62 percent of Hawaii's entire population of 255,881 was composed of Asian immigrants, with the Japanese tallying in at 42.7 percent, Chinese at 9.2 percent, Filipinos at 8.2 percent, and Koreans at 1.9 percent.

JAPANESE AND FILIPINO LABOR UNITE

In December of 1919, the Filipino Federation of Labor and the Japanese Federation of Labor submitted similar demands to their employers. Both groups requested higher wages, an eight-hour day, a retirement insurance fund, and paid maternity leave. The plantation owners rejected both groups' requests.

In response, the leaders of the Japanese union declared: "Let's rise and open the eyes of the capitalists. . . . Let's cooperate with the Filipinos." Though the Japanese and the Filipinos agreed that a strike was the only available recourse, the Japanese felt that both unions should take their time and plan a sound strategy first. The Filipinos, on the other hand, were ready to act.

On January 19, 1920, Filipino labor leader Pablo Manlapit ordered 3,000 Filipino workers to strike on plantations in Oahu. Calling for an interethnic push against plantation owner's abuses, he asked the Japanese to join them:

This is the opportunity that the Japanese should grasp, to show that they are in harmony with and willing to cooperate with other nationalities in this territory, concerning the principles of organized labor. . . . We should work on this strike shoulder to shoulder.

Likewise, Filipino workers on strike called out from the picket lines to Japanese coworkers in the common langue of pidgin English: "What's the matter? Why you *hana-hana* [work]?"

Several Japanese newspapers took up the call to encourage the Japanese union to go on strike with the Filipinos. Editors at the *Hawaii Shimpo* wrote,

Our sincere and desperate voices are also their voices. Their righteous indignation is our righteous indignation. . . . Fellow Japanese laborers! Don't be a race of unreliable dishonest people! Their problem is your problem!

On February 1, 1920, the Japanese finally joined the Filipinos. United, the two unions amounted to 77 percent of Oahu's plantation workforce. Further supported by Spanish, Portuguese, and Chinese laborers, Hawaii's first interethnic strike brought Oahu's plantation system to a standstill.

The plantation bosses, determined to break the precedent-setting strike, decided to deliberately create trouble between the two unions, targeting Filipino union leader Pablo Manlapit. Manlapit accepted a bribe from the planters and called off the strike on February 8, surprising his own rank and file as well as the Japanese. Manlapit reversed his decision on February 10, and made the bribe attempt public. Even without his reversal, many Filipino workers had remained on strike.

The plantation bosses tried to demoralize the Japanese strikers by means of slander. R. D. Read, director of the HSPA's Bureau of Labor, declared, "We have commenced a program of propaganda," and he heckled the Japanese strikers, calling them puppets of Japan. "There is absolutely no race so susceptible to ridicule," he went on, "as the Japanese."

Throughout the strike, plantation owners also hired strikebreakers: Hawaiians, Portuguese, and especially Koreans. Speaking for Hawaii's Korean community, the Korean National Association pledged its cooperation with the planters: "We place ourselves irrevocably against the Japanese and the present strike. We don't wish to be looked upon as strikebreakers, but we shall continue to work. . . . We are opposed to the Japanese in everything."

In another blow to the strikers, in February the planters evicted them from their homes. With no place to go, thousands of strikers flooded into Honolulu, which happened to be undergoing a major influenza epidemic. Thousands of the newly arrived strikers became ill and 150 died.

Labor leaders called off the strike in July 1920. But before doing so, the Japanese Federation of Labor suggested that the two unions merge. On April 23, 1920, the Hawaii Laborers' Association formed, marking the start of interracial unity among Hawaii's immigrant farm laborers.

Though unionism did not radically transform the plantation system overnight, it had, by the second decade of the century, seriously eroded the power of the owners' strategy of "divide and control." When Japanese and Filipino workers decided to join forces in 1920 against plantation owners, a new era dawned for Hawaii's immigrant workers. Though the strike itself failed, the days of unions separated by blood had ended.

TO THE MAINLAND

The Organic Act of 1900 not only granted Hawaii formal status as a U.S. territory it also legally ended Hawaii's system of contract labor. All laborers under contracts were freed from their obligations. Thousands were liberated simultaneously.

Some laborers moved to cities such as Honolulu and opened businesses. The field workers who remained united among themselves and with other ethnic immigrant groups to fight for labor reform.

Many others decided to leave Hawaii altogether. Many Japanese laborers sailed from Hawaii directly for the mainland United States, with the largest period of Japanese remigration occurring between 1890 and 1907. Travel between Hawaii and the mainland United States, defined after the Organic Act as a "coastwise voyage," meant that the Japanese were not subject to immigration procedures. The impact was dramatic: in 1890, 2,039 Japanese immigrants lived on the U.S. mainland; by 1920, that figure had increased to more than 111,000, 40,000 of whom had come from Hawaii.

THE ISSEI IN CALIFORNIA

San Francisco remained the main urban draw for Japanese issei (first-generation Japanese Americans) arriving on the West Coast. California's Fresno and Sacramento grew to be magnet cities for new arrivals, too, as did Portland, Oregon; Salt Lake City, Utah; and Seattle and Tacoma, Washington. By 1900, Japanese neighborhoods, which had been established near urban Chinatowns, began to evolve into areas sometimes referred to as "Japantowns" or "Little Tokyos."

Many Japanese who settled in urban areas worked as domestic servants called "houseboys." Others opened restaurants, hotels, barber shops, pool rooms, laundries, and other retail businesses. As these businesses succeeded, many of the issei earned high status in the community for their achievements, as well as for their generosity in helping their neighbors deal with complicated issues such as legal problems.

Like the Chinese Six Companies and district associations, the Japanese *kenjinkai* played a key role in the lives of Japanese immigrants. Organized according to the district or prefecture of immigrants' origin, these social/cultural groups gave new arrivals assistance and information about housing and jobs. *Kenjinkai* members pooled resources to start businesses, buy land, fight legal battles, and lend money to one another.

The number of Japanese-American businesses in West Coast cities grew rapidly in the first decade of the 20th century—in San Francisco, the number increased nearly

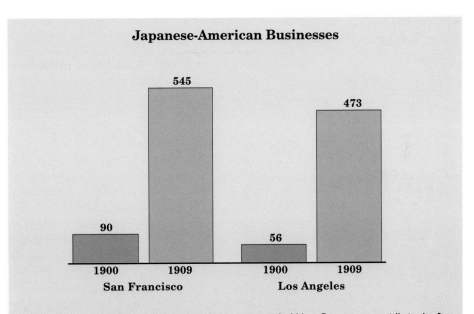

Japanese-American Businesses

The number of urban Japanese-American businesses on the West Coast grew rapidly in the first decade of the 20th century. By 1909, an Immigration Commission survey of the western United States found the following Japanese businesses, mostly in major cities along the Pacific coast, such as San Francisco, Los Angeles, Sacramento, and Seattle:

97 laundries
105 shoe shops
124 provision and supply stores
136 pool rooms
136 tailor and dye shops
187 barber shops
337 hotels and boardinghouses
381 restaurants

Source: Strangers from a Different Shore

Japanese fishermen in San Diego during the early 20th century (Library of Congress)

sixfold (from 90 to 545 businesses) between the years 1900 and 1909. Los Angeles saw a similar jump: from 56 to 473 businesses during the same period.

Nearly 50 percent of the early Japanese immigrants to the mainland United States worked in agriculture. The Vaca valley and the Suisun valley, both near San Francisco in Solano County, attracted many Japanese farmers. Building on skills honed as farmers in Japan, the immigrants first worked as migrant laborers, then gradually arranged to own or lease land of their own. Japanese independent farmers grew fruit, vegetables, and rice. By 1908 Japanese farmers owned 290 acres in California's Vaca valley. Nine years later, California had become one of the world's major rice producers. The Japanese also introduced new fruits and vegetables such as strawberries and celery to California. So adept were the Japanese at agriculture that even though they owned only 4 percent of California's farmland, they produced 10 percent of the state's farm products.

At the turn of the century, nearly 80 percent of America's immigrant Japanese lived in California. But Japanese workers moved to other states, too, such as Washington, Colorado, Utah, and Alaska. Workers in these areas signed on as commercial fisher-

men, fish cannery workers, agricultural laborers, and railroad workers.

Sugar beet farming in Spokane County, Washington, drew Japanese workers at the turn of the century, as did Washington's White River and Puyallup valleys—two areas that grew to become the state's main centers of Japanese truck farming. In Oregon, a number of Japanese cleared Hood River valley land in exchange for uncleared plots of their own, which many turned into berry farms and small orchards. Reclaiming swampy and overgrown land that nobody else wanted provided a backbreaking but sure path to ownership for many issei farmers.

Contract railroad workers imported from 1891 and later supplied much of the labor for the Northern Pacific Railway, the Great Northern, the Seattle and International, and the Rio Grande lines. Japanese railroad crews were sent as far east as Colorado, Idaho, Montana, and the Dakotas.

In California, Japanese immigrants fished along the West Coast near San Diego and at Terminal Island near San Pedro. In fact, the Japanese introduced the use of fishing rods to America's commercial fishing industry. Fish caught by bamboo poles remained in better condition than those caught by nets, and other fishermen soon

THE RAILROADS AND JAPANESE CONTRACT LABOR, 1891–1907

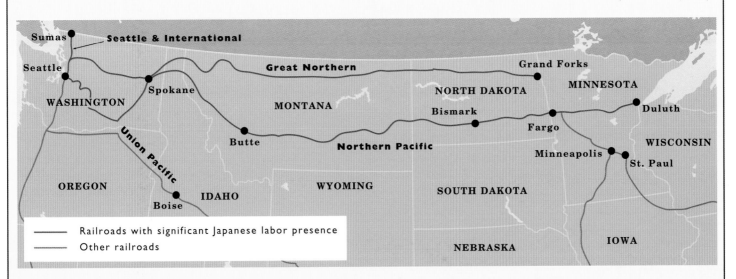

Railroads with significant Japanese labor presence
Other railroads

Between 1891 and 1907, thousands of Japanese arrived in the mainland United States as contract laborers, many of them for the railroads. Recruited by Japanese labor contracting companies (*keiyakunin*) such as the Oriental Trading Company of Seattle, which supplied workers to the Seattle & International, the Great Northern, and the Northern Pacific Railways, they worked for lower pay than their European-American counterparts. Loading freight cars nonstop from 7 A.M. to 6 P.M. each day and living in unsanitary and often freezing conditions, many workers died from accidents, disease, or malnutrition.

Source: Strangers from a Different Shore

The railroad companies themselves were not the only group exploiting Japanese rail workers. The *keiyakunin* also profited at their expense. From a typical daily wage of just $1.10, *keiyakunin* took a commission of 5 to 10 percent. In addition, the labor contracters also charged workers various additional monthly fees, commonly subtracted (at various rates) by individual *keiyakunin* from wages. These extraneous fees included such charges as "office fees," "hospital fees," "translator fees," and room and board charges (workers typically slept in bug-infested railroad boxcars).

also adopted the method. Though barred by law from fishing in Oregon and Washington, many Japanese found work in the salmon canning factories located along the Columbia River, on Puget Sound, and, seasonally, in Alaska.

The Japanese who came to the mainland had to deal with racism and discrimination on a daily basis. Mean-spirited rumors helped to spread anti-Japanese sentiment among disgruntled white Americans. White customers stopped buying vegetables grown by Japanese farmers based on the unfounded fear that the vegetables were purposely sprayed with arsenic. Japan's growing military prowess in the world fired the fear of espionage as white citizens worried that Japanese-American immigrants, so familiar with America's western coastline, were spies. Restaurants, hotels, and stores were physically divided into segregated sections, with special rooms for whites only. Managers and owners often refused to serve Japanese customers altogether.

Japanese immigrants, like the Chinese before them, had to endure racist

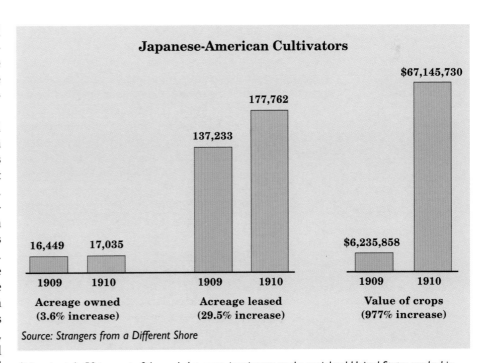

Source: Strangers from a Different Shore

Approximately 50 percent of the early Japanese immigrants to the mainland United States worked in agriculture. The newcomers had extraordinary success. Many started as migrant workers but became independent farmers, cultivating their own fields and orchards. Fast to meet supply and demand, they both sped up and slowed down production of crops to keep ahead of competitors and retained produce when other harvests had been completed. An immigrant named K. Ikuta was the first to successfully cultivate rice in California, and by 1917 California had become a major rice producer.

taunts even when taking a simple walk. Shouts of "Goddamn Jap!", "Dirty Jap!", and "Jap go home!" followed men, women, and children as they went about their daily business. Some whites threw rocks and spat at Japanese people who happened to be in public places. Phrases such as "No More Japs Wanted Here" and "Fire the Japs!" were graffitied near railroad stations, on sidewalks, and in rest-room toilets.

California newspapers reflected and inflamed popular opinion against the Japanese. The *San Francisco Chronicle* published a number of articles delineating the threat of a Japanese "yellow peril." Even though the Japanese population numbered less than 2 percent of California's total population or its immigrant population, newspapermen warned of America's doom at the evil hands of the spies and criminals flooding into the country.

As the Japanese-American population swelled and Japanese farmers and businessmen thrived, suspicious West Coast labor leaders, businessmen, and politicians debated what action needed to be taken. In 1901 Governor Henry Gage publicly referred to Japanese laborers as a "menace" and requested that Congress ban the Japanese from U.S. entry. Opinion was somewhat divided about the issue, with business leaders wanting to keep profit margins high by having a constant supply of cheap labor and unions more concerned that long-term immigration would take away jobs and erode America's standard of living.

White labor outcry against Asian immigrants fell into a variety of small but representative protests. The Native Sons of the Golden West conducted anti-Japanese poster campaigns, among other activities. In 1905, the San Francisco Labor Council organized a major boycott against Japanese businessmen and whites who employed Japanese workers. The Labor Council, made up mainly of white laborers but later dominated by California's elite, enjoyed the full support of Mayor Eugene E. Schmitz of San Francisco.

The group made its stance clear from the beginning:

We have been accustomed to regard the Japanese as an inferior race, but are now suddenly aroused to our danger. They are not window cleaners and house servants. The Japanese can think, can learn, can invent. We have suddenly awakened to the fact that they are gaining a foothold in every skilled industry in our country. They are our equal in intellect; their ability to labor is equal to ours. . . . We are here today to prevent that very competition.

American labor opposition became fully organized on May 14th, 1905, with the formation of the Asiatic Exclusion League, the first large body created with the sole goal of Japanese immigrant exclusion. Delegates from nearly 70 groups gathered that day in San Francisco for an organizational meeting. The league fought for exclusion legislation, distributed anti-Japanese propaganda, initiated boycotts, and helped bring about school segregation and land restriction bills. The league operated under the leadership of mainly European immigrants until 1911, when it disbanded. Later, other groups such as the Japanese Exclusion League of California continued to promote Asian discrimination.

Elected officials also trumpeted anti-Asian views. San Francisco's popular mayor, James D. Phelan (who later became a California state senator), was a leader in both the anti-Chinese movement of the 1880s and the anti-Japanese movement of the early 1900s. Phelan did not hesitate to compare the Japanese and Chinese "problems," proclaiming in speeches, "The Japanese are starting the same tide of immigration that we thought we had checked 20 years ago. . . . The Chinese and Japanese are not . . . the stuff of which American citizens can be made."

As anti-Japanese bias mushroomed throughout the West, the clamor for federal legislation ending East Asian immigration grew to a din. President Theodore Roosevelt had for the most part advanced a position of fairness on Asian-immigrant issues during his presidency. Furthermore, Roosevelt placed good relations with the Japanese government at a premium, and his mediation ending the Russo-Japanese War had helped cement that relationship.

In keeping with his generally pro-Japanese stance, Roosevelt had also reacted strongly against the poor treatment Asian workers endured in Hawaii as those details came to light during an investigation shortly after annexation. In December of 1905, he put forth his position: "The status of servility can never again be tolerated on American soil. . . . Hawaii shall never become a territory in which a governing class of rich planters exist by means of 'coolie' labor."

Just two short years later, however, President Roosevelt's position bent under pressure from the anti-Japanese voting bloc. Other events would contribute to his changing stance, such as a local dispute involving public schools in San Francisco that threatened to erupt into an international crisis.

THE SAN FRANCISCO SCHOOL BOARD CRISIS

Public school segregation was not a new concept to San Francisco lawmakers. American-born Chinese children had long been pushed into separate schools. In 1893, the school board had ruled that Japanese students must attend these Chinese schools.

Although the segregation order was briefly overturned, it was reinstituted several years later. In 1906, San Francisco was devastated by a powerful earthquake that destroyed hundreds of homes, businesses, and other buildings—including public school buildings. In the aftermath of the quake, overcrowding in the schools gave the school board an opening to attempt to resegregate Japanese and Korean children into Chinese schools. To those who favored the policy, the 93 Japanese-American children, or nisei (second-generation Japanese Americans), in the San Francisco public school system posed a particular threat: Since they were born in the United States and were automatically citizens, nisei were entitled to citizenship's rights and privileges. Even though the conflict involved just 93 children, its repercussions would be felt from Wahington, D.C., to Tokyo.

THE GENTLEMEN'S AGREEMENT

The San Francisco School Board crisis was just the kind of situation Theodore Roosevelt had hoped to avoid. Having just negotiated the peace settlement between Japan and Russia to end the the Russo-Japanese War, the president was keenly aware of Japan's military strength, as well as the Japanese government's consistent concern for the well-being of Japanese emigrés and their families. Roosevelt also knew that for Japan, the treatment of Japanese Americans was a matter of national honor.

When the Meiji government asked for his help in the school board matter, Roosevelt sought a compromise. He sent U.S. Secretary of Commerce and Labor Victor H. Metcalf to California, and he met personally with Japan's ambassador, Viscount Suizo Aoki. In December of 1906, Roosevelt not only criticized the segregation order but also called for a federal act allowing issei to become naturalized citizens.

U.S. president Theodore Roosevelt won a Nobel Peace Prize for helping to end the Russo-Japanese War (1904–1905). During his administration, he also negotiated a series of agreements known collectively as the Gentlemen's Agreement that strictly limited Japanese immigration to the United States. (Library of Congress)

Although Roosevelt's public willingness to support Japan and Japanese Americans was not welcomed by California's exclusionist forces, he and Secretary of State Elihu Root commenced negotiations with Japan, California state legislators, and San Francisco school board officials. By March 12, 1907, the delicate diplomatic situation had been finessed. The school board agreed to let most Japanese children attend San

Francisco public schools with white children and promised not to apply further restrictive rules to any alien immigrant group; Roosevelt agreed to limit Japanese immigration; and the California legislature agreed to stop pushing anti-Japanese legislation until the larger immigration issues were ironed out with Japan.

On March 14, the Immigration Act of 1907 became law, banning Japanese migration from Hawaii, Mexico, and Canada to the U.S. mainland. Soon after, Japan promised to stop issuing passports to laborers, except for "former residents, parents, wives or children of residents." This promise formed the core of what became known as the Gentlemen's Agreement of 1908, a treaty which, though deftly negotiated, was only partially successful as an immigration ban. The exceptions to the ban, particularly the one for wives, created a loophole that allowed a new class of Japanese immigrants, known as "picture brides," to continue to arrive in the United States throughout the 1910s.

THE KOREAN INDEPENDENCE MOVEMENT

In the midst of controversies over Japanese immigration and segregation, the constituents of America's small Korean community, both in Hawaii and in the mainland United States, united together in their desire to liberate their homeland from Japan.

Because Hawaii was the point of arrival for most Koreans, it was on the sugar plantations that the Korean independence movement first gathered strength. In 1903 Korean plantation workers founded Sinmin-hoe, the New Peoples' Association, in Hawaii. Four years later, the Korean Consolidated Association formed to fight Japanese colonialism in Korea. This group was headquartered in Honolulu. Oahu's Korean National Brigade began training anticolonial fighters in 1912. Seven years later, Korean immigrants in Honolulu formed the Korean National Independence League. The following year, Syngman Rhee, a Korean immigrant to Hawaii, founded Tongji-hoe, the Comrade Society, again with the express purpose of ending the Japanese colonial stranglehold on Korea. The tactics advocated by the Korean independence movement in America included thoughtful debate, stinging editorials, financial funding, military training, and in several instances, violence.

The Korean National Association of North America, formed in 1909 and headquartered in San Francisco, consolidated and coordinated the efforts of resistance movements in Hawaii and in the mainland United States. The Korean National Association demanded of its members a "complete cessation of any association with the Japanese because normally one does not associate with the murderer of one's parents, and Japan had murdered our fatherland." All Korean immigrants were required to become members and pay dues. Eventually, the Korean National Association transformed into a quasi-government-in-exile and even represented Koreans in dealings with the U.S. government. The Korean National Association also provided welfare assistance to Korean immigrants, as did some of the other Korean independence organizations in the United States.

Korean hatred of the Japanese extended to those who supported Japan in any way. The most notable incident involved a white American lobbyist named Durham Stevens, who was hired by the Japanese government to convince the U.S. government that most Koreans actually supported Japan. In retaliation, California-based Korean patriot Chang In-hwan shot and killed Stevens on March 23, 1908. For his action, Chang was honored as an *uisa*—a national hero martyred for the cause of independence. Many Korean immigrants contributed to help pay for his legal defense.

To Koreans, the murder of Durham Stevens was not merely an isolated act of revenge. It was a necessary response during a time of war. In fact, some Korean-American organizations actively trained soldiers for the day when Korean forces could retake their homeland by force. The Korean Student Federation of North America, founded in 1913 and located in Hastings, Nebraska, trained youth fighters in addition to providing social and educational services to immigrants. Military schools were established in Claremont, Lompoc, and Willows, California. Nineteen students in Willows trained to be pilots using three airplanes provided by a successful agricultural entrepreneur, Kim Chong-nim.

KOREAN LIFE ON THE MAINLAND

Although anti-Asian whites and Korean immigrants shared a hatred for Japanese immigrants, early Korean immigrants

KOREAN INDEPENDENCE ORGANIZATIONS IN THE UNITED STATES

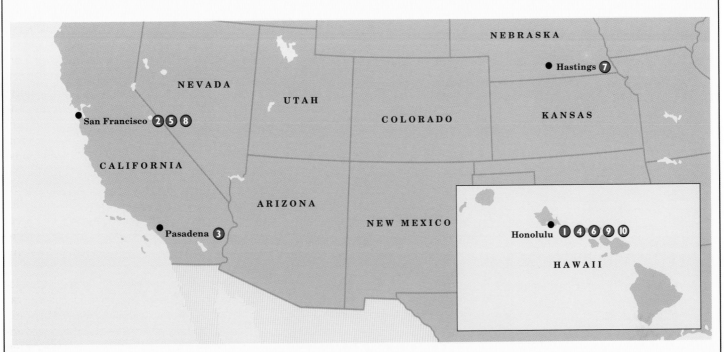

Organzation

① New People's Association

② Korean Mutual Assistance Association (Sinmin-hoe)

③ Korean Restorative Association (Kongnip Hyop-hoe)

④ Korean Consolidated Association

⑤ Korean National Association of North America

⑥ Korean National Brigade

⑦ Korean Student Federation of North America

⑧ Young Koreans' Academy (Heung-sa-dan)

⑨ Korean National Independence League

⑩ Comrade Society (Tongji-hoe)

Purpose

Founded in 1903 by plantation workers to support the independent sovereignty of Korea.

Founded in 1905 to fight Japanese repression and colonialism in Korea and to help immigrants assimilate easily by helping to find housing and work.

Founded in 1905 to fight Japanese repression and colonialism in Korea.

Founded in 1905 to fight Japanese colonialism in Korea.

Founded in 1909 to fight Japanese repression and colonialism in Korea; to consolidate and coordinate the resistance movement; to preserve Korean national identity; to provide welfare assistance, for example, by setting up schools and publishing educational textbooks. All Korean immigrants were required to become members and pay dues. The organization maintained 78 branches in Hawaii alone.

Founded in 1912 to train anticolonial fighters in the struggle against the Japanese.

Founded in 1913 to further the education of Korean immigrants and to offer social services to Korean students. The federation organized military academy to train anticolonial fighters.

Founded in 1913 by Ahn Chang-ho to nurture future leaders of the Korean nationalist movement. The academy promoted loyalty and courage through knowledge, virtue, and good health.

Founded in 1919 to fight Japanese colonialism in Korea.

Founded in 1920 by Syngman Rhee to fight Japanese colonialism in Korea.

faced the same prejudices as their Chinese and Japanese counterparts had before them. In fact, life in the mainland United States was even more difficult in many respects than life on the Hawaiian plantations had been. A migrant from Korea remembered docking at San Francisco in 1906: "One [white] guy stuck his foot out [as we walked down the gangplank] and kicked up my mother's skirt. He spit on my face, and I asked my father, 'Why did we come to such a place? I want to go home to Korea.'" To add the greatest of insults to injury, igno-

rant whites often confused the Koreans with the Japanese, yelling such phrases as "Jap go home!" from street corners at Koreans passing by.

Once again, white labor saw the newcomers as a threat to job security and often reacted violently, engaging in mob attacks. During a 1910 incident in Upland, California, white farmworkers armed with rocks and stones attacked Korean orange pickers. Grassroots hate groups such as the Asiatic Exclusion League and the Japanese and Korean Exclusion League began to include

Syngman Rhee, who became South Korea's first president following World War II, served as a leading figure in the Korean independence movement in the United States to expel Japan from Korea. (National Archives)

all Asians in their definitions of undesirables as they pushed for more exclusionist legislation to be passed.

Ironically, some Koreans responded to this treatment by blaming the Chinese and Japanese immigrants who had come before them. Many Koreans subscribed to the view that the Chinese and Japanese did not try hard enough to assimilate into the American mainstream, which only fostered discrimination and violence against all Asians.

Most Koreans who moved to urban areas in the early 1900s lived in California cities such as San Francisco and Los Angeles. Korean immigrants in these urban areas worked as janitors, gardeners, domestic servants, and restaurant workers. Korean entrepreneurs who borrowed and saved enough money to earn a more independent living eventually opened barbershops, laundries, groceries, bakeries, and photo studios. Korean merchants often went into the hotel business. Many successful Korean hotel owners also worked as labor contractors, providing room and board for those they

signed on to work in the fields as migrant workers. By 1920, Korean-owned hotels could be found in many California cities, including Sacramento, Stockton, San Francisco, Los Angeles, Riverside, and Lompac.

Most newly arrived Koreans found work as farm laborers. They organized themselves into groups of 10 men supervised by a *sip-chang* ("ten-head")—a traditional Korean form of work crew organization. Such teams of laborers moved from town to town wherever work was available. Sometimes the workers picked grapes, plums, or peaches; other times, they planted tomatoes or hoed bean fields. Due to the presence of black widow spiders and yellow-jacket hornets, picking fruit proved to be the riskiest task. To avoid bruising the fruit, peach pickers were required to knock bugs off the fruit with a feather brush, a tedious and sometimes painful job.

Helping one another financially, Korean farm laborers gradually purchased land in small groups to farm on their own. The Koreans used a credit rotating system called

AREAS OF EARLY KOREAN SETTLEMENT, 1903–1920

WASHINGTON

Seattle
(1880s)

Portland
(1870s)

OREGON

MONTANA

NORTH
DAKOTA

IDAHO

SOUTH
DAKOTA

WYOMING

NEBRASKA

Sacramento

NEVADA

UTAH

Denver

COLORADO

KANSAS

San Francisco

CALIFORNIA

Los Angeles

ARIZONA

NEW MEXICO

OKLAHOMA

TEXAS

ALASKA

HAWAII

California: Many Korean immigrants who arrived in California started working as agricultural laborers in gangs, moving from field to field according to the harvest seasons. The work they performed was hot and grueling, with long hours and little pay. Many were able to start their own agricultural enterprises, farming rice and other crops with great success.

One such entrepreneur was Kim Hyung-soon, who started as a fruit wholesaler and later ran his own orchards, nurseries, and fruit packing sheds. He also developed the nectarine and the fuzzless peach.

In urban areas, many worked in service industries in low paying jobs such as janitor or waiter. Many went on to open their own retail businesses, such as laundries, restaurants, grocery stores, and hotels.

Colorado, Wyoming, and Utah: Part of the remigration from Hawaii to the mainland brought Koreans to these western states to work in the coal and copper mines.

Alaska: A small number of Koreans remigrated from Hawaii to the salmon canneries of Alaska.

Arizona: Some Koreans remigrated from Hawaii to Arizona to work on railroad gangs. Eating and sleeping in wagons, these workers moved from one place to another, repairing railroad tracks.

Hawaii: Between 1910 and 1924 approximately 1,100 "picture brides" arrived in Hawaii to marry Korean workers. They brought stability to the Korean community, which had been composed primarily of single men.

---

the *kae*—like the Chinese *woi* and the Japanese *tanomoshi*. Each individual in the *kae* contributed money and allowed group members to borrow and repay one by one on a rotating basis. The last member in line would not be charged interest.

Like the Japanese, Koreans were particularly adept at rice farming. Koreans in the Sacramento area produced 214,000 bushels of rice as early as 1918. Rice acreage owned and worked by Koreans in Willows, California, home to "rice king" Kim Chong-nim, totaled 43,000 acres by the 1920s. Kim Hyung-soon met with great success in the fruit industry. He and partner Kim Ho founded the Kim Brothers

Company, which owned orchards, nurseries, fruit-packing sheds, and wholesale operations. He and his employees also developed new varieties of peaches and invented the nectarine. All successful Korean businessmen practiced *aeguk chongsin* (patriotism) and fought for *kwangbok* (restoration of sovereignty to Korea), donating large sums of money to the Korean independence movement.

Such success did not come about easily, especially after the passage of two anti-Asian laws known as the California Alien Land Acts of 1913 and 1920. The first law prohibited anyone ineligible for citizenship from owning land, and the second outlawed the practice of putting land in the name of American-born children to avoid the ban.

Some turn-of-the-century Korean immigrants migrated deeper into the U.S. interior. Some worked in the coal mines of Colorado and Wyoming, or in the copper mines of Utah. Others repaired railroad track in Arizona. Still others ventured north to Alaska to earn a living in the seasonal salmon canneries.

Unlike the early Chinese settlements, the Korean community was not a bachelor society. Many of those remigrating from Hawaii had already brought their families with them from Korea. Much of family life revolved around the independence movement—membership in political groups, holiday celebrations, courtship practices, language study, religious affiliations, and monetary gifting. Even education was seen as a way to help "crush the enemy"—Japan. According to researcher Hyung June Moon, by 1920, mainland Koreans had the highest literacy rate of all Asian immigrant groups, 92 percent; at that time 96 percent of whites, 89 percent of Japanese, and 80 percent of Chinese were literate.

EARLY ASIAN-INDIAN IMMIGRATION

Asian Indians, the last major Asian ethnic group to arrive in the United States during the turn-of-the-century period, took an entirely different route from the Chinese, Japanese, Koreans, and Filipinos. However, their immigration story shares one thread with the others—colonial domination. Relations between Japanese and Koreans had a significant influence early Japanese and Korean immigration to the United States; American-Filipino relations were a driving force behind Filipino immigration. Likewise, the colonial relationship between Great Britain and India played an important role in the story of early Indian immigration to the United States. For this group of Asian immigrants, however, unlike its predecessors, the plantations of Hawaii had little to do with the story.

Beginning in 1899, a small number of Asian Indians left India for Canada and other British colonies, including British Guiana, Uganda, and the British West Indies. The vast majority of this small wave of migrants came from a region known as the Punjab ("land of five rivers"), an area located in northeast Pakistan and northwest India that is claimed by both countries. The migrants, overwhelmingly male and young (ranging in age from 16 to 35), originated from the districts of Ludhiana, Jullunder, and Hoshiarpur. Those men who were married left their wives and children at home.

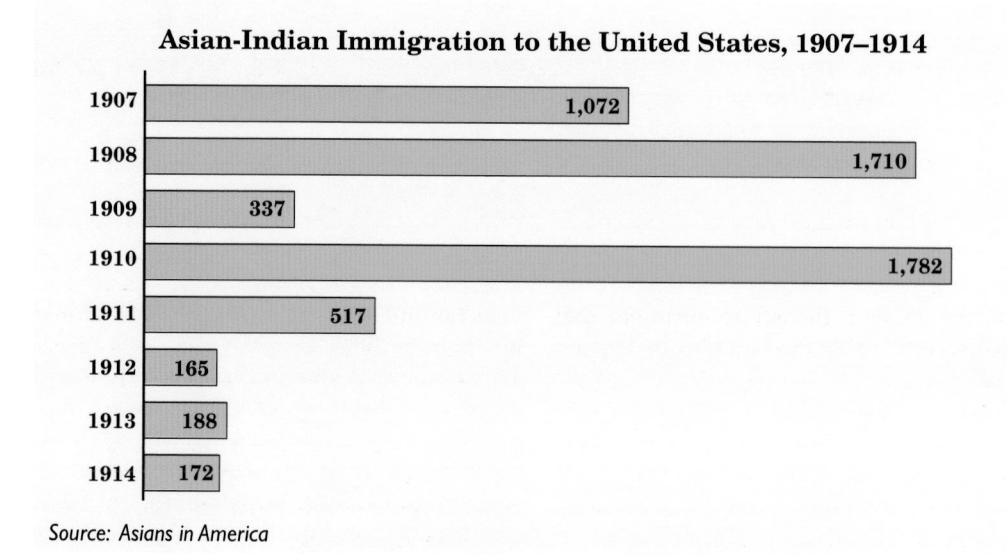

Asian-Indian Immigration to the United States, 1907–1914

Year	Number
1907	1,072
1908	1,710
1909	337
1910	1,782
1911	517
1912	165
1913	188
1914	172

Source: Asians in America

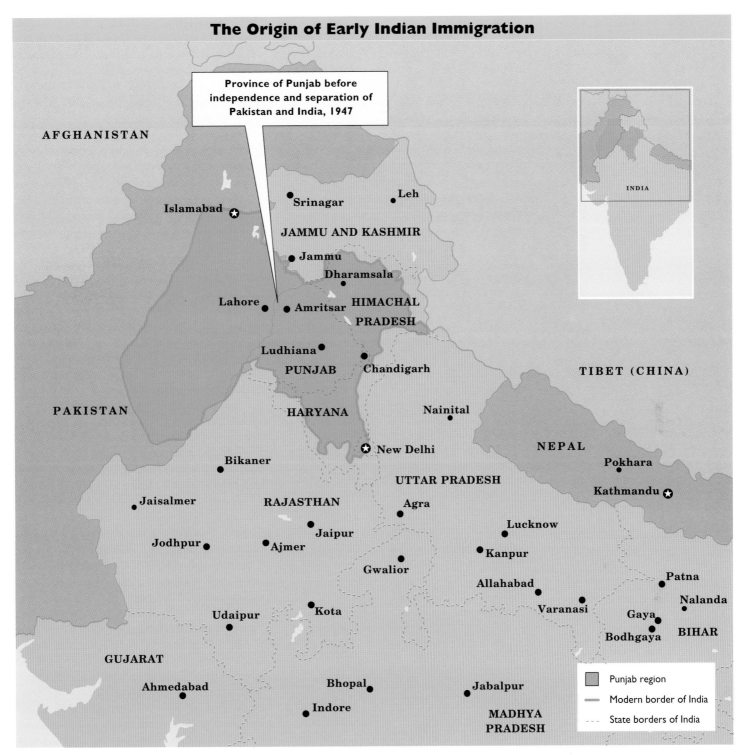

The Origin of Early Indian Immigration

Province of Punjab before independence and separation of Pakistan and India, 1947

AFGHANISTAN

Islamabad

Srinagar • Leh

JAMMU AND KASHMIR

Jammu

Dharamsala

Lahore • • Amritsar   HIMACHAL
                        PRADESH

Ludhiana
PUNJAB   Chandigarh

PAKISTAN   HARYANA   Nainital   TIBET (CHINA)

New Delhi   NEPAL
                      Pokhara

Bikaner   UTTAR PRADESH   Kathmandu

Jaisalmer   RAJASTHAN   Agra
                                Lucknow
Jodhpur   Jaipur   Kanpur
          Ajmer
                  Gwalior   Allahabad   Patna
Udaipur   Kota   Nalanda
                        Varanasi   Gaya   BIHAR
GUJARAT   Bodhgaya

Ahmedabad   Bhopal   Jabalpur

Indore   MADHYA
          PRADESH

INDIA

Punjab region
Modern border of India
State borders of India

Sikh immigrants to the United States originated in the Punjab region, which now encompasses parts of India and Pakistan. Between 1904 and 1923, approximately 10,000 Sikhs settled in California and Oregon, where they found jobs laying railroad track and working in agriculture.

Conditions in the Punjab helped push the young men to the West. In an effort to establish a capitalist form of agriculture in India, the colonial British government had instituted reforms in the land tenure system and agricultural production that placed small Punjabi landholders at risk. In order to pay off short-term debts, many were forced to take out high-interest mortgages that contained clauses stating that lands would be forfeited if payments were not made on time. Exacerbating the situation for Punjabi landowners as well as the Laborers who worked for them was a three-year famine between 1899 and 1902. Urged by their families to return in a few years with enough money to get the family out of debt, many small farmers began emigrating to British colonies overseas in search of work. To the Punjabi, who earned between 5 and 8 cents per day, the prospect of earning 75 cents to $2 per day overseas seemed

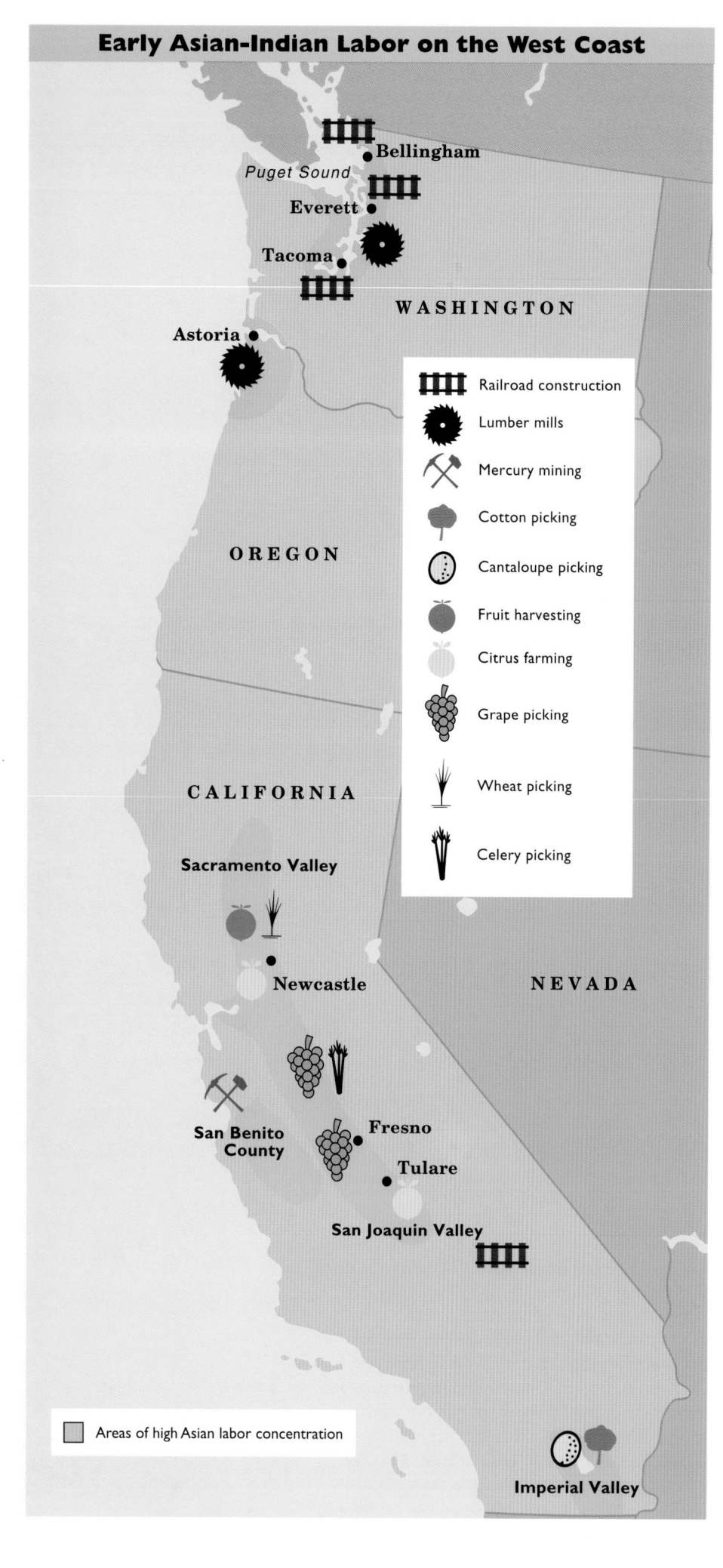

Early Asian-Indian Labor on the West Coast

Bellingham
Puget Sound
Everett
Tacoma
Astoria
WASHINGTON

OREGON

Legend:
- Railroad construction
- Lumber mills
- Mercury mining
- Cotton picking
- Cantaloupe picking
- Fruit harvesting
- Citrus farming
- Grape picking
- Wheat picking
- Celery picking

CALIFORNIA

Sacramento Valley

Newcastle

NEVADA

San Benito County

Fresno

Tulare

San Joaquin Valley

Areas of high Asian labor concentration

Imperial Valley

like a miraculous solution to their families' debt problems.

Canada was one of the most common destinations. After completing a long journey by train to Calcutta, and then by ship to Hong Kong and across the Pacific to Vancouver, Punjabi immigrants—47 percent of whom were illiterate—did find work. Beginning in 1907, many of these laborers headed south from Canada along West Coast railroad lines into Washington State.

Most of these migrant workers—known as *pindi* (village men) and *got* (cousins)—belonged to the Sikh religion. Sikhism rejects the Hindu caste system by which individuals are grouped and separated into a hierarchical social ladder of classes, but it retains the concept of rebirth and reincarnation. Sikhism borrows the Muslim-influenced idea of monotheism (belief in one God), departing from the Hindu concept of pantheism. Sikhs also follow certain strict rules of dress, food, and behavior. Sikhs are not to drink alcohol or smoke cigarettes. Traditional dress for a male Sikh follows the "five k's": *kes* (uncut hair and beard, with hair knotted under a turban), *kacch* (pants hemmed at the knee), *kara* (iron bracelet), *kirpan/khada* (sword/dagger), and *khange* (hair comb).

Even though Sikhs composed the majority of Asian-Indian immigrants to the United States, Americans at the time referred to them as Hindus or "Hindoos." Prejudices previously mounted against Chinese and Japanese immigrants became directed also at this new "menace" to American society, often referred to at the time as "the tide of the turbans."

So when the Asian Indians arrived to work in the lumber yards and sawmills of Washington State, they encountered angry whites, fearful of job competition and prejudiced against Sikhs' skin color, dress, and religion. In September 1907, white workers in the town of Bellingham physically pushed 700 Asian Indians back over the border into Canada. Such mob actions, reminiscent of earlier attacks on the Chinese, recurred in town after town across the state as well as in the mill towns of Oregon.

Continuing south, many Asian-Indian laborers found jobs in California, mainly repairing and laying track for the Western Pacific Railroad. Between 1908 and 1910, Western Pacific imported nearly 1,000 Asian Indians directly into California. By 1910, however, when railroad jobs started to disappear, unionized white railroad employees sought to drive out the newcomers, particularly since they worked longer hours for less money.

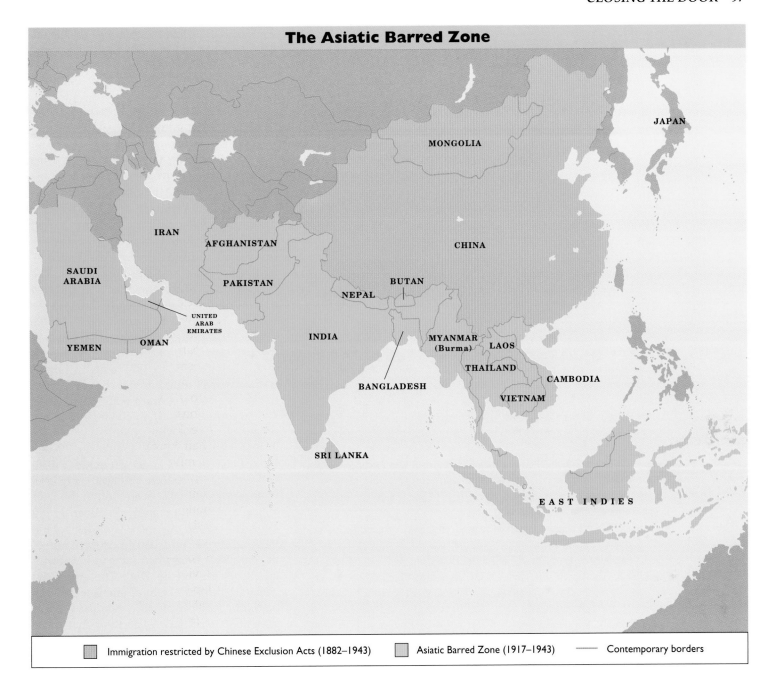

The Asiatic Barred Zone

Immigration restricted by Chinese Exclusion Acts (1882–1943)   Asiatic Barred Zone (1917–1943)   —— Contemporary borders

California's labor shortage in its agriculture industry—a direct result of the Chinese Exclusion Act and the Gentlemen's Agreement—opened opportunities to the Asian Indians, who were experienced at farming. By 1920, 6,400 Asian Indians had migrated to the United States. Their small numbers and the nature of the available work kept the Sikhs relatively dispersed, and no ethnic district or "Indiatown" developed in any particular geographical spot.

Most California agriculture took the form of seasonal contract work. The Asian-Indian farm laborers worked in gangs of three to 50, headed by a gang leader, usually chosen by his proficiency with English. The gang leader found jobs, negotiated contracts with white farm owners, and arranged for the workers' housing, which usually took the form of tents, barns, or sleeping bags on bare ground. For his work, the gang leader earned a commission from the group as well as a wage from the employer.

The Asian-Indian workers migrated with the demands of the seasonal harvests. From July to October, fruits and vegetables needed harvesting; in December and January, trees and plants had to be pruned; in March through May, irrigation canals and ditches needed to be attended to. Sikh laborers spread throughout California's Sacramento, San Joaquin, and Imperial valleys working with grapevines, fruit orchards, rice, asparagus, celery, and cotton plants.

By the 1920s, some Asian-Indian farmworkers, many of them former gang leaders, had saved enough money to buy land of their own. As had the Chinese, Japanese, and Koreans before them, the Asian-Indian immigrants helped one another succeed by pooling their resources. A typical arrangement involved as many as eight men pooling money to buy the land they worked. They chose traditional Indian crops such as rice and cotton and often worked 19-hour days to make their farms thrive. Their ultimate goal was to save enough money to bring their Indian wives and children to America.

EVENTS IN ASIAN-INDIAN HISTORY, 1899–1924

1899–1902	Partly in response to a three-year famine in the Punjab region, some farmers begin to emigrate from their homeland. Many settle in other British and former British colonies, including Uganda, the British West Indies, British Guiana, and Canada.
1907	Punjabi living in Canada head south to Washington State where they find jobs with area lumber mills. Angry whites launch several attacks on Punjabi communities around the state.
	Tarak Nath Das begins publishing a monthly magazine, *Free Hindustan*, in Vancouver, Canada. In it he criticizes American and Canadian immigration laws. After he becomes a naturalized U.S. citizen in 1914, the U.S. government continually threatens him with deportation.
1908–1910	More than 1,000 Hindus are imported to work on the Western Pacific Railroad in California.
1913	The California Alien Land Act of 1913 forbids the ownership of land by aliens "ineligible for citizenship." All Asians are thereby barred from land ownership.
	Hindustan Gadar, the first Asian-Indian newspaper, begins publishing in San Francisco.
1914	The India Home Rule League, which is opposed to British rule in India, founds the first U.S. chapter in New York City.
1917	Adult immigrants are required to show they can read and write, and immigrants from most of Asia and the Pacific Islands, also known as the "Asiatic Barred Zone," are excluded from immigrating entirely.
	The United States enters World War I. White farmworkers leave fields to work in factories, opening up opportunities for Asian immigrants in agriculture.
1920	The California Alien Land Act of 1913 is extended to prohibit the leasing of land by aliens "ineligible for citizenship."
1921	The U.S. Congress passes the Emergency Quota Act. The law restricts the number of annual immigrants admitted to the United States to a percentage based on each nationality's U.S. population in 1910. Japanese and Koreans, whose immigration is already limited by the Gentlemen's Agreement, are exempted.
1922	The Cable Act is passed, allowing the government to punish American women who marry aliens not eligible for citizenship by revoking such women's citizenship. Alien women who are ineligible for citizenship are also forbidden to marry American citizens.
1923	In the case of *United States v. Bhagat Singh Thind*, the Supreme Court rules that Asian Indians are forbidden from becoming naturalized citizens because of their skin color. As a result, all land purchases made by Asian Indians in California are nullified by that state's attorney general, and the former owners are forced from their land.
1924	The Border Patrol is established to prevent unlawful entry along U.S. boundaries.

But a continuous stream of exclusionary laws, passed at both the federal and state levels, thwarted such dreams. Discriminatory legislation aimed at the Sikhs began almost as soon as the immigrants entered Washington State. Between 1908 and 1920, federal immigration officials denied entry to almost 3,500 Asian Indians, the most common justification being that the new arrivals could not earn a living independently and would become a burden to the government. In 1917, the U.S. Congress established an "Asiatic Barred Zone" that banned from U.S. shores all immigrants from India, Afghanistan, Southeast Asia, and the East Indies. The ban included even the wives and children of the immigrant men already living in the United States. Sikh immigrant Moola Singh, recounting the devastating effect of the 1917 law, told of the heartbreak he felt after his wife died in 1921 without him in India: "Lots of time I dream she come close to me. . . . No, she don't want come close, she go round, round, no come close in my dream. . . . That's a life gone."

At the state level, California's Alien Land Laws of 1913 and 1920 made it difficult for Sikhs to acquire and hold on to land by lease or purchase, even though the laws technically did not apply to Asians until 1920. The reason that these laws did not initially apply to Sikhs had to do with one of the earliest immigration laws in U.S. history, the Alien Act of 1790. The Alien Act declared that only "white" aliens were eligible for citizenship. Thus, when the California Alien Land Laws specified that those ineligible for citizenship could not lease (1913) or own (1920) land, the law clearly barred Chinese, Japanese, and Korean immigrants from land lease and ownership. Asian-Indian immigrants, however, presented a difficult complication for white exclusionist lawmakers.

Sikhs fell under the definition of "Caucasian," which to the laws' authors generally meant "white," unlike the Chinese, Japanese, and Koreans, who were therefore technically ineligible for citizenship. To Indians, however, "Caucasian" meant people of Caucasoid ethnicity, which included people not only from Europe, but from northern Africa, Southwest Asia, and the Indian subcontinent as well.

Although Indians were in fact Caucasian, from the beginning of their immigration to the United States, groups like the Asiatic Exclusion League fought to change the definition of that term to exclude them.

In 1910 the league stated that while they agreed that Asian Indians and Europeans both belonged to "the same [Caucasian] family," in a scientific sense, the two groups were "cousins, far removed." The league went on to argue that while the forefathers of white Americans became "Lords of Creation" in the West, ". . . in the everlasting march of conquest, progress and civilization," Asian Indians had become the "Slaves of Creation," having become ". . . enslaved, effeminate, caste-ridden and degraded" in the East. Semantic wrangling over legalities involving the words "white" and "Caucasian" as definitions applied to Asian Indians went on for years, debated in courts and in the press.

The U.S. Supreme Court finally put the matter of semantic definitions to rest in 1923 with the case of *United States v. Bhagat Singh Thind*. The court ruled that Asian Indians were not eligible to become naturalized citizens after all. The court's decision hinged on the argument that the word "white" as it originally appeared had been employed as common speech. Since the word "Caucasian" was not used in 1790, the naturalization law should not include Asian Indians, who were "Caucasian" but not "white."

Thus, in the aftermath of the ruling, all American citizens of Sikh heritage had their citizenship revoked by the U.S. government, and those who had succeeded in purchasing land were forced by California attorney general U. S. Webb to forfeit the farms they had worked so hard to establish. This land included more than 86,000 acres of leased land and approximately 2,000 acres of land owned outright.

Although the Supreme Court ruling drove more than 3,000 Asian Indians to return to India between 1920 and 1930, many who stayed managed to hold on to their land through clever means. Not many Sikhs had children born in the United States, but those who did registered their land in their children's names. Others had white friends and colleagues put their names on deeds in return for a share of the harvest or an equivalent dollar amount. Unlike Japanese farm laborers, who developed business relationships among themselves, the Sikhs' low literacy level forced them to develop more communication with the larger white agricultural community.

Another legal loophole that helped Asian-Indian men maintain their lands involved marriage. Many Sikh laborers had married Mexican-American women, and consequently could—and did—deed their farms in their spouses' names.

THE RISE AND FALL OF THE GHADR PARTY

The discriminatory treatment the Sikhs endured in America and the consequent struggle for civil rights paralleled India's struggle for independence from British colonial rule. The early decades of the 20th century proved to be a fertile time for all kinds of independence and civil rights–related movements around the world. Some groups used peaceful means for change; other groups and individuals resorted to violence. Within the context of the Russian Revolution of 1917–1921 and World War I (1914–1918), fear of anarchist violence and communist "infiltration" in the United States grew to a fever pitch. Immigrant workers such as Sacco and Vanzetti and radical leaders like Emma Goldman were persecuted for their political beliefs and their suspected violent criminal acts.

In India, Mohandas K. Gandhi inspired hundreds of thousands of his countrypeople over many decades to use peaceful methods to press for political and social change. In 1920 he started the non-cooperation movement that included a boycott of all British-made goods, a boycott of elections, and a total withdrawal from government, law courts, and schools.

Nine years later, Gandhi launched the first round of civil disobedience protests, and in 1942 he began his "quit India" campaign, aimed at pressuring the British to relinquish control of India. Though Gandhi's followers practiced pacifist means,

Mohandas K. Gandhi (right) (Hulton-Getty)

The Ghadr Party newspaper (Bancroft Library, University of California, Berkeley)

Two years later, under the leadership of Har Dayal, a weekly newspaper also called *Ghadr* began publication. Dayal, a former lecturer at Stanford University and founder of the Hindustani Association of Students, coined the slogan "Mutiny Comes." During 1913, Dayal visited Washington, Oregon, and California, speaking to Asian-Indian crowds on behalf of the New Hindu Association of the Pacific Coast.

In 1914 Ghadr members took their cause to a more radical—and more violent—level when they began making bombs during strategy meetings held in San Francisco. Nationalistic unrest was widespread in the Indian community, as one immigration official observed: "Most of the Indian students are infected with seditious ideas. Even Sikhs of the laboring class have not escaped their influence." U.S. immigration officials arrested Dayal when he called for sedition against Great Britain, but he fled the United States before facing deportation. That same year nearly 400 Asian Indians left the United States to join in Ghadr-sponsored revolutionary activities in India, which continued in the Punjab region the following year.

By 1917, 105 Asian-Indian immigrants had been arrested in the United States on charges of conspiracy to violate federal neutrality laws. Ram Chandra, who had served as the editor of *Ghadr* since 1914, was assassinated at the end of the trials, which had resulted in the conviction of 14 Asian-Indian activists. The trial—and Chandra's death—effectively ended the Ghadr Party's activities in the United States three decades before India would finally win its sovereignty from Great Britain.

hundreds of thousands, including Gandhi himself, were killed as Hindu and Muslim factions struggled for power on the eve of self-rule. In 1947 India and Pakistan became sovereign nations.

The revolutionary arm of India's nationalist independence movement advocated the use of violence from the beginning, and like those in the anti-Japanese movement for Korean independence, the small Indian immigrant community in the United States played a significant role. In 1911 Asian-Indian activist intellectuals formed the Ghadr (Mutiny) Party in San Francisco to support the push for independence. Ghadr leaders toured Asian-Indian neighborhoods in Sacramento, Fresno, and Stockton to generate support.

WOMEN AND THE SIKH COMMUNITY

The community of early Sikh migrant farm laborers, like the early Chinese mining communities, was almost exclusively male. Sikh work gangs became substitutes for families. The Asian-Indian laborers worked, lived, traveled, and shared life together. Even as late as 1914, women represented less than 1 percent of the 5,000 Asian Indians in California. Nearly half of America's Asian-Indian immigrants had left their wives and children behind in India.

A few Sikh wives did make the journey to America. Their lives in the United States proved far from idyllic, however. Isolation from other Indian women weighed upon them heavily. Mrs. Nand Kaur Singh recalled her feelings about her new home in Utah:

I had come from a village where I was surrounded by family and friends, and here there was no one but my husband, who worked hard all day.... There were none of my countrywomen to speak with, and it was against our custom to talk with men who were not related.

Many states, including California, prohibited Asian-Indian men from marrying non-Hispanic white women. Some Sikh men traveled to distant states to take their vows, but most ended up marrying the Mexican female laborers they worked with in the fields. Between 1913 and 1946, 92 percent of all Asian-Indian men in southern California married Mexican-American women. In central California, the percentage was 76 percent, and in northern California, 47 percent. Half of these Mexican-American women were immigrants themselves, and most of them were as much as 12 to 20 years younger than their husbands. Often the sister of a newlywed would be introduced to the Asian-Indian husband's friends as a potential marriage candidate.

Food, language, and cultural traditions mixed and settled into regular patterns among these families. Similarities in food allowed for some easy substitutions: *chapattis* or tortillas; jalapenos or Punjabi peppers. But as religion dictated the diet of the Sikhs, conflicts did arise.

Both Indian husband and Mexican wife learned bits and pieces of the other's native language, but typically each partner kept his or her own religion. The children, since they were raised primarily by their mothers, were more influenced by Mexican culture. Most spoke both Spanish and English, but few could speak their father's language. Most children therefore bore Spanish first names and were brought up Catholic, with godparents chosen by the mother and charged with religious education.

The Asian-Indian male presence within these households took on a unique characteristic. Many bachelor friends and coworkers, known as "uncles" to the children, lived with the Asian Indian–Mexican American nuclear family. Though the men worked long hours for seven days a week in the fields, in their time off, these Asian-Indian "uncles," many of whom had left their children behind in India, doted on the American-born children living in the home.

The presence of the "uncles" caused conflict as well, however. Many Mexican-American females refused to cook and clean for the many males of the household. But Asian-Indian men were used to women who obeyed their husbands' directives at all times. The women also balked at having to ask their husbands' permission to go on a simple shopping trip. Many times the conflict between cultures proved too great: Two in 10 of these mixed marriages ended in divorce at a time when divorce was uncommon.

Despite the initially awkward cultural melding involved in these interethnic marriages, the fact of such unions demonstrated a successful, though unique, means of cultural adaptation by early Asian-Indian immigrants in the United States.

CLOSING THE DOOR

During the late 19th and early 20th centuries, as immigration from around the world began to skyrocket, the United States began to enact a more restrictive policy toward immigration. While the Chinese Exclusion Act of 1882 (discussed in chapter 2) was the first law to prohibit immigration by people of a specific nationality, policy focused on the exclusion of all "undesirables"—potential charity cases, anarchists, carriers of certain diseases, and those considered to be morally unfit. Southern and eastern Europeans came under sharp scrutiny and attack alongside Asians.

After the Gentlemen's Agreement of 1908 and the creation of the Asiatic Barred Zone, the door to the East essentially slammed shut. Throughout this period, however, Asian immigrants devised a number of means of skirting restrictions, the most important of which were "paper sons" and "picture brides."

PAPER SONS

After the passage of the Chinese Exclusion Act of 1882, many Chinese sought to enter the United States through illegal channels. Some Chinese snuck in across the Canadian or Mexican borders. Others paid bribes to Chinese merchants exempt from the law to falsely claim the workers as their business partners.

The business of such false documentation took on a new dimension in Chinatown after the San Francisco earthquake of 1906. Shouts of "*Aih yah, dai loong jen!*" (The earth dragon is wriggling!) rang out from

The San Francisco earthquake of 1906 (Library of Congress)

Chinatown during the massive quake, which was followed by raging fires that destroyed most of San Francisco's official records— including all immigration files.

With the official records erased, enterprising young Chinese could make a written claim to be another man's son—a "paper son"—enter the United States as citizens, and bring their wives with them. In this way, between 1907 and 1924, approximately 10,0000 Chinese females arrived in America.

It did not take long for immigration officials to catch on to the false "paper son" claims. One State Department report recounted that "every known Chinese woman in San Francisco before the earthquake would have to have had 800 children" for all the submitted claims to be accurate.

Once aware of the deceitful practice, the federal government took elaborate steps to stop the falsification of papers. All Chinese, even Exclusion Act exemptees, such as students and merchants, were subject to rigorous and detailed interrogation. The paper sons went to great lengths to memorize the most minute details about their false family histories, village histories, and all relevant facts and figures. Paper sons became diligent in their study of *hau-kung* (crib sheets) to memorize the information. Many outwitted the authorities even when asked questions such as: "How many of the water buffaloes in your village were male and how many were female?" or "Who occupied the house on the fifth lot of your row in your native village?"

Though successful at their ruse, the paper sons granted citizenship paid a high price for their false entry into the United States: They were left open to blackmail by Chinese and Chinese-American criminals operating in what was known as the "slot racket." U.S. government officials offered immunity to Chinese paper sons who confessed their status if they also fingered other illegal friends and relatives. Many paper sons, having lived in fear of detection all of their lives, carried their secret to their graves, even going so far as to conceal their true identities within Chinese inscriptions written on their tombstones.

PICTURE BRIDES

As early Japanese immigrants succeeded as entrepreneurs, their desire to settle and raise families in the United States sharpened. Around the turn of the century, however, only 7 percent of Japanese mainland settlers were female. Though the Gentlemen's Agreement of 1908 halted further immigration of male Japanese and Korean laborers onto the mainland, loopholes in the law allowed the wives, children, and parents of those already in the United States to immigrate. The loopholes also allowed potential Japanese and Korean brides onto U.S. shores.

To arrange a marriage by mail seemed logical to Japanese and Korean brides as well as to the Asian males working in the United States, as arranged marriage was an honored tradition and commonly practiced in Japan and Korea at that time. In traditional Japan, if the bride and groom lived a great distance apart, pictures and written information were exchanged by hand delivery, and the marriage was arranged in this manner.

The procurement of a picture bride required several steps. The potential groom first sent his photograph to relatives, friends, or marriage agencies in Japan. The groom's family, with the aid of a marriage agency, sought out a bride based on her family background, her age, wealth, and health. Before leaving Japan, the bride actually took part in a ceremony involving a stand-in groom. Her name was then entered in the groom's family registry, making the marriage official in Japan. Upon arrival, the bride went through a series of immigration inspections and if all paperwork was found to be in order, she finally met her new husband for the first time in the United States. Prior to 1917, the U.S. government did not recognize picture bride marriage ceremonies as legal; therefore, a second ceremony—sometimes a mass wedding involving many couples right along the boat docks—had to take place.

Between 1908 and 1920, nearly 20,000 of the 67,000 female Japanese immigrants came as picture brides. By 1920, California's female Japanese population reached 35 percent of the Japanese adult population; in Hawaii that figure reached 46 percent. In addition, from 1910 to 1924, nearly 1,000 picture brides from Korea also arrived. By 1920, women composed 21 percent of the combined adult Korean immigrant population of the mainland and Hawaii.

Never having met their new husbands, many brides were disappointed to find out that these men were considerably older or looked entirely different from the likenesses portrayed in the photos they had received in Japan. "When I first saw my fiancé, I could not believe my eyes," remarked a 15-year-old bride named Anna Choi. "His hair was grey and I could not see any resemblance to the picture I had. He was 46 years old." Some husbands also lied about their jobs in their letters to their wives, pretending to own businesses instead of accurately describing their work as low-paid manual laborers. Korean picture brides landing in Honolulu were often heard to exclaim "*Aigo omani!*" (Oh dear me, what shall I do?)

Japanese picture brides emigrated for a variety of reasons. Some dreamed of wealth and romance to be found in an idyllic life in the United States. Others wished to escape their traditional secondary role to a Japanese mother-in-law or to fulfill their parents' wishes. Some women simply desired to be married; despite Meiji modernization programs that provided Japanese women with greater economic opportunities, many Japanese females viewed marriage as their ultimate goal in life.

Though not nearly as isolated as the few Sikh women who came to the United States in the first years of the 20th century, young Japanese brides also faced extreme loneliness in the new world. A Japanese newlywed described the night view from her new home in the San Joaquin valley:

If I looked really hard I could see, faintly glowing in the distance, one tiny light. And over there, I could see another. And over there, another. And I knew that that was where people lived. More than feeling sabishii [lonely], I felt samui [cold]. It was so lonely it was beyond loneliness. It was cold.

Though a few young women returned to Japan, most felt bound by duty not to shame their families by running away from life in America.

In addition to initial disappointment and loneliness, Japanese and Korean picture brides had to endure racist attitudes toward the marriage practice. White exclusionists defined the procurement of picture brides as a sign of Asian immorality and barbarism, as well as a violation of the spirit of the Gentlemen's Agreement. They also recognized that the practice meant permanent settlement of Japanese and guaranteed citizenship for nisei children. On March 1, 1920, the Japanese government agreed to cease issuing passports for picture brides. For the nearly 25,000 issei single men remaining in the United States, the decision effectively terminated all hope of marriage.

ANGEL ISLAND

Between 1910 and 1940, approximately 165,000 Asian immigrants docked at Angel Island for processing. Ninety-seven percent of those travelers were Chinese. Angel Island, located in San Francisco Bay, is sometimes compared with New York Harbor's Ellis Island, but the two immigrant stations proved very different from each other. Ellis Island officials usually tried to help tens of thousands of European immigrants meet the requirements for entry into the United States, lending the institution the image of a gateway. Angel Island functioned more like a holding cage for prisoners while officials there tried every means possible to legally deny the Chinese entry into America. Between 1910 and 1940, nearly 50,000 Chinese were detained while trying to convince authorities that their papers were in order.

The facilities at Angel Island were somewhat improved over those of "the Shed," a

A Japanese picture bride (National Archives)

Angel Island and Ellis Island, 1910–1940: A Comparison

Ellis Island

Location:	New York Harbor
Immigrants processed:	19 million
Number rejected:	1.2 million
Percentage rejected:	6%
Average length of stay:	1 day

Angel Island

Location:	San Francisco Bay
Immigrants processed:	150,000
Number rejected:	50,000
Percentage rejected:	33%
Average length of stay:	2–3 weeks

Source: U.S. Immigration and Naturalization Service

crumbling two-story warehouse that had served as the previous checkpoint station in San Francisco. Day-to-day operations of the processing center remained the same, however, with detention of immigrants as the primary focus. New arrivals could only be released into the care of a sponsor. If the sponsor lived on the East Coast, an Angel Island detainee would have to wait up to six months or longer to be released because the sponsor had to save enough money for a 3,000-mile journey across the United States to pick up a detained immigrant in person. Some Chinese immigrants were held at Angel Island as long as two years.

Immigration officials subjected all Chinese—men, women, children, merchants, and laborers alike—to rough and degrading physical exams. Afterward, the immigration authorities locked the immigrants in prison-like barracks where detainees waited days, weeks, months, or even years for test results and final decisions regarding their admittance or denial. Due to the paper son phenomenon, Chinese of all ages and both sexes became subject to intense interrogations regarding their identities. Wives were separated from husbands, often for weeks or months. Female detainees were not even allowed outside except for a weekly walk.

By contrast, Ellis Island officials never used interrogation techniques and most European immigrants were admitted within one or two days.

The Chinese government, church groups, the Chinese Six Companies, and the Angel Island detainees themselves often protested the poor treatment, crowded and unsanitary living conditions, and the substandard food to be found at the processing center. "When we arrived," reported a Chinese detainee, "they locked us up like criminals in compartments like the cages in the zoo." From yard and windows, detainees could see San Francisco and Oakland, a cruel view, surely, to those who had come so far only to wait. Protests and riots at Angel Island became common in the early 1920s, finally resulting in somewhat shorter detention stays, but few other improvements.

Not everyone passed the Angel Island admission tests. Some held illegally drafted papers, but some otherwise legal immigrants simply flunked their interrogations. For exampleWong Shee Lum, a Chinese female who arrivedat the island in 1923, made just such a mistake and was sent back to China. She could not accurately remember either the chronological order of her father's job history or whether she was

The immigration station on Angel Island in San Francisco Bay operated between 1910 and 1940, when it was closed due to fire. During that time, more than 150,000 immigrants were processed, most of whom were detained for an average of two to three weeks. Some immigrants, however, were detained on the island for almost two years.

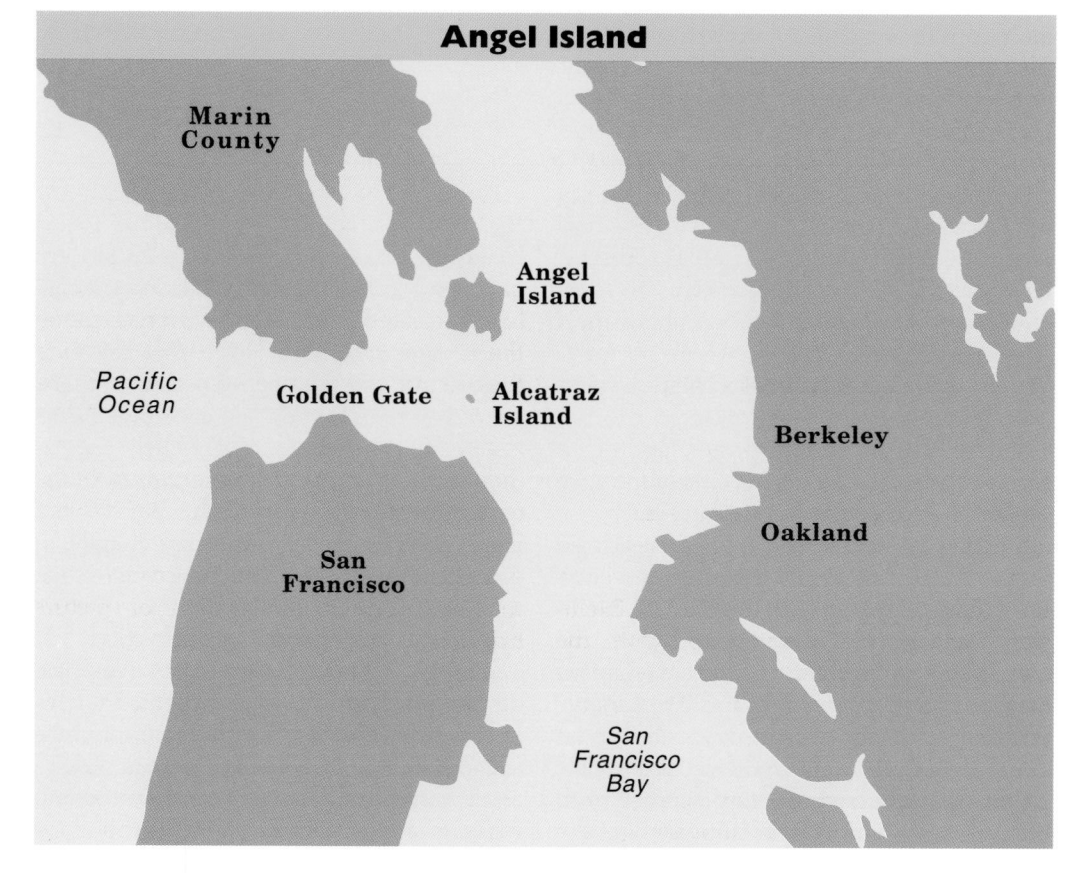

These ramshackle wooden buildings on Angel Island served as a processing center and detainee barracks for Asian immigrants. (National Archives)

alone or accompanied when she got her passport picture taken: "My husband did not send me coaching notes because my papers were real and all I needed to do was to tell the truth. I told the truth and still got into trouble." Nearly 10 percent of all Chinese migrants processed at Angel Island were put on ships headed back to China.

A BAN ON ASIAN IMMIGRATION

By the 1920s, American exclusionists had finally achieved their goal of stopping virtually all legal Asian immigration to the United States. The era of U.S. immigration restrictions that had begun with the Chinese Exclusion Act of 1882, continued with the Gentlemen's Agreement between the United States and Japan in 1908, and been sealed with the creation of an "Asiatic Exclusion Zone" effectively put an end to the first phase of Asian immigration to the United States for all major Asian immigrant groups

at that time (other than Filipinos, who were not considered immigrants since they resided in a U.S. territory). Nonetheless, during the early 1920s, the U.S. government went onto unify these individual pieces of legislation under several new statutes.

In 1921, Congress passed the Emergency Quota Act. This law restricted the annual number of immigrants admitted based on each nationality's population in the United States as of 1910, thus favoring the entry of southern and eastern Europeans over Asians. Although Japanese and Koreans were exempted from the new law (as their opportunities for immigration were already limited by the Gentlemen's Agreement of 1908), that same year, the government also formalized Japan's agreement not to issue further immigration of picture brides by placing a ban on the practice.

The Cable Act of 1922 allowed the government to punish American females who married immigrants ineligible for citizenship. The draconian consequence for engaging in such a marriage ended in the revocation of the bride's citizenship. The

Asian Immigration to the U.S. Mainland, 1900–1925

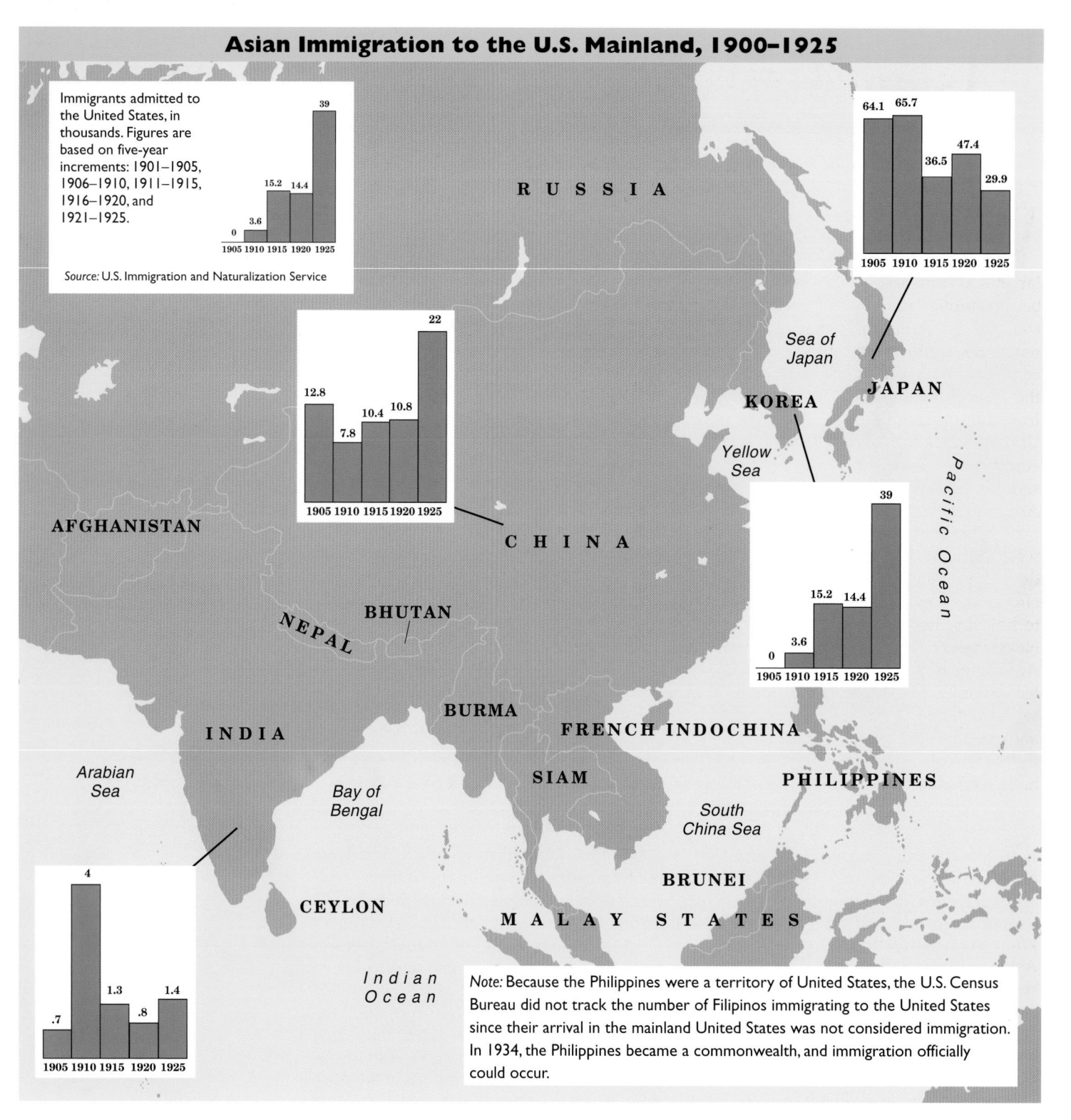

Immigrants admitted to the United States, in thousands. Figures are based on five-year increments: 1901–1905, 1906–1910, 1911–1915, 1916–1920, and 1921–1925.

Source: U.S. Immigration and Naturalization Service

Note: Because the Philippines were a territory of United States, the U.S. Census Bureau did not track the number of Filipinos immigrating to the United States since their arrival in the mainland United States was not considered immigration. In 1934, the Philippines became a commonwealth, and immigration officially could occur.

restriction worked in reverse as well: Ineligible females were forbidden to marry male citizens.

The federal government increased efforts to prevent illegal immigration as well. In 1924, the U.S. Border Patrol was established to prevent unlawful entry along U.S. boundaries in Mexico and Canada. That same year, Congress further limited legal immigration by passing the Immigration Act of 1924. This new law tightened the 1921 act by restricting the number of annual immigrants of any nationality to just 2 percent of the number of foreign-born persons of that nationality residing in the continental United States as of 1890. Since few Asian immigrants other than the Chinese had arrived in America by 1890, the laws effectively ended all Asian immigration.

A QUESTION OF CITIZENSHIP
Asian-American History from 1910 to 1946

4

With the passage of the Immigration Act of 1924, the individual immigration bans on Chinese, Japanese, Koreans, and Asian Indians became unified under a single policy. As citizens of an American territory, Filipinos remained eligible to immigrate to the United States. Otherwise, the central question of the Asian-American experience shifted from who was eligible for entry into the United States to who among the Asian Americans already in the United States should be accorded legal protections as American citizens.

Children of first-generation immigrants were automatically granted the citizenship denied to their parents, and despite the efforts of white exclusionists, they were technically never stripped of this right. Nevertheless, this new generation of Asian Americans had to struggle for the legal protections entitled to them. Hundreds of thousands of Americans of Asian heritage, born and raised in the United States, found that they were considered foreigners in the only homeland they had ever known.

GROWING DISCRIMINATION

Widespread American hostility toward Asians—particularly the Japanese—had begun in the earliest part of the 20th century. The year 1905 marked the start of an orchestrated anti-Japanese movement spearheaded by labor unions whose leaders saw the import of Asian workers as a threat to American job security. Originally localized in California, this movement soon expanded into a national effort that involved all social classes. It was well fueled by the mass media, which disseminated prejudicial sentiments and rhetoric that inflated the population's fears. Thus, anti-Asian sentiment expanded from an economic base to the social and political realms.

After the San Francisco School Board Crisis of 1906 and the Gentlemen's Agreement of 1907–1908 (discussed in chapter 3), state legislation began to center on settlement and land issues. The passage of Cali-

fornia's Alien Land Laws of 1913 and 1920 (discussed later in this chapter) proved critical to the cause, as the measures locked out Asian immigrants from the probable economic success inherent in land ownership. Nevertheless, some Asian Americans found inventive ways to work around the laws that restricted them. The success of the Yamato Colonies is particularly impressive when viewed against the backdrop of growing prejudice and anti-Asian legislation.

THE YAMATO COLONIES

While the majority of rural issei Japanese labored as migrant farmworkers, some tried to put down more permanent roots, even in the early part of the 20th century. These Japanese entrepreneurs purchased and farmed land in regional cooperative efforts known as the Yamato (Japan) Colonies. The immigrant entrepreneurs established these colonies in three different locations: Florida (1904), California (1906), and Texas (1917), with the California colony proving the most successful.

Jo Sakai, a native of Kyoto Prefecture, founded the first Yamato Colony near Boca Raton in 1904, one year after meeting with Florida governor William Jennings. Local businessmen, who viewed the Japanese as expert farmers as well as the solution to their labor shortage, originally welcomed the college-educated Sakai with enthusiasm. Two years after its founding, the Florida Yamato Colony produced a successful pineapple crop. As the enterprise grew to more than 1,000 acres covering three different counties, a railroad station and post office were established for the community. Success, however, was tempered by a major crop blight in 1908 as well as increasing anti-Japanese hostility on the part of white Floridians. By 1919, the number of its members had declined so significantly that the colony officially dissolved, although Japanese farmers continued to work the land through 1930.

The California Yamato Colonies were founded by Kyutaro Akibo, who was born in West Honshu, Japan, and sailed to San Francisco, California, in 1885, not long after

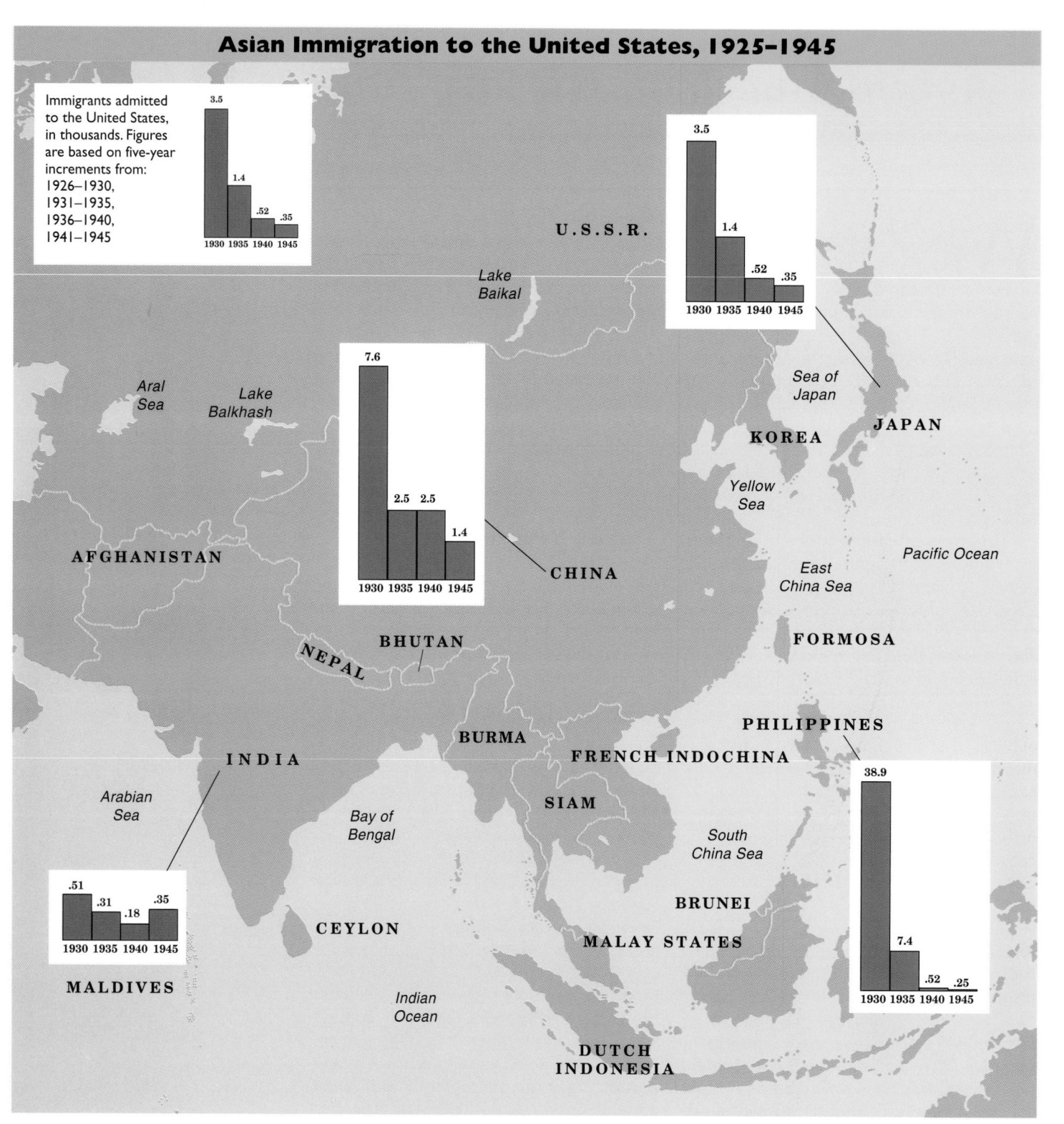

Asian Immigration to the United States, 1925–1945

Immigrants admitted to the United States, in thousands. Figures are based on five-year increments from:
1926–1930,
1931–1935,
1936–1940,
1941–1945

converting to Christianity. In the United States, Akibo made his fortune as the head of a labor contract company and became a strong leader of the Japanese settlement movement in California. By 1899, Akibo had founded the most widely read Japanese-language newspaper published in the United States, *Nichibei Shimbum*. This popular newspaper covered topics ranging from race relations to education, but Akibo's articles pertaining to permanent settlement (*dochaku eiju*) became his hallmark. Even the

name proclaimed the importance of melding the two cultures, with *Nichi* standing for Japan and *bei* for America. Akibo also published the annual *Japanese-American Yearbook* (*Nichibei Nenkan*), a detailed almanac of California's Japanese agricultural enterprises that included farmers' names, crop specialties, acreage, and advice on how to purchase and operate farms.

Akibo put his utopian vision into practice in 1906, when he purchased 3,200 acres near Livingston, California, under the name

The Yamato Colonies

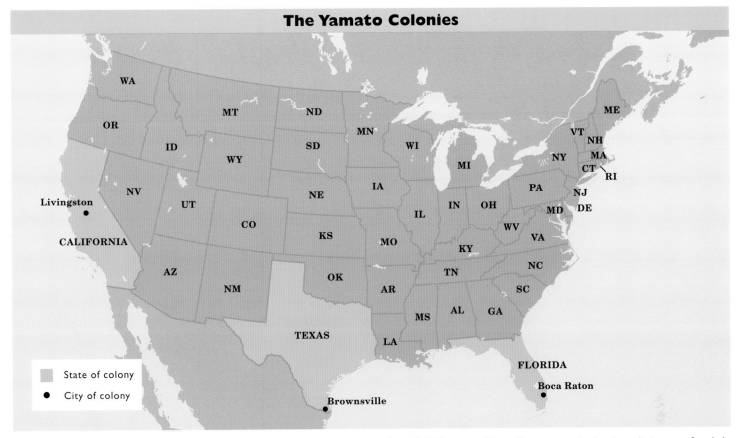

The map above highlights the locations of the Yamato (Japan) agricultural colonies in the early 20th century. These three cooperative farming colonies were founded in 1904 in Boca Raton, Florida, 1906 in Livingston, California, and 1917 in Brownsville, Texas.

of his American Land and Produce Company. Seven years later, the California Yamato colonists had successfully transformed the undeveloped desert land into fruit orchards. In an effort to jointly market their crops, the colonists created the Livingston Cooperative Society. The colony expanded to include 42 families by 1917. Over the next two years, Akibo founded two more California colonies in Cressy and Cortez. The cooperative enterprises continued to succeed until 1941.

The third Yamato Colony near Brownsville, Texas, was founded as a sugar plantation in 1917 by a group of seven Japanese businessmen. Although the colony initially enjoyed success on its 400 acres, the market price of sugarcane fell during a post–World War I depression, resulting in the colony's failure and closure just four years after its establishment.

The Japanese founders of the Yamato agricultural colonies created their communities partly to keep their cultural traditions alive in the United States. They also hoped that land ownership would result in economic self-sufficiency and earn them the respect of white Americans. Successful entrepreneurial pursuits did not result in social acceptance, however, as discrimination continued to grow.

ANTI-JAPANESE DISCRIMINATION

The first two decades of the 20th century marked a turning point in the Asian-American experience—from the hopes and disappointments of the visiting sojourner to the opportunities and obstacles met by Asian immigrants, particularly the Japanese, now intent on settling and attaining the rights of citizenship. They had an uphill battle. Organized labor leaders in the United States had targeted immigrant Japanese workers as an economic threat, just as they had previously targeted the Chinese and were currently fighting the influx of southern, central, and eastern European workers on the East Coast. Western labor unions argued that the Japanese were dirty and unhealthy and could not be assimilated into American society. Above all, the unions charged, Japanese workers were lowering America's standard of living with the threat of "unfair competition" for jobs due to their willingness to work for wages far lower than those of unionized white workers.

The perceived economic threat posed by the Japanese sparked the formation of the Asiatic Exclusion League on May 14, 1905 (discussed in chapter 3), a group devoted to terminating Japanese immigration to the

United States. Immediately, the Asiatic Exclusion League began to reel out anti-Japanese propaganda that often centered on the threat of miscegenation (interracial marriage), and in 1906 it played a key role in the San Francisco School Board Crisis (discussed in chapter 3). The league also instigated boycotts against Japanese businesses and lobbied politicians to pass legislation that limited the ability of Japanese immigrants to settle land, thereby blocking opportunities for economic success.

The media did its part to bolster the discriminatory actions of groups such as the Asiatic Exclusion League and organized labor by broadcasting their messages to a wider audience. Publisher Valentine Stuart McClatchy consistently used his *Sacramento Bee* newspaper as a mouthpiece for anti-Japanese propaganda. The *San Francisco Chronicle* took on an even more influential role by publishing a number of articles regarding the "problem of the day" and delineating the Japanese threat as an invasive "yellow peril." William Randolph Hearst's newspapers, including the *San Francisco Examiner*, fueled hysterical reactions among the populace with "war scare" articles published in 1907 and 1912–1913. Several novels of the period also swayed public opinion against the Japanese. Homer Lea's *The Valor of Ignorance* (1909), for example, chronicled a fictional Japanese attack on the West Coast that was abetted by Japanese-American immigrant informants.

The fear of invasion was unique to the anti-Japanese movement. It was certainly true that Japan's growing military and political strength on the world stage warranted a watchful eye by other global powers, including the United States. This truth, coupled with growing racism against Asians living on the West Coast, carried America's anti-Japanese movement to a level not attained by any other anti-Asian hate wave. The prejudice it fueled led to the passage of two land laws that formed critical blocks against Japanese settlement in California.

THE CALIFORNIA ALIEN LAND LAWS

Anti-Japanese hostility eventually distilled into political legislation known as the California Alien Land Laws of 1913 and 1920. In 1911, California's Progressive Republican Party and Governor Hiram Johnson introduced 27 pieces of anti-Japanese legislation into the state proceedings; two years later, some 40 discriminatory measures were brought to the floor.

The bills fell into two groups: those that sought to keep all aliens from owning land and those that applied only to those "aliens ineligible to citizenship"—words that effectively translated into "all Asians,"since all Asian immigrants were barred from eligibility for citizenship. Despite pressure from President Woodrow Wilson and Secretary of State William Jennings Bryan, the anti-Asian voting bloc grew to dominance. Consequently, California's first Alien Land Law passed through the state legislature and was signed into law by Governor Johnson on May 17, 1913.

The California law severely restricted Asian immigrants from owning or leasing land in the state. Leases could only be drawn for three-year periods by first-generation Japanese, or issei (as well as the small number of Koreans, Asian Indians, and Chinese, to whom the measure technically applied). This limited the immigrants' choice of crops to those that would grow and earn a profit quickly, so most family plans for lucrative orchards and vineyards were scrapped. Some Japanese left the United States altogether at this time, heading for more distant places such as South America, Mexico, and Manchuria.

The 1913 land law also prohibited Asian immigrants from purchasing land in California. This applied to Asian individuals as well as to companies in which one Asian individual held the majority of stock. Thus, the surest method of upward mobility available to the issei immigrants was put out of reach.

Loopholes did exist, however. The laws were difficult to enforce and some local officials allowed Asian farmers to continue as they had been doing previously. Many Asian immigrant farmers registered land deeds in the names of their American-born children, thereby circumnavigating the discriminatory law. Others, especially Asian Indians, enlisted the help of sympathetic whites who put their names on the deeds in a barter arrangement for a share of the crops. Another evasion tactic involved the purchase of land through specially created land companies, a method employed by the Texas Yamato colonists.

Although many issei farmers found ways around it, the new law's message was clear: They were not wanted in their adopted country. Many had already started families in the United States, having worked hard and saved money in order to settle on the land for good.

While issei and their nisei children felt betrayed by the California law, most remained determined to prove their loyalty to the United States. In 1917, when the United States joined the allied effort against Germany, Turkey, and Austria-Hungary in World War I, many issei enlisted, both out of patriotic duty and in the hope that military service might eventually lead to citizenship.

Upon returning home, the issei veterans found their hopes dashed. By 1920, 13 other western states had passed their own versions of California's Alien Land Law; these laws would remain in force until well after World War II. Meanwhile, the anti-Asian forces

This cartoon was created when it was discovered that an attempt to purchase land from Mexico on Magdalena Bay was actually a front for a Japanese plan to use the land for military purposes. The inset shows Uncle Sam approaching an innocent fisherman, wondering if he knows that the land—by reason of the Monroe Doctrine—is protected from foreign intervention. The American fear of Japanese agression culminated in the passage of the Webb Alien Land Holding Bill in 1913, which excluded Japanese persons from owning land in the United States. (Library of Congress)

JAPANESE SERVICE IN WORLD WAR I

While some Japanese-American servicemen during World War I came from the mainland United States, most were from Hawaii. At the time, U.S. troops were still segregated along racial lines, and because so many enlistees were of Japanese descent, the all-Japanese Company D of the First Regiment was formed. In 1917, Company D became the first and only company to recieve its marching orders in Japanese and to march to a Japanese cadence.

Among those who served in Company D was issei Shigefusa Kanda. Kanda, having been rejected for front line duty twice, sailed for London (after having a visa application rejected six times) before finally being accepted into the Red Cross. After serving the humanitarian organization with heroism from July 1918 to July 1919, Kanda received a service ribbon with two stars.

Following the war, issei servicemen hoped that citizenship would come soon. One issei, Hidemitsu Toyota, who had served in the U.S. Coast Guard from 1913 to 1923 and seen action during the war, was in fact granted citizenship by a lower court, based on a federal law passed in 1918 that allowed any alien who had served in World War I to become naturalized. After a circuit court canceled Toyota's certificate of naturalization, Toyota appealed the decision to the U.S. Supreme Court. The Court ruled in its *Toyota v. United States* decision of 1925 that the 1918 law had been intended to benefit Filipinos, not Japanese, and that the categories of aliens eligible for naturalization should not be broadened.

In 1935, a few issei World War I veterans were awarded naturalized U.S. citizenship by Congress, thanks to lobbying efforts by Tokutaro Slocum. Slocum had served as a sergeant major—the highest rank awarded to any Asian-American soldier in the war. However, despite their military efforts, most of the issei veterans would have to wait until the 1950s to become U.S. citizens.

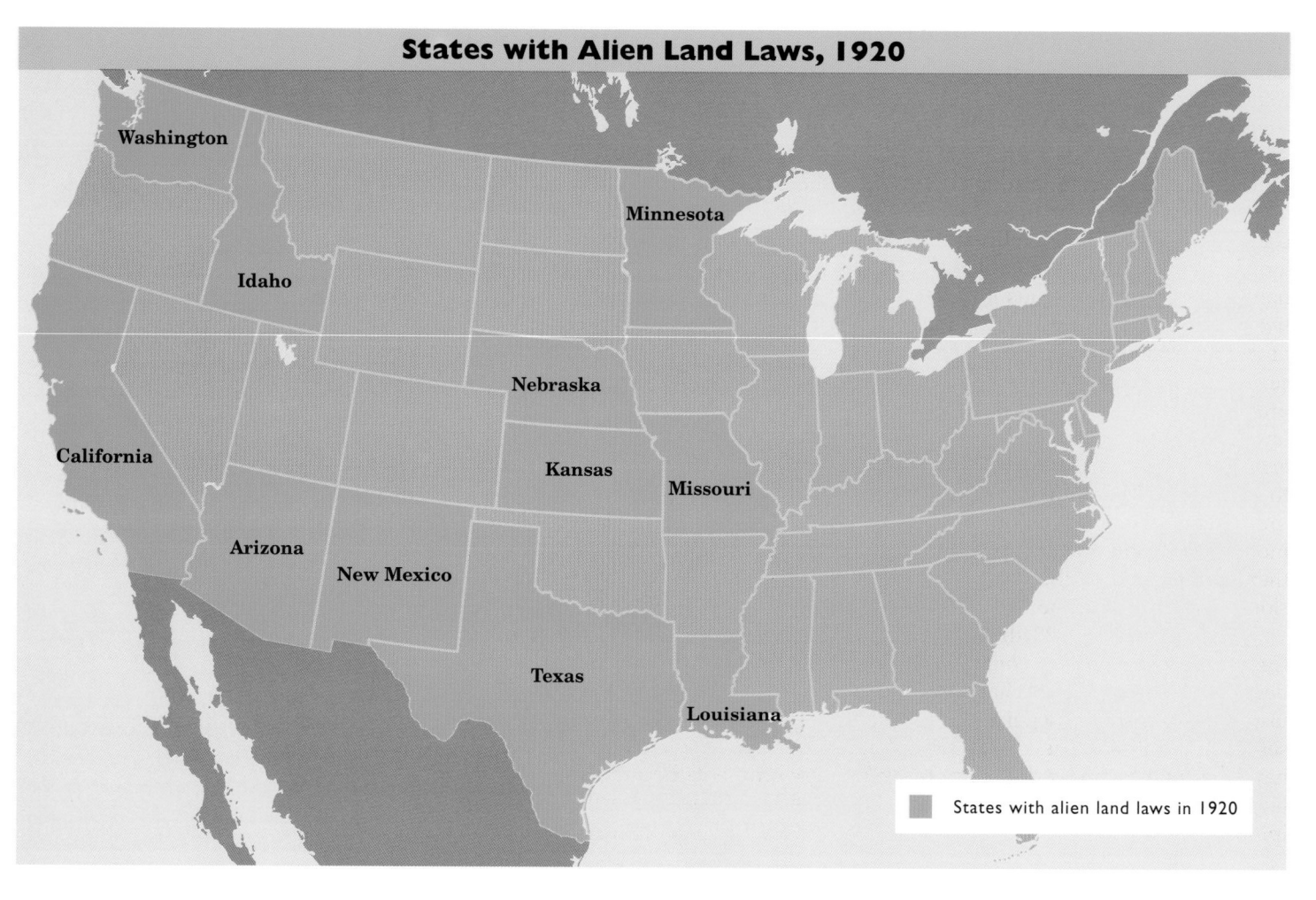

States with Alien Land Laws, 1920

Washington

Minnesota

Idaho

Nebraska

California

Kansas

Missouri

Arizona

New Mexico

Texas

Louisiana

States with alien land laws in 1920

active in California had regrouped to push for an even more stringent land law. Since most issei Japanese had progressed from migrant farm laborer to small farmer, share-cropper, or small business owner, the base of the argument against them had shifted. No longer just a threat to the laboring union man, the Japanese immigrant was now painted as an invader taking prime California farmland away from white farmers.

Once again, popular fiction reflected and heightened prevailing prejudice and fears, as evidenced by the 1920s-era novels of Peter B. Kyne (*Pride of Palomar*) and Wallace Irwin (*Seed of the Sun*). Both books depict harsh issei landowners controlled by the Japanese government and determined to take over California land, as well as any passing non-Asian woman.

The influence of the Asiatic Exclusion League had dwindled by 1911, but other groups—not necessarily dominated by labor unions—had risen to fill the void. The Japanese Exclusion League of California was founded just prior to the passage of the 1920 California Alien Land Law. Composed of several groups that included the Native Sons of the Golden West, the American Legion, the American Federation of Labor, and various women's clubs, the Japanese Exclusion

League of California sought to coordinate the state's anti-Japanese activities.

Politicians—some racist, others merely opportunistic—joined the fray. Beginning in 1910, Hiram Johnson distinguished himself as a leading isolationist during his two terms as governor of California and then 28 years in the U.S. Senate; he played an instrumental role in the passage of the 1913 Alien Land Law and the 1924 Immigration Act. Politician James Duval Phelan also centered his career around anti-Asian sentiments and the drafting of discriminatory legislation. Phelan served as the Democratic mayor of San Francisco for three terms until 1902, when he became a representative of the California State Federation of Labor. He subsequently played a major role in the passage of both land laws. As a state senator nearing the end of his term in 1919, Phelan launched a new anti-Japanese campaign. He called for an end to the procurement of picture brides, which he labeled a "barbaric" practice. He also lobbied for a new land law to combat the Japanese "menace" threatening America's social and economic well-being. Choosing to dispense with any vague wording, such as that found in the Alien Land Law of 1913, Phelan laid all his cards on the table and ran for reelection on the slogan "Keep California White." He lost the race, but California's Alien Land Law of 1920 passed by a three to one margin as a ballot initiative in November 1920.

The new land law—brought to fruition by a coalition of white farmers, anti-Asian associations, opportunist and racist politicians, and the news media—closed the loopholes regarding land ownership that had existed in the previous law. The practice of having deeds drawn up in the names of minor children and land companies ceased. In addition to denying Asian immigrants any means to purchase land, the 1920 law forbade all leasing and sharecropping arrangements. Once more, "aliens ineligible to citizenship"—in other words, Asian immigrants—were locked out of the social mobility that land ownership promised and thereby relegated to the narrow economic slot of migrant farm laborer.

What is more, in 1925, the U.S. Supreme Court ruled in *Toyota v. United States* that despite a 1918 federal law that granted naturalized citizenship to legal aliens who had served in World War I, issei veterans did not have the right to citizenship since the 1918 law had only been intended to cover Filipinos.

VIOLENCE

The early decades of the 20th century saw incidents of mob violence against Japanese immigrants, with mass expulsions taking place in many small towns across California and in Oregon. On July 20, 1921, 58 Japanese laborers were attacked in Turlock, California. The carefully planned operation involved more than 150 people, many armed, who packed the issei workers onto cars and trucks in the middle of the night, drove them out of town, and told them never to return. The police were mysteriously unavailable during the raid, and none of the townspeople admitted to seeing anything. Six men were later charged with the crime. When the trial finally took place after numerous delays on April 26, 1922, only one of eight Japanese witnesses could be found to make a positive identification; the accused men were acquitted in less than 10 minutes by an all-white jury. Other mob incidents of this type took place in California towns and cities such as Delano (1920), Los Angeles (1922 and 1924), Porterville (1922), Hopland (1924), and Woodlake (1926).

In Toledo, Oregon, a mob attack perpetrated by white workers against Japanese immigrants took place at the Pacific Spruce Company in 1925. Pacific Spruce owner C.

D. Johnson had decided to import Japanese laborers to work on the "green chain," a job entailing the sorting of lumber as it left the mill via revolving chains. Although white workers at the company had made it clear that they did not want to work on the "green chain," they also did not want Japanese workers brought into the community. The mill owners ignored their protests. On July 12, nearly 500 protesters gathered by the mill to hear speeches and confront officials. The mob forced the recently arrived issei workers onto trucks and told them never to return. Some time later, pressure from the Japanese government resulted in a grand jury investigation of the incident. Although no indictments were handed down, several civil suits were settled in and out of court.

An incident in Arizona's Salt River valley occurred later than the others, in 1934. First, a parade of 150 cars streamed through Phoenix, broadcasting a deadline for Japanese farmers to evacuate the area. Next came a series of bombings, which continued even after the U.S. and Japanese governments became involved. However, the U.S. State Department did succeed in stopping a revision of Arizona's land law that would have driven all Japanese farmers out of the state.

CITIZENSHIP AND LAND OWNERSHIP

The Japanese community was stunned by the passage of California's second Alien Land Law in 1920 and reacted in two ways. As with the first law, Japanese farmers found loopholes. For instance, they got around the restrictions on leasing land by the use of cropping contracts. Under a cropping contract, an issei farmer would be hired on paper by a sympathetic white landowner to manage a farm and agree to be paid a percentage of the profit. Since the Japanese hired hand was referred to as "manager" instead of "tenant," the issei avoided punishment. However, the practice was declared illegal in July 1921, and in 1923 the U.S. Supreme Court ruled cropping contracts to be in violation of the 1920 land law.

With all legal loopholes closed, Japanese farmers chose to fight the discriminatory land laws in America's courts and to center their fight around the issue of citizen rights. Consequently, the constitutionality of prohibitions against leasing, stock ownership in land companies, cropping contracts, and guardianship were tested in the *Yano Guardianship* case (1922), *Porterfield v. Webb*

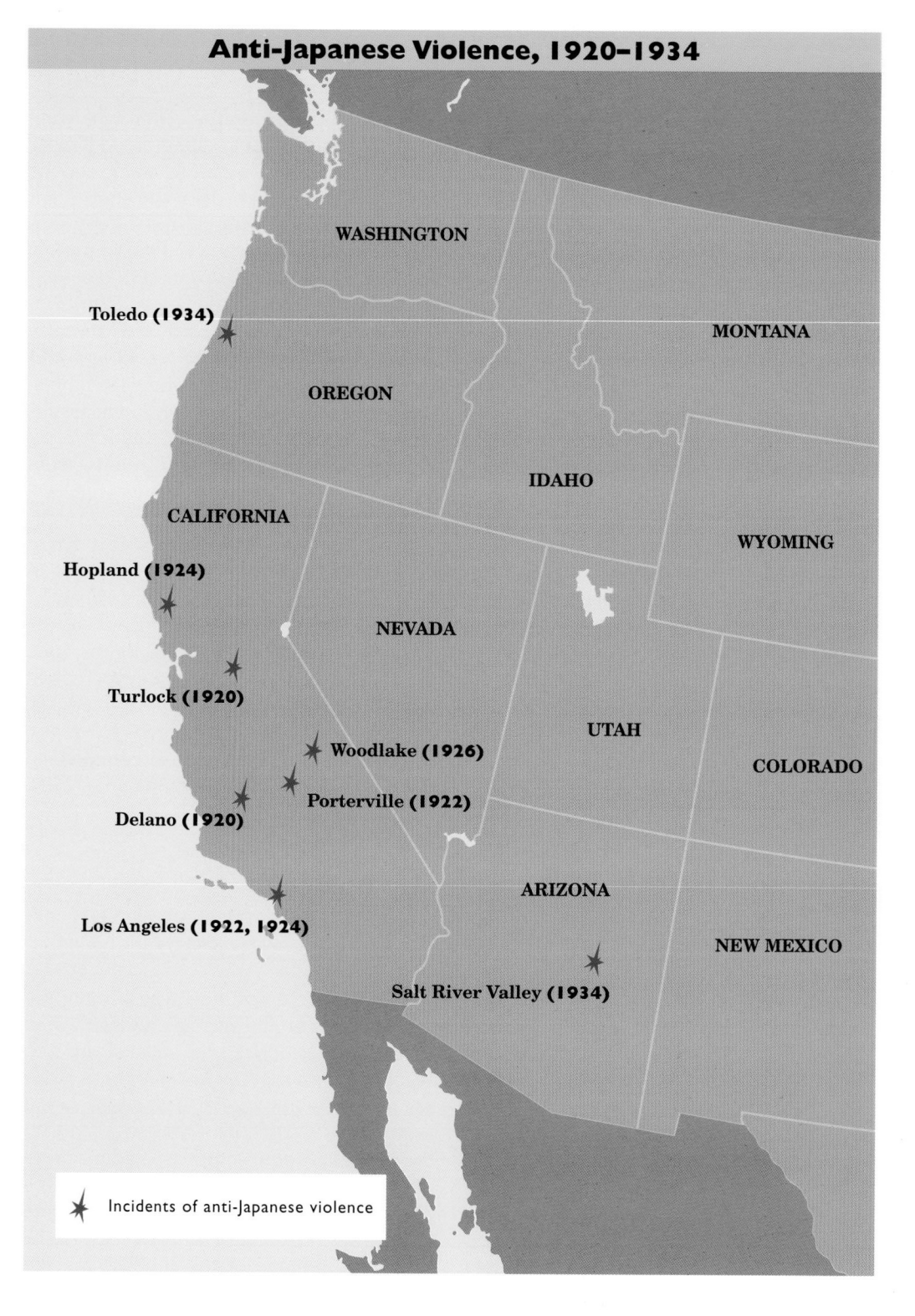

Anti-Japanese Violence, 1920–1934

WASHINGTON

Toledo (1934)

OREGON

MONTANA

IDAHO

CALIFORNIA

WYOMING

Hopland (1924)

NEVADA

Turlock (1920)

UTAH

Woodlake (1926)

COLORADO

Porterville (1922)

Delano (1920)

ARIZONA

Los Angeles (1922, 1924)

NEW MEXICO

Salt River Valley (1934)

✳ Incidents of anti-Japanese violence

(1923), *Frick v. Webb* (1923), and *Webb v. O'Brien* (1923), respectively. The ban on guardianship—or the Japanese practice of buying land in the name of U.S.-born children, since birth in the United States automatically made them citizens—was invalidated by the *Yano* case. All the other cases, however, resulted in defeat for Japanese Americans.

Asians were the only immigrant group in the United States barred from obtaining naturalized citizenship. The Japanese chose to challenge this prejudicial treatment as

well as the constitutionality of the land laws in the courts. The result was *Ozawa v. United States* (1922), a landmark decision.

Takao Ozawa had been a U.S. resident since 1894. A graduate of Berkeley High School, he attended the University of California, married an American-educated Japanese woman, spoke only English at home, had no membership in any Japanese organizations, and worked for an American company. With the encouragement of the Pacific Coast Japanese Deliberative Council, Ozawa filed a petition of intent for natu-

U.S. SUPREME COURT DECISIONS ON CITIZENSHIP AND LAND OWNERSHIP, 1910–1923

Year	Case	Court Decision
1910	United States v. Balsara	Holds that Asian Indians are Caucasians and hence entitled to be considered "white persons" eligible for citizenship under U.S. naturalization laws
1913	United States v. Mazumdar	Reaffirms that Asian Indians are to be considered "white"
1922	Ozawa v. United States	Declares that "Caucasian" and "white" are synonymous, and therefore Japanese immigrants are ineligible for naturalization
1923	Porterfield v. Webb	Upholds the constitutionality of California's alien land laws
1923	Webb v. O'Brien	Rules that sharecropping is illegal because it is a ruse that allows Japanese to possess and use land
1923	Frick v. Webb	Forbids aliens "ineligible to citizenship" from owning stocks in corporations formed for farming
1923	Terrace v. Thompson	Upholds the constitutionality of Washington's alien land law
1923	United States v. Bhagat Singh Thind	Rules that Asian Indians are ineligible for citizenship by arguing that the term "white person" applies only to an immigrant from western or northern Europe

ralization on August 1, 1902. He then filed for naturalization on October 16, 1914, but was denied. After several more appeals and denials, his case went before the U.S. Supreme Court. On November 13, 1922, the justices upheld the lower courts' rulings, and Ozawa was denied citizenship. The ruling proved to be the final blow to the issei citizenship cause.

THE IMMIGRATION ACT OF 1924

In the era following World War I, Americans across the nation sought some kind of immigration quota bill. Anti-immigrant sentiment had spread beyond California and had gained strength nationally. Technically, most Americans did not want a bill that would overtly discriminate against Japan or any other country. Citizens on the East Coast, for example, wanted to restrict European immigration. Consequently, Senator Henry Cabot Lodge of Massachusetts, the chairman of the Senate Foreign Relations committee, played a pivotal role in the development of the Immigration Act, which put quota restrictions for most immigrants into place and definitively ended all Asian immigration. President Calvin Coolidge signed the bill into law on May 24, 1924.

The anti-Asian movement had reached the federal level. Upon hearing of the passage of the Immigration Act, former California state senator James D. Phelan is said to have responded: "I [am] repaid for my efforts—the Japs are routed." California's exclusionists cheered the act, trumpeting it as their final victory. Meanwhile, Asian immigrants reached a new low of despondency. The militarist Japanese government responded with anger, first recounting the years of compromise and negotiation between the two countries, then later using the passage of the law as a reason for increased military buildup. Japan's ambassador Masanao Hanihara and America's ambassador to Japan, Cyrus E. Woods, both resigned in protest, but it was too late—the door had been closed. The act resulted in tense relations between the United States and Japan—the very outcome the federal government had fought for decades to avoid.

After 1924, the active anti-Japanese movement died down. The influence of the exclusionists lived on, however.

THE FIGHT FOR RIGHTS

In addition to land ownership, labor rights became an increasingly important field of battle for Asian Americans during the early 20th century. As was the case with other minorities of the era, Asian-American workers faced the twin challenges of unjust treatment by business owners on the one hand and anti-Asian racism among the members and leadership of the mainstream white unions on the other. Thus, Asian-American labor unions evolved to serve in the forefront of the fight for basic civil rights.

THE HAWAIIAN LABOR MOVEMENT

By the mid-1920s, relatively few Japanese remained on the plantations of Hawaii, and Filipinos made up most of the agricultural labor force. But the fledgling interethnic labor union movement created by the Japanese and Filipino workers during the Oahu Strike of 1920 (discussed in chapter 3) remained a force in Hawaii's agricultural industry. During the 1920s and 1930s, strikes and labor organizing continued sporadically and in a decentralized manner throughout the Hawaiian Islands. Individual strikes often ended in defeat for the workers. However, the consistency of strike actions continued to push the movement forward. By 1930, nervous plantation owners tried to prohibit union activities through various court injunctions and even individual lawsuits.

Although strikes generally began peacefully, violence sometimes prevailed, forcing an end to many walkouts. Such was the case in the Filipino Laborers' Association walkout of 1924, which was called to demand better wages and housing conditions. The strike reached a bloody conclusion at Hanapepe, Kauai, with 20 deaths and numerous injuries reported.

The Hilo Massacre of 1938 occurred on August 1, 1938, nearly five months after the initiation of a peaceful strike. The multiethnic walkout involved Chinese, Japanese, native Hawaiian, Portuguese, and Filipino workers. A variety of unions were involved as well, including the International Longshore and Warehouse Union (ILWU), the Women's Auxiliary of the ILWU, the Metal Trades Council, the Honolulu Waterfront Workers' Association, the Quarryworkers International Union of North America, and the Inland Boatmen's Union. This vast labor coalition challenged the Inter-Island Steamship Company, a shipping company that was backed by the powerful Big Five company of Castle & Cooke, as well as the Matson Navigation Company. (The Big Five, Hawaii's five largest mercantile companies—Alexander & Baldwin; American Factors; C. Brewer & Co.; Castle & Cooke; and Theo. H. Davies & Co.—controlled much of Hawaii's financial sector and was the group responsible for the founding of the Hawaiian Sugar Planters Association, or HSPA.) Demands ranged from wage increases to provisions for closed or union shop hiring practices. By July it was clear that the strike was going nowhere, but the workers held firm.

Violence erupted on August 1, 1938, when nearly 200 union workers gathered at the docks to protest the arrival of a boat christened the SS *Waialeale*, which was piloted by "scabs," or replacement workers not honoring the strike. When protesters did not obey the police warning to disperse, officers fired into the unarmed crowd. Fifty people were injured in the ensuing commotion, including two women and two children. Though the strike ended in bloody failure, the broadly organized action helped build labor solidarity in Hawaii.

In the early 1930s, second-generation Japanese Americans, or nisei, began to earn a toehold in Hawaii's political arena, foreshadowing the importance of political power to the union cause. In November 1930, Hawaiian citizens elected the first Japanese Americans to public office: Republican Party members Tasaku Oka and Masayoshi Yamashiro found seats in the Territorial House, while Noboru Miyake joined the Kauai County Board of Supervisors.

Entrepreneurial businessmen of the 1930s also began organizing cooperative businesses, patterning the success of certain mainland Japanese agricultural growers. The organizational structure of these cooperatives inherently dissolved the roles of worker and boss, providing equal opportunity for all involved in the effort. In 1932, a Japanese cooperative formed at Kauai Homestead near Kapoa and opened a pineapple cannery. The successful experiment later became the Hawaiian Fruit Packers Company.

Hawaii's most significant labor union, a branch of the ILWU, formed in August 1937. Jack Kawano's Honolulu Longshoremen's Association, originally formed because established white unions would not take Asian members, also joined the larger group in August 1937. Kawano speedily rose to prominence as a leader of the ILWU in Hawaii.

The ILWU proved its organizational muscle early on, leading what proved to be the longest strike in Hawaiian labor history. The walkout began in July 1940 at Ahukini landing in Kauai and lasted 298 days. Longshoremen and plantation workers, mainly Japanese and Filipinos, joined together for the action, which resulted in some gains, though minor, for the workers.

Thus, by 1941, the ILWU had successfully unionized almost all of Hawaii's dock workers. Castle & Cooke Terminals subsequently became the first large company to sign an ILWU contract, a negotiation that protected longshoremen in Pearl Harbor—and a significant accomplishment for Hawaiian labor.

By the end of World War II, the hold of the plantation system over the workers and the power of the Big Five Companies had become significantly weakened. Interethnic solidarity thrived under the ILWU's leadership and among nisei laborers. By mid-century, the ILWU had moved beyond the bargaining table to help significantly alter Hawaii's political landscape. In time, through a tightly organized and successful voter registration drive, the ILWU paved the way for Asian Americans to earn labor rights long granted to white workers, such as the right to collective bargaining.

JAPANESE AMERICANS FIGHT FOR LABOR AND CIVIL RIGHTS

On the U.S. mainland, the years between 1903 and 1909 saw a flurry of activity on behalf of issei Japanese rights. Unions, political parties, labor organizations, and civil rights associations were formed to further the Japanese quest for fair treatment in America. Though frequently differing in focus and methodology, all these groups helped to promote the interests of issei and nisei Japanese through unity and cooperation.

The first farmworkers' union in California, the Japanese-Mexican Labor Association, was formed in 1903 and is particularly noteworthy since it served as an example of interethnic unity. That year, the union led 1,200 workers on strike for better wages and working conditions. Over the course of the next decade, Japanese Americans in California would form a number of other unions, professional associations, and political organizations, including the socialist Japanese Fresno Labor League; the Social Revolutionary Party (Skakai Komeito); the Salinas Valley Japanese Agricultural Contractors' Association; and the Delta Agricultural Association.

In 1908, the Japanese Association of America (JAA) formed, uniting local councils into one central organization. The JAA, originally created in 1900 as the Japanese Deliberative Council of America, functioned similarly to the Chinese Six Companies, working to protect Japanese rights in the United States, providing assistance to new immigrants, and coordinating activities promoting political and socioeconomic freedom. The JAA launched moral reforms, instructed new picture brides on "proper" conduct, and exercised the power

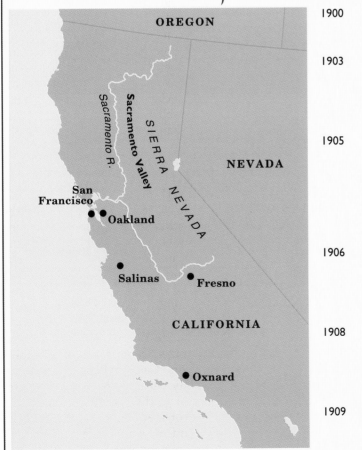

EARLY JAPANESE-AMERICAN LABOR GROUPS

1900	In May the Japanese Deliberative Council of America is formed in San Francisco, California, after a major anti-Japanese meeting. It will later become the Japanese Association of America.
1903	The Japanese-Mexican Labor Association, the first farmworkers' union in California, leads 1,200 on strike for better wages and working conditions in Oxnard, California. One death and several injuries result from a confrontation with the Western Agricultural Contracting Company.
1905	In February the United Japanese Deliberative Council of America—made up of local councils affiliated with the San Francisco–based Japanese Deliberative Council of America—forms as a new, centralized organization of local groups. In August, the Japanese Fresno Labor League, a socialist group, forms with about 2,000 members. It directs the flow of most Japanese laborers to contractors who agree on rates and wages.
1906	The Social Revolutionary Party (Skakai Komeito) is formed in Oakland, California. The group publicly endorses a strike by the International Seamen's Union of the Pacific. Within a year, however, the American Socialist Party and the California Socialist Party resolve to restrict Asian labor immigration into the United States.
1908	Two of the earliest Japanese agricultural groups in California, the Salinas Valley Japanese Agricultural Contractors' Association and the Delta Agricultural Association, are founded. The United Japanese Deliberative Council of America changes its name to the Japanese Association of America.
1909	The Fresno Labor League (Fresno Rodo Domei Kai), formed in 1908, holds a joint rally with the Fresno chapter of International Workers of the World (IWW), which draws Mexican and Italian workers.

to blacklist community members who did not demonstrate appropriate behavior.

Two groups, the Japanese Labor League of America (founded in 1915) and the Japanese Federation of Labor (founded in 1916), sought to work within, rather than against, the limits imposed by whites on Japanese workers. Both groups were founded by Bunji Suzuki, who believed Japanese laborers should work to gain acceptance by organized white labor. Suzuki's goal was to prove that Japanese work-

JAPANESE CIVIL RIGHTS GROUPS, 1902–1937

Name	Origin	Goal(s)	Activities
Association for the America-Bound	Founded in 1902 by Socialist and labor leader Sen Katayama in Tokyo	To generate interest in traveling to the United States	Published and distributed travel guidebooks, with tips such as how to obtain a passport and deal with emigration companies; published the popular *America-Bound* magazine
The Japanese Association of America (JAA)	Launched in 1900 in San Francisco, California, as the Japanese Deliberative Council of America, and broadened in 1905 into a loosely connected umbrella group made up of local Japanese councils around the state, the group was renamed the Japanese Association of America in 1908 when the local councils formally united into one centrally managed organization	Expansion of Japanese rights in United States; assimilation assistance for Japanese in the United States; coordination of activities promoting political and socioeconomic freedom	Each jurisdiction served many functions, including processing certificate applications for Japanese returning to the United States; deferring Japanese military service; registering all Japanese in the United States; blacklisting those deemed detrimental to the community; launching moral reforms; hiring lawyers to challenge discriminatory laws, such as California's Alien Land Acts of 1913 and 1920; sponsoring the opening of a home for orphans of Japanese descent, in conjunction with the Japanese Humane Society of Los Angeles; issuing a guide to picture brides on "proper" conduct; providing loans to farmers for land purchases; sponsoring farmers' conferences; publishing English lessons, information on U.S. culture, and translations of all laws affecting Japanese
Japanese American Citizens' League (JACL)	Having emerged from the American Loyalty League, a student organization founded in California and Washington in 1918, JACL held its first official meeting in Seattle in 1930	To secure the future of Japanese America through nisei loyalty, patriotism, assimilation, and conciliation	The JACL funded successful campaigns in the 1930s to obtain citizenship for issei World War I veterans and to repeal the Cable Acts, which deprived American women of their citizenship if they married aliens
Southern California Farm Federation (Nanka Nokai Renmei)	Founded in 1935 at a meeting of Japanese farmers, the group had a total membership of 1,560	Teamwork between 24 agricultural cooperatives in Southern California	Managed cooperative buying and marketing; negotiated with labor and merchants' associations; produced radio broadcasts of market conditions; began publishing in various agricultural and industrial newspapers; fought for the reversal of the California Alien Land Acts
Southern California Gardeners Federation (SCGF)	After Japanese gardeners' associations were established in Hollywood and West Los Angeles, California, in 1933, they united as the SCGF in 1937	The associations began as social organizations, but with the birth of the SCGF, the group broadened its activities to include settling interassociation route disputes, organizing field trips, and writing articles to educate members about the latest gardening techniques. The group also tried to raise gardening fees and improve rubbish disposal	The SCGF was largely unsuccessful. Most gardeners saw themselves as small businessmen and distrusted anything resembling a labor union. In general, many were satisified with the money they made, despite difficulties. They distrusted joining forces with white gardeners to resolve matters they felt were not pressing

Offices of the Chinese-American Citizens Alliance

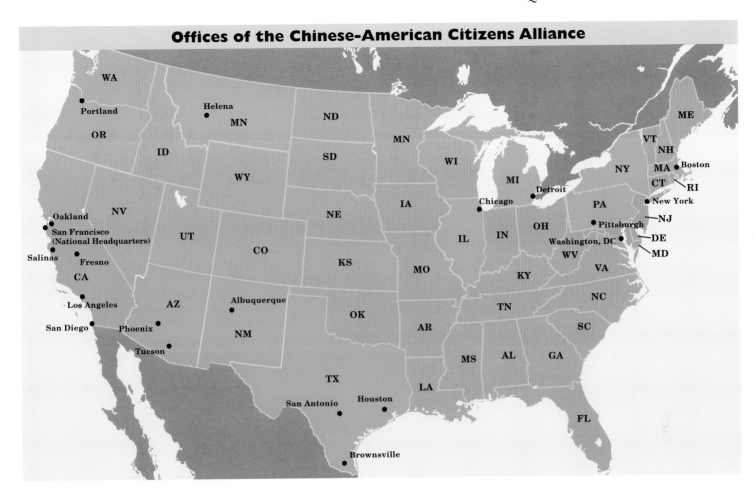

ers understood the principles of organized labor and could raise their standard of living so as not to offend unionized white workers. White unions, however, continued to consistently lock out Asian workers from membership.

By 1930, the student-led American Loyalty League of California and Washington had transformed into the Japanese American Citizens League (JACL). The goal of this group was to secure Japanese-American rights by demonstrating nisei loyalty, patriotism, assimilation, and conciliation. In 1941, JACL national secretary Mike Masaoka summed up the group's philosophy this way:

I am proud that I am an American citizen of Japanese ancestry, for my background makes me appreciate more fully the wonderful advantages of this nation. I believe in her institutions, ideals and traditions; I glory in her heritage; I boast in her history; I trust in her future.... Although some individuals may discriminate against me, I shall never become bitter or lose faith, for I know that such persons do not represent the majority of the American people.... I pledge myself to do honor to her at all times and in all places ... in the hope that I shall become a better American in a greater America.

In addition to these groups, Japanese Americans also continued to form coopera-

tive business associations, particularly in agriculture. Among these were the Southern California Farm Federation (Nanka Nokai Renmei) and the Southern California Gardeners Federation (SCGF).

THE NATIVE SONS OF THE GOLDEN STATE

During the first half of the 20th century, the experience of Chinese immigrants entering the United States was colored by the painful ordeal of Angel Island and detainment (discussed in chapter 3). Once "processed," however, the new arrivals joined the slowly growing numbers of second-generation Chinese in entering a mainstream American lifestyle. More egalitarian dress, manners, and behavior reflected not only their own assimilation into American society but also the increasingly Nationalist nature of their homeland, where revolutionary leader Sun Yat-sen had been installed as president of the new Republic of China in 1912.

In addition to trading Manchu-style dress and queue hairstyles for a more westernized look, Chinese Americans sought to learn English. They also organized Young Men's and Women's Christian Associations

During the presidential campaign of 1932, many Chinese Americans supported Democrat Franklin Delano Roosevelt, seen above during his inauguration the following year. The Chinese-American Citizens Alliance created the Chinese-American Voting League to marshal support for his victorious campaign. (Library of Congress)

and Boy Scout troops, even though as members of an ethnic group they continued to face oppression and rejection by the society at large.

The Native Sons of the Golden State, a pro–Chinese American group, took assimilation efforts to a new level. Although groups like the Chinese Six Companies, the Angel Island Detainees Association, and other benevolent associations continued to push for civil rights protection, the Native Sons of the Golden State pushed even further as the years went on, encouraging education and political participation. The group was founded by three San Francisco–based Chinese American businessmen in 1895. They named their pro-Chinese organization consciously to counter the white, anti-Chinese group of Native Sons of the Golden West.

Dominated by successful American-born Chinese, the Native Sons of the Golden State succeeded in accomplishing many goals, including the publication of the *Chinese Times*, the most popular Chinese language newspaper in America. In 1905, the group changed its name to the Chinese-American Citizens Alliance and continued to open offices in major U.S. cities in the South, Midwest, and East. With each new office, the surrounding Chinese-American community gained political strength, a formidable accomplishment after so many decades of fighting anti-Chinese hysteria and discrimination.

Prior to the 1930s, the Chinese-American community allied itself primarily with the Republican Party, the Democrats being dominated by anti-Asian forces. In 1932, however, the Chinese-American Citizens Alliance created the Chinese-American Voting League in support of Democrat Franklin Delano Roosevelt's first bid for the presidency.

THE INDIA WELFARE LEAGUE AND CITIZENSHIP RIGHTS

The Supreme Court's 1923 ruling in *United States v. Bhagat Singh Thind* revoked Asian Indians' citizenship and forced the settled immigrants to give up the farms they had worked so hard to establish. Between 1920 and 1940, 3,000 Asian Indians returned to India to start over again. Those who stayed continued to press for civil rights protection but were relegated to the migrant laboring class. Their economic progress was further impeded by the Great Depression, a severe worldwide economic downturn that lasted from 1929 to the start of World War II. Due to their alien status, Asian Indians were ineligible for certain federal relief programs available to American citizens.

The India Welfare League, under the leadership of Mubarak Aki Khan, headed the fight for rights. Khan and the league sought redress through congressional measures, which finally resulted in a bill introduced in 1939 that would grant citizenship to all Asian Indians who had been living in the United States since 1924. Paul Scharrenberg of the American Federation of Labor argued against the bill, as did various other anti-Asian group leaders, and the measure never made it off the congressional floor.

Asian Indian Khairata Ram Samras, following the lead of the Japanese immigrants of the 1920s, decided to seek civil rights protection through the U.S. court system. In 1940, Samras legally challenged the *United States v. Bhagat Singh Thind* decision of 1923, stating, "Discrimination against Hindus in respect to naturalization is not only capricious and untenable but in violation of constitutional provisions." Nonetheless, the Court denied his challenge.

It proved to be not the U.S. Constitution but an international agreement that helped settle the matter of prejudice and citizenship for Asian-Indian immigrants. Although the United States had yet to enter the war, World War II had been raging in Europe since September 3, 1939, two days after Nazi Germany's invasion of Poland. In 1940, the Nazis had captured Denmark, Norway, the Netherlands, Belgium, and France, and although Great Britain had managed to keep Germany at bay, British prime minister Winston Churchill recognized that his nation's fate depended on quick relief from the United States. In August 1941, before the Court could pass a ruling in *Kharaiti Ram Samras v. United States*, Churchill and U.S. president Franklin Roosevelt signed the Atlantic Charter. This international document, an unofficial declaration of peaceful alliance against the Axis powers, also declared the right of peoples to determine their own form of government.

The India League of America (headed by Sirdar Jagit Singh) as well as the India Welfare League used the principles espoused by the Atlantic Charter as the basis for their arguments regarding the naturalization of Asian-Indian Americans as well as for their homeland's quest for sovereignty.

Two other war-related factors helped Asian-Indian immigrants to the United States receive due process for their civil rights. After entering World War II, the United States found it increasingly difficult to maintain its own discriminatory policies toward Asian immigrants while fighting Adolf Hitler's racist Nazi regime. The U.S. government was also well aware of the military importance of India's strategic location: It would be easy for Japan to take advantage of the chaos mounting in politically volatile India to advance its position and join German troops in the Middle East territories and then-nations of Aden, Barbary Coast, Irak, Lebanon, Oman, Palestine,

Qatar, Saudi Arabia, Syria, Transjordon, Turkey, and Yemen. Thus, seeing the political need to strengthen relations with India, federal officials began to bend to the demands of Asian-Indian immigrants for fair treatment.

After two years of deliberation, Congress granted naturalization rights to Asian Indians in a 1946 bill that also provided for a small quota of 100 Asian-Indian immigrants per year. The 1946 measure nullified the stranglehold of California's Alien Land Laws as well. Between 1946 and 1964, some 12,000 Asian Indians migrated to the United States, moves that were enabled not just by the naturalization and quota laws of 1946 but also by the McCarran-Walter Act of 1952 (discussed in chapter 5). Without the passage of these bills, it is likely that America's predominantly male Asian-Indian community would have died out.

FILIPINOS ON THE MAINLAND

Filipino laborers began arriving in the United States and Hawaii shortly after annexation of the Philippines in the early 1900s. Most other Asian immigrants usually remained in Hawaii, but nearly 13 percent of Hawaiian-based Filipinos moved on to the mainland. A few thousand came directly from the Philippines as U.S. government-sponsored students known as *pensionados*. As the Immigration Act of 1924 did not apply to Filipinos, who were legally considered U.S. nationals, their numbers spiked greatly between 1920 and 1930.

The mainland experience for *manongs* (first-generation Filipinos) proved to be very different from the experience of those who settled in Hawaii. Unlike the Chinese and Japanese, the Filipinos tended toward Western dress, manners, and religious views, and their American-influenced education helped prepare Filipinos for American culture. Nevertheless, they remained locked out by the larger society and were more often than not treated as strangers. Although they enjoyed the title of "U.S. nationals," immigrants from the Philippines were not allowed to vote, own land, or attain U.S. citizenship. Filipino laborers also had to compete with white workers on the U.S. mainland and were often targeted for attack. Many Filipino immigrants recalled a Tagalog proverb as descriptive of their disappointment upon arrival in a land supposedly symbolized by the Statue of Liberty: *"Isang magandang senora, libot na libot ng espada."*

The *Pensionados*

Following American suppression of the Filipino independence movement in the U.S.-Philippine War of 1899–1902, the U.S. government offered scholarships to Filipino students in a program meant to demonstrate the United States's benevolent treatment of Filipinos. Thus, in the first decade of the 20th century, hundreds of bright Filipino students came to the United States to further their studies. Provided with scholarships or "pensions" by the U.S. government, these students were known as *pensionados*. Upon completion of their studies, most of these students returned to the Philippines, where many obtained high-ranking jobs in the government.

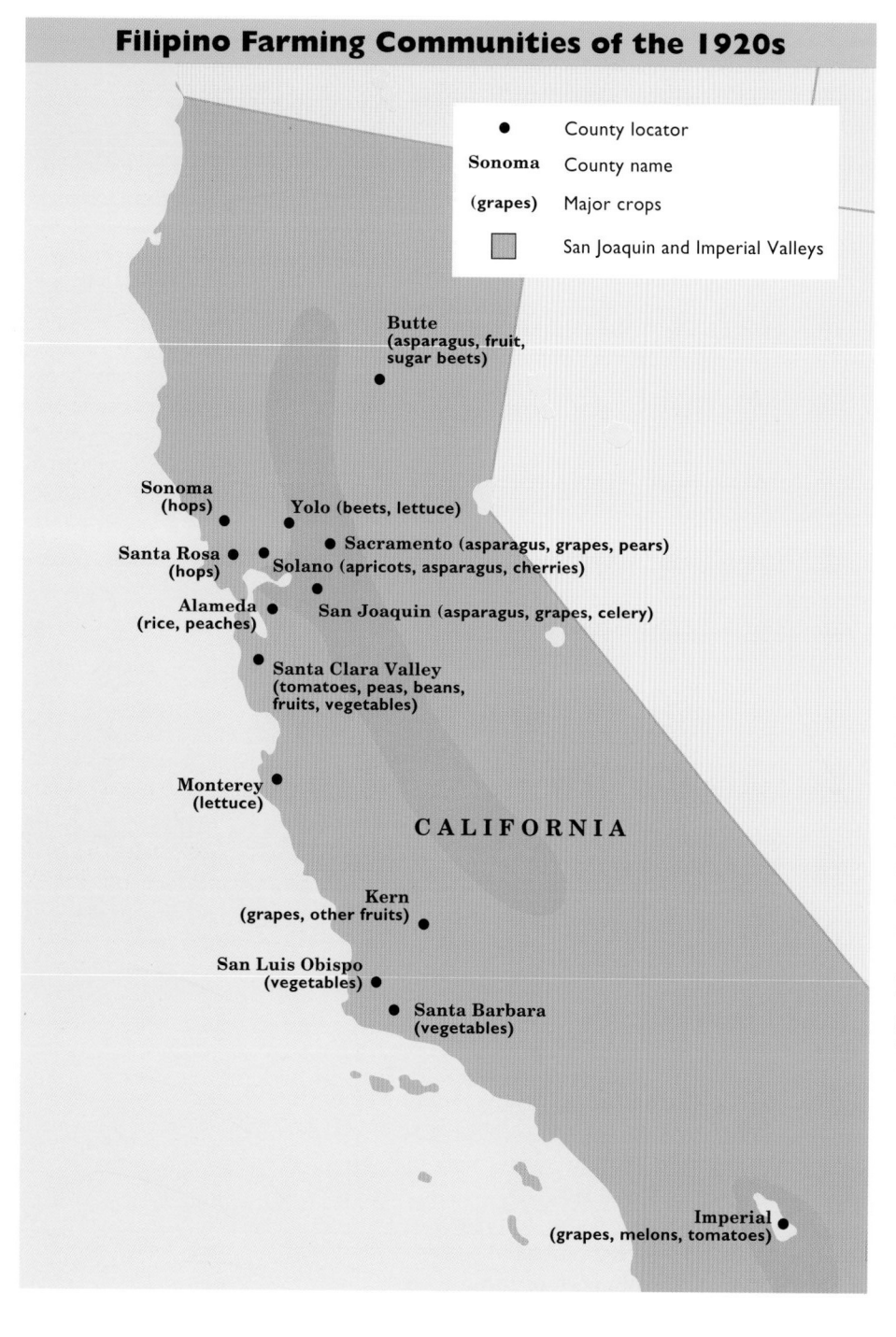

Filipino Farming Communities of the 1920s

● County locator

Sonoma County name

(grapes) Major crops

San Joaquin and Imperial Valleys

Butte
(asparagus, fruit,
sugar beets)
●

Sonoma
(hops) ●
●**Yolo (beets, lettuce)**
Santa Rosa ● ●
(hops) ●**Sacramento (asparagus, grapes, pears)**
Solano (apricots, asparagus, cherries)
●
Alameda ●
(rice, peaches) **San Joaquin (asparagus, grapes, celery)**

●
Santa Clara Valley
(tomatoes, peas, beans,
fruits, vegetables)

Monterey ●
(lettuce)

CALIFORNIA

Kern
(grapes, other fruits) ●

San Luis Obispo
(vegetables) ●
●**Santa Barbara**
(vegetables)

Imperial ●
(grapes, melons, tomatoes)

riages were of mixed ethnicity. Of the Filipino women who emigrated to the United States in the early portion of the century, most were farm laborers who went with their husbands or fathers to Hawaii, where the plantations offered a more settled life than that of the migratory system of mainland agricultural employment.

In addition to migrant farm work, Filipino immigrants secured jobs in the urban-based service industry and in the fish industries of Alaska and the northwest states. Typical service jobs worked by Filipinos in the early 1930s included yardboy, janitor, valet, elevator operator, bellboy, and cook. Approximately 25 percent of Filipino immigrants took on this kind of work.

Those Filipinos who traveled farthest north from Stockton worked in the Alaska fishery industry; by 1930 they composed 15 percent of the Alaska cannery workforce. The "Alaskeros" worked six days a week, from 6 A.M. to 6 P.M., cleaning, cutting, trimming, and packing salmon. It was particularly difficult to save any money working this type of job, as food and other expenses incurred in Alaska left little to live on back in California. Filipinos working this kind of seasonal labor often found themselves signing up for another canning season to pay off a long list of debts from the previous year.

Cannery work was also fraught with health hazards. Carlos Bulosan recalled a gruesome incident he had witnessed while working in an Alaskan salmon cannery in the 1930s:

I was working in a section called the "wash lye." Actually a certain amount of lye was diluted in the water where I washed the beheaded fish that came down on a small escalator. One afternoon a cutter above me, working in the poor light, slashed off his right arm with the cutting machine. It happened so swiftly he did not cry out. I saw his arm floating down the water among the fish heads.

(There is a beautiful lady surrounded with swords.)

Stockton, California, became the center of work and life for newly arrived mainland Filipinos. The *manongs* were overwhelmingly male and young. By 1930, only 6.5 percent of mainland Filipinos were female, and of the 31,092 who arrived in California between 1920 and 1929, 84 percent were less than 30 years of age. Unlike the Chinese and Japanese before them, most migrating Filipino men were single. Also unlike other Asians, Filipino men—who came from a mestizo (mixed race) ancestry—frequently married women of other races, including white women. The 1940 U.S. Census reported that approximately 25 percent of all Filipino mar-

In the 1930s, 60 percent of mainland Filipinos worked in the agriculture industry, which suffered from a labor shortage due in part to the exclusion of the Chinese, Japanese, Koreans, and Asian Indians. Similar to other migrant workers, the Filipinos worked in gangs headed by a crew boss who secured the labor contracts. Their system hinged around large work gangs of 300 or so, and they moved from camp to camp across counties as dictated by the seasonal needs of the crops. The migrants worked in fields filled with asparagus, tomatoes, lettuce, and other vegetables, as well as fruit orchards, grape vineyards, and grain fields of hops and rice. White farmers and writers viewed the Filipinos as particularly suited to the physically exhausting "stoop" work, commenting that their short size allowed for easier bending and that the dust that itched the white workers did not bother the "dark skinned" laborers.

At first, the Filipinos were stereotyped as the most docile and therefore the most sought-after type of Asian worker, but their involvement in the labor movement during the depression years shattered this image. Beginning in 1930 with the growers of the Imperial valley of California, farm owners successively tried to cut the already miserably low wages of farmworkers to make higher profits. Consequently, more than 4,000 Filipinos joined the Filipino Labor Union (FLU) in Stockton and Salinas under the slogan *"Ang lakas aynasa pagkakaisa."* (Strength is in union.) Since the Filipino workers made up 40 percent of the total agricultural workforce in the Salinas valley, their bargaining power was quite strong early on.

White growers countered the strength of the growing FLU by bringing in Mexican, Asian-Indian, and Japanese scabs. Growers on the mainland went a step further than their Hawaiian counterparts and also organized the Filipino Labor Supply Association, filling the group with Filipino labor contractors opposed to the union.

CARLOS BULOSAN

"America is also the nameless foreigner, the homeless refugee, the hungry boy begging for a job and the black body dangling on a tree. America is the illiterate immigrant who is ashamed that the world of books and intellectual opportunities is closed to him. We are all that nameless foreigner, that homeless refugee, that hungry boy, that illiterate immigrant and that lynched black body. All of us, from the first Adams to the last Filipino, native born or alien, educated or illiterate—We are America!"

—Carlos Bulosan, America Is in the Heart

Although he is little known today, Carlos Bulosan was a literary phenomenon during his time. Born in 1911 in Binalonan, a small rural village in northern Philippines, he fled the poverty of his homeland at age 18 for the United States, paying $75 for a ticket in steerage class of the Dollar Line. On July 22, 1930, his ship arrived in Seattle, Washington. Rather than finding a land of golden opportunity in the United States, Bulosan found a nation sinking deeper into an economic depression. With jobs of any kind becoming increasingly scarce, Bulosan found that foreign laborers were far from welcomed. Nonetheless, he was full of hope. As he would later write:

My first sight of the approaching land was an exhilarating experience. Everything seemed native and promising to me. It was like coming home after a long voyage, although as yet I had no home in this city. Everything seemed familiar and kind—the white faces of the buildings melting in the soft afternoon sun, the gray contours of the surrounding valleys that seemed to vanish in the last periphery of light. With a sudden surge of joy, I knew that I must find a home in this new land.

Bulosan did find work—as a migrant laborer. In summers, he worked in Alaska fish canneries, where he earned $13 for the season; in fall, he picked fruit and vegetables in California for little more. His hard life moved him to become active as an itinerant union organizer. He also began to set his feelings in poetry, and in 1932 his work was published for the first time in an anthology.

In 1936, Bulosan was diagnosed with tuberculosis, and he spent the next two years at Los Angeles County Hospital, where he underwent several lung operations, lost the ribs on his right side, and was given—incorrectly, it would turn out—five years to live by his doctors. During his illness, Bulosan, who had arrived in the United States without the ability to speak more than a few words of English, read and wrote feverishly.

After Japan invaded Hawaii and the Philippines in December 1941 and Filipinos fought side by side with Americans, the bitter prejudice against Filipino Americans began to wane. The following year, friends that Bulosan had met in the hospital helped him publish his first two volumes of poetry, *Letter from America* and *Chorus from America.* In 1942, he published another poetry collection, *The Voice of Bataan,* in honor of the men who died on that Pacific island at the hands of the Japanese. That same year, his collection of short stories based on Filipino folk tales, *The Laughter of My Father,* became a runaway best-seller and was translated into several foreign languages. Writers such as Carl Sandburg and William Saroyan hailed his work, and literary magazines such as *The New Yorker* and *Harper's* competed to publish it. In 1945, at the height of Bulosan's popularity, President Franklin Roosevelt handpicked him to write one of the four essays in "The Four Freedoms," a popular wartime collection that appeared in the *Saturday Evening Post.*

In 1946, Bulosan's novel, *America Is in the Heart,* was released. The book gave a gripping account of the bitter poverty in the Philippines and related the heartbreak and discrimination that those looking for a better life experienced on the fringes of American society. *America Is in the Heart* was to be Bulosan's last major published work. By the late 1940s, the political climate in the United States had changed. As an outspoken critic of economic exploitation, Bulosan began to associate with progressive economic and social causes. When he joined novelist Howard Fast and educator W. E. B. DuBois in supporting the publication of the autobiography of Luis Taruc, a leader of Communist rebellion in the Philippines, his friends in the publishing business abandoned him.

Despite the collapse of support for his work, Bulosan continued to speak out for the causes he believed in. In 1948, he returned to Seattle to edit the yearbook of Local 37 of the International Longshore and Warehouse Union (ILWU), which represented the cannery workers. In 1953, however, Bulosan had a cancerous kidney removed and found that his tuberculosis had returned. By this time, Bulosan had also developed an increasingly strong addiction to alcohol and had became subject to bouts of depression. In 1956, he died penniless and largely forgotten by the literary elite. Despite his early death, Bulosan had given voice to the struggles of those at the margins, many of whom had come to America in search of a better life, only to find that promise unfulfilled.

Led by the FLU, white and Filipino lettuce pickers went on strike together on August 27, 1934, but when the whites negotiated separately shortly thereafter, the Filipinos were left to carry on the strike alone. Growers attempted to undermine the strike by disseminating rumors that Communists controlled FLU leadership. Armed vigilantes, highway patrolmen, and "special deputies" joined the growers and tried to run the striking workers off the land. Hand-lettered signs proclaimed "This Is White Man's Country" and "Get Out of Here if You Don't Like What We Pay."

Despite mass arrests and a violent physical attack against FLU leader Rufo Cañete, the strikers held fast, eventually negotiating higher wages and public recognition of the FLU as a legitimate union. FLU strength continued to grow, leading to the formation in 1936 of the Field Workers' Union Local 30326, a Mexican-Filipino agricultural union set up in part by the American Federation of Labor.

THE ANTI-FILIPINO MOVEMENT

Paternalistically referred to by American officials in the Philippines as the United States's "little brown brothers," Filipinos found that the benevolent comparison stopped there. Like the Chinese, Japanese, and Koreans before them, Filipino immigrants encountered prejudicial attitudes, unfair treatment under the law, and the continual threat of violent attack. Furthermore, ignorant and fearful whites often confused Filipinos with other Asian or nonwhite races. Certain theaters allowed "only whites on the first floor [and] Filipinos, Japanese, Chinese, Colored people on the balcony." Landlords discriminated ("Orientals Not Allowed"), as did hotels ("Positively No Filipinos Allowed"). Even other Asians stereotyped the Filipinos, considering them to be "savage" and "filthy" and circulating rumors that all Filipinos were criminals who carried switchblades.

Mob violence against Filipino migrant workers began to occur on the eve of the Great Depression, when 150 armed whites ran 60 Filipinos out of Yakima valley, Washington. The following year, in Ester, California, hundreds of local whites demanded that all farm owners in the area fire their Filipino laborers. The year 1930 witnessed several violent incidents. In Watonsville, California, hundreds of whites angered by the perceived threat to white women posed by Filipinos attacked Filipino men over several days, in

the process killing an immigrant named Fermin Tovera. The day that Tovera's body arrived in the Philippines was proclaimed National Humiliation Day in that country. In the United States, the four whites convicted of the murder ended up serving only one month of jail time.

In Stockton that same year, a car bombing—an unusual occurrence at that time—destroyed the clubhouse of the Filipino Federation of America. Two other bombings occurred in the California towns of Reedley and Imperial, while in West Wapato District, Washington, mobs of armed whites threatened white ranchers with lynchings if they refused to fire their Filipino workers.

The random incidents of violence had a tangible effect: 11,400 Filipinos had come to the mainland in 1929, but that figure dropped down to only 3,200 new arrivals in 1932.

THE TYDINGS-MCDUFFIE INDEPENDENCE ACT OF 1934

Widespread prejudice against Filipinos eventually formed itself into a piece of legislation known as the Tydings-McDuffie Independence Act of 1934. Filipinos' status as U.S. nationals had previously exempted them from the exclusionist laws passed against other Asian immigrants. However, nativists in Congress who wanted to put an end to Filipino immigration succeeded in granting the island independence—a move that effectively solved the Filipino "problem."

When the Tydings-McDuffie Act awarded the Philippines commonwealth status with the promise of independence in 10 years' time, all Filipinos were demoted from "U.S. nationals" to "legal aliens," and the Filipino immigration quota was set at just 50 persons per year. The quota did not apply to Hawaii, where sugar planters were assured of a Filipino labor supply as their needs dictated. However, the limit of 50 per year proved to be the lowest number set for any nation—except for those Asian nations from which immigration was banned entirely—under U.S. immigration laws.

The Tydings-McDuffie Act also placed severe travel restrictions on Filipinos, thus severing ties between those living in the United States and their families at home. By contrast, the Scott Act of 1882 had allowed Chinese merchants to bring their wives with them, and the 1908 Gentlemen's Agreement carried a clause exempting family members of Japanese immigrants.

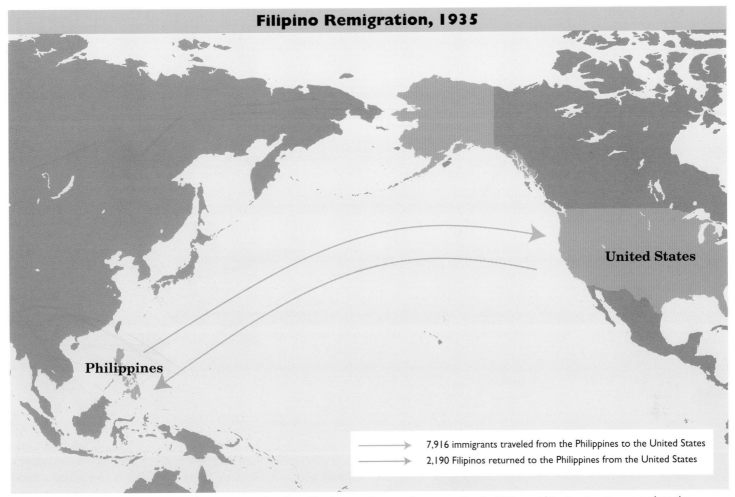

Filipino Remigration, 1935

Philippines

United States

7,916 immigrants traveled from the Philippines to the United States
2,190 Filipinos returned to the Philippines from the United States

In 1935, the U.S. Congress passed the Repatriation Act, a law that offered to pay the cost of transportation for Filipinos wishing to return permanently to the Philippines. The plan was an abysmal failure, as more than three times as many Filipinos arrived in the United States from the Philippines while the law was in effect as left the United States for the Philippines.

Reclassification of Filipino immigrants in 1934 carried another dire economic consequence. Filipinos classified as aliens became instantly ineligible for certain forms of relief assistance. New Deal programs instituted by President Franklin Roosevelt gave hundreds of thousands of people hope as well as work and food during America's Great Depression. Yet after the Tydings-McDuffie Act, Filipinos could no longer enroll in the National Youth Administration or the Works Progress Administration. In addition, because the Supreme Court had ruled that Filipinos were "nonwhite," they could not apply for naturalized citizenship, which kept Filipinos from receiving relief aid under the Relief Appropriation Act of 1937.

THE REPATRIATION ACT OF 1935

By the mid-1930s, white employers no longer desired Filipino workers. Although Filipino labor unions had grown strong, many Mexican laborers were willing to work the lowest-paying jobs without complaint. Exclusionists pressed for still more restrictions against Filipinos, and some even advocated the deportation of those already living in the United States. Los Angeles County Supervisor Roger W. Jessup focused on indigent Filipinos. He reasoned that the $87 per-person cost of deportation would be much less than the cost of maintaining those individuals on welfare. In response to Jessup and others, Congress passed the Repatriation Act of 1935, a law that offered to pay the cost of transportation for Filipinos wishing to return home for good.

The vast majority of all Filipinos in the United States declined the government's offer—and for many reasons. First of all, the law stipulated that they could never return to the United States. Second, the Philippine economy remained weak and stagnant, discouraging return. Finally, many Filipinos felt that going home would be a sign of defeat, and any such return would be made in a cloud of shame. In the end, only 2,190 Filipinos went home under the 1935 act.

The *Honolulu Star-Tribune announces the attack on Pearl Harbor.* (National Archives)

ASIAN AMERICANS AND WORLD WAR II

The entry of the United States into World War II following Japan's surprise attack on Pearl Harbor brought about many consequences for Asian Americans, whose loyalty as Americans was immediately called into question. Nevertheless, for Filipinos, Chinese, and Koreans, the war presented an opportunity to strike back at Imperial Japan, while also allowing them the chance to prove their loyalty to their adopted land.

PEARL HARBOR

On December 7, 1941, the Oahu port of Pearl Harbor—a major base of the U.S. Navy—was suddenly attacked by a squadron of Japanese planes in two successive bombings that lasted less than three hours. Simultaneously in other parts of the Pacific, Japan also attacked U.S. bases in the Philippines, Guam, and the Midway Islands. When the air had cleared over Pearl Harbor, 2,335 soldiers and sailors and 68 civilians were dead, and 1,178 Americans were wounded. Of the eight battleships stationed at Pearl Harbor, three had been sunk and the remainder heavily or partially damaged. About 120 U.S. planes were also destroyed in the sneak attack. Congress declared war on Japan the following day, and the United States official-

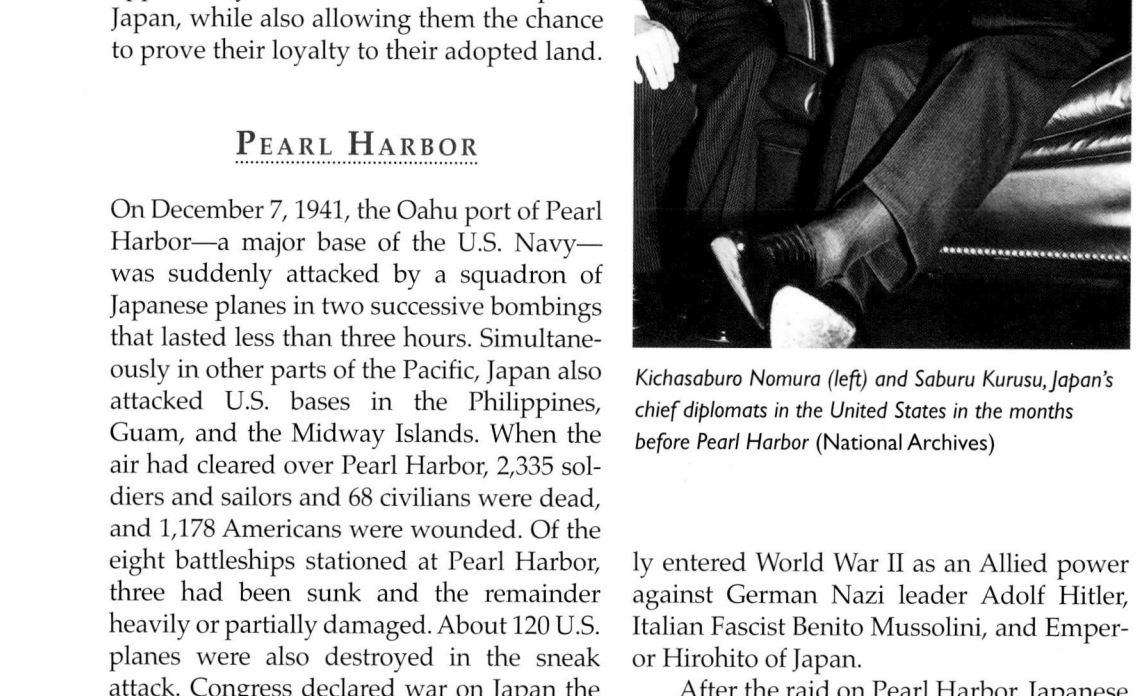

Kichasaburo Nomura (left) and Saburu Kurusu, Japan's chief diplomats in the United States in the months before Pearl Harbor (National Archives)

ly entered World War II as an Allied power against German Nazi leader Adolf Hitler, Italian Fascist Benito Mussolini, and Emperor Hirohito of Japan.

After the raid on Pearl Harbor, Japanese Americans grew especially apprehensive

Smoke and flame rises above American ships at Pearl Harbor. (National Archives)

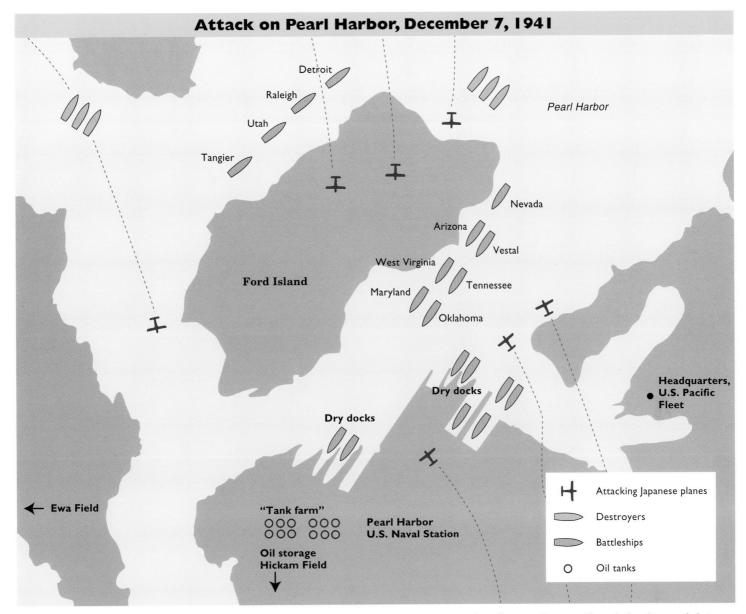

Attack on Pearl Harbor, December 7, 1941

Pearl Harbor

Detroit
Raleigh
Utah
Tangier

Ford Island

Nevada
Arizona
Vestal
West Virginia
Maryland
Tennessee
Oklahoma

Dry docks

Dry docks

← Ewa Field

"Tank farm"
○○○ ○○○
○○○ ○○○

Oil storage
Hickam Field
↓

Pearl Harbor
U.S. Naval Station

● Headquarters,
U.S. Pacific
Fleet

⊣⊢ Attacking Japanese planes

Destroyers

Battleships

○ Oil tanks

The Japanese air attack on Pearl Harbor caught the U.S. Pacific fleet completely unprepared. The map above illustrates the route of attack that the overwhelming Japanese force of 103 bombers, 40 torpedo bombers, 139 dive-bombers, and 69 fighters took—and locations of major targets.

about their future. Anti-Japanese sentiment had been growing exponentially over the last few decades, both in America and abroad, and with the U.S. entry into the conflict, it seemed certain that prejudice against Japanese living in the United States would only increase.

Indeed, the reaction against Japanese Americans proved swift and fierce and was inflamed immediately by remarks made by Secretary of the Navy Frank Knox. At one time the general manager of the blatantly anti-Asian Hearst newspaper chain, Knox allowed his own prejudice to skew his military inspection of the damage at Pearl Harbor. Without any proof, he charged that the Japanese Americans of Oahu had engaged in sabotage and espionage that had enabled the Japanese to carry out a successful attack. Knox also called for the Japanese on Oahu to

be relocated to another Hawaiian island. Rumors spread quickly across the nation that Oahu's Japanese had cut special paths among rows of pineapple and sugarcane to guide Japanese bombers and had parked their cars on highways to block traffic.

Naval intelligence and FBI investigations subsequently absolved Hawaii's issei and nisei population of wrongdoing. However, fears of Japanese spies and informants active on American soil continued to grow, especially on the West Coast of the U.S. mainland.

The anti-Japanese views of other Asian-American groups figured significantly in their responses to America's entry into the war. The Chinese- and Korean-American communities cheered the prospect of fighting against their longtime enemy under the strength of the American flag. Because the Philippines had also been bombed by

Emperor Hirohito of Japan (National Archives)

The shared experience of captured Filipino and American troops during the forced Bataan Death March solidified a sense of comradeship between soldiers. Some of those captured troops are shown here. (National Archives)

A Japanese bomber hits the USS Yorktown at the Battle of Midway in June 1942. (National Archives)

Japan, Filipinos living in the U.S. mainland looked forward to fighting both for their country of origin and for their adopted homeland. Nevertheless, although President Roosevelt would soon allow Filipino Americans to serve in combat, the U.S. military—at least initially—denied all Asian Americans the opportunity to fight alongside their non-Asian contemporaries. Arguments over American hypocrisy in regard to racism and oppression therefore framed each group's entry into the war against the Axis forces.

THE FIGHTING FILIPINOS

When the Japanese bombed Pearl Harbor, they also simultaneously attacked the Philippines, Guam, and the Midway Islands. Clark Field, a U.S. air base constructed in northern Luzon in the Philippines, was destroyed just hours after the Pearl Harbor attack. General Douglas MacArthur's troops were caught off guard and retreated from Manila to the Bataan Peninsula. Filipino Americans rushed to join in the fight for their homeland and for democracy.

Initially, though, Filipinos living in the United States were rejected for service by the U.S. armed forces. Having been classified as "legal aliens," they were considered ineligible to fight. In response to Filipino protests, however, President Franklin Roosevelt changed the law. Thus, on February 19, 1942, Secretary of War Henry Stimson announced the creation of a new unit: the First Filipino Infantry Regiment.

Nearly 40 percent of California's Filipino population registered for the first draft. "On to Bataan" became the regimental song of the First Filipino Infantry, and a Second Filipino Infantry Regiment was quickly formed, lifting the total of men in both regiments to more than 7,000. After the Filipino Commonwealth government also joined the U.S. forces, Filipinos and Americans fought side by side.

Under General MacArthur's leadership, the combined troops battled the Japanese for four long bloody months on Bataan. The First and Second Regiments joined Filipino resistance fighters to play key roles in the conflict, sneaking behind enemy lines and sabotaging Japanese com-

Although they were eventually defeated by Japanese invaders, Filipino soldiers heroically defended their homeland, inspiring posters such as this one. (National Archives)

munications. However, Bataan fell into enemy hands on April 9, 1942. At the battle's conclusion, the Japanese marched 80,000 Americans and Filipinos 120 miles to prison camps erected in San Fernando. Those too tired to complete the six days' journey were executed. The exodus came to be known as the Bataan Death March. Thousands of Filipinos and Americans also died from starvation, disease, and torture over years spent in Japanese prison camps.

Though Bataan was lost early on, the "Fighting Filipinos" won the respect of mainland Americans for their bravery. The Bataan troops also earned a special tribute from Eleanor Roosevelt, who proclaimed:

Fighting in Bataan has been an excellent example of what happens when two different races respect each other. Men of different races and backgrounds have fought side by side and praised each other's heroism and courage.

Other doors opened for Filipinos in the United States during the war years. Returning soldiers were granted U.S. citizenship.

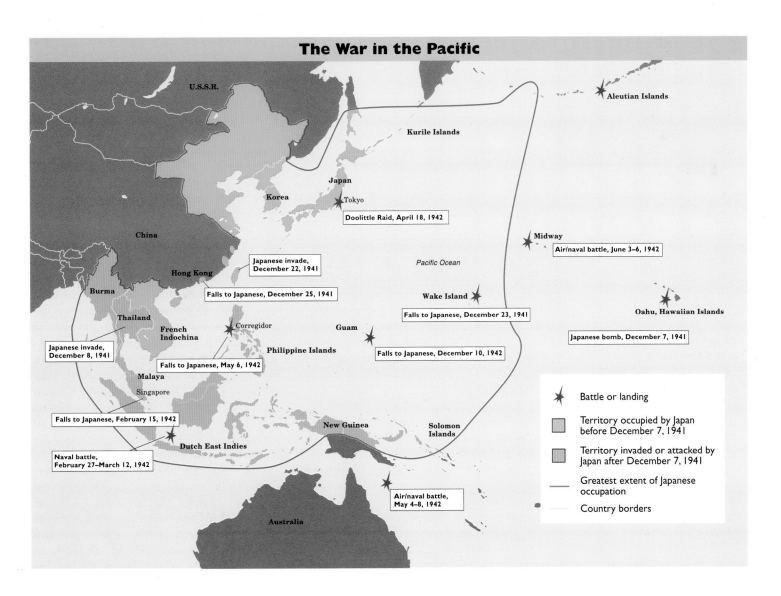

California's attorney general reinterpreted the state's alien land laws and allowed Filipinos to sign land leases. Filipinos were encouraged to take over farms abandoned by interned Japanese. White-collar employment opportunities opened up in the defense industry, and for the first time mainland Filipinos had a chance to work as technicians, engineers, and clerks.

General MacArthur returned to help liberate the Philippines on October 20, 1944, but it took nearly a year for American and Filipino troops to fully defeat the Japanese. More Filipinos lost their lives in the liberation than had in the original invasion of December 7, 1941. Following the war, the Philippines formally earned independent status from the United States on July 4, 1946.

CHINA: CIVIL WAR AND JAPANESE INVASION

Because Japan had conquered much of China before its attack on Pearl Harbor, and because Chinese Americans had been concerned about the ongoing war in Asia, they were more than willing to join the effort against Japan, both in battle and on the home front in America. Like the Filipinos, the Chinese found opportunity as well as hardship during the war years. Economic doors opened and prejudice against the Chinese declined somewhat as troops and civilians distinguished themselves in the fight against their longtime enemy.

The antagonism between China and Japan had deep roots. Following the Chinese Revolution of 1911 which toppled the imperial monarchy, Sun Yat-sen, leader of the National People's Party, or Kuomintang, became the first president of the Provisional Chinese Republic in 1912. Espousing policies of nationalism, democracy, and reform, Sun was forced from office by conservative opponents who installed Yuan Shih-k'ai as his successor. Yuan, who failed in his attempts to make himself emperor, died in 1916, beginning a period of civil war began among China's military and civilian leaders.

From exile, Sun Yat-sen attempted but failed to establish an independent Chinese republic based in Guangzhou (Canton). In 1925, Sun died and was followed as leader of the Kuomintang by General Chiang Kai-shek, who succeeded in uniting China again under one government in 1928 in the city of Nanking. However, even then, Chiang's hold on power was threatened—by the Chinese Communist Party (CCP) and by territorial aggression from Japan.

Among the leaders of the Chinese Communist Party was the young Mao Zedong. Ideologically at odds regarding the country's direction, the Nationalists and the Communists eventually came to blows. Chiang and his forces prevailed after shooting down thousands of Communists in the streets of Shanghai and other cities.

Upon taking power in Nanking, Chiang outlawed the Chinese Communist Party, making membership punishable by death. By April 1929, the party's rosters had dropped from 50,000 to 10,000. Meanwhile, although Chiang stressed modernization and nationalism in his rhetoric, he gave first priority to the big-business interests of his supporters both at home and abroad. He even punished non-Communists who had supported Sun Yat-sen.

By the mid-1930s, however, tensions between the two rival political camps had once again reached a boiling point. Although the Nationalists had succeeded in uniting the country, they lost some support as they continued to fight China's Communist rebels even after Japan invaded Manchuria in 1931 and threatened the country's security. That same year, the Communists hiding in the mountains of Kiangsi and Hunan gathered support among the peasants and proclaimed a Chinese Soviet Republic in Kiangsi with Mao Zedong established as chairman. By 1933, membership in China's Communist Party had swelled to more than 300,000, and Chiang Kai-shek had vowed to do everything possible to "stamp out the bandits."

Within a year, Nationalist forces had again gained the upper hand, trapping the Communist guerrillas with a western and southern blockade of Kiangsi Province. In a desperate and daring move, on October 16, 1934, the rebels broke through the line and began what is now known as the Long March. During this epochal event, Mao and his Red Army led more than 100,000 men, women, and children on foot over 6,000 miles of harsh terrain. Less than a quarter of the group survived the grueling trek across high mountains and raging rivers, but their courage and fortitude won the Poor People's Army the support of millions. The survivors of the journey settled around the city of Yan'an. At this time, Mao consolidated his power as leader of the revolution.

While Chiang's Nationalists tried to subdue the growing strength of Mao's Communists, both groups also fought their common enemy: the invading Japanese. Following World War I, Japan had taken over territory previously held by the Germans on Shantung Peninsula. Next, in 1931, Japan invaded Manchuria. Rather

Chinese revolutionary leader Sun Yat-sen, seen above with his wife, served as China's first president after the nation became a republic in 1911. (Hulton-Getty Archives)

Commemorative buttons showing Chinese leader Chiang Kai-shek, like the one above, were popular among Chinese Americans during World War II. (private collection)

A terrified Chinese infant cries amid the rubble of Shanghai, China, following Japan's decimation of that city. (National Archives)

than focus on the Japanese threat, however, Chiang's government continued to focus on combating Mao's Communists.

By 1936, anti-Japanese sentiment was so strong in China that Chiang Kai-shek's own generals kidnapped and forced him to join with the Communists to form a united front against Japanese imperialism in China. Japan countered with a massive invasion and soon conquered Nanking as well as Shanghai. Within another year, the Japanese controlled most of eastern China. Chiang kept a number of Japanese divisions at bay over the next few years. He resumed offensive attacks when the United States entered World War II in 1941.

CHINESE AMERICANS AND THE WAR EFFORT

The day after Japan's attack on Pearl Harbor, the United States and the People's Republic of China declared war on Japan, becoming allies against the common enemy. As a result, those who earlier had been looked down on now became recognized in America for their courage in battle and loyalty to the cause. Within a year after Pearl Harbor, President Franklin Roosevelt publicly praised Chiang Kai-shek and the Republic of China, remembering that "the Chinese people were the first to stand up and fight against the aggressors in this war."

When their draft notices started arriving, Chinese Americans responded. Military protocol specified that able-bodied men with no dependents would be the first drafted. Most Chinese men living in the United States had not started new families and therefore fit the criteria for first pick. Almost 40 percent of New York City's Chinese population were called in the first round of drafting. Some Chinese boys too young to serve tried lying about their ages in order to enlist. Altogether, nearly 13,500 Chinese males served in the U.S. armed forces during the war.

Chinese women and children also joined the war effort. They collected tin cans and tin foil scrap metal to be converted into military parts, learned first aid, drilled in civilian defense techniques, and joined groups like the Women's Army Auxiliary Corps (WAAC). Thousands donated money to help fight Japan. Dr. Margaret Chung, the first licensed Chinese-American physician, helped lead national fundraising drives and lobbied Congress for the creation of WAVES (Women Accepted for Voluntary Emergency Service), an auxiliary unit of the U.S. Navy.

Madame Chiang Kai-shek, the Nationalist leader's wife, also lobbied in the United

Dr. Margaret Chung, the first licensed Chinese-American physician, helped lead national fundraising drives and lobbied Congress for the creation of WAVES (Women Accepted for Voluntary Emergency Service), an auxiliary unit of the U.S. Navy. (National Archives)

The Chinese and U.S. militaries did their best to promote the alliance between the United States and China among the people of China. This Chinese leaflet issued in early 1945 reads, "This American pilot helped you to chase the Japanese out of the Chinese sky . . . but he and his Chinese colleagues need your help when they are hurt or lost or hungry." Such appeals were used to alert rural Chinese people to which nations were friendly to China. (Library of Congress)

States for money and legislative change. In the spring of 1942, Madame Chiang spoke in front of Congress for the repeal of America's immigration laws. The following year she visited San Francisco to successfully raise money for the Chinese war effort.

When the United States entered the global conflict, the Chinese living in America had reason to fear being mistaken for the enemy. *Time* magazine, in a tone typical of the time, featured a story dedicated to educating the average American on how to tell "friend from foe"—that is, how to distinguish between Chinese and Japanese people. The article and accompanying photographs detailed differences in body build, facial expressions, and walking movements. Thousands of Chinese took to wearing buttons that proclaimed "I Am Chinese," and many shopkeepers put up signs stating "This Is a Chinese Shop."

For the most, however, prejudice against the Chinese declined in America throughout the course of the war. Discriminatory legislation remained in force, but economic changes took place quickly. Fueled by the war, major defense industries opened the doors of opportunity to all Asian Americans, as well as to African Americans and women. Prior to the conflict's outbreak, the Chinese in America worked mainly in restaurants and laundries. During the war, defense industry jobs abounded from the shipyards of Washington, Delaware, and Mississippi to the airplane factories of New York's Long Island. By 1942, 300 Los Angeles laundry workers had closed their shops to construct the warship *China Victory*. Second-generation college-educated Chinese were hired to work in their chosen fields, and Chinese women found work opportunities that ranged from aircraft mechanic to office typist.

Nevertheless, the Chinese were not treated equally under the law. Koreans and Asian Indians joined the Chinese community in pressing for the repeal of the exclusion laws. Ironically, it was Japan that tipped the scales in their favor. In an effort to turn the vast complexities of World War II into a race war, Japan had called repeatedly for all of Asia to unite against white America. Reports broadcast by the Japanese into China told tales—based on truth, yet exaggerated—of the racist treatment of Asians by Americans in the United States. Congress saw the danger in Japan's "Asia for Asiatics" campaign and finally repealed the exclusion acts in 1943. A new law allowed for a quota of 105 Chinese to enter the United States annually and extended the right of

Chinese-American school children welcome Madame Chiang Kai-shek, the wife of the Chinese Nationalist leader, to San Francisco. (Library of Congress)

naturalized citizenship to Chinese immigrants who passed certain tests and possessed the right documents. All the same, only 1,428 Chinese became naturalized citizen between 1944 and 1952.

"I AM KOREAN"

Korea had been held under Japanese control since 1910. Koreans in America and abroad therefore hoped that World War II would end Japanese imperialism and Korea would finally gain independence. Until this occurred, however, Japan used the land and people of Korea as an arsenal and a food production factory throughout the war. Many Korean citizens were forced to work for the Japanese war effort in factories and on farms. Others were drafted and forced to fight in the Japanese armed forces.

In the United States, various Korean nationalist groups—active decades before Pearl Harbor was bombed—merged into the United Korean Committee and issued the Declaration of the All-Korean Convention, which pledged support of the Allied

powers. Just hours after the Pearl Harbor bombing, the Korean National Association of Los Angeles resolved to promote unity during the war, work for the defense of their country of residence, purchase war bonds, and volunteer as needed.

At the start of the war, the U.S. government classified Koreans as Japanese nationals because Korea was a Japanese possession. Koreans in America were therefore categorized as potential enemies of the state. To counter potential harassment, Koreans on the mainland started to wear miniature Korean flags on their shirt collars or badges that read "I Am Korean." Some also wore signs declaring "I'm No Jap!" Koreans employed in Hawaii's defense plants were especially insulted by their Japanese classification. When ordered to wear badges with black borders to signal their restricted-category status, they staged massive protests until they were finally granted the right to print "I Am Korean" on the emblems.

Many Korean nationalists suspected the Japanese, their long-standing enemy, of espionage against the United States. The Sino-Korean People's League, under

Madame Chiang Kai-shek on her visit to the United States (Library of Congress)

At the Yalta Conference in February 1945, U.S. president Franklin D. Roosevelt (center) and Soviet premier Josef Stalin (right) agreed to divide Korea into the two hostile nations of North Korea and South Korea. Seen with them is Winston Churchill, prime minister of Great Britain. (National Archives)

T. Z. SHIOTA
IMPORTER
ORIENTAL OBJECTS OF ART

Phone DOuglas 5791
515 GRANT AVENUE

MARCH TWENTY-SIXTH
1 9 4 2

Dear San Franciscans & Friend Customers:

Time has come for us to say,
"Au Revoir" after faithfully created the
world renown Chinatown by serving with
quality merchandise for 43 years.

To you, San Franciscans and
friend customers, the members of the
firm of T. Z. SHIOTA, wish to acknowledge
each and every one of you for your past
patronage and co-operation.

At this hour of evacuation when
the innocents suffer with the bad, we bid
you, dear friends of ours, with the words
of beloved Shakespeare, "PARTING IS SUCH
SWEET SORROW".

Till We Meet Again,

T. Z. SHIOTA

A letter in the shop window of T. Z. Shiota, a Japanese-American purveyor of Asian objets d'art in San Francisco's Chinatown, reads, in part, "At this hour of evacuation when the innocents suffer with the bad, we bid you, dear friends of ours, with the words of beloved Shakespeare, 'PARTING IS SUCH SWEET SORROW.'" Shiota, who had operated his shop for 43 years, had just received orders to evacuate his home and business. (National Archives)

the leadership of Kilsoo Haan, spread rumors of collusion between Hawaiian Japanese and the imperial government. In 1942, Haan pressed for the internment of all West Coast Japanese.

Since most Koreans spoke and wrote Japanese, they served a vital function during World War II. Koreans decoded classified documents, spread propaganda over the radio, and taught the Japanese language to others. They also served as underground agents in Japanese-occupied parts of Asia. On the home front, Koreans in Los Angeles formed the Tiger Brigade (Manghokun), a special unit of the state National Guard that comprised nearly one-fifth of Los Angeles's Korean population. Elderly Koreans of both sexes volunteered for the war effort, and between 1942 and 1943 alone, Koreans purchased $239,000 worth of war bonds—a very significant amount of money for a population of only 10,000.

As with the Filipinos and Chinese, white Americans began to treat Koreans with more respect in light of their war service and patriotism. Korean Americans' economic status also improved during the war years. Many bought farms vacated by interned Japanese. Legislatively, however, no progress was made on their behalf, and they remained technically classified as Japanese throughout the war. When World War II had ended, Hawaii's Joseph R. Farrington introduced a congressional bill that would grant naturalization rights to Koreans, but it did not pass.

To make matters worse, at the Yalta Conference the Soviet Union and the Unit-

ed States formed a partnership that led to Korea's postwar division into two hostile countries, North Korea and South Korea, which subsequently became controlled by the Soviet Union and the United States, respectively. The original aim had been to jointly govern the country to eventually achieve a united, independent Korea, but cold war tensions intervened, and the split set the stage for the Korean War in the early 1950s.

JAPANESE INTERNMENT

Inevitably, the surprise attack on Pearl Harbor stirred up America's long-simmering anti-Japanese bias. White America's fear of Japanese Americans' disloyalty resulted in an executive order that forced more than 110,000 Japanese Americans to leave their homes and move into relocation camps. The confinement of the Japanese, which violated both the U.S. Constitution and the U.S. legal system of due process, lasted for nearly three years and would prove to be a particularly black mark in the U.S. government's dubious history of race relations.

EXECUTIVE ORDER 9066

The fear of a Japanese invasion on the United States's West Coast after the bombing of Pearl Harbor was a realistic military concern. As a matter of course during wartime, governments implement emergency procedures to ensure national security. Thus, within a few hours of the Pearl Harbor attack, the local Hawaiian law enforcement authorities and the FBI began rounding up some 1,291 issei community leaders in Hawaii. Holding the issei without charge, law enforcement officials forbid them from even contacting their families.

The emergency incarceration did not stop there, however. Newspaper portrayals of the Japanese as "Jap" spies and disloyal "yellow vermin" perpetuated hysterical rumors, fanned fear, and increased prejudice toward the Japanese, especially on the mainland. Calls for the mass evacuation of all Japanese on the mainland grew in number and intensity.

Hearings on the matter of evacuation were to be held before the newly formed Select Committee Investigating National Defense Migration on February 22, 1942. President Franklin Roosevelt, however, signed a document known as Executive Order 9066 two days prior to the start of the hearings. Though no reference to Japanese Americans or native-born Japanese is made in the document, Executive Order 9066 served as the basis for America's wartime curfew and internment measures against the Japanese, as well against smaller numbers of Germans, Italians, and various Eastern Europeans.

Two-thirds of America's Japanese affected by Executive Order 9066 were U.S. citizens—second-generation Japanese born in the United States. The Japanese American Citizens League (JACL), the main nisei rights advocacy group, encouraged Japanese Americans to cooperate with the order. Though Executive Order 9066 clearly violated the civil liberties of the nisei, many felt that protest would only harm their cause, as prejudiced whites might view their resistance as a sign of disloyalty. The JACL also urged cooperation in order to reduce or, preferably, avoid possible bloodshed over the matter.

A new government agency, the War Relocation Authority (WRA) organized the forced internment. Nearly 70,000 of those held were U.S. citizens—second-generation Japanese born in the United States, or nisei. Those who resisted the relocation were sent to prison.

The lives of Japanese on the mainland were greatly altered by Executive Order 9066, but local leaders, politics, and economics allowed the issei and nisei of Hawaii to largely escape the experience of mass internment. Hawaii's military governor General Delos Emmons took a strong stand against the mass evacuation and internment of Hawaii's Japanese population. Many factors figured into his position, which he maintained throughout the war.

The first issue revolved around numbers. While the Japanese made up only 1 percent of America's mainland population, they composed 40 percent of Hawaii's population. A mass evacuation of that many people would impede crucial wartime transport, equipment, construction, and housing needs, leading to decimation of Hawaii's economy. General Emmons also repeatedly emphasized the civil rights violations involved in such a move. Hawaii's white population supported him and actively opposed mass internment. Consequently, only 1,444 out of about 158,000 Japanese Americans from Hawaii—979 aliens and 525 citizens—were deemed "dangerous" enough to be interned during the war.

Lieutenant General John L. DeWitt, head of the Western Defense Command on the mainland, behaved very differently from General Emmons. He was convinced that the presence of Japanese on the West

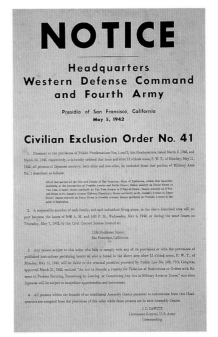

Executive Order 9066, which provided for the creation of "military areas . . . from which one and all persons may be excluded," did not specifically mention Japanese Americans but did open the door to forced relocation. It was followed on the West Coast by Civilian Exclusion Order No. 41, which specifically ordered Japanese Americans to leave their homes and report for relocation. (National Archives)

The Mochida family prepares for relocation to an internment camp. (National Archives)

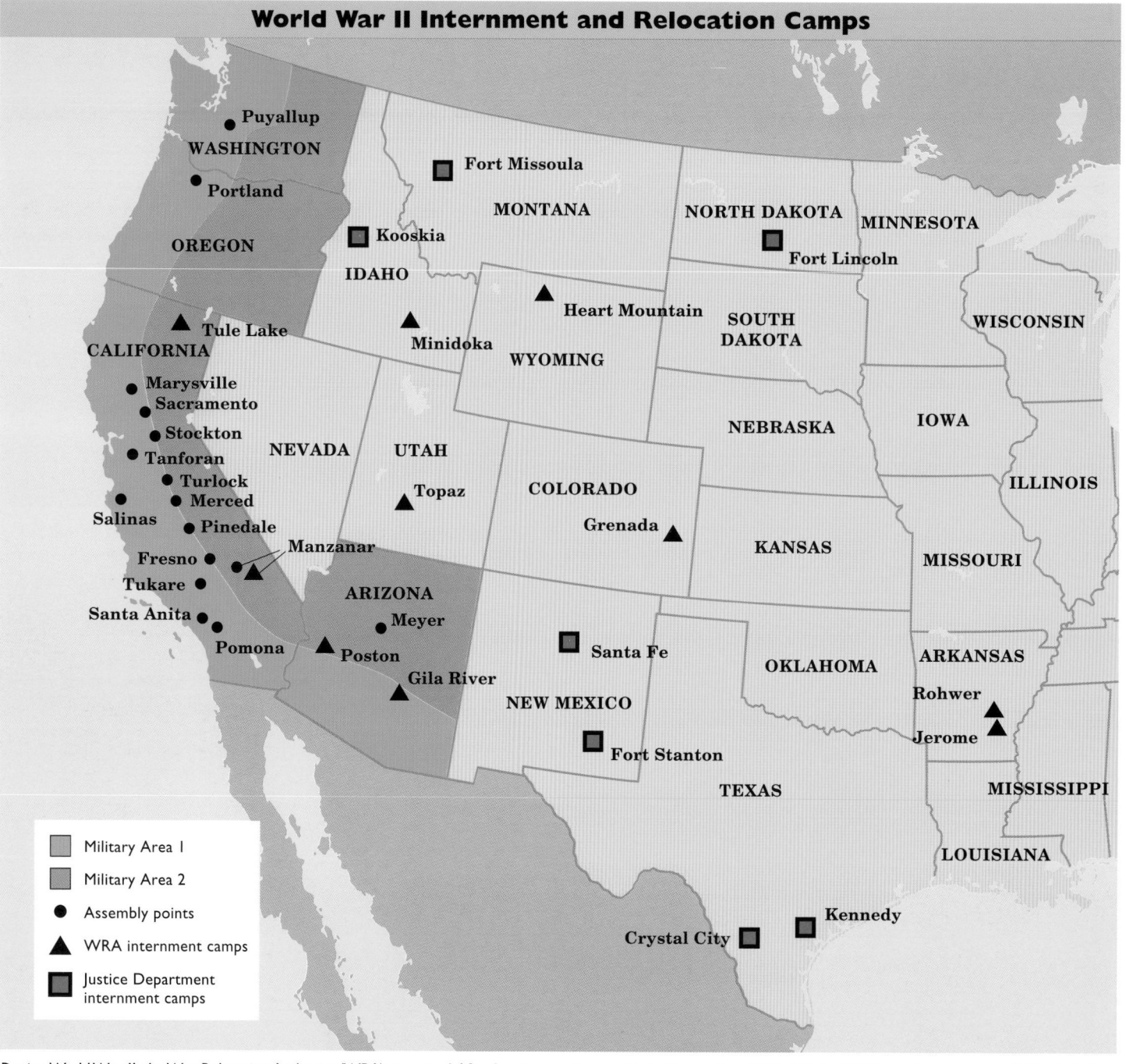

World War II Internment and Relocation Camps

Legend:
- Military Area 1
- Military Area 2
- ● Assembly points
- ▲ WRA internment camps
- ■ Justice Department internment camps

During World War II, the War Relocation Authority (WRA) managed 10 relocation camps, mostly in the western United States. WRA camps were occupied exlusively by Japanese Americans relocated from their homes on the West Coast, which the U.S. military declared Military Area 1 following the attack on Pearl Harbor. (The military named the eastern portions of Washington, Oregon, and California, and the northern portion of Arizona Military Area 2.) Japanese Americans living in this district were ordered to report to their nearest assembly point for transport to a "relocation center" operated by the WRA. The U.S. Department of Justice ran a second set of camps, referred to as internment camps. These camps housed those "enemy aliens" who were suspected by the FBI as posing a danger to the United States. While the vast majority of internees were Japanese issei, some were German, Italian, or Eastern European.

Coast threatened national security, though no evidence to support this contention had ever been presented. The social climate of the American West also differed vastly from that of Hawaii. *Time* magazine and newspapers such as the *San Diego Union*, the *Los Angeles Times*, and the Hearst syndicates helped circulate anti-Japanese rumors, and editorial writers called for mass evacuations. Patriotic groups such as the Native Sons and Daughters of the Golden West and various state American Legions, as well as certain farming associations, also joined the demand for internment. Encouraged by the pervasive anti-Japanese mentality, therefore, General DeWitt pushed through a quick and forceful program that involved house-to-house searches without warrants and the confiscation of weapons and cameras.

General DeWitt's Proclamation Number 1, announced on March 2, 1942, designated California, Washington, Oregon, and

TYPICAL INTERNMENT CAMP LAYOUT

When Japanese Americans arrived in internment camps in May and June of 1942, they found that the U.S. Army had used construction plans for housing unmarried army recruits. Thus, as many as four to six families were forced to crowd into long army barracks, with simple partitions to separate each family's living space of little more than 20 by 20 feet. Most of the camps included primitive recreational, social, and health facilities, but overcrowding, poor food that usually did not include staples of the Japanese-American diet such as fresh vegetables and fruit, and long lines for virtually everything were commonplace. Internees persevered by trying to focus on the future. Many referred to their stays as "vacations."

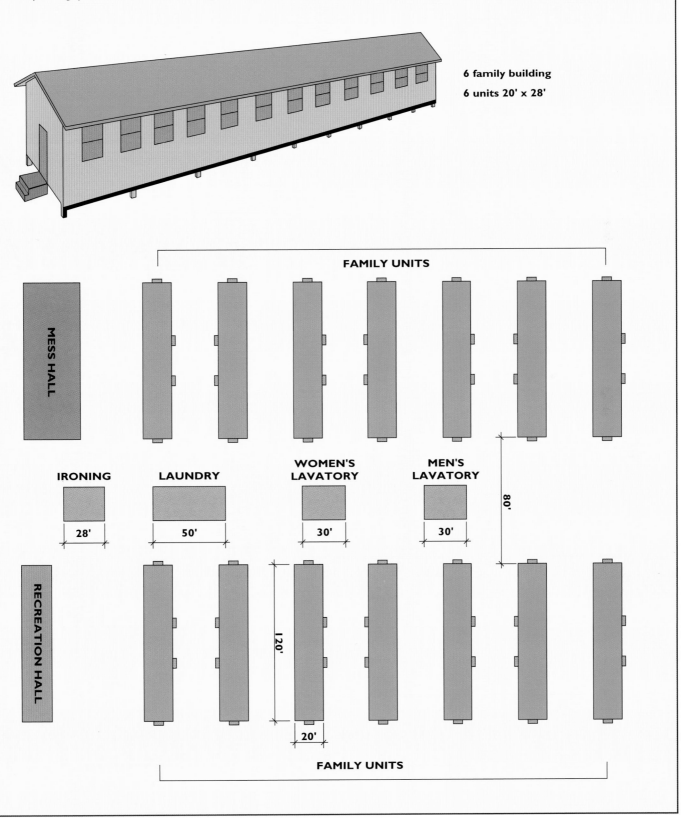

6 family building
6 units 20' x 28'

FAMILY UNITS

MESS HALL

IRONING — 28'
LAUNDRY — 50'
WOMEN'S LAVATORY — 30'
MEN'S LAVATORY — 30'

80'

RECREATION HALL

120'

20'

FAMILY UNITS

On the night of December 5, 1942, at Camp Manzanar (shown above) in California, Fred Tayama, a leader of the Japanese American Citizens League (JACL), was beaten by six men. Tayama identified one of his assailants as Harry Ueno, a vocal critic of the JACL. When Ueno was taken to a nearby county jail, a crowd of protesters gathered to demand his release and to read aloud a list of suspected inu, or informants. In response, camp guards fired on the crowd, killing two. (National Archives)

Arizona as Military Areas 1 and 2, with the land in Area 1 being the most likely site of an enemy launch of attack. (General DeWitt devised a further complicated land division under the heading Proclamation Number 2, but even the War Department thought it was too extreme to release to the public.) After President Roosevelt granted him the military power to govern the designated zones three weeks later, General DeWitt issued Proclamation Number 3. This measure created a curfew system that applied to all residents of Japanese ancestry and "enemy" aliens. DeWitt ordered the Japanese to stay indoors between 8 P.M. and 6 A.M. and restricted daytime travel to a five-mile radius around the home, excluding travel to and from work. Proclamation Number 4 soon followed, upon which movement out of Military Area 1 became restricted.

The first Japanese Americans to be moved by the WRA lived in Washington State. DeWitt's armed soldiers escorted 54 families to California's Manzanar Reloca-tion Camp via train. DeWitt's rigid system subsequently completed the forced evacuation of 120,000 Japanese in less than six months. The WRA created 10 camps in all: California's Manzanar and Tule Lake, Heart Mountain in Wyoming, the Topaz in Utah, Poston and Gila River in Arizona, Jerome and Rohwer in Arkansas, Grenada in Colorado, and Mindoka in Idaho.

LIFE IN THE CAMPS

Once the decision to intern the Japanese had been made, the WRA gave families only a few days to sell or safeguard their possessions, businesses, and farms before reporting to designated control centers. Notices posted onto telephone poles instructed the Japanese on where to report for processing. The signs recommended that each individual bring clothes, bedding, and toilet articles.

At the control centers, each family was registered and given a number, such as

"Family 16754." Issei and nisei, young and old, were then crowded into assembly centers located at fairgrounds, stockyards, racetracks, or stables. The dirty and noisy assembly centers featured long lines, patrol guards, roll calls, and curfews. After a brief stay at the assembly center, the Japanese families packed onto special WRA trains bound for the camps. At this point, none of the Japanese Americans knew where their families' final destination might be.

The 10 internment camps were basically the same in routine and design. Each camp barracks consisted of four to six rooms, each measuring no more than 20 feet by 28 feet. An entire family lived in a single room, furnished with a pot-bellied stove, a single electric light, and an army cot for each family member to sleep on. Barbed wire and guard towers framed each camp.

All awoke to the sound of a siren blast at 7 A.M. Families were not allowed to eat together and spent most of the day separated from one another. Children went to school after breakfast, beginning each day with the song "My Country 'Tis of Thee." Most of the adults housed in the camp worked for the government at wages of $12 to $19 per month—a harsh adjustment for the thousands of Japanese entrepreneurs whose self-reliance and independence had enabled them to succeed in America in the first place.

Days spent in the desert heat proved long and boring; incarceration was demoralizing and the injustice of imprisonment was emotionally draining. Most evacuees, however, tried to maintain some sense of normalcy, scheduling recreational events such as dances and athletic contests. The phrase *"shi-ka-ta-ga nai"* (it can't be helped) framed the pattern of their adjustment, but the open-endedness of the length of stay wore down even the most accepting personalities. Young families became especially worried about the fate of babies born within the camps. Many nisei and sansei (third-generation Japanese-American) babies entered the world imprisoned, for the majority of inmates remained interned for the duration of the war.

THE LOYALTY QUESTIONS

Despite the federal government's program of internment and anti-Japanese hysteria before and during the war years, the War Department and the WRA came to realize that most Japanese Americans in internment camps were in fact loyal to the United States. The moral pressure of America's obligation to put democratic ideals into practice pushed Roosevelt to open the draft to all eligible U.S.-born Japanese-American citizens. In order to accomplish this, the WRA and the War Department launched a joint program to separate the "loyal" internees from those classified as "disloyal." The War Department therefore created a voluntary questionnaire entitled "Statement of Japanese Ancestry." Two "loyalty questions," numbers 27 and 28, were written into the form with the intent of weeding out the "disloyals" from the rest of the group. Question 27 read: "Are you willing to serve in the armed forces of the United States on combat duty, wherever ordered?" Question 28 asked: "Will you swear unqualified allegiance to the United States of America and faithfully defend the United States from any or all attack by foreign or domestic forces, and forswear any form of allegiance or obedience to the Japanese Emperor, or any other foreign government, power or organization?" Only nisei Japanese Americans of draft age who agreed to it were asked to fill out the document.

The WRA, on the other hand, hastily created a questionnaire entitled "Application for Leave Clearance" that all internees were required to complete. The questionnaire posed enormous problems—primarily because of its poorly adapted wording of the War Department's loyalty questions. For example, question 27 asked internees if they would be willing to volunteer for women's military organizations such as the Army Nurse Corps or Women's Army Auxiliary Corps. It was impossible for many Japanese-Americans to know how to answer the question correctly, since most men of that or any era would never join a women's military group. Yet any negative answer to question 27 spelled disloyalty to the United States in the eyes of the WRA bureaucrats.

Thus, a program intended to reward those loyal to America often resulted in their punishment. Thousands of law-abiding Japanese Americans earned the brand of "disloyal" based on their answers to two confusing and poorly worded questions. Those who answered one or both loyalty questions negatively, or refused to answer at all, were sent to a special facility for "disloyals" known as the Tule Lake Segregation Center.

UNREST AT TULE LAKE

While many Japanese Americans at all relocation camps were offended, angered, or confused by the loyalty questions, opposition to the questions was strongest at the Tule Lake

Many Japanese Americans, interned to prevent anti-U.S. spying or sabotage, had sons serving in the U.S. armed services during their internment. (National Archives)

Relocation Center in California. Among the American public at large, however, the news that large numbers of Japanese in the United States had refused to declare their loyalty to the nation in time of war was greeted with anger. In response, the WRA decided in July 1943 to convert that center into a special facility in which to hold those considered "disloyal" to the United States based on their responses, or lack thereof, to the loyalty questions. Among the "disloyal" were 7,222 people who had applied for repatriation to Japan; 4,785 people who had either refused to answer the loyalty questions or had answered negatively; those denied clearance to leave their relocation centers for any reason; aliens paroled from Justice Department internment camps who were recommended for further detention; and anyone else in any center that was believed to be a troublemaker. Added to this mix were family members of all of the above, as well as about 6,000 residents of the former Tule Lake Relocation Center who decided to stay where they were rather than being forced to pick up and move again. Thus, when in September 1943, "disloyal" Japanese Americans from other camps began arriving at Tule Lake, the WRA had unwittingly created a volatile camp population in which the residents held widely divergent levels of "loyalty" and "disloyalty" to the United States.

Conflict began almost immediately. On November 26, 1943, the camp administration arrested members of the Daiyho Sha Kai, a group elected to represent the camp population, and then declared martial law Some of those arrested are beaten with rubber hoses. Other leaders went into hiding, only to have camp guards conduct 24-hour searches for 12 days, leading to the arrest of another 450 internees, often on little pretext. Martial law finally ended at Tule Lake in May 1944, when the U.S. State Department investigated the situation.

THE 442ND REGIMENTAL COMBAT TEAM

Despite all the problems created by the "loyalty questions," the U.S. military did finally admit nisei Japanese for service. In addition to opening the draft to American-born Japanese, the War Department also succeeded in creating a segregated regiment. The 442nd Regimental Combat Team went on to serve with distinction and honor throughout the war.

Many Japanese Americans in Hawaii—including more than 2,000 nisei already enlisted in the U.S. Army—had participated in the defense of Pearl Harbor on December 7. Throughout the day, Japanese civilians lined up to donate blood to help the wounded. Later that night, members of the Hawaii Territorial Guard, a group composed of thousands of high school and college-aged nisei youth, guarded key locations on the waterfronts as well as power plants and water reservoirs.

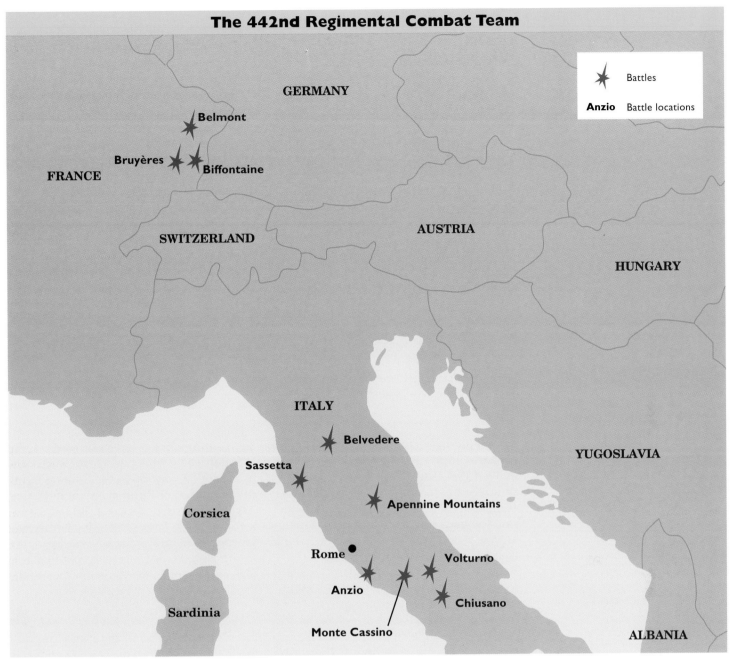

The 442nd Regimental Combat Team

✶	Battles
Anzio	Battle locations

GERMANY

Belmont

Bruyères   Biffontaine

FRANCE

SWITZERLAND

AUSTRIA

HUNGARY

ITALY

Belvedere

Sassetta

YUGOSLAVIA

Corsica

Apennine Mountains

Rome

Volturno

Anzio

Sardinia

Chiusano

Monte Cassino

ALBANIA

Perhaps no group of Americans sacrificed more during World War II than the Japanese Americans who served in the all-nisei 100th Battalion, 442nd Regimental Combat Team. This unit, which included a number of soldiers whose own parents, wives, and children had been interned back home as security risks, saw action in Italy and southern France in 1944 and 1945. Rallying behind a Hawaiian dice-game call, "Go for Broke!," the 100th/442nd became the most highly decorated U.S. military unit of its size during the entire war.

Nevertheless, fear and distrust of Japanese Americans put some 4,000 nisei soldiers into limbo. Though inducted before the bombing of Pearl Harbor, the soldiers were afterward excluded from active duty. Japanese-American citizens classified as "IV-C" could not be drafted or accepted as volunteers because of their Japanese ancestry. Many nisei sought to prove their loyalty to the United States through military service and fought to change the IV-C classification ruling. Though pressure from various Japanese civil rights associations remained consistent on this point, the change, when it finally came, was sparked mostly by Amer-

ica's desire to improve its image abroad. The Japanese propaganda machine was continually broadcasting exaggerated tales of discrimination faced by Asians in America. The United States found it difficult to present itself as one of the leaders of democracy while discriminating against nisei soldiers who wanted to fight.

In January 1943, Hawaii's General Emmons asked for 1,500 nisei to volunteer for military service. His office was immediately swamped with 9,507 ready and willing applicants. More than 2,600 were inducted. Many of that group traveled to Camp Shelby, Mississippi, where they embarked on 10

General Mark Clark reviews the men of the 100th Battalion, 442nd Regimental Combat Team. (Library of Congress)

You fought for the free nations of the world along with the rest of us.... You fought not only the enemy, but you fought prejudice and you won. Keep up that fight, and we will continue to win to make this great republic stand for what the Constitution says it stands for: "The welfare of all the people all the time."

The influence of the 442nd Regimental Combat Team extended beyond the war years. Lobbyists wanting to overturn discriminatory legislation such as the alien land laws cited the unit's heroism to support their arguments for fair treatment. In Hawaii, veterans of the 442nd became involved in the rise of the ILWU and the Democratic Party. In the 1980s, key legislation of the internment redress movement passed under the name "H.R. 442" in honor of the veterans' service.

JAPANESE-AMERICAN INTERNMENT AND THE SUPREME COURT

months of basic training with 800 nisei inductees from the mainland. The recruits fulfilled President Roosevelt's order for an all-nisei unit, forming the 100th Battalion, 442nd Regimental Combat Team. Their slogan, the gambling phrase "Go for Broke!" expressed to the world the fervor behind their intent.

While many of these soldiers' parents, wives, and children languished in internment camps, the members of the 442nd fought the Axis powers around the world, particularly on the front lines of Italy and in the air invasion of Germany. Their most heroic duty took place in France during the Rhineland campaign in the fall of 1944. In the face of heavy Nazi opposition, the 442nd liberated the towns of Bruyères, Belmont, and Biffontaine. Their daring rescue of America's "Lost Battalion" from behind enemy lines has become legendary; their action saved 211 soldiers, most of them Texans, at the cost of 800 nisei casualties.

In recognition of their skill and courage, the 100th/442nd became the most highly decorated U.S. military regiment of the entire war. The unit's 18,143 decorations included 3,600 Purple Hearts, 47 Distinguished Service Crosses, 350 Silver Stars, 810 Bronze Stars, three Presidential Unit Citations, and one Congressional Medal of Honor. When they were honored at the White House on July 15, 1946, President Harry Truman told the men:

Four separate cases regarding the internment of America's Japanese reached the U.S. Supreme Court during the war years. In each of the four cases, the Court avoided ruling on the constitutionality of detaining Americans based on race. In all cases, including *Ex Parte Endo,* in which the Japanese-American plaintiff was freed, the Court issued very narrowly defined rulings, leaving open the larger question of the legality of internment based on race.

Yasui v. United States came before the Supreme Court in 1943. Minoru Yasui tried to voluntarily enlist in the U.S. Army following the bombing of Pearl Harbor. He was rejected on racial grounds. After the federal government forced his father into an internment camp, Yasui, an American lawyer, challenged General DeWitt's curfew law. He purposefully sought arrest and was taken to trial for violating the curfew. A lower court ruled that the curfew law was unconstitutional when applied to American citizens but deemed that this did not apply to Yasui as an individual because he had forfeited his citizenship by working for the Japanese consulate earlier in Chicago.

The Supreme Court reversed the ruling, rejecting the proposition that Yasui had relinquished his citizenship. The Court proclaimed the curfew constitutional, however, and sent the case back to a lower court for resentencing. Minoru served nine months in prison.

The case of *Hirabayashi v. United States* also came before the high court in 1943.

The heroism shown by members of the 442nd Regimental Combat Team help reshape the popular perception of Japanese Americans in the eyes of the white majority. The unit was awarded more medals per capita than any other unit that served in World War II, and it suffered enormous casualties. Above, mothers of nisei killed in battle are awarded their sons' medals. (Library of Congress)

Gordon Hirabayashi, a 24-year-old student at the University of Washington, challenged the evacuation order. While he was imprisoned, authorities read his personal journal and found that Hirabayashi had also purposefully violated the curfew orders. They therefore charged him with that crime as well. The jury of a lower court found Hirabayashi guilty on both counts. He spent 90 days in jail.

The Supreme Court avoided ruling on the legality of evacuation in *Hirabayashi v. United States*. However, the Court ruled unanimously that Congress had the right to make and enforce curfew laws, as per the congressional mandate to "repel invasions" prescribed by Article I, Section 8 of the U.S. Constitution.

In the 1944 case of *Korematsu v. United States*, the Supreme Court finally ruled specifically on the legality of the evacuation order. After the Pearl Harbor bombing, Fred Toysaburo Korematsu lost his job as a welder because the Boiler Makers Union had expelled all Japanese-American members. He decided to marry his Italian-American fiancée and move to the Midwest to start over, but Korematsu felt that the harassment they would face as an interracial couple would be too hard to bear. His solution was to disguise his race from the world through plastic surgery. Despite his claim of Spanish-Hawaiian ancestry, authorities arrested him for violating a law that banned Japanese Americans from relocating without permission of the U.S. Army. A lower court found him guilty and passed a sentence of five years' probation. A military police officer then forced him at gunpoint to join his family at the Tanforan Assembly Center. The Supreme Court subsequently upheld Korematsu's conviction by a six-to-three vote. The grounds for the decision were the idea that the evacuation order was made out of "military necessity."

The case of *Ex Parte Endo* began in 1942, when the Japanese American Citizens League (JACL) hired a lawyer to oppose the firing of California's Japanese-American employees. The state had fired the workers on the grounds that they posed threats to U.S. security. The JACL also decided to challenge the legality of racial detention and toward that end brought suit against

Milton Eisenhower, the director of the federal WRA.

The case was brought in the name of Mitsuye Endo, a former employee of the California Department of Motor Vehicles. As a second-generation Japanese American, Endo was born into citizenship. She did not speak Japanese; she had never been to Japan; she had a brother in the U.S. Army; she had obeyed all laws passed in wartime; and she had been raised a Methodist. Eisenhower was asked to show why Endo was being detained, since she clearly did not pose a security threat. The government took the position that since Endo had not complied with a WRA leave program structured around the loyalty questions, she had no case. However, in 1944, the day before the court's ruling was to be handed down, federal officials announced that detainees not considered "disloyal," like Endo, were free to leave internment. On December 19, 1944, the Supreme Court ruled unanimously that is was unlawful to detain a law-abiding citizen and ordered Endo's release. As the Court stated:

A citizen who is concededly loyal presents no problem of espionage or sabotage. Loyalty is a matter of the heart and mind, not of race, creed or color. He who is loyal is by definition not a spy or saboteur.

Mitsuye Endo won her case, but once again the Supreme Court did not address the central question of the constitutionality of detainment by race. The Court's reluctance to address this question in all four cases underscored the depth of America's institutional racism.

The Japanese-American internees were finally released on January 2, 1945. Some were ultimately able to reclaim their former property. For example, the three Yamato Colonies in California had banded together, formed a corporation, and hired a white administrator to continue operations during the period that Japanese Americans were interned. Such foresight allowed the colonies to survive; after World War II, nisei generation farmers worked to reclaim colony land, finally uniting in 1956 in the Livingston Farmers Association. However, many internees had lost their farms, homes, possessions, and businesses and had to begin all over again. Most returned to the West Coast to rebuild their lives and communities. Some of the 35,000 nisei who had been cleared by the government for earlier release in 1943 rejoined their families on West Coast after the closing of the internment camps.

Several decades later, America's Japanese community finally succeeded in obtaining redress for their imprisonment during the war. The Commission on Wartime Relocation and Internment of Civilians, created by Congress in 1980, ruled that the internment of Japanese Americans had been unjust and that monetary compensation was due to the families who had suffered. The government issued a formal apology in 1988 and awarded those who had been incarcerated in the camps $20,000 each. (The apology did not include the thousands of German, Italian, Bulgarian, Czechoslovakian, Hungarian, or Romanian immigrants who were also detained in American camps during the war.) Though Asian Americans had made economic and social gains during the war years, and so many had distinguished themselves in battle, legislative change to protect their rights and improve immigrants' eligibility for citizenship still proved slow in coming.

FROM RED SCARE TO YELLOW POWER
Asian-American History from 1946 to 1972

Although Asian Americans—especially the Japanese of the 442nd Battalion—had distinguished themselves during the Second World War, and the country's Caucasian majority had largely begun to exercise more objectivity in their treatment of their Asian neighbors, perceptions of loyalty nevertheless remained an issue for some time following the war's end. This was particularly true for Chinese Americans as the cold war got under way. In the aftermath of the Communist takeover of China, they were no longer regarded as allies but as possible spies and were therefore viewed with suspicion and distrust.

On the other hand, for many Asian-American groups, the 1950s and 1960s became a period of stability despite the turmoil of the cold war. Like American society at large, these groups were experiencing a baby boom, and the new generation benefited from increased educational and job opportunities; consequently, they worked harder for greater academic and social achievement. Hawaii finally achieved statehood during this period, becoming the first state to elect a nonwhite governor. And in the late 1960s, a new youth activism, proclaimed under the banner Yellow Power, flowered throughout the mainland Asian community.

AFTER INTERNMENT

The internment camps of World War II, created due to American fears of espionage and disloyalty, altered the lives of 120,000 Japanese Americans. Yet none of those interned—not even those individuals identified as "dangerous" in December 1941—was ever formally charged or found guilty of an act of disloyalty against the federal government. The War Department finally rescinded its evacuation order on December 16, 1944, a day before the Supreme Court ruling in *Ex Parte Endo* (discussed in chapter 4) announced that all detainees not considered "disloyal" should be released. The War Department subsequently declared that all internees would be freed after January 2, 1945. By March 1945, all Japanese Americans had relocated, and the camps were closed.

Thousands of second-generation Japanese students and laborers, however, had already won part or all of their freedom from the War Relocation Authority (WRA) through an early release program. Nearly 35,000 of these nisei had left the camps by 1943. Between 1942 and 1946, 4,084 students met the stringent criteria for release and resettled in America's interior states or eastern coastal regions. The release process included an FBI security check and required proof of acceptance at an approved college and sworn testimony as to each student's character and loyalty as a U.S. citizen. Females composed an estimated 40 percent of all students released.

During the war, the WRA had also allowed nisei to work in defense-related industries and seasonally in the farm fields. The labor shortage caused by the global conflict carried a special benefit for all American women, including nisei Japanese, as job opportunities opened up in both blue collar and white collar industry segments. Japanese-American women had long been relegated to work as domestic servants, but by 1950, 47 percent of all Japanese-American women occupied jobs as secretaries, factory workers, and sales representatives.

Chicago became a popular destination for nisei freed in the early release program. Major cities in New York, Minnesota, Michigan, Idaho, Utah, Ohio, and Colorado attracted thousands looking for work and educational opportunities. After the demise of the internment system, many moved back to California and other states along the West Coast to join their newly freed families and try to rebuild the lives and businesses that had been snatched away from them.

After the war, the nearly 50,000 returning internees were surprised to encounter the same level of racism they had endured before the war. Although discriminatory attitudes against the Japanese had eased nationally, the tenor of anti-Asian feeling held by West Coast whites had changed little. Families returned to signs and comments of "No Japs Allowed" and "No Japs Welcome." Even Captain (later Senator) Daniel K. Inouye, who had lost his right arm fighting on the Allied side, was snubbed by a San Francisco barber who proclaimed to the soldier's face: "We don't serve Japs here." The weight of the comment was especially heavy, as Captain Inouye had been wearing his highly decorated U.S. Army dress jacket at the time.

Returning issei and nisei were also shocked to discover ruin where just a few years earlier there had been plenty. In their absence, family farms and businesses had met with vandalism, fire, theft, and neglect. Some financial institutions had even frozen bank accounts. Although urged by the Japanese American Citizens League (JACL) to offer more assistance to released internees, the WRA provided only transportation home and $50 cash per family. Elderly issei and their families thus found themselves in the position of having to start all over again, as if they had just arrived from across the sea.

Financial losses sustained by internees reached $400 million by some estimates. The greatest loss, especially for the nisei, came in terms of land. Upon receiving the evacuation order in 1942, thousands of Japanese Americans had been forced to sell their land for whatever price they could find. What is more, during the internment period, the California government used the Alien Land Act of 1920 as pretext for seizing property from Japanese Americans. Because that law prevented Japanese-born issei from buying property in the names of their U.S.-born nisei children, (who were U.S. citizens by merit of having been born in the United States), the state seized thousands of acres of property, asserting that such nisei-owned lands violated the law. By 1946, more than 60 Japanese families had had their lands confiscated in this manner.

The Oyama family of San Diego took their case against the land seizure practice all the way to the Supreme Court, in the process challenging the 1913 and 1920 California Alien Land Laws. Fred Oyama's issei parents, Kajiro and Kohide, had been labeled as "aliens ineligible to citizenship." Therefore, when the couple bought six acres of land, they registered the title in their son's name. In 1935, the Superior Court of San Diego County granted the elder Mr. Oyama guardianship of his son's estate. Two years later, the Oyamas purchased two more acres, again in Fred's name. When Executive Order 9066 proclaimed the military-governed evacuation of Japanese Americans, the Oyamas were forced to abandon their land in 1942. Two years later, the state of California declared an escheat (confiscation) of the property, arguing that registering the title in the son's name violated the Alien Land Laws. In a 1946 ruling, the state supreme court upheld the escheat action. The Oyamas then appealed at the federal level.

On January 19, 1948, the Supreme Court of the United States reversed the state court's ruling by a six-to-three margin, declaring the Alien Land Laws of California to be ". . . nothing more than outright racial discrimination . . . [based] on the fact that Fred Oyama's father was Japanese and not American, Russian, Chinese, or English." The court then cited the 14th Amendment to the U.S. Constitution, which transferred the protection of individual liberties from the states to the federal government and granted citizenship rights to freed African-American slaves after the Civil War. Supreme Court Justice Hugo Black pushed the point even further with a significant and timely reminder that the United States had only recently agreed ". . . to cooperate with the United Nations to 'promote universal respect for, and observance of, human rights and fundamental freedoms for all without distinction as to race, sex, language, or religion.'" Justice Black then went on to ask, "How can this nation be faithful to this international pledge if state laws which bar land ownership and occupancy by aliens on account of race are permitted to be enforced?"

The decision in favor of the Oyama family set an important precedent for the protection of individual liberties and helped pave the way for debates and rulings in other landmark court cases of the civil rights era, such as *Brown v. Board of Education*, a 1954 school desegregation case. The Oyama ruling also made possible other successful legal attacks on California's Alien Land Laws. In both *Fujii Sei v. State of California* and *Masaoka v. State of California*, the California Supreme Court ruled that state laws could not deny land ownership to first-generation Japanese immigrants labeled "aliens ineligible to citizenship."

Another important piece of legislation for former internees was the Evacuation Claims Act of 1948, which had been spearheaded by the JACL. Passed on July 2, 1948, the act was intended to compensate Japanese Americans for financial losses sustained during their forced confinement in the internment camps. It fell far short of its goal, however, as many restrictions hampered the measure's effectiveness. Claimants first encountered a payment lid of $2,500. Those seeking damages in excess of that amount—some 40 percent of the internment victims—were required to petition for special appropriations from Congress, which meant long time delays. Such

IMPORTANT COURT DECISIONS IN ASIAN-AMERICAN HISTORY, 1948–1967

Year/Case	Background	Outcome
1948 *Oyama v. State of California*	In 1935, the Superior Court of San Diego agreed to allow Kajiro Oyama, a Japanese-born immigrant, to become guardian of his U.S.-born son Fred's estate. The elder Oyama had purchased six acres of farmland in the name of his young son and in 1937 purchased two more acres the same way. In 1942, the Oyamas were forced from their home and into an internment camp. Two years later, the California government declared an escheat on the property (a legal term referring to the reversion of property to the state in the absence of legal heirs) and in 1946 the California Supreme Court upheld the state's action. The state argued that the elder Oyama had purchased the land with the intent to violate California's Alien Land Act.	The U.S. Supreme Court ruled that the section of California's Alien Land Act that allowed for escheat actions was in violation of the equal protection clause of the 14th Amendment to the U.S. Constitution. The Court ruled that the law discriminated against minors whose parents happened to be ineligible for citizenship.
1948 *Shelly v. Kraemer*	This case centered around two instances in which African Americans had been denied occupancy of housing on the basis of race. One instance involved a 1911 agreement signed by property owners in a St. Louis, Missouri, neighborhood forbidding the occupancy of the property "by people of the Negro or Mongolian Race." A second, similar case involved the contested sale of a property in Detroit, Michigan, to African Americans. Because the St. Louis case specified the "Mongolian race," the case was significant for Asian Americans as well as African Americans.	Specifically citing its *Oyama v. State of California* decision from earlier in the same year, the Court ruled that the enforcement by the government of restrictive housing agreements violated the equal protection clause of the 14th Amendment, thus setting a legal precedent against Asian-American discrimination.
1948 *Takahashi v. California Fish and Game Commission*	In 1943, while Japanese Americans were being held in internment camps, the state of California passed a law that denied Japanese aliens the right to obtain fishing licenses. In response, Torao Takahashi, an issei who had been in the commerical fishing business for 21 years, sued. Although a Los Angeles court sided with him, the California Supreme Court reversed the decision.	Finding that Takahashi had been denied his license solely because he was Japanese, the U.S. Supreme Court again used the equal protection clause of the 14th Amendment to overturn this descriminatory law.
1952 *Fujii Sei v. State of California*	When Fujii Sei, an issei newspaper publisher, purchased land in his own name in violation of California's Alien Land Act, the state attempted an escheat action, as it had in *Oyama v. State of California*. With backing from a superior court, Fujii appealed to the California Supreme Court.	The California Supreme Court struck down the Alien Land Act on the basis that it violated the equal protection clause of the 14th Amendment.
1954 *Brown v. Board of Education*	When Linda Brown, an African American, was turned away from an all-white school in Topeka, Kansas, her father challenged the action in court.	The U.S. Supreme Court ruled that the doctrine of "separate but equal," used to justify racial segregation in public schools and other public facilities, was unconstitutional. The Court's reasoning was again based on the equal protection clause of the 14th Amendment. Although the specific case involved African Americans, the ruling extended to all racial segregation, including that involving Asian Americans.
1967 *Loving v. Virginia*	When Mildred Jeter and Richard Loving, an interracial couple, were found guilty of violating Virginia laws forbidding miscegenation (interracial marriage), their case was appealed to the U.S. Supreme Court. Among those filing arguments in favor of overturning the Virginia statute were lawyers for the Japanese American Citizens League.	The U.S. Supreme Court ruled that laws against interracial marriage violated the 14th Amendment's equal protection clause and its due process clause. The Court argued that because "the freedom to marry [is] one of the vital personal rights essential to the orderly pursuit of happiness by free men, to deny this ... freedom deprive[s] all the State's citizens of liberty without due process of law."

lags between promise and delivery of restitution made it especially difficult for elderly, destitute, or ailing issei to carry on. In addition, those seeking monetary compensation from the U.S. government were asked to produce proper documentation and witness testimony. Many internment victims found it difficult to produce the necessary papers, as the evacuation process had been conducted in haste during a chaotic time.

By 1950, more than 22,000 claims had been filed. However, the federal government had processed only 211; of those, only 137 Japanese Americans received cash payments. Furthermore many of those claimants received far less than $2,500; the average payment tallied at $450. Government bureaucracy subsequently became so entangled that the final claims were not processed until 1965. Survivors of the internment system and their families would have to wait until 1988 for a public apology and until 1990 to receive a substantial monetary payment as compensation for the years of suffering they endured.

A REVOLUTION IN CHINA

Mao Zedong's Communist triumph in China's civil war in 1949 transformed the political, economic, philosophical, and social structures of one of the world's most ancient civilizations. Hundreds of thousands of poor and struggling Chinese peasants supported and participated in the Communist Revolution, perceiving it as a means to the radical reform necessary to modernize their nation. Others, especially those living comfortably under Chiang Kai-shek's Kuomintang (Nationalist) regime, worried that Mao's Red Army would usher in an era of ruthless oppression. Repercussions from the dramatic ideological shift in China reverberated across the globe and throughout U.S. Chinese communities as well.

MAO'S VICTORY

Following the Second World War, the Chinese civil war between Nationalist and Communist forces increased in intensity, until Chiang was forced to flee with his supporters to the island of Formosa (now Taiwan). On October 1, 1949, Mao announced the formation of the People's Republic of China. The Chinese Communist Party had emerged victorious after 22 years of bloody guerrilla warfare. Some Nationalists switched sides, while others joined Chiang in Taiwan, where he created the Republic of China and ruled until his death in 1975.

Mao's victory in China affected the geopolitical balance of power on a global scale. The rise of communism in China alongside the Communist-controlled Soviet Union put the capitalist powers of the West into an adversarial position, thus heightening the cold war, an era of high tension between the United States and the Soviet Union.

THE CHINESE-AMERICAN RESPONSE

The reaction to Mao's Communist takeover of China varied among America's Chinese. The Communist victory was celebrated by some Chinese-American groups, mainly those focused around workers' rights and leftist politics. An exuberant Chinese Workers' Mutual Aid Association proclaimed:

Under the leadership of the Chinese Communist Party, the masses of Chinese people and the People's Liberation Army thoroughly unfettered the yoke of imperialism, destroyed the reactionary dictatorship of the inept and corrupt Kuomintang and established people's rule.

The Chinese Six Companies, on the other hand, publicly declared firm support of the Kuomintang, as well as Chiang's active, though sporadic, campaign to invade the mainland and unseat Mao's Communist government. Also supporting the Koumintang were the Chinese Consolidated Benevolent Association of New York and the Chinese American Citizens Alliance, which had formed in 1895 as the Native Sons of the Golden State before changing its name in 1905.

Most Chinese Americans, however, experienced Mao's Revolution as a direct threat to their own security due to American prejudice against them, especially after the start of the Korean War and the passage of the Internal Security Act of 1950 (discussed later in this chapter). The Chinese in America therefore once again felt pressured to prove their loyalty to the individualist and free-market ideals of the United States. Groups like the Anti-Communist Committee for Free China, established in 1951, soundly denounced communism and proclaimed strict loyalty to the United States. The All-American Overseas Chinese Anti-

A young Mao Zedong addresses his followers. (Frankin D. Roosevelt Library)

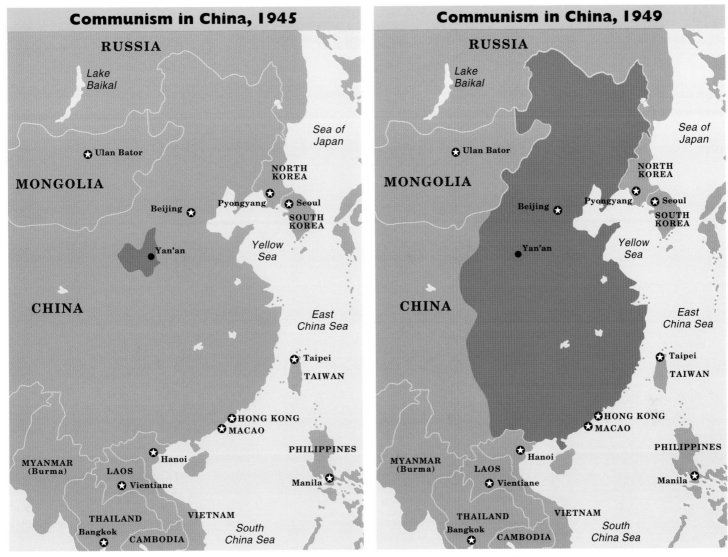

Communism in China, 1945

RUSSIA

Lake Baikal

Sea of Japan

Ulan Bator

NORTH KOREA

MONGOLIA

Pyongyang

Seoul

SOUTH KOREA

Beijing

Yan'an

Yellow Sea

CHINA

East China Sea

Taipei

TAIWAN

HONG KONG

MACAO

PHILIPPINES

MYANMAR (Burma)

Hanoi

LAOS

Vientiane

Manila

THAILAND

VIETNAM

Bangkok

CAMBODIA

South China Sea

Communism in China, 1949

RUSSIA

Lake Baikal

Sea of Japan

Ulan Bator

NORTH KOREA

MONGOLIA

Pyongyang

Seoul

SOUTH KOREA

Beijing

Yan'an

Yellow Sea

CHINA

East China Sea

Taipei

TAIWAN

HONG KONG

MACAO

PHILIPPINES

MYANMAR (Burma)

Hanoi

LAOS

Vientiane

Manila

THAILAND

VIETNAM

Bangkok

CAMBODIA

South China Sea

The maps above show the spread of Communist territorial control in China between 1945 and Mao's victory in 1949.

Communist League formed in New York in 1954, solely to reassure white Americans that those Chinese living among them were not Communists. More politically liberal-minded Chinese Americans created other groups, such as the Chinese-American Democratic League, formed in 1954.

THE DISPLACED PERSONS ACT OF 1948

After the Red Army seized control of China in October 1949, nearly 5,000 university students and professionals visiting the United States found themselves stranded on American soil. Many of these business-people, scientists, teachers, and students had supported China's fallen Nationalist government. Fearing for their safety, they did not return to Communist China.

The Chinese students of the 1940s, unlike the early Chinese immigrant laborers from Kwangtung Province, came from China's upper class. Their American education would have prepared them for high-ranking jobs in Nationalist China. Now locked out of their homeland, some went to Taiwan and others to Hong Kong and Singapore. Most, however, sought refuge in the United States. Despite their high level of education and obvious non-Communist political stance, however, many suffered harassment from white Americans during the Red Scare—the period from the late 1940s to the 1960s during which fear of Communist invasion was at its height in America. Nevertheless, the U.S. federal government passed legislation in an effort to help the stranded Chinese in their country.

The Displaced Persons Act of 1948 granted the stranded Chinese immigrant status. This was the first law in U.S. history to admit those fleeing political persecution (as defined by the International Refugee Commission). Under the act, nearly 205,000 displaced persons were

In addition to causing a great many deaths, the Korean War damaged a numerous historical buildings, including this Buddhist shrine. (National Archives)

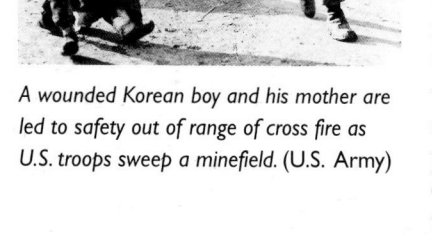

A wounded Korean boy and his mother are led to safety out of range of cross fire as U.S. troops sweep a minefield. (U.S. Army)

allowed into the United States during a two-year period beginning in July 1949. This figure included 15,000 Chinese. The Displaced Persons Act formally expired in 1954, though two other legislative measures, the Refugee Relief Act of 1953 and the Refugee-Escape Act of 1957, also granted entry to refugees from Communist China and North Korea.

Many of the originally stranded Chinese settled in New York City's Chinatown, which by mid-century had become second in Chinese population only to San Francisco's Chinatown. In New York, the displaced Chinese of the 1940s joined second-generation Chinese-American high school students who were excelling in New York City public schools. More second-generation Chinese pursued a college education than any other ethnic group living in New York City at the time. The merger of these two highly educated groups, along with the increasing numbers and importance of Chinese women in the community, consequently transformed the economic, social, and political lives of America's Chinese living on both coasts.

FEAR ON THE RISE

By the late 1940s, the people of the United States had become seized by cold war panic in the face of the sudden and seemingly unstoppable growth of Communist power in the world. The government of the Soviet

Union had successfully detonated an atomic bomb, and in China Mao had succeeded in the overthrow of the pro-Western Nationalists. Meanwhile, the outbreak of war in Korea amplified the struggle between the two ideological standpoints of Communist and capitalist. These and other circumstances all combined to create and fuel growing fears of the "red menace" among Americans—fears that sometimes led to extreme reactions.

INTERNAL SECURITY ACT OF 1950

The Internal Security Act of 1950 was a controversial bill passed almost immediately after, and partly in response to, the start of the Korean War. The post–World War II division of Korea into northern and southern sections—governed by the Soviet Union and the United States, respectively—was originally intended as only a temporary measure until free elections that would unite the country could be held under the supervision of the United Nations (UN). After a series of delays, South Koreans proceeded with their election, choosing Syngman Rhee as the first president of the Republic of Korea in 1948. Following the election, the United States began a gradual withdrawal of its troops from the country. The Soviet Union, meanwhile, installed Communist Kim Il Sung as leader of North Korea.

The two sides coexisted this way until June 25, 1950, when North Korean troops

North Korean tanks roll into Seoul, South Korea in 1950. (National Archives)

invaded the south, capturing the capital city of Seoul within three days. Both the Soviet Union and the People's Republic of China sent advisers and supplies to their Communist allies in North Korea; China also sent more than 750,000 combat troops. South Korea was aided in the war by the United States and 14 other member countries of the UN.

Territory was continuously seized and surrendered, passing back and forth between the two sides throughout the conflict, but by the time of the 1953 cease-fire, the borders of the two Koreas had changed very little. Some 1.5 million Koreans lost their lives during the war, as did 54,000 Americans, with an additional 100,000 wounded or declared missing. The tense split remained in effect into the 21st century, with 1 million North and South Korean soldiers stationed in a perpetual face-off along both sides of the border known as the DMZ (Demilitarized Zone).

Korea's physical division reflected the then-new ideological split of the world into the cold war era of Communist-allied versus capitalist-allied nations. As a result, Chinese involvement in the Korean War fanned the flames of anti-Chinese bias on American soil, and all Chinese Americans, regardless of political affiliation, became suspected Communists and therefore potential enemies of the United States.

Following the outbreak of the Korean War, and in response to charges by Senator Joseph McCarthy that Communists had infiltrated the State Department, Congress passed the Internal Security Act (also called the McCarran Act after its chief sponsor, Senator Pat McCarran). Among other provisions, the act permitted the internment of suspected Communists during a national emergency. President Harry S Truman vetoed the bill, declaring that it "would make a mockery of our Bill of Rights [and]

President Harry Truman vetoed the Internal Security Act of 1950 on the grounds that violated the Bill of Rights. Dismissing his objections, Congress overrode his veto by a wide margin. (National Archives)

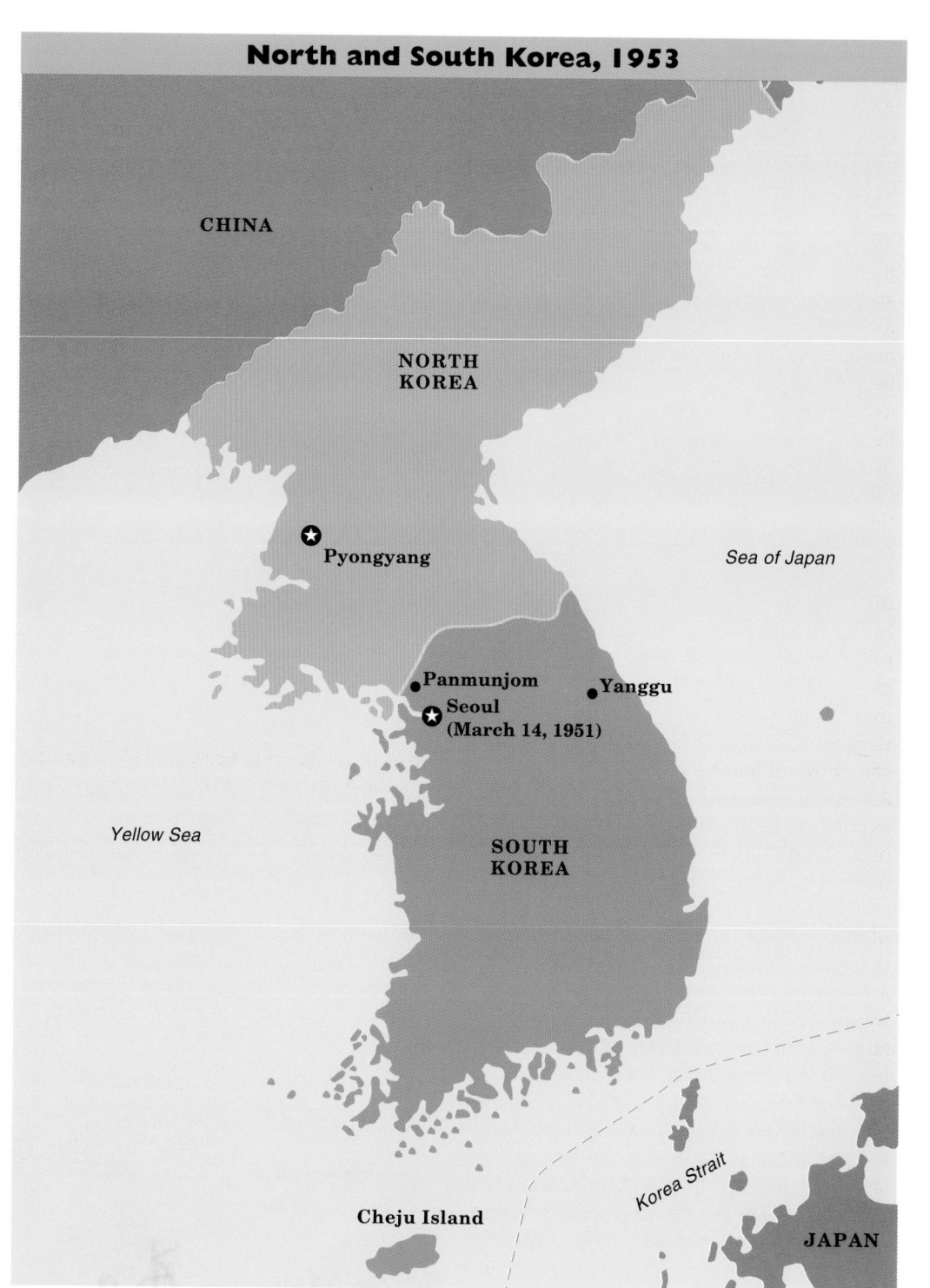

North and South Korea, 1953

CHINA

NORTH
KOREA

Pyongyang

Sea of Japan

Panmunjom   Yanggu
Seoul
(March 14, 1951)

Yellow Sea

SOUTH
KOREA

Korea Strait

Cheju Island

JAPAN

Following the end of World War II, the Soviet Union occupied the northern part of Korea and set up a Communist government. The United States occupied the southern portion and set up an anti-Communist government. In 1948, the north and south became the independent nations of North Korea and South Korea, with the dividing line at the 38th parallel. Both countries claimed to be the legitimate government of all Korea. Despite the Korean War of 1950–1953, which was fought to resolve the issue, the two nations remained separate into the 21st century.

would actually weaken our internal security measures." In 1950, Congress, however, overrode the veto by a wide margin.

Title II of the act gave the attorney general of the United States power to "apprehend and detain each person as to whom there is a reasonable ground to believe that such a person will engage in, or probably will conspire with others to engage in, acts of espionage or sabotage." One of the six detention centers opened by the Justice Department under Title II was Tule Lake, an internment camp previously used to detain Japanese Americans during World War II. The Chinese community in America feared they would face a similar fate as anti-Communist fervor grew increasingly intense in the United States.

The McCarran-Walter Act

As a consequence of anti-Communist provocation by Joseph McCarthy in the Senate, the House Un-American Activities Committee (HUAC) in the House of Representatives, and others, some government officials had grown obsessed with the threat of suspected Communist agitators and spies living in the United States. The resulting clash between internal security needs and the protection of civil liberties became a central—and controversial—debate in 1950s America. In 1948, HUAC held nationally televised hearings focused on allegations that U.S. State Department official Alger Hiss was a Communist spy. (Hiss was convicted.) In 1950, the Senate convened a special investigating committee, led by Senator McCarthy, which conducted a series of investigations and public hearings intended to expose hidden Communists working within the U.S. government and army. The overzealous and misguided senator even went so far as to suggest that President Eisenhower was somehow in league with the Communists. Although Senator McCarthy failed to expose a Communist conspiracy, the people of the United States became divided in their reactions, with pro-McCarthy supporters charging that Americans who were against McCarthy had to be pro-Communist and therefore subject to investigation. McCarthy was eventually discredited, but by then many law-abiding Americans had suffered the loss of their careers and reputations as a result of the false accusations he insisted upon perpetuating.

While McCarthy and HUAC were searching for possible Communist subversives, Congress passed the McCarran-Walter Act (officially known as the Immigration and Naturalization Act) in 1952. The act's passage was emotionally charged for many Asian Americans, but particularly for the Japanese and Chinese. First of all, it granted naturalized citizenship to foreign-born Asian immigrants who had previously been deemed ineligible—a cherished goal for the Japanese-American community and for the JACL in particular, which had long fought to achieve a repeal of the 1924 Immigration Act. Consequently, in the 13 years between the passage of McCarran-Walter in 1952 and 1965, 46,000 issei became naturalized citizens of the United States.

The McCarran-Walter Act also ended the 1924 ban on Asian immigration by establishing a quota system based on national origin. At the same time, however, it reaffirmed the use of racial preference in immigration laws and gave the attorney general the power to revoke the citizenship and undertake the deportation of any immigrant suspected of Communist affiliations. Civil rights groups as well as portions of the Asian-American community criticized McCarran-Walter, as did President Truman, who commented on its "totalitarian approach" and remarked as he vetoed the bill: "If this is equalization, I do not know the definition of discrimination!" Nevertheless, Congress again overrode Truman's veto.

The main provisions of the McCarran-Walter Act included an annual quota of 105 immigrants from each Asian country. European immigrants, however, were not limited by such numerical quotas. The act also established a four-category selection system for Asian immigrants, giving 50 slots to those with high educational levels or exceptional abilities and the remainder to relatives of U.S. citizens or legal resident aliens.

Joseph McCarthy, who headed a special Senate investigation into Communist infiltration of the U.S. government, poses with a gift of "Northern Spies," apples from Red Wing Orchards, a Canadian apple grower. (Library of Congress)

The Communist Control Act

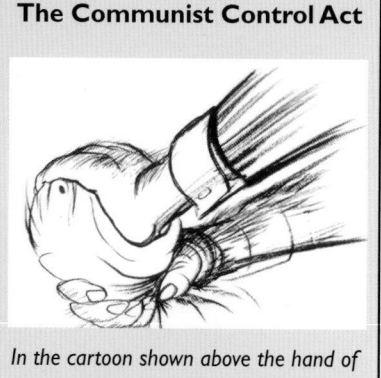

In the cartoon shown above the hand of government is seen stopping the free speech of the ordinary citizen. (Library of Congress)

In 1955, Congress passed the Communist Control Act, which deprived the Communist Party of rights and privileges guaranteed by the Constitution. It also subjected Communists to penalties under the Internal Security Act and provided that Communist-infiltrated organizations would lose their rights under the National Labor Relations Act. More than 2,500 Americans designated as security risks were fired from federal positions and another 4,000 resigned before investigations were completed regarding "unfavorable" information in their files. Among these Americans were, not only people suspected of radical political ties, but also those accused of being heavy drinkers, homosexuals, or of having other "character defects."

Although Asian Americans benefited in some ways from the passage of the McCarran-Walter Act, the immigration provisions revealed the continuing strength of racist attitudes against Asians as an ethnic group. The bill's cosponsor, Senator Pat McCarran, freely expressed his views, warning against "opening the gates to a flood of Asiatics." Senator McCarran also added the anti-Communist provisions to the bill, commenting that "if this oasis of the world should be overrun, perverted and contaminated, or destroyed, the last flickering light of humanity will be extinguished." In the anti-Communist enviroment of the postwar United States, the Chinese Revolution helped make Chinese and other Asian immigrants suspect.

CHINATOWN RAIDS AND THE CONFESSION PROGRAM

Anti-Asian sentiment, complicated and inflated by American fears of a global Communist takeover, continued to build well into the mid-1950s. In 1955, the U.S. general consul in Hong Kong, Everett F. Drummond, informed the State Department that an elaborate passport and visa fraud existed among Chinese trying to immigrate to the United States. Despite little evidence, Drummond argued that the system was a Chinese Communist conspiracy to infiltrate and weaken the United States. In response, the U.S. Immigration and Naturalization Service (INS) launched a series of raids into Chinatowns throughout the country in search of Communists and illegal aliens.

The raids terrified Chinese Americans, especially those who had arrived in the country decades before as "paper sons." Claiming to be the children of Chinese already in America, "paper sons" entered the United States with citizenship status (as discussed in chapter 3). Though largely successful at the time, "paper sons" lived in constant fear of discovery.

Thus, tensions over the need for secrecy exploded into panic in 1956, when the raids into America's Chinese communities began. Federal agents investigated thousands of Chinese Americans, charging that passports had been obtained with false birth certificates. Those Chinese found guilty of passport fraud were deported.

The INS orchestrated its search for Communist spies and illegal aliens through its Confession Program—a system that echoed in some ways the notorious HUAC investigations into alleged Communists in Hollywood, during which writers, directors, actors, and others were forced to testify in front of Congress and name any associates who may have expressed interest in or been somehow connected to Communist politics. U.S. officials promised immunity to Chinese illegals who confessed their status if they also betrayed illegal friends and relatives. In further reward for their cooperation, informers would be granted legal status, provided that they were not involved in subversive activities. (Ironically, the programs coercive methods were eerily similar to those later employed by Mao Zedong's Red Guard during China's Cultural Revolution [1966–1976]. That such a program operated in the name of protecting American liberty against the threat of Communist dictatorship was clearly lost on its creators.)

The INS conducted its raids and Confession Programs on both coasts. Up to 10,000 Chinese Americans confessed and named others in San Francisco alone; the vast majority were granted legal alien status for doing so. But the cost of cooperating with the INS program ran high, as friends and family turned on one another, splintering the strength of the Chinese community in America.

HAWAII GAINS STATEHOOD

When Congress declared Hawaii a U.S. territory with the passage of the Organic Act on June 14, 1900, the federal government appointed planter Sanford Dole as Hawaii's first governor, ensuring that the business interests of plantation owners would have a legislative voice. The Republican Party, heavily dominated by plantation owners, subsequently controlled Hawaii's territorial government for more than 50 years.

Nevertheless, workers in Hawaii continued to press for radical change in the exploitative plantation system, building on their earlier successes. By the end of World War II, the hold of the plantation system over the workers and the power of the Big Five Companies had been significantly weakened. Interethnic solidarity thrived under the leadership of the International Longshore and Warehouse Union (ILWU) and among nisei-born laborers.

The plantation bosses, however, did not give up their power easily, and they continued their drive to smash Hawaii's unions, the ILWU in particular. Their strategy moved from the importation of strikebreakers to "red-baiting," denoucing the unions as Communist organizations. Similar scare tactics were used during the McCarthy era of the early 1950s. The plantation owners' ongoing attack on the ILWU leadership resulted in the weakening of Hawaii's union movement. The dramatic rise of the Democratic Party in Hawaiian politics, however, caused its own "revolution" within Hawaiian society, breaking the stranglehold of the Republican Party and securing statehood for Hawaii, which was finally granted in 1959.

THE ILWU AND ELECTORAL POLITICS

In the years following Hawaii's establishment as a U.S. territory, the Republican Party worked to secure the political interests of Hawaii's plantation owners. Eventually the ILWU countered, expanding the tools in its arsenal by including the power of the labor vote alongside the strike in its campaign for workers rights. As the nisei generation came of voting age, the necessity of a well-organized voter registration drive had become apparent: In 1920, only 3 percent of eligible voters in Hawaii were Japanese Americans. By 1940, that figure had risen to more than 30 percent due to the increase in the nisei population. Nonetheless only 30 percent of that group of eligible voters were even registered to vote. The ILWU therefore launched a highly successful voter registration drive that year, a move bolstered by a series of tightly organized political rallies conducted among the Asian workers, with speeches and literature translated into all the appropriate Asian languages.

The ILWU also introduced the political action committee (PAC) to Hawaii. PACs endorse and raise money for candidates; in return, they expect their demands to be addressed by the candidate. On election day in 1944, 16 out of the 21 candidates endorsed by labor-dominated PACs were elected to the Hawaiian House of Representatives; in the Senate, six out of eight PAC-endorsed candidates won. Two ILWU members, Joseph Kaholokula Jr. (Maui) and Amos Ignacio (Hawaii), won seats in Hawaii's territorial legislature.

The electoral victories paved the way for the passage of the Hawaii Employment Relations Act of 1945. The act secured the right of union organization and collective bargaining for Hawaii's multiethnic workforce. Having won this key liberty, the workers—Japanese, Chinese, Filipino, Puerto Rican, Portuguese, and Hawaiian—went out on strike in 1946, demanding higher wages and a 40-hour work week. The strike lasted 79 days, involved 28,000 workers, and shut down 33 out of 34 plantations. The multiethnic group of workers emerged victorious, turning the vision of a big interracial union into reality and further cementing the power of the ILWU in Hawaii. By 1947, the union's membership in Hawaii had reached 30,000.

Contract negotiations between sugar workers and plantation owners proceeded smoothly in 1948, and agreements were made without a strike. However, talks between dock workers and their employers did not result in the same easy agreement. Consequently, beginning in March 1949, the ILWU led a longshoremen's strike, with 2,000 workers walking out on their jobs. By June, 20,000 faced unemployment, many small businesses had gone under, and food shortages had occurred. Hawaiian officials called on President Truman and the U.S. Congress for help. As violent clashes occurred amid media allegations of the supposed subversive political intent of the ILWU, public opinion of the union began to sour. The dock workers secured a raise in the end but lost several months' worth of wages and sustained irreparable damage to the ILWU's image.

THE HAWAII SEVEN

In repeated attempts to undermine the ILWU in Hawaii, conservative forces in Hawaii put out claims that the Communist-dominated union threatened national security. Disgruntled former ILWU leaders helped fan the flames of rhetoric against the organization. Former ILWU leader Ichiro Izuka's pamphlet, *The Truth About Communism in Hawaii*, published in 1947 and distributed among Filipino workers by the Hawaiian Sugar Planters Association (HSPA), also helped sway public opinion against the ILWU.

Jack Kawano, a former ILWU leader, inflicted the most damage to the group's reputation. Kawano, who had helped lead the ILWU to power, quit both the union and the Communist Party in 1951, when he lost an internal power struggle to mainland colleague Jack Hall. Kawano's testimony in 1951 before the House Un-American Activities Committee about the workings of the Communist Party and the ILWU led to the trial of seven suspected Communists, including Jack Hall, accused of intent to overthrow the government by force.

The defendants, who became known as the Hawaii Seven, were tried in Hawaii

LEADING HAWAIIAN POLITICIANS

John Anthony Burns (1909–1975)

Burns served as governor of Hawaii from 1962 to 1973. A consistent advocate for statehood, over the years he worked closely with the Japanese-American community and nisei politicians of Hawaii. Burns moved to Hawaii at age four from his birthplace of Assinneboine, Montana. He attended public schools and graduated from the University of Hawaii in 1931. The oft-described "stubborn, stone-face Irishman" consistently defended the loyalty of Japanese Americans during World War II. Burns served as police officer and captain in Honolulu, then as Traffic Safety Commission chairman (1950–1954) and Honolulu Civil Defense administrator (1951–1955). He also chaired the Honolulu County Democratic Committee (1948–1952) and the Territorial Democratic Central Committee (1952–1956). He played a key role in the rise of the Democratic Party during the mid-1950s and emerged as a leader. Burns served five times as a delegate to the Democratic National Convention (1952, 1956, 1960, 1964, 1968). His defeat of Republican incumbent Elizabeth P. Farrington in 1956 by a landslide victory set the stage for his election as delegate to the 85th and 86th Congresses. Diagnosed with cancer, Burns passed the governorship over to Lieutenant Governor George Ariyoshi, who succeeded thereafter in earning election to the post for three full terms.

Dan Aoki (1916–1986)

Aoki, a key Democratic Party leader, worked with Governor John Burns for nearly 30 years, serving as his administrative assistant from 1956 to 1978. Hawaiian-born Aoki attended public schools in Maui, then graduated from the University of Hawaii with a degree in sociology. Aoki had no interest in a political career until his return from World War II with a Bronze Star. He met then congressional candidate John Burns at a meeting of the 442nd Veterans' Club, which Aoki had helped found. After Burns's victory in 1956, Aoki traveled with Burns to lobby for statehood in Washington, D.C.

Daniel K. Inouye (1924–)

Daniel K. Inouye, a decorated World War II veteran and six-term senator, is one of the most influential and best-known Japanese-American politicians in U.S. history. Inouye was born in Honolulu and attended public schools in Hawaii. He was awarded the Distinguished Service Cross for service in the 442nd Regiment. Inouye had dreamed of becoming a surgeon, but lost his right arm during combat in 1945. He graduated from the University of Hawaii in 1950 and earned his law degree two years later from Washington University Law School in Washington, D.C. Inouye, a lifelong Democrat who had campaigned for John Burns in the late 1940s, served as majority leader in the territorial house of representatives in 1954 and as a member of the territorial senate, 1958–1959. Inouye was elected in 1959 as Hawaii's first congressional representative. After his second term in the House, Inouye began his long Senate career, earning election in 1962 and six times thereafter (1968, 1974, 1980, 1986, 1992, 1998). Over the decades, Inouye sat on several congressional committees, including those that investigated the federal government's wrongdoing in the Watergate and Iran-Contra scandals.

Masayuki "Spark" Matsunaga (1916–1990)

Spark Matsunaga, legislative leader in the redress movement and a well-known peace issues advocate, served seven terms as U.S. congressman and three terms as U.S. senator. Matsunaga, born to a poor Japanese immigrant family on the island of Kauai, worked his way through high school and college. He graduated with honors from Harvard Law School in 1951. A decorated World War II veteran of the 100th Infantry Battalion, Matsunaga was elected to Hawaii's territorial house of representatives in 1954. He went on to serve seven consecutive terms as a U.S. congressional representative of Hawaii, beginning in 1962. During his tenure, Matsunaga pushed for the repeal of the Emergency Detention Act (also known as Title II of the Internal Security Act of 1950), which gave the attorney general power to intern any Chinese or other immigrant suspected of Communist ties. Matsunaga defeated his colleague Patsy Takemoto Mink in 1976, beginning his long career in the Senate where he served on several committees. After 22 years of lobbying, he finally succeeded in winning congressional approval for the establishment of a U.S. Peace Institute in 1984. Matsunaga spearheaded the passage of the Civil Liberties Act of 1988, which garnered a public apology and $20,000 compensation for internment camp survivors. Matsunaga also created various opportunities and site locations for joint ventures between the United States and the former Soviet Union regarding space exploration and research.

George Ryoichi Ariyoshi (1926–)

George Ariyoshi became the first Japanese American to serve as lieutenant governor and governor of Hawaii. Ariyoshi, John Burns's right-hand man for decades, never lost an election. His father, a Sumo wrestler and small businessman, arrived in Hawaii in 1918. Ariyoshi attended public schools in Hawaii, briefly studied at the University of Hawaii, then earned a degree in history and political science from Michigan State University in 1949. In 1952, Ariyoshi returned from University of Michigan Law School to open a practice in Hawaii. He joined other major Democrats in the dramatic election of 1954, winning a seat in the territorial house of representatives. Ariyoshi eventually became majority leader after his first territorial senate win in 1958. He became John Burns's lieutenant governor in 1970, stepping in as governor three years later. He subsequently earned election to three full terms as governor, the longest in Hawaii's history.

Patsy Mink (1927–)

After Patsy Takemoto Mink earned her law degree from the University of Chicago in 1951, she found that her status as an Asian woman made finding a position as a lawyer at an established firm difficult. Therefore, Mink opted to strike out on her own by setting up her own practice. By 1956, Mink, who had become active in Hawaii's Democratic Party, won election to the state house of representatives. Two years later, she moved up to the Hawaiian Senate. Then, in 1964, five years after Hawaii was admitted to the United States, she became the first Asian woman elected to the U.S. House of Representatives. Although he was defeated in 1976 by Spark Matsunaga, she was later reelected. In 2000, she won election to her eighth term in the U.S. Congress, where she has focused on providing greater access to education and health care for all Americans.

over the course of two years (1951–1953). They were found guilty on June 19, 1953, of violating the Smith Act, a 1940 law that made it illegal to belong to any organization that advocated the overthrow of the U.S. government. Six men—Jack Hall, John Reinecke, Dwight James Freeman, Charles Fujimoto, Jack Kimoto, and Koji Ariyoshi—were sentenced to five years in prison and $5,000 fines. A woman, Eileen Fujimoto, was also found guilty but sentenced to only three years in jail and $2,000. All seven convictions were overturned on appeal in 1958. Ironically, Kawano suffered the most personally from the fallout related to his testimony against the Hawaii Seven: He failed as a businessman and died in virtual exile in 1984. Hall, on the other hand, went on to succeed as a labor rights organizer, empowering workers through Democratic electoral politics and playing a key role in the elections of 1954. Ariyoshi founded a prolabor newspaper, the *Honolulu Record*, in 1948 and was appointed president of the Hawaii Foundation for History and the Humanities in 1974. Charles Fujimoto was blacklisted and never worked again as a chemist, but he continued to publicly advocate left-wing political views.

The ILWU itself, though fallen from its glory days, became less radical and gradually more involved in mainstream politics. Its influence dwindled in the 1960s, but the union has survived into the 21st century.

THE REVOLUTION OF 1954

The 1954 elections held in the Territory of Hawaii proved to be revolutionary in that they significantly altered the balance of political power between the Republicans and the Democrats. Republicans in Hawaii had long dominated the scene and for the most part protected and advocated the interests of a white ruling class that controlled the plantation system (and therefore Hawaii's economy). The 1954 elections ushered in Democratic majorities not only in the territorial house and senate but also in many local legislative bodies for the first time.

Three factors coalesced to create the dramatic shift in Hawaiian politics. First, an entire generation of American-born Japanese, Chinese, and Filipinos had reached voting age, and their political interests reflected both their higher level of education and a prevailing civil rights–oriented worldview. Second, the ILWU combined the electoral power of this generational voting bloc with that of the committed labor bloc it had established through decades of union activity. This two-pronged tactic advanced the interests of workers fighting for fair labor practices in Hawaii. Third, World War II veterans of Asian ethnicity, including those of the highly decorated 442nd Regimental Combat Team (discussed in chapter 4), returned from battle with a hard-earned and well-deserved sense of pride that would no longer tolerate racial discrimination and inequality.

Although Hawaiians had begun to favor the Democrats as early as 1948,

Patsy Mink (Library of Congress)

Republicans continued to dominate. The Democratic Party found itself divided due to disorganization and infighting as various factions jockeyed for control of the party platform. In addition, many liberal Democrats were discredited as subversive Communists during the Red Scare era of the 1950s. By 1952, leaders of a more moderate position—such as John Burns, Dan Aoki, Daniel K. Inouye, Spark Matsunaga, and George Ariyoshi—emerged to carry the Democrats to victory.

With the dramatic election of 1954, Democrats swept two-thirds of the seats in the territorial house and nine out of 15 seats in the territorial senate. Nearly half of the new legislators were nisei. No second-generation Asian Americans had served in Hawaii's territorial legislature prior to the

Daniel Inouye (U.S. Senate)

revolution of 1954. Locally, the Democrats secured control on the islands of Maui, Kauai, and Oahu.

In addition to securing political representation for Asian-American, labor, and liberal interests, the election of 1954 ushered in legislators intent on securing statehood for Hawaii—a goal finally reached in August 1959.

THE 50TH STATE

Although territorial legislators petitioned Congress for statehood regularly from 1903 to 1959, they were consistently denied. This surprised many, as U.S. territories commonly became states as soon as their populations grew to a high enough level to warrant representation in the federal government. Opposition to statehood for Hawaii centered around prejudice against Asians as an ethnic group, an attitude exacerbated by the anti-Japanese climate of World War II and the anti-Communist hysteria of the 1950s. Others argued over the years that Hawaii was too distant from the mainland to become a state.

Unlike mainland residents, people living in Hawaii during World War II had to endure life under U.S. military rule. For three long years, blackouts, curfews, wage freezes, cen-

sored news, and rationed food and gas made up the daily routine for Hawaiians. Wartime security concerns negated the basic civil liberties ordinarily inherent in the social structure of a U.S. territory.

The Japanese-American experience in Hawaii also differed radically from that of mainland residents. Japanese composed nearly 40 percent of Hawaii's labor force, and internment of the entire Hawaiian Japanese population would have completely destroyed the islands' economy. The pivotal role of Japanese workers and the recognition of their economic importance not only kept the majority of Hawaii's Japanese out of internment camps but also cemented the power of the unions in the 1940s and the political power of Hawaii's Democrats in the mid-1950s.

After years of lobbying, Hawaii's Democrats finally secured the right of the islands to become America's 50th state. Statehood was made official by President Eisenhower's signature on August 21, 1959. Hawaii's first elections reflected the racial diversity that characterized the fledgling state. William F. Quinn, a Caucasian, became its first governor; Quinn's lieutenant governor, James K. Kealoha, was of Hawaiian descent. Hawaiians elected a Chinese American, Hiram L. Fong, as one of two senators and Daniel K. Inouye, a decorated war veteran and second-generation Japanese American, as their first congressman.

THE POSTWAR BOOM

America's postwar era was characterized by dramatic growth: The economy boomed, the population soared, and educational achievement reached unprecedented levels. The Asian community in the United States prospered, as did all ethnic segments of postwar society. In some instances, Asian Americans' education and income levels even surpassed those for whites (a situation that would later fuel a new wave of anti-Asian resentment and stereotyping).

The population boom and sudden increases of females in America's Asian community resulted from the passage of favorable congressional legislation, beginning with the War Brides Act of 1945. This measure allowed for the entry of Chinese, Filipino, and Korean wives and children of American servicemen into the United States. The G.I. Fiancées Act, which passed on August 9, 1946, expanded the provisions of the War Brides Act to include fiancées and also exempted the wives of servicemen from the racially based immigration quota system. All of these measures, in combination with a rising birth rate among Asians already in America, transformed the demographics of America's Asian community.

Like other Asian Americans, Filipinos had proven their loyalty to the United States with devoted service during World War II, both in combat and on the home front. Widespread prejudice had waned, and by the end of the war, Congress had extended naturalization rights to those Filipinos who had come to the United States before 1934. Then, on July 4, 1946, the U.S. government declared the Philippines to be a sovereign nation.

Although the strict quotas enacted with the Tydings-McDuffie Independence Act of 1934 (described in chapter 4) remained in force, the Filipino population on the U.S. mainland skyrocketed. During the prewar decade of 1930 to 1940, the Filipino mainland population grew by only 668 people. By contrast, between 1940 and 1960, their numbers increased by nearly 78,000. Most of the immigrants from the Philippines were women—some war brides, others the wives of Filipinos already living in the United States.

Like all citizens and aliens living in the United States, Filipinos took advantage of the abundant employment opportunities available during the postwar era. The economic situation in the United States was especially attractive to Filipinos, who came from a country that had fallen into disarray after the ravages of war and the initial chaos of sudden independence.

The War Brides Act led to an increase in the U.S. Korean population as well. The vast majority of the 5 million Americans stationed in Korea during the Korean War (1950–1953) were male recruits. Many servicemen married Korean women and brought their new wives back to the United States at the end of their tour of duty. These war brides were the first Korean immigrants since 1924 legally allowed to enter the United States. Because U.S. Armed Forces remained stationed in South Korea at the end of the conflict, marriages between Korean women and American GIs continued for many years. Between 1951 and 1964, more than 28,000 Korean women settled and began their families in the United States.

War brides legislation also spurred the growth of the female population among America's Chinese community, as did the 1943 repeal of the Chinese Exclusion Act of 1882. In addition, many Chinese women took advantage of the Displaced Persons Act of 1948 and the Refugee Acts of 1953,

1957, and 1959 to make the United States their home. The impact of increasing numbers of Chinese women in America was dramatic. Families, unheard of in the "bachelor society" Chinatowns of a century earlier, grew to be commonplace.

WOMEN RESHAPE THE CHINESE COMMUNITY

Many Chinese immigrants of the postwar period settled in established urban Chinatowns, as in New York City, Boston, San Francisco, and Los Angeles. The Chinatown locations offered familiarity, supportive relatives, and job opportunities. Although the arrival of large numbers of women led to a more stable and family-oriented social structure, the population

During the late 1940s, the ratio of male to female Chinese immigrants of began to shift dramatically, eventually transforming the Chinese-American community. The cause of the shift was a series of laws that allowed women married to American servicemen to immigrate to the United States. Although the growth of female immigration from China peaked in 1948, Chinese women continued to outnumber men in the years that followed.

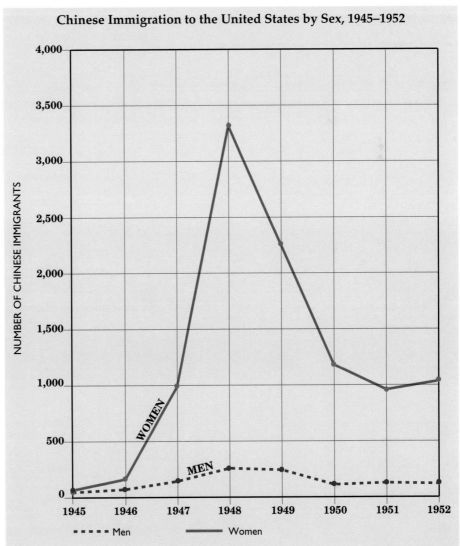

Chinese Immigration to the United States by Sex, 1945–1952

NUMBER OF CHINESE IMMIGRANTS

- - - - Men   —— Women

A mother strolls with her children in New York City's Chinatown. (Library of Congress)

boom caused overcrowding, which led to problems of inadequate housing and social services, poor health conditions, and underemployment.

Those women with poor skills and little English-speaking ability found menial, nonunion jobs, often in Chinatown restaurants or in the sweatshops of the garment industry. However, Chinese women such as Dong Zem Ping did not complain about the dirty and unsafe working conditions, as they saw these jobs as their only possible means of earning money.

I can still recall the times when I had one foot on the pedal [of the sewing machine] and another one on an improvised rocker, rocking one son to sleep while the other was tied to my back. Many times I would accidentally sew my finger instead of the fabric because one child screamed or because I was falling asleep on the job.

Although daily life for some female Chinese immigrants echoed the hardships experienced by the first wave of Chinese men in the mid-19th century, many Chinese females found greater opportunity in the postwar economy. Young immigrant women who were married to white or Chinese servicemen often had an easier time

assimilating into the new culture. Since discrimination had lessened, life outside of Chinatown became an attractive option to many. Those highly educated professionals allowed to stay in or come to the United States under the Displaced Persons or Refugee Acts arrived at a time when their scientific and technical skills were in demand. For example, Dr. Chien-shiung Wu, after graduating in 1936, decided to do her graduate work in the United States at Berkeley; she became one of the world's top experimental physicists. Highly educated Chinese—mainly Mandarin speakers—often moved to suburban areas and did not associate with the primarily Cantonese-speaking inhabitants of America's Chinatowns.

The influx of Chinese women unsurprisingly led to a postwar baby boom. Chinese-American children growing up in the 1950s and 1960s, like the second-generation children of the 1930s and 1940s, experienced conflicts between their two cultures and struggled with the shape of their identities. For example, individualism, assertiveness, and gregariousness were prized in American culture, whereas in Chinese culture, females were honored for their quiet reserve and obedience to their elders and husbands.

Per Capita Annual Asian-American Male Income v. Caucasian American Male Income
(Median Income for Total Population, age 15+)

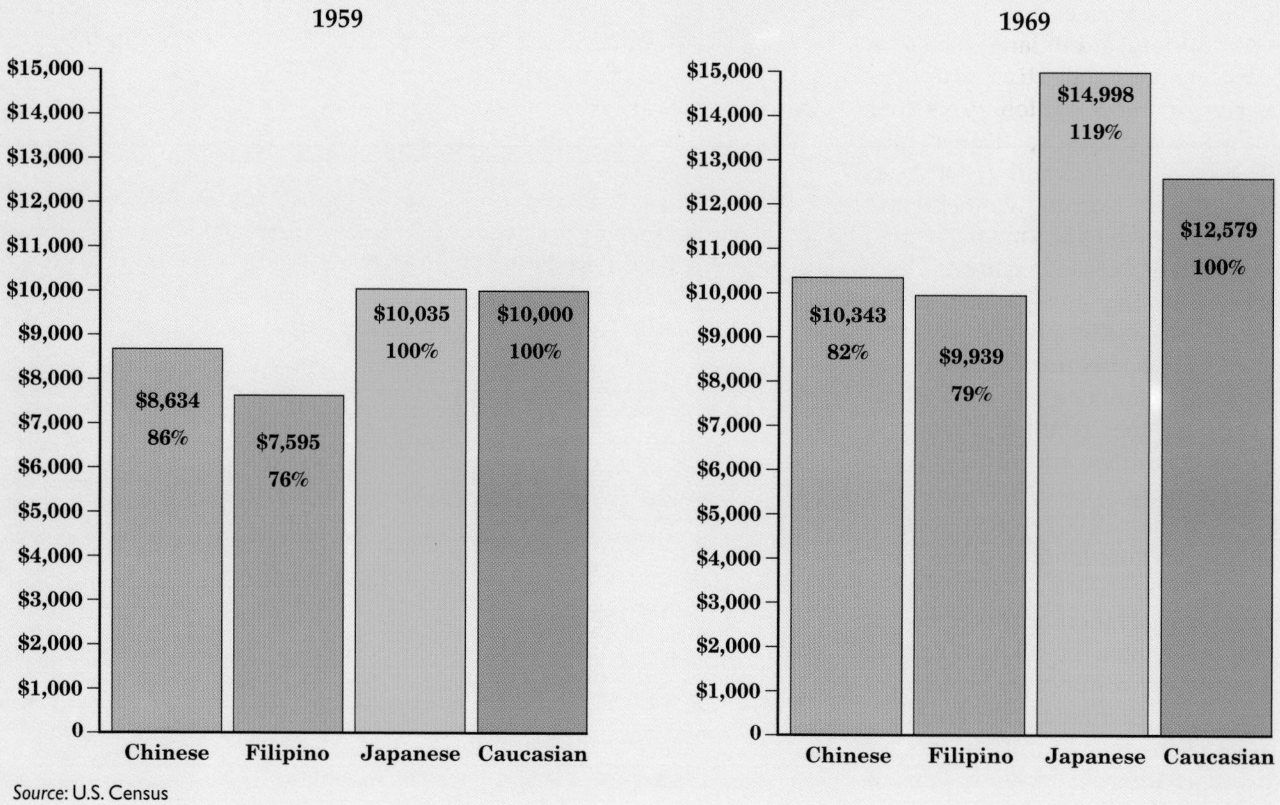

1959

Chinese	$8,634 / 86%
Filipino	$7,595 / 76%
Japanese	$10,035 / 100%
Caucasian	$10,000 / 100%

1969

Chinese	$10,343 / 82%
Filipino	$9,939 / 79%
Japanese	$14,998 / 119%
Caucasian	$12,579 / 100%

Source: U.S. Census

Chinese families also continued to value sons over daughters, even in the United States. Nevertheless, rising incomes and greater educational opportunities, along with the simple passage of time, led to increasing assimilation in attitude, thought, and behavior among Chinese Americans, many of whom became more American than traditionally Chinese.

RISING INCOMES AND EDUCATION

In many ways, the greater economic and social stablility of the Asian-American community in the late 1940s and 1950s was a function of the generational shift from first-generation immigrants to their second-generation, U.S.-born children. In the early 20th century, most newly arrived immigrants to the United States took what work they could get, since it was the only way to survive. Those born later to settled immigrant families had more educational and economic choices—a situation as true today as it was then.

However, the gap between Asian and white incomes began to close during the 1950s. The U.S. economy blossomed in postwar expansion, creating more opportunities for all Americans. More highly educated Asians arrived, securing top job offers in highly specialized and high-paying fields. Second- and third-generation Asians achieved academically, thereby bettering their employment options. And women—both white and Asian—who had honed job skills and assertive attitudes during wartime, put their intelligence and

skills into the job market as well as the home. In time, the income levels of Asian women who had to supplement the family income often surpassed those of white women.

Historically, educational levels among Asian immigrants have varied by ethnicity. While most early Filipino and Chinese

Educational Attainment Among Asian Americans, 1960 v. 1970				
Level of Education Completed (by percentage)	Japanese	Chinese	Filipino	Caucasian
1960				
Males				
Elementary school	26.9	46.6	62.3	39.5
Some high school	14.3	10.9	12.7	18.9
High school graduate	34.6	15.5	12.7	22.2
Junior college or some four-year college	10.4	8.8	6.3	9.1
Four-year college graduate	13.9	18.2	6.0	10.3
Females				
Elementary school	29.6	42.4	39.0	35.7
Some high school	13.6	10.1	16.9	19.6
High school graduate	41.4	24.3	20.0	29.2
Junior college or some four-year college	9.1	9.4	10.4	9.5
Four-year college graduate	6.3	13.9	13.7	6.0
1970				
Males				
Elementary school	17.9	29.0	38.0	27.8
Some high school	11.2	10.7	13.9	18.2
High school graduate	34.8	18.8	19.5	28.5
Junior college or some four-year college	13.9	10.6	12.0	11.1
Four-year college graduate	22.3	30.8	16.6	14.4
Females				
Elementary school	19.8	36.5	23.6	25.6
Some high school	13.0	8.7	12.7	19.4
High school graduate	42.7	23.8	20.4	35.5
Junior college or some four-year college	13.3	11.4	12.8	11.1
Four-year college graduate	11.1	19.6	30.5	8.4

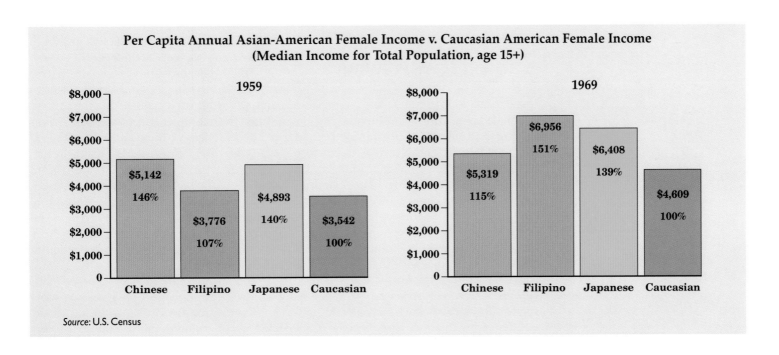

Per Capita Annual Asian-American Female Income v. Caucasian American Female Income (Median Income for Total Population, age 15+)

1959

Chinese $5,142 146% — Filipino $3,776 107% — Japanese $4,893 140% — Caucasian $3,542 100%

1969

Chinese $5,319 115% — Filipino $6,956 151% — Japanese $6,408 139% — Caucasian $4,609 100%

Source: U.S. Census

immigrants had little formal schooling, many Japanese immigrants came to the United States well educated. The emphasis that Asian-American parents often placed on educational achievement (and still do) had generally resulted in high success rates for their children, thereby leading to higher-paying jobs, especially for males. The percentage of Asian Americans enrolled in university-level study increased dramatically during the 1960s, a change pushed forward, in part, by the success of the African-American civil rights movement. Although the education of Asian women and girls remained a lower priority, gains were made among second- and third-generation Asian females, many of whom finished high school and attended college during the 1960s.

Between 1960 and 1970, the percentage of Asian and white females completing four years of college increased greatly. During the passage of a single decade, the percentage of Japanese women earning bachelor's degrees jumped from 6.3 percent to 11.1 percent; the share of Chinese females increased from 13.9 percent to 19.6 percent; and that of white female Americans rose from 6.0 percent to 8.4 percent. Filipinas saw the most dramatic leap in degree earners—from 13.7 percent in 1960 to 30.5 percent in 1970.

The percentage of Chinese males earning four-year college degrees increased the most between 1960 and 1970, rising from 18.2 percent to 30.8 percent. Japanese male college graduates tallied in at 13.9 percent in 1960 and 22.3 percent in 1970. Among Filipinos, the share of degree earners increased from 6.0 percent to 16.6 percent and that of white males rose from 10.3 percent to 14.4 percent.

YELLOW POWER

During the 1960s, many Asian-American youths became heavily influenced by the shifting cultural and political mood of the United States. At the same time, the majority youth culture also embraced certain aspects of Asian culture. For example, Asian-Indian sitar music, incorporated into the music of the Beatles as early as 1965, became a popular sound during the "psychedelic era" of the 1960s, a time of experimentation by youth with drugs as well as with alternative dress, music, and lifestyles. Various aspects of Asian-based religions and health practices, such as yoga and transcendental meditation, also became fashionable, and the martial arts found new devotees among American youth.

Both the African-American civil rights movement and activism against the Vietnam War provided young Asian Americans the impetus to stand up for greater recognition and rights. One of the goals of the Yellow Power movement, as it became known, was to foster a new awareness of ethnic heritage and pride.

ASIAN CULTURE GOES POP

Today it is not unusual to hear a chorus of multiethnic children chanting *kiai* yells from suburban karate studios, nor is it uncommon to hear of patients seeking "alternative" health treatments such as acupuncture or medicine based on Chinese herbs. Words such as *ginseng, yoga,* and *yin/yang* have entered the American vernacular. All of these Asian-based cultural influences, once considered exotic, strange, and foreign, are now familiar parts of American culture.

Introduced to mainstream America in the 1960s and early 1970s through the movies of martial arts master Bruce Lee movies and television shows such as *Kung Fu,* martial arts in the United States grew dramatically in popularity for adults and children alike. (*Kung Fu* was initially conceived of by Lee, although the leading role was denied him by television executives who believed white audiences would not accept an Asian actor as a popular television star.) Because martial arts training places a high value on strength of character as well as physical strength, many parents have found that the classes provide their children which particularly enriching experience. Once only practiced by males, participation in the martial arts has grown to include girls as well as their mothers.

What became known as alternative medicine also began to gain popularity among America's youth in the 1960s. Young people eager to explore alternatives to the practices of their parents embraced Chinese medicine and Asian-Indian Ayurvedic health practices. Many found that the Asian emphasis on holistic medical approaches—in which the individual focuses on the health of the interconnected body, mind, and spirit rather than simply reacting to the symptoms of a particular illness—appealing. These practices, once viewed as the province of "kooky" and "cultish" religious groups, gained respect and some mainstream American insurance plans began to pay for them.

INDIAN MUSICAL INSTRUMENTS

Although Indian music was little known to the general public in the West before the 1960s, since that decade it has become increasingly popular worldwide. After rock musicans such as The Beatles began using Indian rhythms, Indian musicians such as Ravi Shankar began finding increasingly receptive audiences in Europe and the United States. Indian music is based on raga (melody) and tala (rhythm). Talas are rythmic cycles ranging from three to 108 beats. Ragas, complex and detailed series of notes, each have their own mood (such as tranquility, loneliness, or heroism) and association with season and time of day. The musician often meditates on these before playing, becoming fully enveloped in the music while improvising and communicating the mood of the raga to the listener. In this way, playing the instruments becomes a vehicle for expressing the spiritual word of God.

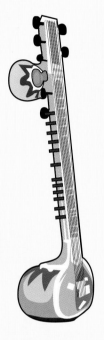

Sitar
The sitar is the most popular stringed instrument of India and has been in use since the 13th century. It has between seven and 20 strings and about 20 metal frets, is carved of wood, and is attached to a large gourd. The strings are plucked using a wire plectrum (*mizrab*) that fits over the forefinger. The instrument has been popularized in the United States by Ravi Shankar.

Tabla
A tabla set consists of two drums—the tabla (treble, right hand drum, at top) and the dagga (bass, left hand drum, shown below). The tabla is usually made from clay, sheesham wood, tum wood, rosewood, or mango wood. The dagga is made from copper or brass. Goat or deer skin stretches across both drums, which are tuned to different pitches. The tabla is played by striking the fingers and palm against various parts of the drums. This instrument is an essential ingredient of Hindustani classical music and dance.

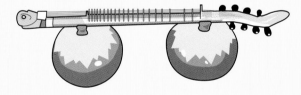

Vina
One of India's oldest instruments, the vina can be traced back to the earliest of India's written records. Three kinds of these stringed instruments are used today:
1. Rudra vina: This type has seven strings and 24 movable frets and is played with finger picks.
2. Vitchitra vina: A comparatively new version, this vina has four main strings, three drone and rhythm strings, and 11 to 13 resonating strings. There are no frets.
3. Saraswati vina: This version has seven playing strings with fixed frets set in wax.

Mridanga and *Pakhawaj*
Two popular drums are the mridanga (above, left) and *pakhawaj* (above, right). The mridanga is a double-ended barrel drum with metal tuning hardware, usually used in ashrams, or religious retreats, for accompanying chanting. It is the most popular drum in south India. The *pakhawaj* is also a double-ended barrel drum, but with a leather strap. It is used to accompany vocal music and is the oldest drum of north India.

One practice that became particularly closely associated with the youth culture of the 1960s was transcendental meditation (TM), a religious movement based on Vedanta, an orthodox Hindu philosophy, founded by Maharishi Mahesh Yogi, who left the Himalayas to bring his message to the West in 1959. His expressed goal was to help individuals reach a higher level of consciousness and thereby create more

CHINESE AND JAPANESE MARTIAL ARTS

There are many different kinds of Chinese and Japanese martial arts. The martial arts judo, aikido, and karate were all popularized in the United States by the Japanese in the 1960s, and they are practiced today by Americans of all heritages. Judo emphasizes throws and holds, aikido focuses on wrist and hand locks, and karate emphasizes punches and kicks. All three martial arts have spiritual, mental, and physical compo-nents, mastered only after years of rigorous training. Among the many Chinese martial arts are kung fu, t'ai chi, tae kwon do, *pakua*, and others. They divide into "internal" techniques (with strength focused on the legs and torso) and "external" techniques (with strength coming from train-ing of specific leg and arm muscles). Kung fu and t'ai chi are examples of these, and both are widely practiced in the United States.

Name of Form	Year Developed	Meaning of Name	Basic Principles and History
Kung fu	2600 B.C.	"ability"	Kung fu is a more physical, "external" Chinese system of self-defense, which, like t'ai chi, uses circular movements. Believed to originate from about 2600 B.C., it includes many different fighting styles based on animal movements, such as the monkey, white crane, tiger, dragon, and praying mantis. The praying mantis technique, for example, emulates certain physical characteristics of the insect, such as the "mantis claw"; here, the hands imitate the insect's claws. They are supplemented with throwing, grasping, and pulling moves, and locking joints. Kung fu means "ability," a concept that may be applied to any of the martial arts. This notion of ability includes strength, speed, endurance, agility, and coordination.
T'ai chi ch'uan	ca. A.D. 200	"supreme ultimate fist"	One of the most difficult "soft" or "internal" martial arts to master, t'ai chi ch'uan is based on a meditative series of postures and circular movements that continuously flow together. Almost balletlike in form, it incorporates 108 different positions. The fundamental concept behind its practice is *chi*, which the Chinese consider the universal energy flowing in the body. T'ai chi ch'uan helps to maintain the right balance of *chi* in the body.
Karate	ca. 16th century	"empty hand"	Karate derives from a Chinese-based fighting technique which came to, and was modified in, Japanese-occupied Okinawa. This early Okinawan fighting emphasized hand and foot movements to destroy Japanese armor. This style of fighting soon became popular in Japan. Karate was brought to the United States in the 1920s. Karate teaches defensive and offensive moves; combatants also use a yell, called a *kiai*, when punching and kicking, to help the muscles contract at the point of contact and thus give added strength through focused physical and mental energies.
Judo	1882	"the gentle way"	Judo is based on the ancient Japanese technique of jujitsu and the principle of least resistance. It is based on a combination of throws and holds with hand and foot blows; the goal is to immobilize opponents by breaking their balance, making them fall, and locking them in a hold. It was introduced in the United States in the early 1900s and gained recognition as an Olympic sport in 1964. Judo emphasizes spiritual precepts through principles such as "maximum efficiency with minimum effort for the mutual welfare and benefit of all," which can be translated to a way of life.
Aikido	1943	"way of harmony" or "way of the spirit"	Aikido emphasizes the principle of nonresistance. This Japanese martial art focuses not on kicks or punches, but on using one's energy to gain control of opponents or throw them away from one's body. The technique is to neutralize opponents' attacks by flowing with their motions; for example, if pushed, a person will allow himself or herself to be pushed and bring the opponent along, knocking the opponent off balance. Training focuses on four areas: developing physical strength; adopting and practicing a disciplined and peaceful attitude; increasing suppleness; and increasing coordination and improved physical health through refined posture. Spiritually, the goal is to focus on defeating negative characteristics in one's own mind rather than on the defeat of others. This philosophy is tied to the Zen school of Buddhism, which teaches that all people are in harmony with the physical world.

In addition to leading India as its first prime minister, Jawaharlal Nehru also lent his name to the Nehru jacket, which became a popular garment among stylish Western youth during the late 1960s. (Hulton-Getty Picture Collection)

highly evolved societies. TM became a distinct subculture during the 1960s and attracted a huge following among American youth. Many creative individuals prominent at the time began to follow TM, including writer Marshall McLuhan; actress Mia Farrow; and musicians Donovan, the Beach Boys, and the Beatles. Members of the Beatles, joined by Farrow, Mike Love of the Beach Boys, and others, went so far as to make several high-profile retreats to learn from the Maharishi in 1968.

The movement influenced fashion as well as religious practice. It was around the time of these retreats that the Nehru jacket, a dressy, silk or linen Indian garment with a short turned-up collar (named for Jawaharlal Nehru, India's first prime minister following independence from Great Britain), became a popular clothing style in the United States. It was often worn over brightly colored pants and topped with many long strands of "love beads," a common accessory of the time.

Asian Activism in the 1960s and Early 1970s

Although the pop culture of the 1960s and 1970s focused on love, peace, and the expansion of limits, the harsh fervor and swell of violence of the period revealed a severely troubled American society. Early in

the decade, President John F. Kennedy engaged many Americans by offering a vision of new American frontiers, in which the American democracy would provide a purposeful beacon of hope to the world; in 1963, the youthful leader was assassinated. Just five years later, in 1968, Dr. Martin Luther King Jr., the leading figure in the African-American civil rights movement, was shot dead on a Memphis, Tennessee hotel balcony. Just two months later, President Kennedy's younger brother Robert, on the verge of winning the Democratic Party nomination for president, was also killed by an assassin. Although the Democratic National Convention did convene in August in Chicago to nominate Vice President Hubert Humphy for the presidency, violence erupted on the streets of that city as police clubbed young antiwar protesters and bystanders alike in what many has since termed a police riot. Meanwhile, as Americans struggled to make sense of the violence threatening to spin out of control around them, thousands of others found themselves doing the very same thing, only in the jungles of Vietnam.

The Vietnam War began in 1955 when Ngo Dinh Diem, leader of the southern portion of partitioned country, refused to recognize the election victory of Ho Chi Minh, the Communist leader of the northern region. Having sent military advisers to assist the South Vietnamese a few years earlier, the United States intervened directly by sending troops in 1965. Before the U.S. withdrawal in 1973, more than 55,000 Americans would die in a losing effort to prevent Ho Chi Minh's forces from assuming control of all of Vietnam.

As U.S. involvement in Vietnam increased to hundreds of thousands of young men and women sent to fight a war that seemed to be leading to stalemate at best, a growing number, and then finally a majority of Americans began to criticize U.S. policy in Vietnam. Never before in American history had so much of the citizenry come to question so seriously and so publicly the wisdom of Washington's decision makers in time of international military conflict. Although many certainly rallied around the war effort, giving voice to the slogan "My country, right or wrong," more Americans simply saw their country as wrong.

Together with the African-American civil rights movement, the anti–Vietnam War movement led a growing number of Americans to question the status quo in U.S. society. The Chicano, Native American, and feminist movements, as well as

A CHRONOLOGY OF ASIAN-AMERICAN ACTIVISM, 1968–1972

1968

April — Sansei Concern, an Asian-American student group, begins meeting at the University of California, Los Angeles (UCLA).

September — Oriental Concern, previously known as Sansei Concern, organizes an Asian-American conference at Lake Arrowhead, California. More than 200 Asian Americans attend the conference, which is named "I Am Yellow, Curious."

November — A student strike over the issue of student and community control of San Francisco State College begins. By month's end, president Robert R. Smith resigns. He is replaced by professor S. I. Hayakawa. Hayakawa wins applause from conservatives for his no-nonsense handling of the affair, including tactics like ripping wires from protesters' loudspeaker systems.

1969

February — One hundred and twenty-five Japanese Americans from the Asian American Political Alliance picket a public speaking engagement by S. I. Hayakawa.

March — Dr. Thomas Noguchi is fired as the Los Angeles County coroner. He is reinstated in July after a six-week investigation and public charges of racism.

March 21 — The San Francisco State College strike ends when the college establishes the country's first school of ethnic studies.

April 3 — Asian Americans for Action, the first Asian-American political group in New York City, is founded.

April — The first edition of *Gidra* is published by Asian-American students at UCLA. Publication of the monthly newspaper, which becomes known as "the voice of the Asian-American movement," continues until 1974.

September 28 — A "One Hundred Year Celebration of the Issei" is held in Los Angeles. The event is sponsored by the Pioneer Project and the Japanese Pioneer Community Center in Los Angeles. The Pioneer Community Center, a senior citizen center established primarily by third-generation (sansei) Japanese Americans for aging first-generation Japanese Americans (issei), opens the following month.

November 15 — A contingent of 300 activists from Ad-Hoc Japanese Americans for Peace participates in the Anti-Vietnam Peace March in San Francisco.

December 27 — The first annual Manzanar Pilgrimage takes place, as Japanese Americans visit the site of the Manzanar World War II internment camp.

1970

January 17 — A group of 200 Asian Americans holds an "Asian Americans for Peace" march in Los Angeles's Little Tokyo neighborhood.

March 9 — A group of students from the Oriental Student Union at Seattle Central Community College occupies administration offices to protest the lack of Asian administrators. The school agrees to fill the next vacancy with an Asian.

1971

May 16 — A group called Asian Americans for Peace organizes a "Peace Sunday" rally in Los Angeles. Two thousand gather to hear speakers that include actress and peace activist Jane Fonda.

1972

March 25–28 — Asian-American students at the City College of New York occupy the building that houses the Asian studies department. The three-day protest ends when the school administration grants most of the students' demands.

August 20 — The annual Nisei Week parade in Los Angeles is interrupted by the Van Troi Anti-Imperialist Youth Brigade, a group of 150 antiwar student activists. They are joined by another antiwar group, the Thai Binh Brigade, which passes out leaflets and chants slogans.

---

the ecology movement, all gathered strength during the peak years of the antiwar movement. Not surprisingly, the late 1960s and early 1970s were also a time when many young Asian Americans took up the banner of protest. Victories won during the African-American civil rights movement energized young Asians, especially Chinese and Japanese, to speak out on a variety of issues and to fight for minority rights. Many young Asians, who shared all of the reasons common to others in the antiwar movement, were also moved by a sense of solidarity with the Vietnamese, and became active in the movement against the war. When leaders of the Black Power movement, such as Malcolm X and Stokely Carmichael, encouraged African Americans to find empowerment through increased knowledge of "self and kind," young Asians, too, became inspired to develop a sense of ethnic pride and positive self-esteem. Many Asian-American students fought for and won the inclusion of Asian-American studies into college-level curricula.

The Yellow Power movement burst onto the scene in November 1968, when militant African-American students at San Francisco State College went on strike over the issue of student and community control of the institution. When college president Robert R. Smith resigned in the midst of the strike, his replacement Samuel Ichiye Hayakawa, a politically conservative Japanese-American professor of semantics, took a hard line against the strikers, calling in the police to clear the campus by force. Rather than end the protests, however, Hayakawa's response helped broaden the range of student groups involved in the protests. A group of 125 Japanese students belonging to the Asian American Political Alliance disrupted a public speech by Hayakawa in February 1969 to protest the Caucasian-focused curricula of the school. The conflict finally ended on March 21, 1969, when the college established the first school of ethnic studies in the United States. Similarly, students calling themselves the Third World Liberation Front at the University of California, Berkeley, staged a "Third World Strike" that same year and succeeded in calling attention to the need for the inclusion of ethnic studies at the university. Also in 1969, the first edition of a newspaper called *Gidra* was launched. Produced by Asian-American students at UCLA, the paper soon became known as "the voice of the Asian-American movement" and continued to run monthly until 1974.

New York City became another focal point for the development of Asian ethnic power and political protest groups. On April 6, 1969, the antiwar group Asian Americans for Action formed in New York City to push for U.S. withdrawl from Vietnam. Three years later, in March 1972, Asian-American students at the City College of New York took over the building that housed the Asian studies department. The protest lasted three days and succeeded in securing almost all student demands for revisions of the curriculum to include ethnic American studies.

Some Chinese-American youths, inspired by the Third World Strikes, the civil rights movement, and the peace movement, decided to effect change through social service, specifically by establishing community centers that provided such services as housing assistance, food and clothing drives, and assistance with translating written or spoken communication from government agencies. Young

Asian-American activists turned to community work in America's urban Chinatowns and Little Tokyos to foster ethnic pride, as well as to give back to their communities. Winnie Tang of Boston remembered:

I was going to college during the time of a lot of demonstrations and the peace movement was very much alive in Boston. It certainly did have an effect on the direction that I took, in terms of a concern for my community and my involvement in Chinatown rather than elsewhere. . . . I feel I can raise consciousness, either with people within the community or outside the community, and effect some level of change.

Tang later worked as the executive director of the Chinese American Civic Association Multi-Service Center and as executive director of the Chinese Consolidated Benevolent Association of New England.

Japanese Americans also gave back to their communities. In 1969, Japanese Americans living in Los Angeles began the Pioneer Project, which in turn established Japanese Pioneer Community Centers. These organizations were established as senior citizen centers by sansei (third-generation Japanese Americans) to care for the aging issei in the community. The initial stirrings of the redress movement also began during the late 1960s and early 1970s. The Organization of Southland Asian American Organizations led the first annual Manzanar Pilgrimage on December 27, 1969, when Japanese Americans visited the site of the Manzanar internment camp. Asian-American youths also protested against the war in Vietnam, marching alongside Americans of many ethnicities. Three hundred members of the Japanese Americans for Peace picketed in San Francisco during the Anti-Vietnam Peace March of November 15, 1969. On May 16, 1971, Asian Americans for Peace held a "Peace Sunday" rally in Los Angeles. This rally attracted more than 2,000 people of all races to hear a variety of speakers, including actress and antiwar activist Jane Fonda.

By stimulating ethnic pride, the Yellow Power movement sought to link the issues and concerns common to all generations of Asians living in the United States. Those involved in it often successfully employed the American rights of free speech and peaceful assembly to get their points across to the government and society at large. Young Asian Americans worked diligently, as did their African-American and white counterparts, to secure their rights so that their voices would be heard alongside those of the white establishment.

6 / A NEW WAVE OF AMERICANS

The impact of the Vietnam War on American history has been dramatic. Not only did it lead to the deaths of more than 50,000 American servicemen, the failed American effort to roll back Communist advances dealt the United States a significant psychological blow as well. Though the Korean War had ended in stalemate, never before had the U.S. military lost a war.

The war also led to dramatic changes in the makeup of the Asian-American community in the United States. In the aftermath of the U.S. withdrawal and the North Vietnamese takeover of South Vietnam, hundreds of thousands of Vietnamese would come to the United States—both legally and illegally. By the 1980s, these Vietnamese refugees would be joined by other Southeast Asians fleeing repression at home, most particularly Cambodians fleeing the genocidal rule of Pol Pot.

Ironically, the same year that the U.S. government sent ground troops to Vietnam, it also opened the door to new, large-scale Asian immigration, for the first time since the early 1900s. The Hart-Celler Act of 1965 did away with ethnic-based restrictions that had been in place for much of the 20th century. In the years following the act's passage, hundreds of thousands of new Asian immigrants—largely from India, China, Korea, and the Philippines—surged into the United States.

CONFLICT IN SOUTHEAST ASIA

Even into the 21st century, a quarter century after the United States withdrew from combat in Vietnam, U.S. involvement in that conflict remains controversial. As discussed in chapter 5, the war profoundly shook virtually all all elements of American society as it dragged on from one year to the next, and the nightly news broadcast a constant count of casualties. By the late 1960s, a majority of Americans had concluded not only that the U.S. policy in Vietnam was wrong but that the government could not always be trusted to level with the American public.

In the aftermath of the war, returning American GIs found themselves the target of scorn from many segments of the American public. Rather than being welcomed proudly back to the United States and honored for service to the country, Vietnam veterans found themselves in the impossible situation of representing a conflict that many Americans wished to forget.

As difficult as the transition back to civilian life was for returning American GI, the collapse of South Vietnam helped create an even more difficult transition for South Vietnamese citizens, many of whom had worked side by side with Americans, either in the military or as civilians. When U.S. Congress passed legislation allowing many of these Vietnamese to leave their homelands as refugees and resettle in the United States, many thousands of Vietnamese, as well as Lao, Thai, and other Southeast Asians, took advantage of the opportunity.

THE VIETNAM WAR

Since its inception as the Kingdom of Nam Viet in 207 B.C., Vietnam has been the target of foreign conquest and has consequently suffered long periods of internal instability due to forced occupation. By the late 1800s, the French had taken control of Vietnam and made it a part of their colony of Indochina, which also consisted of Cambodia and Laos. In 1940, Japan assumed control of military bases in the country. Finally, during World War II, the Communist-led national front known as the Vietnam Independence League (or Vietminh), under the leadership of Ho Chi Minh, fought to put an end to French colonial rule and Japanese occupation. In 1945, Ho Chi Minh declared Vietnam's independence and asked, unsuccessfully, for recognition from President Harry S Truman, just as he had previously asked for support from President Franklin D. Roosevelt, also unsuccessfully.

The relationship between Ho Chi Minh and the United States was complicated and troubled. Although the CIA's predecessor, the U.S. Office of Strategic Services (OSS), had trained Ho Chi Minh's guerrilla forces in

A South Vietnamese villager, watched by U.S. forces (U.S. Marine Corps)

the jungles of Vietnam during World War II, the United States was also allied with France, which wanted to recolonize Vietnam after the war. President Roosevelt initially promised that the French would regain control of its colonies at the war's end. However, he subsequently proposed that Indochina be placed under international stewardship or under the control of Chinese Nationalist leader Chiang Kai-shek, who did not support the idea. Roosevelt's final approval of French repossession of Vietnam hinged on France's promise to grant its colonies independence in due course.

Thus, backed by the United States, the French ignored Ho Chi Minh's declaration of independence in 1945 and proceeded to recolonize Vietnam. Over the ensuing years, resistance to the French regime was fierce and marked by the threat of a Communist takeover of Indochina. Fearful of this possibility, the United States provided support to France, spending over $2.5 billion by 1954. Nevertheless, the French finally conceded defeat and withdrew from the country. With the signing of the Geneva Accords in 1954, Vietnam at last became an independent nation—albeit one that was, like Korea, divided into north and south sections.

As was the case with North and South Korea, Vietnam was split between the two warring political ideological camps of Communist and anti-Communist. By the terms of the Geneva Accord, Ho Chi

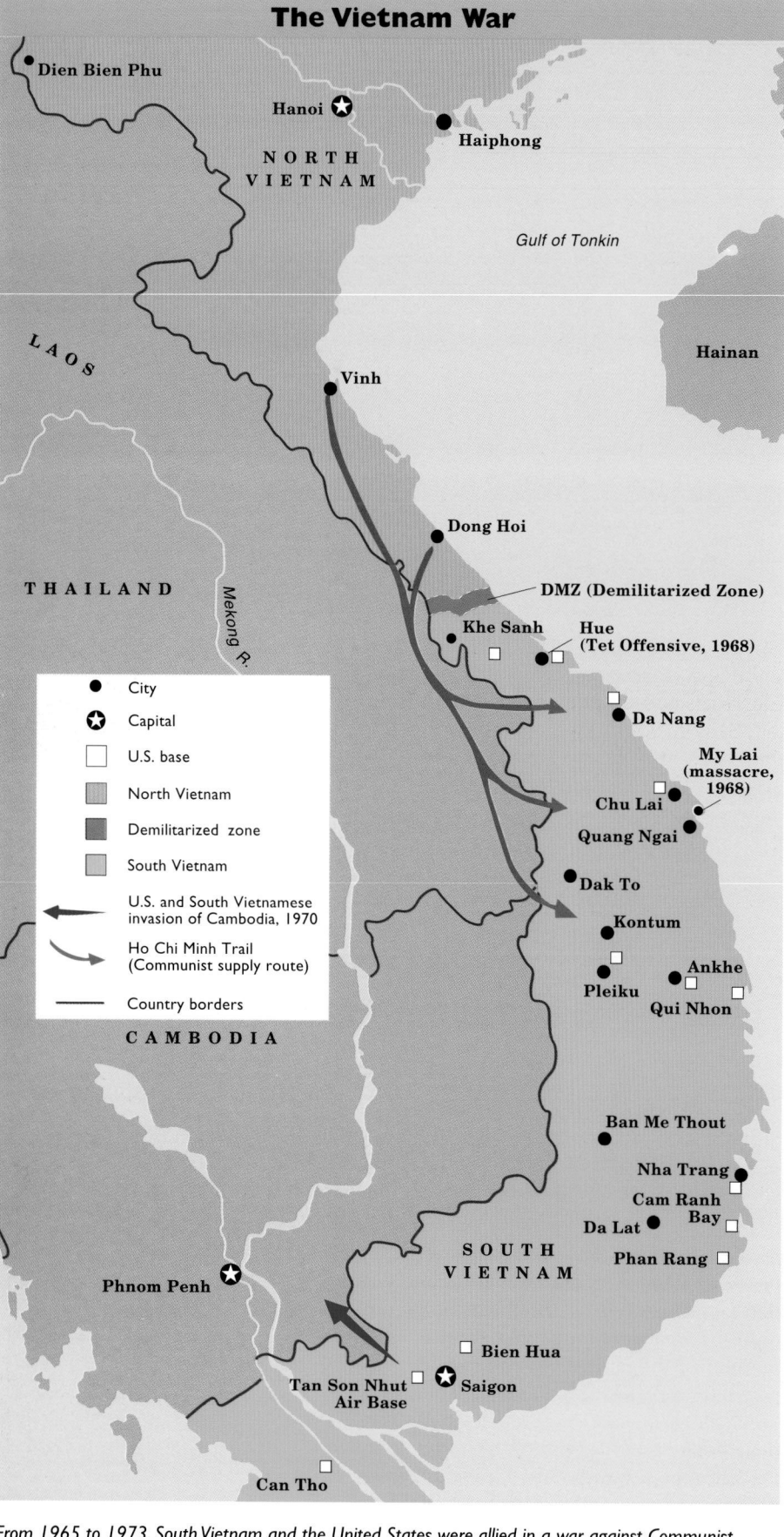

The Vietnam War

Dien Bien Phu

Hanoi

Haiphong

NORTH VIETNAM

Gulf of Tonkin

LAOS

Hainan

Vinh

THAILAND

Dong Hoi

DMZ (Demilitarized Zone)

Khe Sanh

Hue (Tet Offensive, 1968)

Da Nang

My Lai (massacre, 1968)

Chu Lai

Quang Ngai

Dak To

Kontum

Ankhe

Pleiku

Qui Nhon

CAMBODIA

Ban Me Thout

Nha Trang

Cam Ranh Bay

Da Lat

Phan Rang

SOUTH VIETNAM

Phnom Penh

Bien Hua

Tan Son Nhut Air Base

Saigon

Can Tho

Mekong R.

Legend:
- ● City
- ★ Capital
- □ U.S. base
- North Vietnam
- Demilitarized zone
- South Vietnam
- → U.S. and South Vietnamese invasion of Cambodia, 1970
- ↷ Ho Chi Minh Trail (Communist supply route)
- — Country borders

From 1965 to 1973, South Vietnam and the United States were allied in a war against Communist North Vietnam and South Vietnamese rebel forces known as the Vietcong. By 1969, the United States had 540,000 stroops stationed in Vietnam but was still unable to subdue the enemy. The guerilla warfare tactics of the Vietcong made conventional war difficult. Because both the Vietcong and North Vietmamese Army received supplies via the Ho Chi Minh Trail, a supply route that entered Laos, U.S. efforts to destroy the route widened the war to neighboring countries. In 1973, the United States withdrew. South Vietnam collapsed two years later.

Minh's Communist Vietminh were to control the area north of the 17th parallel from 1954 to 1956. An anti-Communist government headed by Ngo Dinh Diem was to rule the region south of the 17th parallel, renamed the Republic of Viet Nam. Between 1954 and 1956, Vietnamese citizens were allowed to choose which side to live in. More than 850,000 civilians moved south during this period.

After two years, the two sides were to hold national elections that would reunite the country. However, when the time came, South Vietnamese president Ngo Dinh Diem refused to comply with this term of the Geneva Accords. Tensions between north and south escalated and finally exploded into war in the early 1960s, when North Vietnam conducted a series of insurgent attacks into the south and secured its military position with the installation of the Communist National Liberation Front (NLF). The United States, which had framed all foreign policy decisions since 1947 through the lens of the containment of communism, soon found itself embroiled within the conflict. President John F. Kennedy sent military supplies and advisers to support the South Vietnamese effort. By 1963, nearly 16,000 U.S. soldiers were stationed in Vietnam. Under President Lyndon B. Johnson, that number escalated sharply by 1966 to more than 190,000 ground troops and by 1969 to nearly 550,000.

Initially many anti-Communist South Vietnamese welcomed the involvement of the United States in their war with the Communist Vietcong. As time went on, however, the ethnocentric and paternalistic attitude of U.S. military advisers as well as numerous military errors dampened South Vietnamese enthusiasm. And from the beginning, many Vietnamese students and religious leaders living in South Vietnam protested the war. Some held that U.S. intervention in the south coupled with that of the Soviet Union and China in the north smacked of a superpower ideological battle fought at the expense of yet another developing world nation. Others criticized the United States's indiscriminate use of dangerous chemical weapons such as napalm and Agent Orange in civilian areas as racist and inhumane. There was also a faction in the south that favored the promises of the Vietnamese Communists over the colonialist domination they had experienced under the thumb of the industrialized countries.

The war raged on for years, as did protests against American involvement in it, both in the United States and in South Vietnam. On January 31, 1968, as part of

CONFLICTS IN SOUTHEAST ASIA, 1941–1975

1941–1945 The United States aids Vietnamese nationalists in their fight against Japanese occupation.

1945–1954 The United States supports France in its war against Vietnamese nationalists.

1954 Following defeat at the Battle of Dien Bien Phu, France withdraws from Vietnam, Cambodia, and Laos. Under the terms of the peace treaty, Vietnam is split into Communist North Vietnam and non-Communist South Vietnam, which is backed by the United States.

1960 Former prince Norodom Sihanouk becomes leader of Cambodia. The number of U.S. troops in Vietnam reaches 900.

1963 President Ngo Dinh Diem of South Vietnam is assassinated.

1964 After the government of North Vietnam is accused of attacking an American spy ship in waters off North Vietnam, the U.S. Congress passes the Gulf of Tonkin Resolution, which gives President Lyndon Johnson authorization to "take all necessary measures to repel any armed attack against the forces of the United States and to prevent further aggression."

1965 The United States sends combat troops to South Vietnam and begins bombing North Vietnam.

1968 More than 500,000 U.S. troops are now in Vietnam. The Vietcong and the North Vietnamese army overrun most major South Vietnamese cities during the Tet Offensive. U.S. troops massacre 450 unarmed civilians in the village of My Lai.

1969 The United States begins a policy of "Vietnamization," or gradual withdrawal from Vietnam.

1970 Without authorization from Congress, the Nixon administration orders an invasion of Cambodia.

1973 The United States withdraws from Vietnam.

1975 The North Vietnamese capture Saigon, reuniting the nation. In Laos, the Pathet Lao gain control, while the Khmer Rouge, led by Pol Pot, take over Cambodia. Over the next two years, millions of Cambodians die as a result of efforts to reshape the country into a self-sufficient socialist state. More than 130,000 Cambodian, Laotian, and Vietnamese refugees come to the United States.

what came to be known as the Tet Offensive, the Vietcong overran the U.S. embassy in Saigon—an event that was televised worldwide. At that point, even mainstream America began to doubt the federal government's generally rosy characterization of the war. In addition to Saigon, 36 provincial capitals were attacked during the Tet Offensive, as were 72 district towns, various airfields, and military bases and headquarters. With 14,000 killed, 22,000 wounded, and 500,000 refugees driven from their homes, the war's end seemed far from sight. Public support for it was increasingly on the wane; hundreds of thousands of Americans decried the high number of U.S. casualties, the war's exorbitant cost ($25 billion per year as of 1968), and war crimes such as the My Lai massacre, in which U.S. soldiers murdered a large number of unarmed Vietnamese villagers. Consistent protests and public denouncements of the war by peace activists and key politicians such as Robert F. Kennedy, James W. Fulbright, and George McGovern also played a key role in turning American opinion against it.

In early 1968, President Johnson finally ceased his massive buildup of American troops in Vietnam, though the war raged on, even after the death of Ho Chi Minh in September 1969. Under President Richard M. Nixon, North Vietnam and the United States negotiated a cease-fire that was cemented with the signing of the Paris Peace Agreement on January 27, 1973. Since the United States could not declare any kind of victory, its troops were withdrawn under the face-saving slogan of "peace with honor." The fighting in Vietnam continued, however, and soon spread to Laos and Cambodia. (The war's effect on these countries is discussed in detail later in this chapter.) Saigon, South Vietnam's capital, fell to the Communist Vietcong on April 30, 1975, causing hundreds of thousands of Vietnamese to flee their homeland.

Vietnam formally reunified under Communist control in 1976, and Saigon was renamed Ho Chi Minh City. During the era of direct U.S. involvement in the war (1961–1972), American casualties reached more than 50,000. Estimates of the death toll in Vietnam numbered more than 400,000 South Vietnamese and more than 900,000 Vietcong and North Vietnamese.

VIOLENCE IN CAMBODIA

Like those of Vietnam, the political and social histories of Cambodia and Laos—once part of Indochina—have been characterized by foreign occupation and border disputes. Both the Cambodians and the Laotians fought against French colonial rule until World War II, when the Japanese gained control of the region. At the signing of the Geneva Accords in 1954, both Laos and Cambodia gained their independence from France, which had already begun granting more autonomy to those countries as early as 1947. In both cases, however, the internal struggle for power between factions set the stage for chaos and bloodshed. Also, as with Vietnam, the struggle played out between Communist and anti-Communist ideologies, and the countries had to endure U.S., Chinese, and Soviet involvement in their affairs.

Although the administration of corrupt South Vietnamese president Ngo Dinh Diem was unpopular with his people, the U.S. government initially supported him. In 1957, U.S. president Dwight Eisenhower and John Foster Dulles (to Eisenhower's left), the U.S. secretary of state, accorded him a hero's welcome. (Indochina Archives, Berkeley)

North Vietnamese artillery crashes into Khe Sahn during the Tet Offensive of 1968. (U.S. Marine Corps)

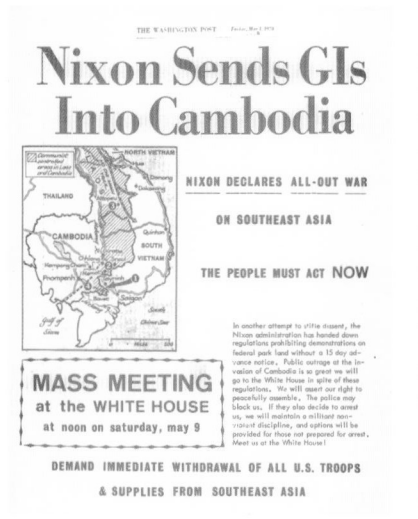

In 1970, without the authorization from Congress required by law, the Nixon administration ordered an invasion of Cambodia, widening the Vietnam War. Nixon's decision was met with anger by many in the American antiwar movement. The protest announced by the flyer above took place shortly after news of U.S. bombing runs in Cambodia were made public. (Library of Congress)

After France recognized Cambodia's sovereignty, the nation's former prince, Norodom Sihanouk, became its legal authority. Sihanouk mistrusted the United States, and during the Vietnam War he allied Cambodia with China and North Vietnam and allowed the transport of North Vietnamese troops and supplies across Cambodia, even as internal dissent festered within his country. In March 1970, Sihanouk lost power to the U.S.-supported General Lon Nol during a coup.

Under Lon Nol, Cambodia severed ties with Communist North Vietnam and became the Khmer Republic. Sihanouk, forced to live in exile, created a Communist guerrilla organization called the Khmer Rouge and received funding from the North Vietnamese. In the meantime, the United States had pushed the Vietnam War lines into Cambodia with air-bombing raids targeted on Vietminh and Khmer Rouge strongholds. During the raids, the U.S. Air Force dropped three and a half times as many conventional bombs as it had rained on Japan during World War II. The bombings destroyed hundreds of thousands of homes, farms, and livestock, creating a mass of angry, displaced young

people ready to join the Khmer Rouge against the United States and Lon Nol.

As North Vietnamese troops stormed Saigon in early 1975, the Khmer Rouge overran Phnom Penh, the capital of Cambodia, thus deposing Lon Nol. Under the Communist leadership of the Khmer Rouge prime minister Pol Pot, Cambodia became Democratic Kampuchea. (Pol Pot had joined the Cambodian Communist Party after having met and been inspired by Ho Chi Minh in 1949 while in France studying radio technology. After returning to Cambodia, he worked to build the Communist Party until ultimately he and his forces came to power.) The Khmer Rouge sought to convert Cambodia into a self-sufficient agrarian utopia that would attain the Communist ideal of a classless society. To do so, Pol Pot made several swift changes, using methods similar to China's Chairman Mao. Execution of perceived enemies of the state began immediately.

Thus the nation entered a time commonly referred to as the years of "the killing fields"—a nightmarish period of violent oppression and death through a program of gruesome social engineering and attempted brainwashings. Estimates of the death toll during Pol Pot's two-year reign range from 1.5 million to 2 million people, almost one-third of Cambodia's entire population. Any Cambodian involved with the U.S.-supported Lon Nol government, as well as anti-Communists, outspoken intellectuals, students, the wealthy, and even doctors, were labeled enemies of the state and summarily executed. Amid disease and death, physicians trapped in Cambodia had to pretend to be unskilled to survive.

The Khmer Rouge banned religious practice, invalidated the country's monetary currency, and burned books. No one outside of the elite government circle was allowed to read or write. Even the wearing of eyeglasses became a crime under Pol Pot, for it signified an intellectual, pro-Western connection. All Cambodians were to be reeducated in the Khmer Communist philosophy. Those who questioned any of the changes or refused to obey were killed instantly, as the value of individual life became meaningless. According to survivors, soldiers became indifferent to the routine slaughter they carried out. "To preserve you is no gain," chanted the soldiers, "to destroy you is no loss."

Pol Pot instantly secured complete physical control of the population of Cambodia. As soon as they took over Phnom Penh in 1975, Khmer Rouge soldiers told the city's 2 million residents that they had to leave at once to avoid bombing by U.S. forces. The citizens, who received this report at gunpoint in the midst of mass chaos, accepted the lie and evacuated the city by foot in a matter of three days. The government emptied all the hospitals, forcing the recovering wounded to be carried or pushed along the roads in hospital beds, their IVs held aloft by relatives. Khmer Rouge soldiers ordered doctors in the middle of surgery to stop immediately and leave the city. Those who questioned orders were shot on the spot.

Once relocated to the remote rural regions of their ancestors, the former urbanites discovered that they were trapped within a newly created collectivized farming system. Former city dwellers with no knowledge of farming were expected to work 12 or more hours a day, seven days a week, tilling rice fields and caring for fruit orchards using only the crudest methods of cultivation. The constant threat of execution, substantiated by the rotting corpses and skeletal remains of previous victims that lined roads and lay stacked in fields, served as a grim reminder to the living of the need for strict obedience. Cambodia's "classless utopia" had turned into an elite-led two-class system composed of "old people"—those revered for their simple, uneducated agrarian lifestyle—and "new people"—educated, skilled, nonfarming former city dwellers who would be executed if they did not change their beliefs and way of life immediately.

STRIFE IN LAOS

Although France recognized Laotian independence in 1954, an internal power struggle between the Pathet Lao and the Royal Lao tore the country in two. The Communist Vietminh supported the Pathet Lao faction in order to keep the Ho Chi Minh Trail, a military supply line, running through Laos to North Vietnam. The United States, again acting on a foreign policy of Communist containment, bolstered the non-Communist Royal Lao faction within Laos's civil struggle.

When the Vietnam War expanded into Laos during the 1960s, the U.S. Central Intelligence Agency (CIA) recruited the Hmong (meaning "free people") to fight against the Pathet Lao and Vietcong. Tribal elders, wooed by what turned out to be false promises of mutual care and aid on the part of the CIA, ordered all young men to join the fight. The CIA-managed Hmong military operations are often referred to as the "secret war" of the Vietnam era. Hmong mountain tribespeople were recruited en masse and in some cases paid directly by the U.S. government. The Hmong fighters endured a casualty rate five times higher than that of U.S. soldiers in combat, as they were ordered to conduct the riskiest operations, such as disrupting the flow of arms along the Ho Chi Minh Trail and rescuing captured American soldiers. Hmong villagers suffered from heavy bombing as well.

A specially created U.S. Air Warfare Unit based in Thailand trained Lao and Thai pilots to conduct air strikes against the Pathet Lao and Communist supply line trails. By the end of 1964, the United States had stationed 75 aircraft in Laos and filled camps with 3,000 U.S. Air Force personnel. By 1971, air strikes on Laos had reached a rate of 700 to 1,000 bombing missions per day. Despite such intense military action and $40 million per year from the United States, the Pathet Lao still controlled four-fifths of the land and two-fifths of the population in 1972.

SOUTHEAST ASIAN REFUGEES

The Vietnam War was not only a watershed event in U.S. political history; it also led directly to a dramatic shift in the course of U.S. immigration history. In the aftermath of the war, hundreds of thousands of Vietnamese, Cambodian, Laotian, and other refugees and immigrants from Southeast Asia began arriving in the United States. Some came through official government-facilitated programs and others by escaping from their homelands to refugee camps in Thailand via any means possible—whether borders by land or by sailing dangerous, overcrowded, and only marginally seaworthy boats.

THE FALL OF SAIGON

While direct U.S. engagement in the Vietnam War ended in 1973, the last Americans were not withdrawn from South Vietnam until the fall of Saigon in 1975. Even before the North Vietnamese army captured the city, however, the U.S. government began admitting South Vietnamese nationals—particularly those who had worked directly with the American forces—into the United States as refugees.

The first evacuation program began in the last few days of April 1975. The federal government had initially planned to evacuate only about 17,000 people—all of them U.S. employees and their families. But as the streets of Saigon turned to chaos and the U.S. embassy became flooded with desperate Vietnamese, the program expanded to include Vietnamese employees and those whose lives were immediately threatened by the change in power. In a few short days, nearly 86,000 people fled the country, cramming themselves into helicopters and airplanes, with some attempting to grab onto the outside of an aircraft in desperation as the vehicles lifted off the roof of the American embassy. With less than 10 hours to decide on a course of action, the panicked Vietnamese had no idea where they would end up or how long they would be away from their homeland and loved ones.

By December 1975, the U.S. government had granted entry to 125,000 Vietnamese refugees. Many of this first wave were soldiers, government officials, and urban professionals who feared for their future at the hands of the Communists. Most spoke English and had worked with the South Vietnamese or U.S. governments

Vietnamese refugees arrive in the United States in 1975. (National Archives)

during the war. Others feared that their high social status or religious beliefs would place them at the mercy of the Communists. Nearly 50 percent of this first wave of refugees were Christians who had moved from the Communist North to South Vietnam at the time of the Geneva Accords in order to escape religious persecution.

Since the needs of Vietnamese refugees were strikingly different from those of ordinary immigrants, three earlier pieces of legislation helped to set the groundwork for their admission to the United States. The McCarran-Walter Act of 1952 (discussed in chapter 5) gave the U.S. attorney general the power to "parole" into America any alien for "emergency reasons or for reasons deemed strictly in the public interest." Two other pieces of immigration legislation focused on the specifics of refugees fleeing Communist regimes: the Refugee Relief Act of 1953 and the 1965 Immigration Act. The attorney general had previously used the power of parole to aid Chinese fleeing Mao's Communist takeover in 1949, as well as to help Hungarian refugees leaving Soviet-occupied Hungary in 1956 and Cubans abandoning Cuba after Castro's coup in 1959.

Between April and December 1975, more than 100,000 refugees from Vietnam and Cambodia were admitted to the United States as parolees, so declared by the U.S. attorney general. The following year, 50,000 Vietnamese government employees, 75,000 relatives of U.S. residents, and 4,000 Vietnamese orphans were granted asylum. The classification was later extended to include Vietnamese "boat people" (discussed later in this chapter).

The parole program was scrapped in March 1980 with President Jimmy Carter's signing of the Refugee Act. The establishment of a refugee quota of 50,000 per year from 1980 to 1983 streamlined a system operating within the chaos of Southeast Asians fleeing for their lives. The Refugee Act of 1980 also granted the president power to admit more people than the quota allowed after first consulting Congress. Another intent of the 1980 Refugee Act was to include all individuals with a "well-founded fear of persecution," not just those fleeing Communist-controlled nations.

When refugees first leave their troubled homelands, they generally head for "first-asylum" countries. These nations are located near the refugees' homeland and declared safe places in which to relocate. During the Southeast Asian refugee crisis of the mid-1970s, first-asylum countries for those fleeing Vietnam, Laos, and Cambodia included Thailand, Hong Kong, and the Philippines. Many times, however, first-asylum countries are not able to adequately handle the huge influx of people needing food, clothing, shelter, medical attention, and emotional support. The Red Cross and United Nations help out in such times of crisis, but the scope of a crisis is often too large for the world's humanitarians to handle all at once.

Countries that permanently resettle refugees on a voluntary basis are known as "second-asylum" countries. The United States became the leading second-asylum country for Southeast Asian refugees dur-

ing the mid-1970s—not surprisingly, since many felt that the United States had a moral obligation to help those whose suffering the U.S. government had helped create. Other nations, such as France, China, Canada, and Australia, have also opened their doors to Southeast Asian refugees.

THE BOAT PEOPLE AND SECOND-WAVE REFUGEES

Although the United States granted entry to many Vietnamese in 1975, many others remained trapped in Vietnam, unable to leave because they lacked the government or American connection, the money to buy one of the scarce seats available on the airplanes still allowed out of the country, or both. As a result, in the first few weeks of May 1978, thousands of Vietnamese refugees began to flee the country by boat. Most of these people were rescued by U.S. naval personnel. They were then taken to Guam and the Philippines to await resettlement. Compared with the first wave of Vietnamese, these refugees, known as "boat people," were as a group less educated and primarily from poor, rural areas, though some were educated professionals. In addition, the vast majority of the second wave, unlike the first, did not speak English.

Amid the chaos, some Vietnamese decided to stay in their homeland, hoping that the Communists would bring peace to Vietnam. But in 1979, the Communist government under the leadership of President Nguyen Van Thieu began to exert tighter control over the country, instituting oppressive measures

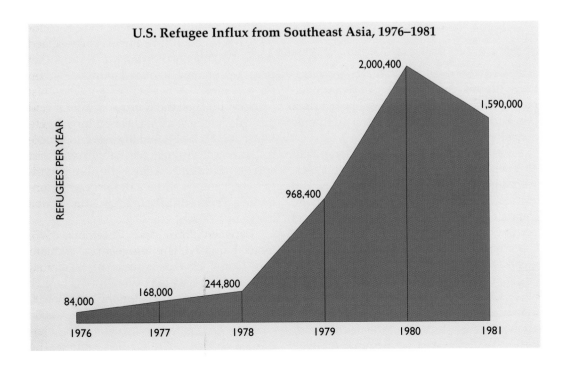

U.S. Refugee Influx from Southeast Asia, 1976–1981

REFUGEES PER YEAR

84,000 — 1976
168,000 — 1977
244,800 — 1978
968,400 — 1979
2,000,400 — 1980
1,590,000 — 1981

Refugee Camps of Southeast Asia, 1970s

CHINA

UNION OF MYANMAR (BURMA)

VIETNAM
Hanoi
Haiphong

LAOS

Vientiane

THAILAND

Hue

Bangkok

CAMBODIA

Ho Chi Minh City (Saigon)

Phnom Penh

George Town

MALAYSIA

Kuala Lumpur

- ◉ Lao refugee camps
- ▣ Cambodian refugee camps
- ◬ Vietnamese refugee camps
- ✪ Capitals
- — National borders

Packed aboard rickety, leaky, overcrowded vessels, the refugees faced starvation; uncertain destinations; rough, stormy seas; and vicious Thai pirates, who raped and killed many Vietnamese boat people. Refugee Thai Dang remembered what she experienced on one of these boats at the age of 13:

The pirates, wearing almost nothing but frightening tattoos, jumped into our boat with axes and guns to rob and beat us. The air was saturated with the most disheartening cries.... We were literally begging on our knees.

Survivors of the arduous journey were then forced to live in refugee camps when they reached Thailand. Most stayed there for months, some even for a period of years. From there, most refugees moved to the United States, although Australia, Canada, and France also accepted the crisis victims.

THE CAMBODIAN REFUGEES

In addition to Vietnamese, the second wave of Southeast Asian refugees into the United States included Laotians and Cambodians who were also escaping oppressive governments. Like second-wave Vietnamese, these refugees tended to be poor, undereducated farm people who had a difficult time adjusting to life in the United States.

Hundreds of thousands of Cambodians tried to flee the terror of certain death by sneaking into Thailand, but due to Pol Pot's iron control of physical movement, relatively few succeeded until his overthrow in 1979, when the Vietnamese invaded and occupied Cambodia. Though weak from torture, illness, stress, and starvation, Cambodian refugees flooded into Thailand, and the magnitude of Pol Pot's extermination program became known to the world for the first time.

Life in Thailand's refugee camps was difficult. Overcrowding, unsanitary conditions, and lack of adequate food and medical care contributed to the physical and emotional trauma suffered by Cambodian refugees. Some had to wait for years before finding a sponsor to help them move out of the camps.

Between 1975 and 1990, more than 100,000 Cambodian refugees made their way to the United States, with the years between 1981 and 1985 showing the largest influx, at 69,726. The Cambodian population in the United States, including those born as U.S. citizens, totaled more than 200,000 by 2001.

such as press restrictions, the collectivization of farms, the takeover of private businesses, and the forced relocation of urban populations into newly created "economic zones."

Ethnic Chinese made up approximately 40 percent of second-wave refugees. Although ethnic Chinese living in South Vietnam composed only 7 percent of the country's population, they owned nearly 80 percent of the retail trade industry. The Communist-driven economic changes greatly affected this group, who feared government repression even more in 1979, when China and Vietnam became engaged in military disputes over border divisions.

Vietnamese refugees who escaped by boat after 1979 faced a perilous journey.

THE LAOTIAN REFUGEES

Refugees from Laos, though not subjected to the extreme violence of Pol Pot's regime, had to leave their country under much the same chaotic and frightening circumstances as the Vietnamese and Cambodians.

When the Americans pulled out of Vietnam, they also pulled out of Laos. As in Vietnam, the U.S. Air Force undertook a massive airlift of local U.S. allies—Hmong soldiers and their families. Entire Hmong villages disappeared into the freedom of the sky as the Pathet Lao quickly secured control of Laos. Also as with Vietnam and Cambodia, a Laotian refugee crisis mushroomed overnight.

Like the Vietnamese who had helped U.S. operations, any Laotians who sided with the United States or the Royal Lao faction during the civil war became immediate targets for the new Communist government. Hmong guerrilla fighters faced particular danger as the Pathet Lao focused on violent revenge against them. Many Laotians, though not in immediate danger, fled the country fearing the threat of political repression, religious persecution, and forced labor at Communist "reeducation" camps. Hundreds of thousands poured into Thailand's overtaxed refugee camps to await sponsorship for relocation in the United States. To reach Thailand by way of the Mekong River, some Laotians bought illegal boat tickets; others swam or floated across strapped to tree trunks. Entire families floated across by way of huge rubber tires taken from military vehicles.

In addition to the 70,000 ethnic Lao and 10,000 ethnic Mien, 60,000 ethnic Hmong migrated to the United States in 1975. By 1983, it was estimated that 300,000 to 400,000 Laotians had fled their Communist-controlled homeland. Hmong, while composing only 10 percent of the population of Laos, made up nearly half of the U.S. Laotian refugee population by 1996. By 2001, more Laotians lived in the United States than in Laos's capital, Vientiance. Only about 100,000 Hmong remained in Laos.

THE AMERASIAN HOMECOMING ACT

Amerasian is the term used to refer to children born to American servicemen and Asian mothers. Most mothers of Amerasian children are Vietnamese. When U.S. troops were pulled out of Vietnam in the mid-1970s, most Amerasian

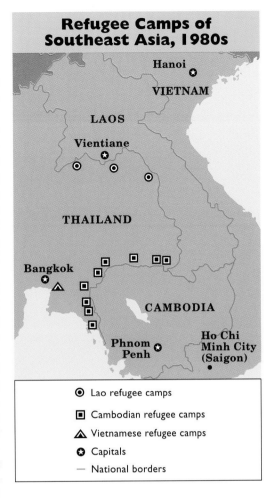

Refugee Camps of Southeast Asia, 1980s

- ◉ Lao refugee camps
- ▣ Cambodian refugee camps
- △ Vietnamese refugee camps
- ✪ Capitals
- — National borders

children were left behind. Amerasians met with racist treatment in Vietnam, since both the government and the public disapproved of the children's American parentage. Many of these children came from unplanned, out-of-wedlock pregnancies and were therefore not welcomed by their mothers' families. Some were born with birth defects as a result of poisoning by Agent Orange—an herbicide sprayed over the jungles of Vietnam by U.S. troops. Orphaned and abandoned Amerasian children in Vietnam begged for food on the streets or tried to survive by doing odd jobs. Some 12,000 Amerasian children struggled in South Vietnam this way for years.

In 1987, Congress passed the Amerasian Homecoming Act. This piece of legislation granted special provisions for the immigration of 46,000 Amerasian offspring who by that time were teenagers. The act affected Amerasian children born between January 1, 1962, and January 1, 1977. By 1994, more than 75,000 Amerasians and their families, also allowed under the Homecoming Act, had resettled in the United States. This wave of Amerasian refugees was rounded out by former prisoners of Vietnamese reeducation camps and other detainees.

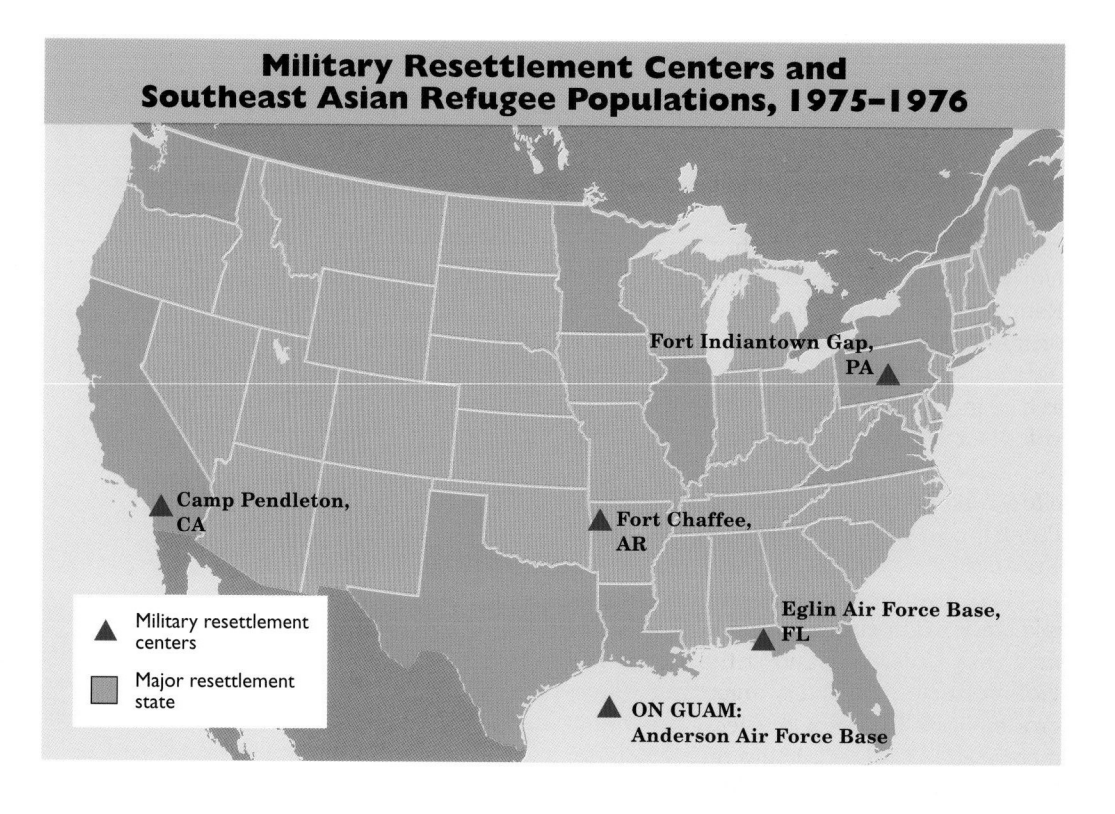

Military Resettlement Centers and Southeast Asian Refugee Populations, 1975–1976

Fort Indiantown Gap, PA ▲

Camp Pendleton, CA ▲

Fort Chaffee, AR ▲

Eglin Air Force Base, FL ▲

▲ Military resettlement centers

▢ Major resettlement state

▲ ON GUAM: Anderson Air Force Base

RESETTLEMENT IN THE UNITED STATES
....

Prior to the refugee crisis of the mid-1970s, small numbers of Vietnamese students, teachers, and diplomats lived in the United States. In 1964, around 600 Vietnamese were residing in the country with the intent of only a temporary stay. In the aftermath of the war, the United States's existing refugee quotas could not begin to meet the need generated by the Vietnamese refugee crisis. Therefore, in 1975, Congress passed the Indochina Migration and Refugee Assistance Act. The temporary program authorized special admission of Indochinese refugees and created an aid program to assist their domestic resettlement. By 1985, the demographics had transformed radically with the permanent settlement of more than 640,000 Vietnamese.

The evacuation of Vietnamese and other Southeast Asians from their war-torn homelands in the immediate aftermath of the Vietnam War presented an enormous logistical problem for U.S. officials. The speed of the liftoff effort and the sudden surge in numbers stretched the limits of the plan that was in place. The U.S. military transported most of the first wave of evacuees to Andersen Air Force Base in Guam, a U.S. territorial island located in the western Pacific. From Andersen, the refugees were divided into four groups, each destined for a different federal military base: Camp Pendleton, California; Fort Chaffee, Arkansas; Eglin Air Force Base, Florida; and

Fort Indiantown Gap, Pennsylvania. The U.S. government and the Interagency Task Force handed out identification numbers and registration papers and provided housing, food, and clothing. They also conducted interviews and physical examinations. Between 1975 and 1992, the United States spent nearly $11 billion to resettle the refugees, of whom 128,000 came from Vietnam, 11,000 from Laos (most of Hmong ethnicity), and 5,700 from Cambodia.

Of the first wave of Southeast Asian refugees, 21 percent settled in California. The remainder scattered across the country with at least 100 in every state except Alaska. The federal government made an effort to spread new refugees across the nation in order to minimize the harsh economic impact on a local community that a sudden, sharp influx of refugees would generate. This meant, however, that some Southeast Asian families were split apart. The resulting isolation and emotional trauma led many refugees to relocate after their government resettlement. By 1980, nearly 45 percent of the initial wave had joined others to create ethnic enclaves, located mainly in California and Texas.

The U.S. government created several different programs and organizations to conduct its wide-scale resettlement effort. Of the eight federal resettlement programs enacted between 1975 and 1992, three were especially significant in altering the lives of Southeast Asian refugees. The Special Parole Program of 1975 provided aid to 129,792; the Indochinese Parole Programs of 1977–1980 aided 268,482; and the Refugee Act of 1980 aided 1,029,572 between the years of 1980 and 1992.

In addition to federal government programs, numerous international, national, and private organizations help refugees relocate in the United States. The Office of the United Nations High Commissioners for Refugees (UNHCR), created in 1951, is one of the leading international groups to provide assistance to refugees. The UNHCR acts as a coordinating house, networking various volunteer agencies and nations worldwide to cooperate efficiently in resettlement efforts. In 1981, the UNHCR earned a Nobel Peace Prize for its work in resettling Southeast Asian refugees in the United States.

The Office of Refugee Resettlement takes a leading role in providing information, cash assistance, and critical social services to newly arrived refugees. Volunteer groups contracted by the federal government (called VOLAGs) help refugees resettle through sponsorship programs. Sponsors, who are usually families or church groups, provide emergency assistance in the form of housing and clothing and also help refugees find jobs, enroll their children in public schools, and learn to negotiate the rules, customs, and language of U.S. culture. Organizations within the VOLAG system include the United Hebrew Immigrant Aid Society, the United States Catholic Conference, the Lutheran Immigration and Refugee Service, the International Rescue Committee, the American Council for Nationalities Services, and Travelers' Aid International Social Services. Each VOLAG receives $500 per refugee to help ease the process.

Mutual Aid Associations (MAAs), created in 1975 and funded by private donations as well as the U.S. government, have played a significant role in helping Southeast Asian refugees resettle in the United States. Refugees who have successfully assimilated into life in the United States volunteer to help new refugees find needed social services, learn English, and understand the ways of American culture. MAAs are especially attractive to new arrivals since volunteers know how to speak the native language and are familiar with specific issues of conflict and confusion that arise in the gulf between the culture of their native land and American culture. MAAs lobby Congress on relevant political issues and also help organize festival celebrations that keep native traditions alive.

The problems faced by refugees at any time are similar in many ways to those of other immigrants. Language and cultural

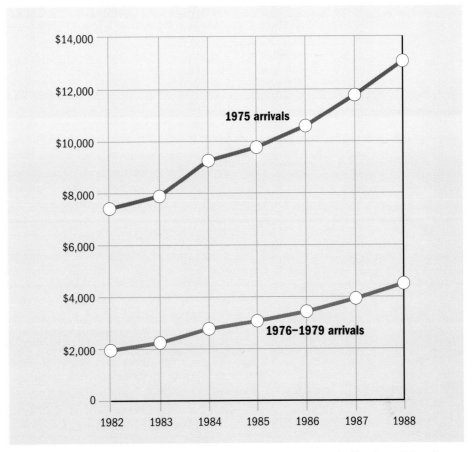

Because the members of the first wave of Vietnamese refugees were more highly educated than those who followed them, their incomes tended to be higher on arriving in the United States, although still far lower than the average mean income for all Americans; that figure rose from $9,940 in 1980 to $18,666 in 1990. In fact, the income level of 1975 refugees barely kept pace with the United States poverty rate, which rose from $8,414 in 1980 to $12,674 in 1989.

barriers as well as prejudiced reactions on the part of the host communities can affect immigrants and refugees alike. Psychologically, however, the differences are pronounced. Immigrants, though often "pushed out" of their homelands by poverty, famine, and war, generally have the time and inclination to dream, save, and plan for their journey and new life—a luxury not afforded refugees, for whom destinations are unknown. And even once settled, refugees face emotional and logistical problems that exacerbate their already precarious economic positions in their new communities. For Southeast Asian refugees—especially the first wave to flee the area in 1975—there was no time to plan. The only decision to be made was between life and death.

VIETNAMESE RESETTLEMENT

Vietnamese refugees have had varied success rates in acculturation to life in the United States. The first wave of refugees from Vietnam spoke English, were well educated, and were generally familiar with Western ways. Many have built successful careers or established thriving small businesses, although most have never attained the same level of career status that they enjoyed in Vietnam.

For most Vietnamese refugees, however, income levels have remained low. By 1988, those who left Vietnam in 1975 had reached an average annual income level in the United States of only $13,000. Those who came to the United States between 1976 and 1979 fared even worse, reaching an average income level of only $4,200 per year. Refugees of the second wave were less educated and skilled than the earlier group, though some achieved success through small business ventures. Between 1982 and 1987, the number of Vietnamese-owned small businesses increased by 415 percent. However, many second-wave Vietnamese refugees remained stuck in low-paying jobs and isolated from American society at large due to cultural differences and language barriers. Many Vietnamese families relied on their American-born, English-speaking children to negotiate the culture for them.

Traditional family life has been almost impossible for the Vietnamese to maintain in America. Traditionally, the needs of the Vietnamese family have priority over those of the individual, and large groups consisting of cousins, uncles, aunts, and grandparents always lived together in Vietnam. Few sponsors could scrape together enough cash to keep even nuclear families intact, let alone such extended familial groups. Even Vietnamese who managed to rejoin their extended families faced problems, as U.S. zoning regulations prohibit large groups of people technically defined as "unrelated" from living together in single households.

By 1980, however, isolation was eased as nearly half of the first wave of Southeast Asian refugees had relocated to ethnic enclaves, mainly in California and Texas. By 1988, a two-mile stretch of Bolsa Avenue in Westminster, California, had sprouted so many Vietnamese-American businesses that the district became officially titled "Little Saigon." In Orange and Los Angeles Counties, Vietnamese doctors, dentists, restaurants, and food stores abound, including the large Vietnamese-run Wai Wai and Man Wah supermarket chains. Tony Lam, Westminster city councilman, became the first Vietnamese American to serve in elected office.

As ethnic neighborhoods became established, many of California's run-down urban areas have been reinvigorated with life. Vietnamese Americans have turned run-down areas in San Francisco, San Jose, Santa Ana, and tiny parts of Los Angeles (as well as Arlington, Virginia) into vibrant neighborhoods filled with homes and businesses. Though the Vietnamese make up only 10 percent of San Jose's population, almost 40 percent of all retail businesses in downtown San Jose are owned by Vietnamese.

Vietnamese children have succeeded in the U.S. public school system in many instances. Many have gone on to college. A study conducted in 1988 revealed that Vietnamese students made up 25 percent of the valedictorians and salutatorians in San Diego high schools, even though the Vietnamese constituted only 7 percent of the graduating classes. The same study also noted that only Chinese-, Japanese-, and Korean-American students academically outperformed the Southeast Asians in San Diego's public high schools.

Some Vietnamese youths, however, have fallen prey to a lifestyle dominated by gang membership. Most of this "lost generation" arrived in the United States without adult relatives or supervision and unable to speak, read, or write English. Both male and female Vietnamese gang members are known as *bui doi*, "the dust of life." Unlike other U.S. youth gangs, they have demonstrated more interest in robbing other Vietnamese than in defending their territory from other gangs. Many post-1975 Vietnamese refugees hide their money at home due to a lack of trust in the security of banks rather than deposit it and thus are regularly subject to gang attack.

By 1985, after the arrival of the second wave of Southeast Asian refugees, the United States had accepted an additional half-million Vietnamese, Cambodians, and Laotians. As the camps in Southeast Asia emptied during the 1980s, the number of refugees declined. However, with the end of the cold war, warmer relations between the United States and Vietnam encouraged another sizable Vietnamese influx. Under the Orderly Departure Program, a joint agreement between the United States and Vietnam signed in 1979, 20,000 Vietnamese per year enter the United States as immigrants rather than as refugees. The agreement also applies to family members of those Vietnamese already living in the United States.

The Socialist Republic of Vietnam, though still under the strict control of the ruling Communist Party of Vietnam, has shown signs of improvement in the area of human rights and has cooperated at times with United Nations guidelines. Political

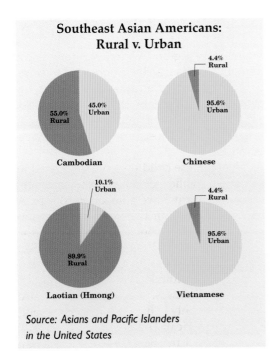

Southeast Asian Americans: Rural v. Urban

Cambodian
55.0% Rural
45.0% Urban

Chinese
4.4% Rural
95.6% Urban

Laotian (Hmong)
10.1% Urban
89.9% Rural

Vietnamese
4.4% Rural
95.6% Urban

Source: Asians and Pacific Islanders in the United States

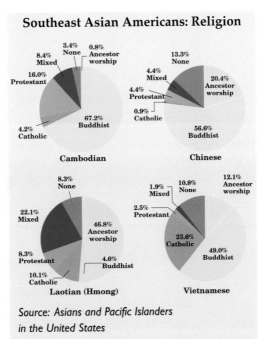

Southeast Asian Americans: Religion

Cambodian
3.4% None
0.8% Ancestor worship
8.4% Mixed
16.0% Protestant
4.2% Catholic
67.2% Buddhist

Chinese
13.3% None
4.4% Mixed
4.4% Protestant
0.9% Catholic
20.4% Ancestor worship
56.6% Buddhist

Laotian (Hmong)
8.3% None
22.1% Mixed
8.3% Protestant
10.1% Catholic
4.6% Buddhist
46.8% Ancestor worship

Vietnamese
1.9% Mixed
10.8% None
2.5% Protestant
23.6% Catholic
12.1% Ancestor worship
49.0% Buddhist

Source: Asians and Pacific Islanders in the United States

dissent continues to be repressed, but there are glimmers of social and economic change internally. Unified Vietnam has also released tens of thousands of political detainees and allowed the return of thousands of Vietnamese who had fled abroad as refugees.

CAMBODIAN RESETTLEMENT

Adjustment to life in modern America has been especially difficult for Cambodian refugees due to the horror of their experiences under Pol Pot's rule. Many Cambodian refugees lost their spouses during the time of the killing fields. Thus, they arrived in America as single parents, charged with the solitary task of raising their children in a new culture.

Many Cambodians have also suffered post-traumatic stress disorder, a psychological illness that afflicts victims of torture, rape, physical abuse, and other atrocities. Symptoms of this disorder include depression, emotional numbing, social withdrawal, nightmares, sleep disorders, and poor appetite. Many Cambodian women living in the United States during the 1980s suffered a form of blindness diagnosed by American doctors as psychosomatic rather than a physical condition. For the victims, though, the effects of the blindness are physical as well as emotional. It is generally believed that they lost their sight after witnessing, experiencing, or being forced to participate in the violent acts characteristic of Pol Pot's Cambodia.

Such psychological problems exacerbated the already difficult transition faced by refugees challenged with the need to develop job skills and language proficiency, gain education, and assimilate into a new culture. As Khmer Rouge survivor Haing Ngor reflected:

... in 1975 the Communists put an end to our [traditional and stable] way of life. We lost everything—our families, our monks, our villages, our land, all our possessions. Everything. When we came to the United States we couldn't put our old lives back together. We didn't even have the pieces.

Cambodian refugees scattered around the United States at first, but later relocated in an effort to find better job opportunities, warmer climates, and the support of a network of ethnic peers. The majority eventually resettled in California. As of 2001, Long Beach, California, was home to the largest Cambodian community outside of Cambodia, and the Cambodian district along Anaheim Street is known as "Little Phnom Penh."

Lowell, Massachusetts, was home to the second largest number of Cambodian settlers in the United States. A Buddhist temple constructed in 1984 in Lowell attracted many refugees to the working-class town, as did the promise of job opportunities offered by Wang Laboratories, the town's largest employer in the 1970s. The population of Cambodians in Lowell leveled off, however, as the public school system became overloaded with the special needs of refugee children and the local economy nosedived in the late 1980s when Wang Laboratories ordered massive layoffs.

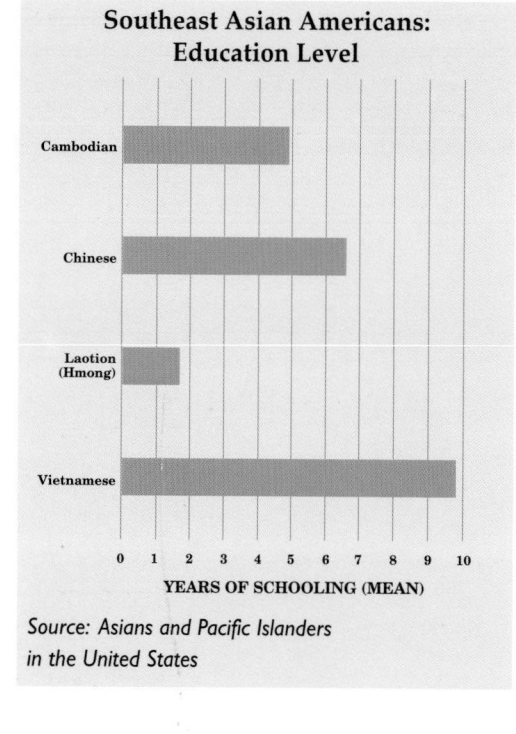

Southeast Asian Americans: Education Level

YEARS OF SCHOOLING (MEAN)

Source: Asians and Pacific Islanders in the United States

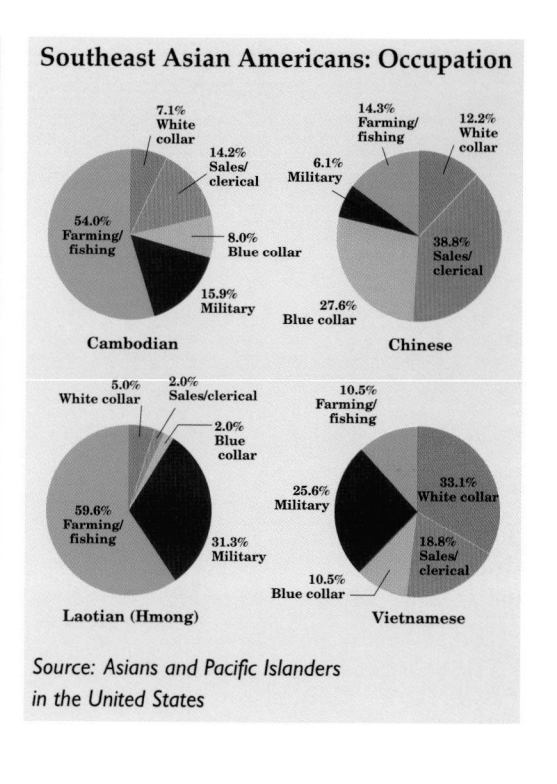

Southeast Asian Americans: Occupation

Source: Asians and Pacific Islanders in the United States

Higher-paying skilled job opportunities for recent immigrants—especially refugees—are usually hard to come by. Many Californian Cambodians, however, benefited from the employment opportunities sparked by Bun Tek Ngoy, who became a millionaire during the 1980s with the successful opening of a chain of doughnut shops. His nephew, Bun H. Tao, became a successful distributor of doughnut-making supplies. Bun Tao's customers, mainly Cambodian, sought to follow a similar economically successful path. In 1996, nearly two-thirds of all California-based doughnut shops were owned and operated by Cambodian families.

Ethnic Mien Laotians have settled in Portland, Oregon, and Seattle, Washington, as well as Sacramento, Oakland, San Jose, and Long Beach, California. More than half of America's Hmong refugees live in California, while others have also settled in Missoula, Montana; Providence, Rhode Island; Minneapolis-St. Paul, Minnesota; and La Crosse and Eau Claire, Wisconsin.

Hmong Laotians, in particular, have had an extremely difficult time adjusting to life in contemporary America. Until the arrival of missionaries in 1953, the agrarian Hmong had no written language of their own. Thus, nearly 70 percent of Hmong refugees arrived in the United States illiterate in their own language. The very concept of written symbolism was nearly incomprehensible, but in order to survive in the United States the refugees had to become literate in their own language, then learn how to speak, read, and write in English, too. Even a task as simple as paying a utility bill was daunting for people unfamiliar with letters, numbers, stamps, envelopes, and deadlines.

Other Hmong cultural customs conflicted greatly with societal norms in the United States. For example, among Hmong, it was customary for men to marry girls aged 12 to 14, an illegal practice in the United States. It was also traditionally not necessary for a man to gain a female's consent for premarital sexual relations—something that would be considered rape in the United States, and therefore illegal. These practices, however, still continue among the Hmong in the United States, resulting in high birth rates in the community.

High numbers of children coupled with low levels of education and no or low-paying jobs have placed a high percentage of Hmong refugees on American welfare rolls. Unemployment for the Hmong stood at 90 percent as recently as 1996. Jobs for this group generally fall into domestic service work, seasonal migrant work, and the selling of handmade jewelry or needlework.

Although most Laotian refugees farmed independently in their homeland, their success at farming in the industrialized United States has been very low. The use of pesticides, the day-to-day business of marketing produce, the mechanics of modern farm equipment, and even the concept of irrigation—all are foreign to the Hmong refugees. As one Hmong refugee commented to author Ronald Takaki during an interview in 1988:

When I stayed in Laos I was a farmer....I had all things I wanted. I never begged anyone for food. Only when I came to the country of America I had to beg.

Like earlier Asian immigrants, the Mien and Hmong have encountered racism in their new communities. Most Americans have no idea who they are as a people and no grasp of the depth of their sacrifice and involvement in the Vietnam War. Nearly every Hmong refugee family lost a father or brother fighting the CIA's "secret war" in Laos, yet Laotians are subjected to racial harassment and threats of violence.

Like Cambodians and Vietnam veterans who suffer from post-traumatic stress disorder as a result of their Vietnam War experiences, Hmong males have died from an mysterious illness called sudden unexplained nocturnal death syndrome (SUND). Among Hmong men aged 30 to 50 living in the United States, sudden death during sleep is an unexplainable and regular occurrence. The men, all soldiers in Vietnam for 15 to 20 years, were otherwise physically healthy. American doctors have agreed that nerve gas used during Vietnam is not the cause of SUND, but no physical explanation has been found. Some believe that the men are literally dying of grief over the loss of their traditional way of life. Relocation depression is common to refugee populations and is especially widespread among the elder Hmong. Nightmares, uncontrollable sobbing, listlessness, and apathy are all symptoms common to depressed adult Hmong, torn from the land to which they had not only happy familiarity, but a spiritual attachment.

Hmong youth, however, are gradually adjusting to life in modern America. Having fled the mountains of Laos while still young children, their attachment to the traditional tribal life is far weaker than that of their parents. Hmong youth have learned to read and write English in U.S. public schools and therefore have wider job opportunities and a chance to go to college. Unlike their parents, children of Hmong refugees generally define themselves as Hmong Americans and plan to stay in the United States.

The slow process of adjustment for Hmong Americans, as well as for other Southeast Asian refugees, immigrants, and their children, is in many ways, yet another legacy of U.S. military involvement in Southeast Asia. Clearly, the impact of the Vietnam War has had a ripple effect that has reached well beyond the U.S. servicemen and women who served in the war, only to come home to face a difficult readjustment.

Those ripples have also helped pull a new wave of Asians to the United States. While many of the wounds suffered by those who experienced the trauma of conflict in Southeast Asia may even now remain unhealed, a new generation of U.S.-born Americans of Southeast Asian descent has reached adulthood and is broadening the definitions of what it means to be American.

KOREAN, INDIAN, CHINESE, AND FILIPINO IMMIGRATION SINCE 1965

Southeast Asians may be the most recent group of newcomers from Asia to the United States, but they are far from the only one. Since 1965, the number of all Asian immigrant groups has increased. Changing immigration laws, beginning with the Hart-Celler Act of 1965, have had a tremendous impact on Asian immigration, especially for Koreans and Asian Indians, who were a disappearing minority in America before World War II. Increased population, community activism, educational achievement, assimilation, economic success and reinvestment, and urban renewal programs have all contributed to change and growth within America's Asian communities.

THE HART-CELLER ACT

The legislative and legal victories that the African-American civil rights movement of the 1960s pushed to success set the stage for continued progressive reform. The year 1965 saw the passage of the Voting Rights Act, the creation of several antipoverty programs under the leadership of President Lyndon B. Johnson, and the passage of the Hart-Celler Immigration Act, also known as the Immigration Act of 1965.

Hart-Celler amended the 1952 McCarran-Walter Act, which had ended the outright ban on Asian immigration and established U.S. entry quotas of 2,990 Asian immigrants per year and 149,667 European immigrants per year. Under Hart-Celler, the use of quotas based on national origins ceased. The new system allowed an annual admission of 170,000 immigrants from the Eastern Hemisphere (with a maximum of 20,000 per country) and 120,000 from the Western Hemisphere. As soon as the immigrants earned citizenship, their immediate families could enter freely as permanent residents and bring other extended family

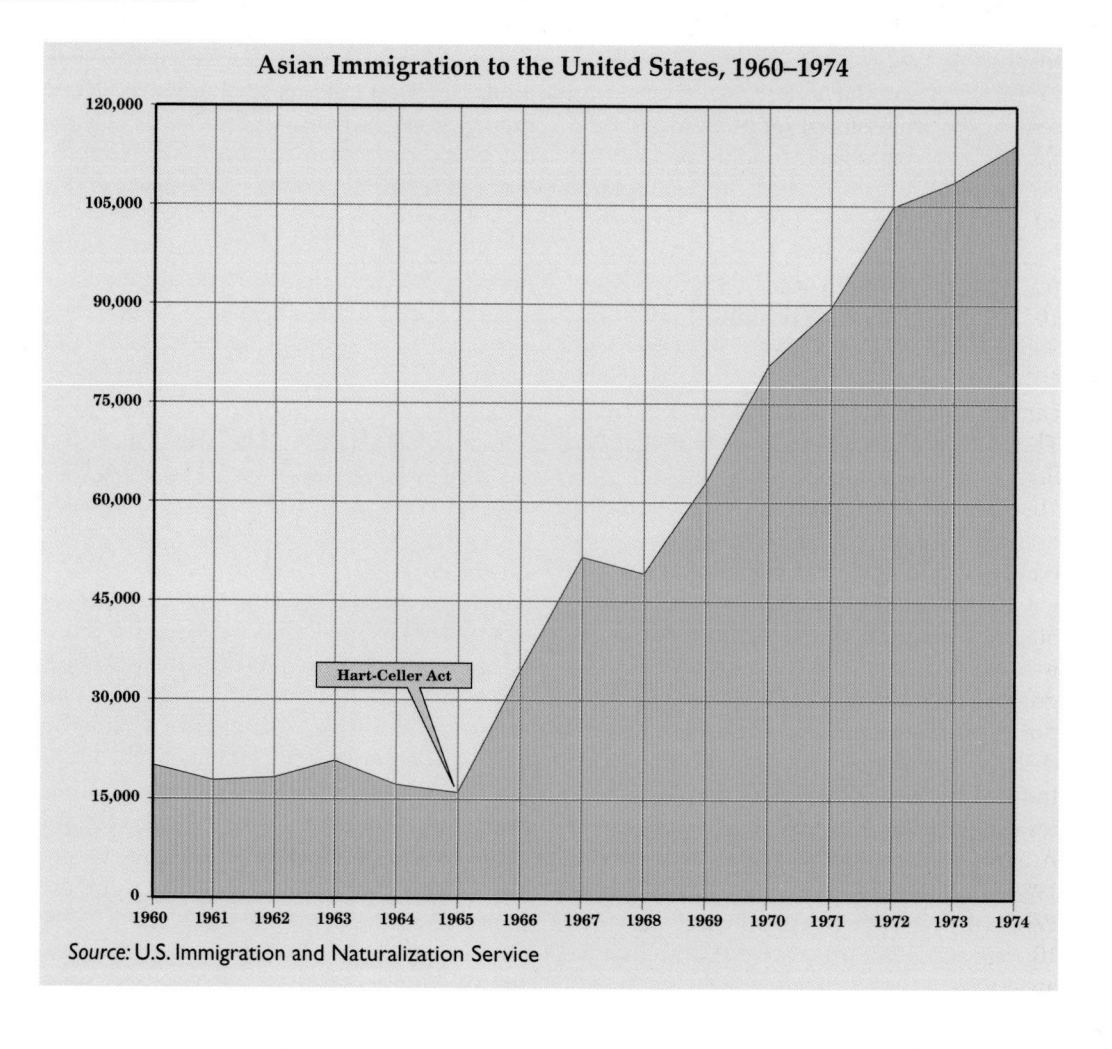

Asian Immigration to the United States, 1960–1974

Hart-Celler Act

Source: U.S. Immigration and Naturalization Service

members along in a new practice called chain migration.

The Hart-Celler Act based admission to the United States on an ordered system of seven preferences, as follows: first—unmarried foreign-born children of U.S. citizens over age 21; second—spouses and unmarried children of permanent resident aliens; third—professionals, scientists, and artists of "exceptional ability"; fourth—married children of U.S. citizens over age 21; fifth—siblings of U.S. citizens; sixth—workers, skilled and unskilled, in occupations for which labor is in short supply in the United States; and seventh—refugees. The bill stipulated that non-Western workers could be admitted only if the U.S. secretary of labor certified that a shortage existed in that occupation and that the entry of immigrants would not lead to lower wages or working conditions for resident U.S. citizens.

In the mid-1960s, Asian Americans totaled less than 1 percent of the U.S. population. The architects of Hart-Celler believed that Europeans would continue to take up most immigration slots and that the number of immigrants from Asia would remain small, with few taking advantage of the bill's family reunification provisions.

This belief proved grossly inaccurate, however, as immigration statistics changed dramatically after the passage of the Hart-Celler Act. In 1965, Asian immigration to the United States totaled 16,062; the year 1975 saw the entry of 116,521 Asians. Since Hart-Cellar, most immigrants to the United States have been from Asia and Latin America.

ASIAN INDIANS

In 1946, the Asian-Indian population in the United States numbered only 1,500. Within a few years after the passage of the Hart-Celler Act, however, the population increased significantly. By 1970, 20,000 Pakistanis had arrived in the United States; half of these were Punjabi. By 1980, the total Asian-Indian population, including those from Pakistan, Sri Lanka, and Bangladesh, had risen to 525,000; it had increased to 815,447 by 1990.

Unlike the first wave of turn-of-the-century Sikh laborers, who on average were less educated, late 20th-century South Asian immigrants were largely highly educated, English-speaking professionals from urban areas. Most were of the Hindu religion. Due to overpopulation and high unemployment in India, many have left the country in search of professional opportunities, and they have brought their families with them.

India is a struggling nation with limited job opportunities for its well educated. In 1970, 20,000 doctors found themselves unemployed in their native land; in 1974, 100,000 engineers could not find work. Salaries in India are also low—in the mid-1970s, physicians in the United States earned 15 times what they would in India. Thus, many chose to emigrate to the United States, a phenomenon referred to as a "brain drain." For India, as for other developing countries, this exodus of the highly educated is an unfortunate loss of talent.

Asian Indians living in the United States averaged a yearly income of $18,707 in 1979, making them the highest income group among America's recent immigrant population. In addition, no matter what the field, the unemployment rate for Asian Indians in the United States has been very low. Less than 5 percent of Asian-Indian Americans lived below the poverty line in 1980 and few received public assistance. While the national average for savings was 10 percent, Asian Indians typically put away 20 to 40 percent of their annual incomes, with self-employment and home ownership as primary goals.

Asian-Indian professionals who have come to the United States since 1947 have met with great success. A higher percentage of Asian Indians occupied more managerial and professional positions than any other Asian-American group. In 1980, 47 percent of adult Asian Indians held professional or managerial jobs in the United States, whereas 30 percent of Chinese, 28 percent of Japanese, and 22 percent of Koreans held such jobs. Asian-Indian women have come to the United States in roughly the same numbers as male Asian-Indian immigrants. The women, too are highly educated and eager to seize professional satisfaction and economic opportunities offered in the United States. In India, only about 13 percent of females worked outside the home in 1980.

Since the 1980s, entrepreneurship has risen among Asian Indians. Many have been especially successful in the hotel business. Others have opened convenience stores, Indian grocery stores, restaurants, travel agencies, and gas stations. Many Asian Indians in New York City drive taxicabs; by 1996, more than 40 percent of all New York City cab drivers were Asian Indians.

Most post-1965 Asian-Indian immigrants have chosen to live in or near cities in the Northeast such as New York City, where the Asian-Indian community numbers more than 40,000, or in midwestern cities such as Chicago, which boasts an Asian-Indian population of 23,000. College towns throughout the country have attracted Asian-Indian intellectuals, and San Francisco and Houston have drawn many engineers and other scientists. Although almost none live in Hawaii, Asian Indians generally prefer the warmer climates of states such as California, where their population has

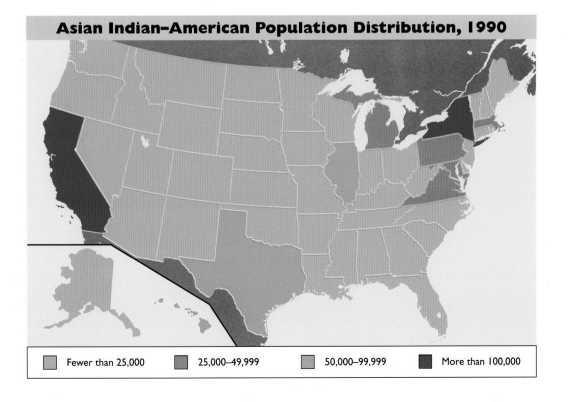

Asian Indian–American Population Distribution, 1990

Fewer than 25,000   25,000–49,999   50,000–99,999   More than 100,000 risen to nearly 60,000. Since 1970, many Sikhs have moved to family farms that by 2001 were part of a growing California Punjabi community, breathing life back into a once-thriving Asian-Indian locale. As of 2001, the Sacramento Valley was home to more than 7,000 acres of Sikh-owned and operated farmland.

KOREAN AMERICANS

In 1960, America's Korean population stood at only 10,000, but by 1985 that figure had shot up to 500,000. The passage of the Hart-Celler Act, coupled with Korea's ongoing economic difficulties since the Korean War, led many Koreans to emigrate. Between 1965 and 1980, approximately 299,000 Koreans moved to the United States. These numbers included skilled laborers, engineers, accountants, chemists, technicians, and other professionals encouraged by the success of Korean doctors who had already fashioned successful careers, especially in the New York metropolitan area. Since 1976, the immigration numbers for Koreans come to an annual average of 30,000 or slightly more.

The largest Korean enclave outside of Seoul is in Los Angeles, where approximately 150,000 Korean Americans have settled and created a Koreatown on Olympic Boulevard between Hoover and Western Avenues. Korean Americans have met with success in a variety of fields, especially in entrepreneurial business endeavors. Figures from 1992 showed that more than 3,200 Korean-American businesses were located in Los Angeles's Koreatown.

By 2000, New York City had become home to nearly 100,000 Korean Americans, many of whom had also set up thriving small businesses in a Koreatown stretching from 23rd Street to 32nd Street between Fifth and Sixth Avenues in Manhattan. More than 3,500 of Manhattan's Korean-owned small businesses were 24-hour corner stores. In the late 1960s, only a handful of stores belonged to Korean owners. However, as third-generation Jews and Italians moved into other occupations, they left a void in the greengrocery business, which the Koreans filled. By 1983, Koreans owned three-fourths of the city's greengroceries, a retail sector worth approximately $500 million per year. Start-up costs are minimal and proprietors do not need to hone their English-speaking skills in order to succeed.

Korean groceries have succeeded similarly in the inner-city regions of Newark, New Jersey; Atlanta, Georgia; Washington, D.C.; and Chicago, Illinois. Korean families are known to work literally around the clock to make their groceries, dry cleaners, fish stalls, and other businesses succeed. Almost all Korean greengroceries in New York City stay open 24 hours per day. New York's Koreatown is also the headquarters for larger endeavors, including several Korean corporations, three newspapers, wholesale businesses, and import-export companies.

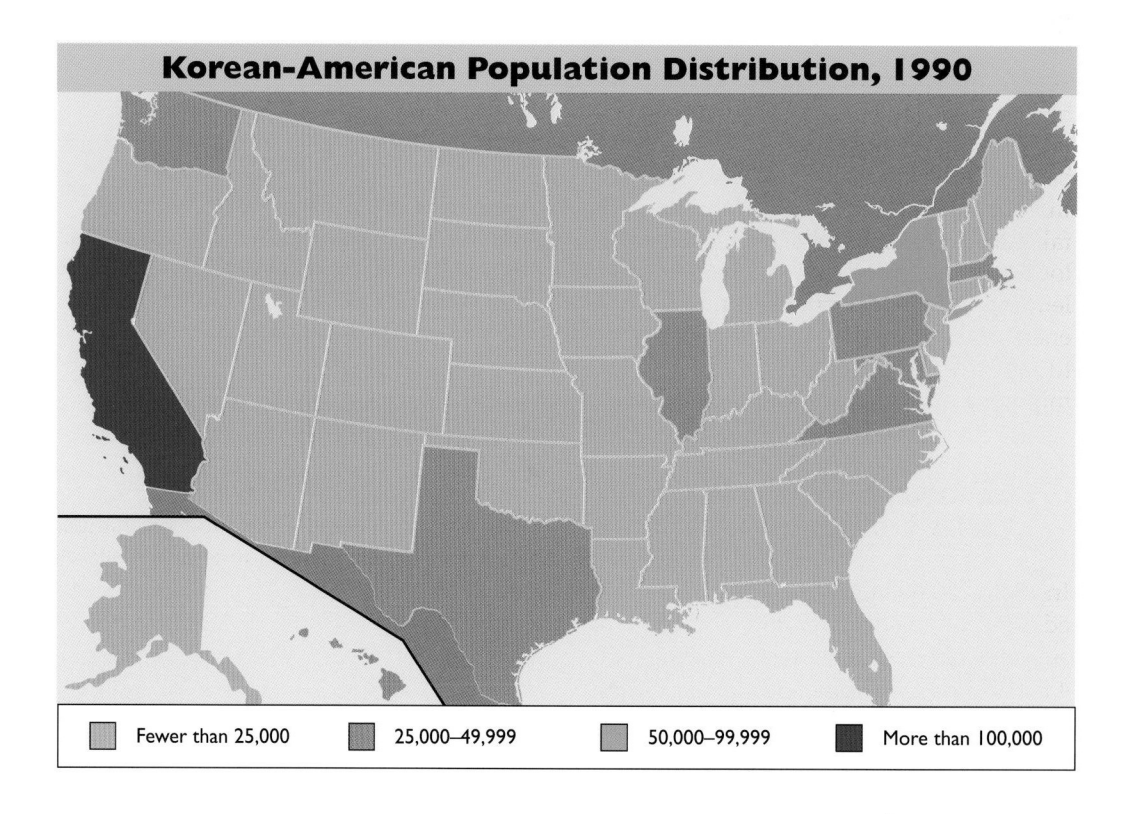

Korean-American Population Distribution, 1990

Fewer than 25,000   25,000–49,999   50,000–99,999   More than 100,000

Korean Retail Outlets in New York City

Source: From the Land of the Morning Calm:
The Koreans in America

The number of Korean-owned retail establishments in New York City rose dramatically between the late 1960s and late 1980s.

One reason Korean Americans have succeeded to such a high degree in the business world is their use of a credit-rotating system called a *kae*, similar to the Chinese *woi* and the Japanese *tanomoshi*. This system allows those who have been successful to help new arrivals—and therefore the community as a whole—through a mutually beneficial lending and borrowing system. In addition, many Korean-American banks fall under the umbrella of a parent bank located in Korea. Thus, the bank's risk in lending to newly arrived Koreans is lessened, and the new immigrants do not have to face over the prejudicial treatment they might encounter at an American bank.

CHINESE *SAN YI MAN* AND URBAN RENEWAL

In 1950, 150,000 Chinese lived in the United States. Each decade, the population has steadily climbed, reaching 237,000 in 1960, 435,000 in 1970, 860,000 in 1980, and 1,600,000 in 1990. By 2000, the Chinese-American population stood at more than 2,430,000. Chinese Americans referred to post-1965 immigrants from China as *san yi man* ("new immigrants"). Earlier waves of Chinese immigrants known as *lo wa kiu* ("old overseas Chinese") were mainly poor peasants from rural areas of China. As it had done with other Asian immigrants, the Hart-Celler Act encouraged a wider socioeconomic variety of newcomers. Though some migrated to the United States to escape the repression of Maoist Communist China, especially before the normalization of relations between the United States and China in 1979, many chose to move to the United States in order to achieve their professional and personal goals.

Between 1965 and 1975, nearly half of all Chinese immigrants came to the United States as managers, professionals, and technical workers. Unlike their uneducated bachelor predecessors (discussed in chapter 2), who came to Gold Mountain to make their fortunes and return, *san yi man* came with their families and the intention to stay. Approximately 700,000 *san yi man* moved to the United States between 1965 and 1990—a figure almost double that of Chinese immigrants who came between 1849 and 1930.

By and large, the *san yi man* coming from China were blue-collar and white-collar urban workers who spoke either Mandarin or Cantonese. The arrival of dual classes has split the Chinese-American community along the same lines. The well-educated, professional-level Chinese have assimilated quickly into mainstream America and live in middle- and upper-middle-class suburban communities. Many of their children attend top schools such as Yale, Harvard or the University of California at Berkeley.

On the whole, *san yi man* blue-collar workers have settled in urban Chinatowns. Like their predecessors, they tended to hold menial and low-paying jobs. Lack of education and English language skills have compounded their economic problems. Many lived below the poverty line in substandard housing, even though they worked long hours. Chinese-American youth gangs have flourished in such areas, as have drug use and the illegal activities of the ancient secret societies.

U.S. Chinatowns revived during the 1980s and 1990s, however, due to changes generated by larger economic and political forces. Nationally, urban renewal programs were implemented in the 1970s alongside the social activism of young Asians who sought to revitalize America's urban Chinatowns and Little Tokyos. International forces took the shape of overseas investment. During

New York's Chinatown doubled in size during the 1980s, as the number of new immigrants increased rapidly. (photograph courtesy of Erin Smith)

the 1980s, wealthy Chinese from Taiwan and Hong Kong worried that the impending return of Hong Kong to the People's Republic of China might generate an economic upheaval. (Even after the Communist takover of mainland China in 1949, the territory of Hong Kong remained a colony of Great Britain, as it had since 1898, when Great Britain leased the 398-square-mile territory for a 99-year term. Since 1997, Hong Kong has had the status of a "special administrative province" within China, allowing it to continue to operate within the capitalist system as a global trade and financial center.) Consequently, those residents of Taiwan and Hong Kong with great financial means decided to move to the United States—specifically, to Monterey Park, California, which is so characterized by the Chinese presence that the city is often referred to as "Chinese Beverly Hills" and "Little Taipei." Meanwhile, big-business interests from Taiwan and Hong Kong set off a real estate boom in New York City's Chinatown, drawing large amounts of money and potential into the area. Simultaneously, new businesses mushroomed. Advertising agencies, real estate offices, accounting firms, and law practices abounded within the community. As a result, New York's Chinatown doubled in size over 10 years (1980–1990), pushing its borders into parts of Little Italy and the historically Jewish Lower East Side.

FILIPINO AMERICANS

While Asian-Indian, Chinese, and Korean immigrants have arrived in the United States in large numbers since the passage of the Hart-Celler Act of 1965, no Asian group has arrived in larger numbers than Filipinos. Because the Philippines have had a long history of association with the United States, most Filipino immigrants are English speakers. Unlike recent Chinese and Korean immigrant communities, Filipinos have not formed separate "Filipinotowns." At the same time, the Filipino-American community is highly concentrated geographically, with more than half of all Filipino Americans settling in California.

Of the nearly 900,000 Filipino immigrants to the United States between 1970 and 1990, fully two-thirds were educated professionals, with many of them concentrated in the medical professions. Since the 1970s, U.S. hospitals, especially in urban areas, have come to rely on Filipino nurses to fill staff shortages. Throughout the 1970s and 1980s, many graduates of Filipino nursing schools began their studies with the intention of emigrating to the United States for work upon graduation, since few job opportunities were available at home.

Thus, as has often been the case in Asian-American immigration history, economic opportunity served as a magnet pulling Filipinos to the United States. As discussed in previous chapters, the pull of economic opportunity is often coupled with the push of turmoil at home. For educated Filipinos during the 1970s and 1980s, this "push factor" existed in the form of economic and political turmoil brought on by the Philippines' corrupt and repressive president, Ferdinand Marcos. By the mid-1970s, professionals had grown alarmed by Marcos's increasingly frequent violations of human rights. In 1976, Amnesty International, an international human rights watchdog organization, published reports on the use of torture in the Philippines. For many Filipino professionals, the turning point came when Marcos ordered the assassination of Benigno Aquino, his chief political opponent, in 1983.

In 1986, Begnino Aquino's widow, Corazon, ran against Marcos for the presidency. When Marcos attempted to declare himself the winner through voter fraud and intimidation, thousands of Filipinos took to the streets in protest. After the Filipino military announced its support of Mrs. Aquino, Marcos and his wife were forced to flee the country. Corazon Aquino served as president of the Philippines until 1992.

While Marcos was president, however, he, his wife Imelda Marcos, and his associates looted hundreds of millions of dollars from the nation's treasury to pay for New York City real estate investments and extravagant luxury items. Marcos's corrupt rule helped weaken the economy of his nation. Immigrants to the United States reported paying as much as $7.50 for a pound of chicken during the early 1980s due to food shortages. Partly because so much money intended to support the economy ended up in the private coffers of the Marcos family, many businesses had little money to hire needed professional workers. Thus, to stand any chance of finding employment during the 1970s and 1980s, Filipinos looked to the United States.

THE REDRESS MOVEMENT

After World War II, most Japanese former internees focused on rebuilding their lives—socially, economically, and psychologically. In the years following the war, few felt it possible to publicly discuss the shame they felt from the experience of mass incarceration and the related losses. Not until the 1970s did a new generation of Japanese Americans take up the cause of winning compensation from the U.S. government for the internment episode. Even then, it was almost 20 years before they won a victory (of sorts) for the 100,000 Japanese Americans who had been interned.

The struggle for redress proved to be a long one, hampered by in-fighting within the Japanese community as well as by congressional foot-dragging on the issue. Edison Tomimaro Uno, along with a handful of other members of the controversial Japanese American Citizens League (JACL), first raised the idea of redress at the group's 1970 national convention. Although Uno's resolution passed at that meeting and two subsequent conventions, the JACL leadership took no further action. This conservative approach reflected the political stance of the group's aging nisei leadership, who at the time had not even publicly issued the JACL's stand on the Vietnam War, much less taken a leadership role in the national, multiethnic civil rights movement then at its height.

By the mid-1960s, the JACL had established itself as the most influential Japanese-American association in the United States. The organization's power began to crumble, however, as the issue of redress gathered grassroots support and sansei (third-generation Japanese-American) youth pushed for more representation within the organization. The conflict over redress reflected the growing political divide between nisei and sansei generations and eventually led to the formation of two other Japanese-American groups: the National Council for Japanese American Redress (NCJAR) and the National Coalition for Redress/Reparations (NCRR).

By the early 1970s, dissatisfied JACL members in Seattle had formed their own splinter group to push for individual reparations. On November 19, 1975, they unveiled their "Seattle Plan," which called for reparations to be paid to all Japanese-American individuals who had suffered internment, including "voluntary resettlers" and those living beyond the bounds of the Western Defense Command. The following year, President Gerald R. Ford repealed Executive Order 9066, the curfew and internment measure enacted at the start of World War II. While he did not issue a formal apology, President Ford defined the internment period as a "national mistake."

The JACL, meanwhile, finally took action and in 1976 formed the National Committee for Redress (NCR). The committee's proposal for redress conflicted with that of the Seattle group's plan in that it initially called for payments to be funneled through community "block grants" and did not include "voluntary resettlers" nor Japanese Americans relocated from Hawaii, Alaska, and other nonwestern states. By 1978,

Corazon Aquino, president of the Philippines from 1986 to 1992 (Library of Congress)

THE REDRESS MOVEMENT

1945–1946 Thousands of interned Japanese decide to settle away from the West Coast, though the majority return to old communities.

1948 President Harry S Truman signs the Japanese American Evacuation Claims Act, allowing internees to file claims for up to $2,500 for losses incurred due to internment. Because many internees had lost homes, businesses, and many other possessions, actual losses were usually far higher. Those who decide to make higher claims—40 percent of all claimants—are forced to wait for Congress to make special appropriations before receiving payment. In 1950, when the first claims are paid, only 211 of more than 22,000 claims are processed. The last claim is not processed until 1965.

1970 Edison Uno and several other delegates to the 1970 Japanese American Citizens League (JACL) convention introduce a resolution seeking reparations from the U.S. government for wrongs committed against the 110,000 Japanese Americans who were interned during World War II. Although the resolution passes (as do similar ones at the 1972 and 1974 conventions), no further action is taken.

1975 The Seattle Evacuation Redress Committee of the JACL presents the "Seattle Plan," which calls for a $5,000 payment to each person interned during the war with an additional payment of $10 for every day spent in internment. The national JACL, on the other hand, proposes that any reparations money should be paid to Japanese-American organizations, such as itself, rather than to individuals.

1976 The national JACL establishes the National Committee for Redress (NCR) to research the reparations issue and prepare legislation to be voted on at the 1978 convention. President Gerald R. Ford repeals Executive Order 9066 (the presidential order that initiated the internment camp policy) and calls internment a "national mistake," words that anger many Japanese who want a formal apology.

1978 At the national JACL convention, a plan to seek reparations payments to be paid into a block grant fund that would then be redistributed to community organizations is defeated in favor of a plan to seek $25,000 payments to be distributed by a commission to each person forcibly moved to an internment camp. Despite opposition, the plan passes.

1979 The NCR backs away from the plan endorsed at the 1978 convention and favors the creation of a federal government commission to study the matter of internment reparations and redress and recommend a solution. The change of strategy is due in part to Senator S. I. Hayakawa of California, a conservative Japanese-American opponent of redress measures.

1979 In response to the NCR's shift in policy, members of the Seattle JACL form the National Council for Japanese American Redress (NCJAR) to lobby Congress for support of direct payments to former internees. All four Democratic Japanese-American congressmen support the govern-ment commission plan. Representative Mike Lowry of Seattle sponsors the first reparations bill to be introduced in Congress; Lowry's bill never makes it to a vote.

1980 Congress creates the Commission on Wartime Relocation and Internment of Civilians (CWRIC) to study the internment and redress issue. Hearings begin in cities nationwide the following year. The National Coalition for Redress/Reparations (NCRR) is founded by a number of grassroots local and regional groups out of concern that the JACL will abandon the goal of monetary compensation.

1981 Historian Peter Irons begins researching the internment camp cases of Fred Korematsu, Gordon Hirabayashi, and Min Yasui. In doing so, he discovers that the government had purposely suppressed evidence during the trials of the three resisters. After meeting with the men, he and a group of third-generation U.S.-born Japanese-American (sansei) lawyers win the overturn of the wartime convictions using a little-known legal procedure called a writ of error *coram nobis*.

1981–1982 The CWRIC holds hearings on the internment camps. Many former internees provide emotional testimony regarding their experiences. For the Japanese-American community, the hearings provide an opportunity to finally open a dialogue on an era that few internees had been willing to discuss.

1982 The CWRIC issues its report entitled *Personal Justice Denied*. Although it makes no specific recommendation, it is sympathetic to the redress cause.

1983 The CWRIC recommends that individual internees be compensated with a payment of $20,000 and given a formal apology by the U.S. government.

1983 The NCJAR files a class action suit on behalf of all internees. Although the case is ultimately dismissed, it serves to pressure the federal government to follow the CWRIC recommendations.

1987 Redress bills are introduced in both houses of Congress. The NCR sends a large delegation to lobby members of Congress in support of the bills.

1988 Although President Ronald Reagan initially vows to veto any redress bill that reaches his desk because of fiscal restraints in the federal budget, he signs the Civil Rights Act of 1988, which establishes the Office of Redress Administration (ORA) and includes a formal U.S. government apology for internment.

1990 The ORA begins making payments to former Japanese-American internees and their heirs. Final payments are made eight years later, in August 1998.

however, the NCR finally agreed with part of the Seattle Plan, calling for payments of $25,000 for each individual forcibly removed. The proposal passed at the 1978 JACL convention, despite arguments against redress made by older nisei leaders such as the JACL's Mike Masaoka and Senator S. I. Hayakawa of California.

The JACL did not push forward on the issue of redress, however, and in March 1979, the NCR made an abrupt about-face in its plan for action. The committee dropped its support for individual payments and advocated the creation of a federal government commission to research World War II internment camps and recommend solutions to requests for redress. This proposal was supported by the four Japanese Americans then seated in Congress.

In response, the NCJAR, composed of Seattle members and led by William Hohri of Chicago, formed in May 1979. NCJAR secured Seattle congressman Mike Lowry to sponsor a redress bill almost identical to the Seattle Plan. However, with no support from nikkei (fifth generation and beyond) congressmen, the bill died in committee.

The next year, on July 12, 1980, the NCRR formed in Los Angeles. This national Japanese-American organization grew out of a local redress rights group known as the Los Angeles Community Coalition for Redress/Reparations (LACCRR). The LACCRR was one of many local redress groups that had sprouted up across the nation, many having grown out of civil rights conflicts raised by urban renewal programs of the 1970s.

The NCRR included many grassroots community groups such as Concerned Japanese Americans in New York and the Asian Pacific Student Union of the West Coast. The NCRR, like the NCJAR, disagreed with the idea of a government commission to investigate the internment camp system. When Congress created the Commission on Wartime Relocation and Internment of Civilians (CWRIC) on July 30, 1980, both new national alliances viewed the move as a delaying tactic at best. The CWRIC had no power to rule for change; its mission was simply to gather information through national public hearings, during which internment survivors were to recount their experiences publicly.

As the hearings began, so did another force for redress. While researching material for a book, law historian and author Peter Irons reviewed the wartime cases of internment resistors Fred Korematsu, Gordon Hirabayashi, and Min Yasui (discussed in chapter 4). In so doing, he found documents revealing that the U.S. government had suppressed evidence in the convictions of the three men. Under the petition procedure known as *coram nobis* (meaning "error before us"), he worked with a group of sansei lawyers to get their convictions overturned.

Irons's success helped spur further support for the redress movement, which received its final push toward success via the CWRIC hearings. For the vast majority of the camp survivors, these hearings became the first opportunity to publicly tell of their experiences. Consequently, even earlier opponents of redress, such as Mike Masaoka, were won over by the detailed and emotional testimony. In December 1982, the CWRIC published its report, entitled *Personal Justice Denied*, and the following year recommended payments of $20,000 per individual wronged and a public apology from the government. These recommendations formed the basis of the redress bills that followed.

Fearing that the sluggish pace for change would continue indefinitely, the NCJAR decided to register its grievances through the judicial arm of the federal government. On March 16, 1983, the organization filed a class action law suit against the U.S. government on behalf of all former internees. The suit was eventually dismissed, but it helped to keep pressure on the federal government to act on the redress issue. In 1987, the push for redress through legislative action finally met with success.

After intense debate on the congressional floor and lobbying by hundreds of NCRR members, Redress Bill H.R. 442 passed the House of Representatives by a vote of 243–141 on September 29, 1987; the Senate version passed on April 20, 1988. Although President Ronald Reagan at first threatened a veto due to fiscal restraints on the federal budget, he changed his mind and signed the redress bill into law on August 10, 1988. Called the Civil Rights Act of 1988, the bill included an official government apology for the internment of Japanese Americans and established the Office of Redress Administration (ORA) to administer reparations. Two years later, on October 9, 1990, the oldest living survivors of America's wartime internment camps received the first redress payments.

The long struggle for redress helped to both create and reveal major shifts in America's social and political climate during the decades between the 1960s and the 1990s. The mobilization of Japanese youth to use legislative and judicial processes in addition to organized protest as means for change illuminated the assimilation of the sansei generation into the national culture of American democracy. And the push for redress, actively supported by some powerful whites and derided for many years by some influential Japanese Americans, showed the blurring of ethnic lines that had for so long characterized the relationships between groups of people within U.S. society. Though cash payments and apologies could not erase the injustice and suffering experienced by camp survivors, the success of the redress movement helped restore pride to the Japanese-American community.

President Ronald Reagan initially threatened to veto any bill authorizing redress for Japanese Americans interned during World War II. Ultimately, however, he signed into law a bill that granted an official government apology for the internment of Japanese Americans and established the Office of Redress Administration (ORA) to administer reparations. (private collection)

7 ASIAN AMERICA TODAY

As the United States crossed into the 21st century, it also reached the 150-year anniversary of the arrival of the first Chinese sojourners to Gam Saan—the Gold Mountains of California. Since that time, new groups of Asian immigrants—from Japan, India, Korea, the Philippines, and finally Southeast Asia—have made similar journeys, leaving their homelands, some in search of riches, some in search of safety. By the start of the 21st century, some of these immigrants, such as the Japanese, have seen generation after generation born and raised in the United States, as issei have passed on to nisei, and nisei to sansei, sansei to yonsei, and most recently yonsei to nikkei.

With each passing generation since the first Asian Americans immigrated to the United States, a greater and greater number of Americans of Asian descent have become household names in virtually all fields of endeavor. From boardrooms to ball fields, and from research laboratories to Hollywood soundstages, many Asian Americans are helping to shape American society in a variety of ways.

At the same time, the success of many Asian Americans has been a double-edged sword leading some to pronounce the entire Asian-American population a "model minority." While significant numbers of Asian Americans have achieved at high levels in the classroom and elsewhere, this label misrepresents the many diverse peoples of Asian ancestry in the United States as a monolithic group. It not only unfairly saddles all Asian Americans with unjust expectations but has also occasionally led to greater economic tension between Asian Americans and other ethnic groups. What is more, the model minority label has also marginalized many Asian-American communities that have not succeeded as universally as others. Newer arrivals, such as recent refugees from Southeast Asia, have found themselves largely isolated from the mainstream, lacking knowledge of or trust in the bewildering new land in which they come to live.

Like the early Chinese miners of the 19th century, many Hmong, Vietnamese, Cambodians, and others arrived in the United States for what they expected to be a temporary stay. Though most in their communities have yet to assimilate into the majority culture of the United States, an increasing number have begun that process, just as generations of Asian Americans did before them, overcoming prejudice and all too often violence to do so.

ANTI-ASIAN VIOLENCE

Anti-Asian violence has been a constant feature of Asian-American history, but in recent years it has assumed an increasingly high profile. This is partly due to the rapid increase in Asian immigration and partly to greater economic competition between various segments of American society. Consequently, the number of incidents involving anti-Asian sentiment has been on the rise, occurring coast to coast throughout the 1980s and 1990s. Through groups such as the American Citizens for Justice, Asian Americans of the new millennium are uniting to stop the tide of hate and violence through legal recourse, education, and media attention. But it is an uphill climb, since many cases now defined as hate crimes unfortunately garner little attention outside local communities. The Vincent Chin case in Michigan and the case of the Dotbusters in New Jersey are two incidents that did receive national attention.

THE VINCENT CHIN CASE

Although anti-Asian violence has occurred in the United States since the first Chinese arrived during the California gold rush of the 19th century, the wave of violent acts in the latter part of the 20th century has not only illustrated America's problem of racism but also tested the fairness and equity of the U.S. justice system. As with most racist incidents, a climate of economic hardship frames the nature of the problem.

In 1982, Michigan's once-dominant automobile industry was in the throes of a severe economic downturn. The import of Japanese cars into the United States had taken a huge bite out of U.S. automaker profits, and massive layoffs had occurred in Michigan and other states. On June 19, 1982, Vincent Chin and two friends went to a bar in Highland Park, near Detroit, Michigan. The trio were celebrating Chin's upcoming wedding. Ronald Ebens, an unemployed auto worker who blamed Japan for Michigan's unemployment problem, observed Chin across the room and began to shout out obscenities and racial epithets in the mistaken assumption that Chin was Japanese. Ebens, seeking a scapegoat, blamed Chin for the loss of his job, and a fight broke out between the two, upon which all patrons involved were thrown out of the bar. Ebens and his stepson, Michael Nitz, chased Chin through the streets, eventually catching up with him at a nearby fast-food restaurant. They then beat Chin with a baseball bat, shattering his skull. The 27-year-old Chin, an engineering student, died four days later.

Ebens and Nitz plea-bargained their case from a second-degree murder charge down to a lesser charge of manslaughter. Judge Charles Kaufman of the Wayne County circuit court sentenced the killers to three years' probation and a fine of $3,780 each. The Chinese-American community, seeing immediately the parallels between the contemporary incident and the mob violence of a century earlier, reacted with outrage at the verdict and sentencing. Lily Chin, the victim's mother, remarked: "If two Chinese killed a white person, they must go to jail, maybe for their whole lives. . . . Something is wrong with this country." Many Americans wondered why Asians would be blamed for

ANTI-ASIAN HATE CRIMES, 1981–2001

1981	In a wave of arson attacks, the Ku Klux Klan of Texas burns several boats belonging to Vietnamese to symbolize their resistance to the immigration of the "boat people."
1982	Two unemployed autoworkers in Detroit beat 27-year-old Chinese American Vincent Chin to death with a baseball bat after they mistake him for Japanese.
1984	After taunting Thong Hy Huynh and three other Vietnamese students for several weeks, white students at Davis High School in Davis, California, fatally stab Huynh.
1985	Two white Boston teens beat a Vietnamese-Chinese restaurant owner and scratch a racial epithet on his window
1987	Thugs from an anti-Asian gang known as the Dotbusters beat Asian-Indian immigrants Navrose Mody and Kaushal Sharan in Jersey City, New Jersey, killing Mody. The gang's name referred to the *bindi*, a dot worn by some Hindu women as a sign of sanctity.
1988	A vandal scrawls the words "Japs and Chinks Only" on a door of the Ethnic Studies Department at the University of California at Berkeley.
1989	Patrick Purdy fires 105 rounds into a Stockton, California, schoolyard, killing five Southeast Asian children, before turning the gun on himself. Purdy had blamed immigrants for his personal problems and specifically targeted Southeast Asians.
1990	Two whites beat Yan Than Ly, a Laotian-American restaurant employee, with a hammer in Yuba City, California, after he gives two white women a ride.
1990	Congress passes the Hate Crimes Statistics Act to allow gathering and reporting of information on racially motivated crimes.
1990	Two white skinheads kick a Vietnamese-American youth to death in Houston, Texas.
1992	Luyen Phan Nguyen, a 19-year-old Vietnamese American, is beaten to death in Coral Springs, Florida.
1993	A gang of a dozen whites beats Cambodians Sophy Soeung and Sam Nhem, in Fall River, Massachusetts, as they take out trash from their apartment. Nhem is killed.
1993	A group calling itself the Aryan Liberation Front claims responsibility for firebombing the Sacramento office of the Japanese American Citizens League as well as for an attack on the Jewish Temple B'Nai Israel and the local office of the National Association for the Advancement of Colored People (NAACP).
1995	Robert Page stabs Eddy Wu as Wu carries a bag of groceries from a supermarket in Novato, California, to his car, Wu survives with stab wounds to his back and shoulder and a punctured lung.
1996	Gunner Lindberg, age 21, and Dominic Christopher, age 17, stab Thien Minh Ly, a 24-year-old Vietnamese-American UCLA graduate after selecting him at random for murder.
1998	Kanu Patel and Mukesh Patek, two Asian-Indian Americans, are killed in their doughnut shop. The killer allegedly ridiculed their English skills, murdered them, and doused them with gasoline.
2000	Won-Joon Yoon, a 26-year-old graduate student from Korea, is killed in a Bloomington, Indiana, shooting spree that also leaves an African American dead and nine other ethnic or religious minorities wounded. The shooter is a member of a white supremacist group.
2000	Filipino American Joseph Ileto, a postal worker, is shot dead by a man who minutes earlier had wounded five people at a Jewish community center in Granada Hills, California.
2000	In San Francisco, 60-year-old Vietnamese American Hien Nguyen is collecting cans in his neighborhood when he is beaten to death by a man who allegedly also spat and urinated on him.
2001	Christopher Charles Hearn, 20, fatally stabs his next door neighbor Kenneth Chiu, 17. Police find racial epithets scratched on a car at the scene.

taking away auto assembly jobs. Critics argued that poor corporate decision-making and the export of U.S. jobs to countries like Mexico seriously derailed the successful path of America's auto industry, and not Japanese automakers. George Wong of the Asian American Federation of Union Membership pushed this point further, noting, "When corporate heads tell frustrated workers that foreign imports are taking their jobs, then they are acting like an agitator of a lynch mob."

The Justice for Vincent Chin Committee formed to push for a more equitable outcome. The U.S. Department of Justice investigated and came to the conclusion that Ebens had committed a racially motivated crime and thus deprived Vincent Chin of his civil rights. Ronald Ebens was sentenced to 25 years in prison after a federal jury rendered a guilty verdict, but the conviction was reversed by an appellate court appeal in May 1987. After another retrial, Ebens was acquitted but settled a civil suit out of court for $1.5 million. Neither Ebens nor Nitz has ever spent any time in jail for their crime.

THE DOTBUSTERS

Another well-known case of anti-Asian violence in recent history illuminates the widespread nature of anti-Asian bias in the United States. An anti-Asian gang known as the Dotbusters first surfaced in Jersey City, New Jersey, home to nearly 15,000 Asian Indians. Its name referred to the red *bindi* dot worn by some Hindu women between their eyebrows as a sign of sanctity, with the addition of "busters" intentionally implying violence. Beginning in the mid-1980s, the Asian Indians of Jersey City endured regular racial taunting from gangs of white, black, and Hispanic youths. The Dotbusters took their harrassment a step further and physically assaulted Asian Indians in traditional Indian dress in addition to damaging Asian Indian–owned property and businesses.

On September 27, 1987, Indian immigrants Navrose Mody and Kaushal Sharan were beaten in Jersey City by two white Dotbuster gang members. Sharan lived but suffered extensive brain damage; Navrose Mody lost his life as a result of the attack. The youths, when interviewed, remarked that they had beaten the two men because Asian Indians were "taking over."

Around the time of the attack, the *Jersey Journal* newspaper printed a letter signed by the Dotbusters that read:

We will go to any extreme to get Indians to move out of Jersey City. If I am walking down the street and I see

a Hindu and the setting is right, I will just hit him or her. We plan some of our extreme attacks, such as breaking windows, breaking car windows, and crashing family parties. We use the phone book and look up the name Patel. Have you seen how many there are?

In response to the threats, the leaders of the Indian community in Jersey City organized a series of protests to demand greater police protection. Eventually, several youths were convicted for some of the beatings, and indictments were handed up in September 1992 against three men—one of whom had become a police officer since the 1987 beating.

HATE CRIMES ON THE RISE

Tensions continued to mount between ethnic groups in America, and violent hate crimes were on the rise, even during the relative economic prosperity of the 1990s. The Hate Crime Statistics Act of 1990 states that a violent action may be considered a hate crime if victims are targeted because of their "race, religion, sexual orientation, or ethnicity." The vast majority of hate crimes are directed at individuals, though businesses and religious organizations are also targeted.

In 1999, nearly 8,000 hate crimes were reported to the Federal Bureau of Investigation (FBI). Of these, 54 percent of the incidents were found to be motivated by racial bias, 17 percent by religious bias, 16 percent by sexual-orientation bias, and 11 percent by ethnicity/national origin bias. Intimidation was the most frequently cited hate crime offense (35 percent of the total) with property damage/destruction tallying in at 28 percent. In 1999, 17 people were murdered in hate-motivated incidents.

Almost every U.S. state has some form of legislation that can be used to prosecute hate crimes. President Bill Clinton drew national attention to the problem with the first White House Conference on Hate Crimes, which took place on November 10, 1997. At the conference, the president praised the successes of community programs and outlined new law enforcement initiatives. President Clinton also reminded the participants that teenagers and young adults account for a significant proportion of America's hate crimes—both as victims and perpetrators.

Due to the resurgence of Ku Klux Klan activity in the last decades of the 20th century, the Southern Poverty Law Center (SPLC) created its Klanwatch arm in 1981. Klanwatch monitors the activities of racist groups and neo-Nazis, who model themselves after Hitler's Third Reich. In 1994, the SPLC warned the federal government of the dangerous rise in a new blend of armed hate groups and created its Militia Task Force. The Militia Task Force monitors more than 400 such groups espousing extreme antigovernment views. Some of these groups have racist agendas and leanings; others do not. On April 19, 1995, Timothy McVeigh, a former U.S. soldier with ties to the militia movement, bombed a federal building in Oklahoma City, killing 168 adults and children. Although McVeigh blamed the U.S. government for his actions and was not specifically targeting minorities in his attack, racist materials were found in his possession upon his capture. As always with racist hatred, economics play a significant role: Many of the young white males belonging to racist hate groups suffer from unemployment and low education. The speed and generally anarchic nature of modern Internet communication has allowed many white supremacist groups to organize and grow quickly. One such group, the Aryan Liberation Front, firebombed the Sacramento office of the Japanese American Citizens League in 1993, causing $20,000 in damage.

A 1995 study conducted by the Asian Pacific American Legal Consortium shows that anti-Asian violence in Southern California increased from 63 incidents in 1994 to 113 in 1995. Of the 458 anti-Asian incidents reported nationwide in 1995, nearly one-quarter occurred in Southern California. In 1997, the California attorney general counted 226 hate crimes against Asian Americans. Between October 1998 and August 1999, five Asian Americans lost their lives to racially motivated violent attacks. Margaret Fung, executive director of the Asian American Legal Defense and Education Fund commented: "For five people to get killed in a year is a phenomenal number; that's [the sharpest rise] we have seen in a decade." The FBI reported that the total number of all hate crimes in the United States topped 50,000 between 1991 and 1999, yet only 37 cases were brought to trial by the Department of Justice.

Acts of violence by white hate groups are not the only terrorist acts that have had an impact on Asian Americans, of course. In the wake of the terrorist attacks on the World Trade Center in New York City and the Pentagon outside of Washington, D.C., on September 11, 2001, federal law enforcement officials identified Islamic extremists from the Middle East as prime suspects. Immediately thereafter, some angry Americans targeted anyone who appeared to be Middle Eastern in ethnicity. Not only were mosques attacked, but a number of Middle Eastern and Asian Americans were killed. Five days after the attacks on New York and Washington, a man shot and killed a Lebanese gas station attendant in Mesa, Arizona, after first having killed a Sikh American at another gas station. Because they wear turbans that have been confused with headresses worn by some Muslim fundamentalists, Sikhs were specifically targeted. As these attacks mounted, President George W. Bush met with Muslim leaders at the Islamic Center of Washington, where he denounced the attacks, saying:

Those who feel like they can intimidate our fellow citizens to take out their anger don't represent the best of America, they represent the worst of humankind, and they should be ashamed of that kind of behavior.

RACE AND ECONOMIC TENSION

Racial tensions flared between the African-American and Korean-American communities in both New York City and Los Angeles during the early 1990s. With the continued rise in Korean-owned businesses located in the inner cities, some African Americans resented the lack of employment opportunities available to them at the new stores. As a rule, Korean businesspeople have hired other Korean immigrants for clear financial reasons: low wages, long hours, no vacations, and no health benefits combine into a labor package that is undesirable to the vast majority of American-born workers, whereas new immigrants with low-level English skills will take what they can get, no matter what their level of education.

Differing socioeconomic levels have also led to tension between the Korean- and African-American communities. A Korean immigrant shop owner with an advanced college degree has little in common with an African-American inner-city youth who might be a high school dropout. Difficulties in communicating are exacerbated by language barriers as well as the tight-knit nature of Korean communities, which separates the immigrants from the natives of the neighborhood. Over time, such poor communication and estrangement between neighbors breeds mistrust.

Between 1978 and 1987, the number of Korean retail outlets in New York City jumped from 350 to 6,160. This was achieved through the daily struggles of many Koreans to earn $17,000 to $35,000 annually per family, as well as through the credit rotating system and the strong Korean neighborhood network. But such means have generally not been available to generations of inner-city African-American youth who have had to struggle within neighborhoods dominated by violence, gang activity, drug use, and despair, with no place for them to emigrate. There are few if any local banks (and certainly no ethnic-driven credit systems such as the *kae*) to provide loans for the business dreams of such youth. As a result, despair often wins out over ambition for young African Americans who have observed the contrasting success of their Korean-American neighbors.

The combination of economic struggle, poor communication, estrangement, lack of education, and simple jealousy resulted in two significant racial incidents in the early 1990s: the Brooklyn greengrocer boycott and the destruction of Korean-owned businesses during the Los Angeles Riots.

THE BROOKLYN GREENGROCER BOYCOTT, 1990

In January 1990, a Haitian American named Ghislaine Felissaint accused Brooklyn-based Korean greengrocer Bong Jae Jang of verbal and physical assault. Bong's store employees claimed that Felissaint became enraged and shouted racial epithets when they waited on another customer while she searched for money to pay for her purchases. Members of the neighborhood's black community organized a full-scale boycott of the Korean grocery store and later demanded that the Koreans vacate the neighborhood permanently. Tensions simmered for months. At one point a group of young African Americans attacked three Vietnamese Americans with baseball bats, bottles, and knives after mistaking the trio for Koreans. Five months later, 10,000 Korean Americans rallied in protest of the boycott and as an appeal for racial harmony. Then-mayor David Dinkins, an African American, attended the rally and made an antiboycott statement by purchasing items at Bong Jae Jang's store.

The boycott finally ended in March 1991, and Bong Jae Jang was acquitted of any criminal wrongdoing. However, the incident, which had garnered national attention, seriously affected business: On his worst day, he sold only 38 cents' worth of merchandise.

THE LOS ANGELES RIOTS

Racial tensions exploded on multiple fronts in the spring of 1992, during the Los Angeles Riots. The clash was spurred by the beating of African-American motorist Rodney

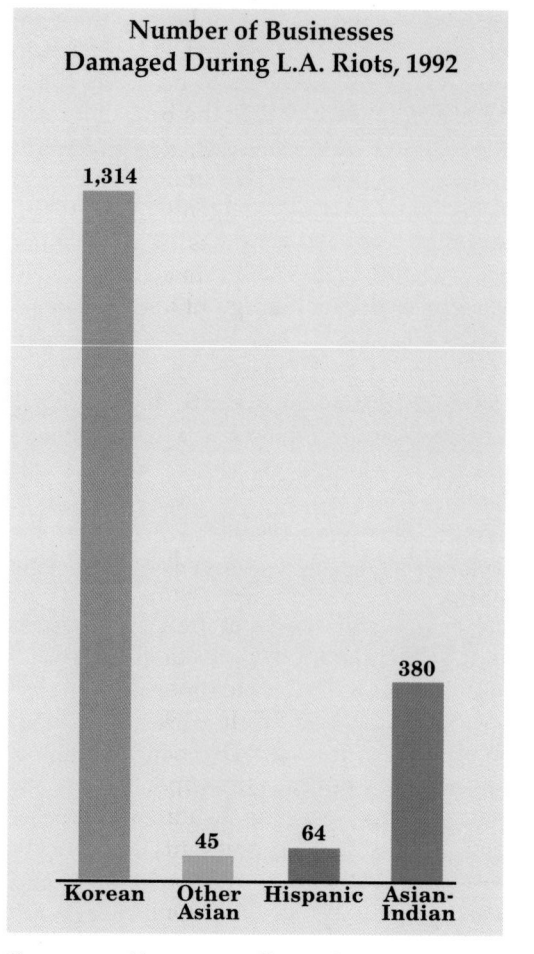

Number of Businesses Damaged During L.A. Riots, 1992

Korean-owned businesses suffered a far higher proportion of damage in the Los Angeles Riots of 1992 than did stores owned by other Asian Americans or Hispanics.

King by white Los Angeles police officers, an event that was captured on videotape and broadcast around the world. The notorious videotape demonstrated what many African Americans have argued is a common occurrence in their communities—police brutality and abuse. When the officers involved were found innocent of any wrongdoing in April 1992, riots erupted in South Central Los Angeles. Over the course of three days, the violence spread, resulting in 54 deaths: 25 African American, 2 Korean, 15 Hispanic, 10 white, and 2 of unknown ethnicity. By time the riots ended, 10,000 arrests had been made, 10,000 businesses had been damaged or destroyed, and nearly 5,000 fires had been set. The financial toll reached almost $1 billion. Two thousand three hundred Korean-owned businesses were destroyed or damaged, amounting to a loss of $500 million.

Circumstances such as the Los Angeles Riots, the Brooklyn boycott, and the economic recession of the 1980s combined to hurt the *kae* system and therefore the financial core of the Korean-American business community. Those Koreans who suffered great monetary losses could not repay their *kae* loans, with the result that less money was available for others to borrow. Fraud, too, has played a role in the breakdown of the Korean credit system, as increasing numbers of members are strangers to those already involved. Consequently, the Korean-American success story has become somewhat tarnished but still remains a positive example for other immigrant communities.

ASIAN AMERICANS AND THE CLINTON ADMINISTRATION

During the presidency of Bill Clinton (1993–2001), a number of controversial events directly affecting Asian Americans took place. After the Democratic Party lost control of both houses of the U.S. Congress in the 1994 midterm election, President Clinton made an effort to reposition himself as a political centrist. In 1996, he bucked many members of the Democratic Party to join with Republicans in supporting a bill to overhaul the nation's welfare laws. The new law made all immigrants—even legal residents—ineligible for food stamps and other government benefits. Only by submitting to the naturalization process and becoming a U.S. citizen could an immigrant restore these benefits. Although the new law convinced many immigrants to register for naturalization, many others, particularly in the Southeast Asian community, did not—largely due to distrust and lack of understanding of U.S. government authority. Thus, even greater hardship was added to the lives of the nation's most vulnerable Asian-American community.

The same year, President Clinton also signed a new, tougher immigration law. The new law, aimed at cracking down on illegal immigration, allowed government officials to expel illegal immigrants without hearings. Although Clinton forced Congress to drop several provisions that would have reduced legal immigration and denied public schooling to illegal immigrants, the combiniation of the welfare reform law and new immigration restrictions served to confirm the perception of many recent Asian immigrants that the U.S. government did not consider them Americans.

During the 1996 presidential campaign, tensions between the Asian-American community and some members of the general public grew when revelations surfaced that the Clinton administration had benefited from illegal contributions from wealthy Asian-American residents of the United States. Likewise, when a Chinese-American former physicist at Los Alamos National Laboratory was indicted on charges of violating the Atomic Energy and Espionage Act—even though there was no evidence he had ever passed information on to anyone—many in the Asian-American community were angered, particularly after the FBI was forced to drop the case for lack of evidence.

THE MODEL MINORITY STEREOTYPE

Statistically speaking, Asian Americans are the most highly educated ethnic group in the United States. On average, more Asians have attended both college and graduate school than any other ethnic group, including Caucasians. In 2000, 44 percent of Asian and Pacific Islander Americans had completed four years of college as compared with 28 percent of white Americans. Asian Americans have also scored consistently higher on the math section of the Scholastic Aptitude Test (SAT) taken by college applicants. While the average score on the mathematics portion of the test was 482 for all American students during the 1994–1995 school year, Asian Americans scored an average of 538. On the verbal portion, Asian Americans scored 418, which was higher than the scores for African Americans (356), Mexican Americans (376), Puerto Ricans (372), and Native Americans (403), and just below the national average for all students of 428. (White Americans scored an average of 448.)

Beginning in the 1960s, the media began focusing on this overall success in academics by branding Asian Americans as the "model minority." Though it was initially intended as a compliment of Asian-American success, many Asian Americans and others object to this designation, as it glosses over the very real problems that individual Asian Americans face.

The lumping of Filipinos, Japanese, Chinese, Koreans, Southeast Asians, and Asian Indians into one group also tends to ignore the vast differences between the many, very different cultures that make up the Asian community and contribute to the "inability" of whites to learn about and honor each ethnic group's native culture and history. It also blurs the differences in assimilation achieved by the various Asian ethnic groups and their economic and social impact upon the United States. For example, of the post-1965 immigrant populations, Asian Indians and Filipinos have integrated themselves within the larger society, while the Koreans, Chinese, and Southeast Asians have evolved economically and socially within their own ethnic enclaves.

The negative consequences of the "model minority" stereotype are many. Generalizations about Asian-American academic success minimize the seriousness of the difficulties faced by those Asians in need of public and private assistance programs. "Model minority" stereotyping ignores the dire needs of elderly Japanese, aging Filipino farmworkers, "downtown" Chinese, unemployed Hmong, and others. Stereotypical views of Asian Americans as math- and science-oriented overlook the contributions of those individuals skilled in the creative arts. And the pressure to succeed placed upon Asian-American youth as a result of "model minority" stereotyping takes on an unrealistically intense bent, leading to poor self-esteem and skewed perceptions of true achievement.

The "model minority" stereotype also downplays the racism, discrimination, and increasing threat of hate crime violence often faced by Asian Americans. In May 1991, the results of a *Wall Street Journal* survey revealed that most Americans did not believe that Asian Americans encountered racial bigotry. Some respondents to the poll felt that Asian Americans were given "too many special advantages." The characterization of Asians and other American minorities as receiving special treatment through public and private agencies has become a common refrain used by those opposed to affirmative action programs originally designed to ensure that minorities were not discriminated against in the workplace or in college admissions procedures.

The perception of Asian Americans as untroubled by problems that struggling whites and African Americans face completely ignores the difficulties faced daily by recent Asian-American immigrants. Those Asians arriving from nondemocratic countries have an especially hard time understanding their legal rights within America's democratic system. Affordable legal assistance, ideally provided in the client's native language, is a crucial service for new arrivals, as are social services, housing, welfare, and food stamp programs for those new arrivals finding themselves to be unskilled, highly stressed, and poorly educated within the context of modern American society.

Asians who reach a high level of success within American corporate culture also encounter discrimination. Just as women have hit the invisible limit commonly referred to as the "glass ceiling," so too have Asian Americans, finding that the absolute top corporate positions are seemingly unavailable to them. For example, in January 1992, the *New York Times* reported that while a Silicon Valley–based Hewlett Packard plant reported 26 percent of its engineers and 12 percent of its managers as Asian American, not one Asian American held the position of senior executive. Like many well-educated and highly motivated corporate female managers, many Asian Americans have turned to entrepeneurship as a solution to corporate discrimination. For example, David Lam, an MIT-educated China native, resigned from Hewlett Packard to found his own company, Lam Research, a highly successful multimillion-dollar technology company.

Highly skilled professionals who move to the United States also encounter a unique problem that afflicts doctors in particular: They find that their credentials are viewed as substandard in the United States. Each individual is thus forced to choose either many more years of higher education or an entirely different career path. Such a choice, often having to be made at midlife, is disguised by the "model minority" stereotype and belies the success rate of the highly skilled contemporary Asian-American immigrant.

Within the various Asian ethnic subcultures alive in America, residents face serious problems. In addition to hate crime violence, many Asian Americans have encountered or worry about crimes perpetrated by Asian youth gangs and the entrenched tong societies still active in contemporary Chinatowns. Generalizations about Asians as "model minorities" in the media and in the culture at large obscure both these complex problems and the need for the larger society to empower its Asian-American citizens with legally backed long-term solutions.

CELEBRATING ASIAN-AMERICAN CULTURE

As the United States moves into the 21st century, the nation's concept of what it means to be an American continues to expand—thanks in large part to diverse Asian-American communities that range from first-generation immigrants to those families whose roots in the United States go back more than a century.

As demonstrated in previous chapters of this book, each national group of Asian Americans carries its individual history of migration and adaptation, of acculturation and contribution. Asian Americans in all

Asian-American Population Distribution, 2000

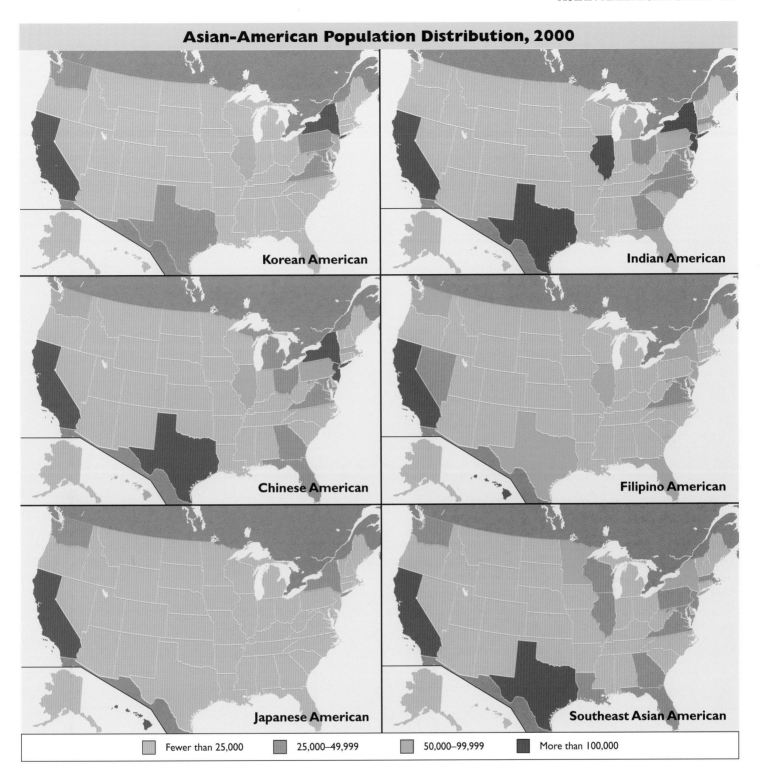

Fewer than 25,000 25,000–49,999 50,000–99,999 More than 100,000

walks of life have contributed significantly in an array of disciplines, becoming heroes to Americans of all backgrounds in the process. At the same time, many Asian cultural, religious, health, and even culinary practices have become widespread in the United States.

ASIAN-INDIAN AMERICANS

Asian Indians living in the United States try to maintain traditional family values. Arranged marriages are still common, and many travel to India for matchmaking or the taking of vows. Divorce, which is rare in India, is also unusual among Asian-Indian Americans. Extended family life is important to Asian Indians; since 1975, almost half of U.S. Asian-Indian households have included at least one nonnuclear relative. Long visits between family and friends are an important tradition and therefore common. Naturalized citizens also sponsor other family members to make a permanent move to the United States. The high success rate of

Asian Indian–owned businesses is due in large part to families working long hours together to make their businesses thrive.

Education is highly valued among Asian-Indian immigrants. The 1990 census revealed that 52 percent of adult Asian Indians were college graduates, compared with a rate of 35 percent of all adult Asian Americans. Three out of four Asian-Indian Americans earned above-average grades by 1990, their academic achievements bolstered by their fluency in English.

In addition to the establishment of special schools to educate young people in traditional language and cultural arts, Asian-Indian Americans have created ethnic organizations to advance their needs and protect their civil rights. Since the 1980s, the Association of Indians in America (AIA) has worked on a variety of issues affecting the community, such as promoting participation in the U.S. census for an accurate count, so that Asian-Indian Americans can take advantage of affirmative action programs. The Fed-

eration of Indian Associations, created in the early 1990s, represents the interests of Asian-Indian businesspeople living in America.

Asian-Indian Americans who have risen to prominence include Nobel Prize–winning astrophysicist Subrahmanyan Chandrasekhar, ethnic studies professor Jane Singh of the University of California at Berkeley, California congressman Dalip Singh Saund, Honolulu-based retail giants Gobindram Jhamandas and Watumull Jhamandas, conductor Zubin Mehta, and holistic physician and author Deepak Chopra.

Increasingly, Indian cultural traditions are also finding new audiences among non–Asian Indian Americans. Though still unknown to many Americans, Indian cuisine, with its characteristic hot curries and sweet coconut milk flavors, is growing in popularity.

Also increasing in popularity among a wide variety of Americans are Ayurvedic health practices. Although the

SELECTED ASIAN-AMERICAN ARTISTS

Name	Ethnicity	Description
Isamu Noguchi (1904–1988)	Japanese	An internationally renowned sculptor, Noguchi blended Eastern and Western influences in his series of Akari lamps, lending modern meterials and designs to these traditional paper laterns. He also worked as a furniture maker and set designer for choreographer Martha Graham.
I. M. Pei (1917–)	Chinese	A renowned architect, I. M. Pei has designed the John F. Kennedy Library in Boston, the East Building of the National Gallery of Art in Washington, D.C., the Rock and Roll Hall of Fame in Cleveland, and the Bank of China in Hong Kong.
Nam June Paik (1932–)	Korean	A musician, performance artist, and installation artist, Paik has shown his work at such notable insitutions as the Museum of Modern Art and the Whitney in New York City, and the Museum of Contemporary Art in Chicago. One of his best-known works is *Video Fish* (1975).
Seiji Ozawa (1935–)	Japanese	Ozawa is the conductor and music director of the Boston Symphony Orchestra.
Zubin Mehta (1936–)	Asian Indian	Zubin Mehta joined the Los Angeles Philharmonic in 1962, becoming the youngest conductor in the United States appointed to a major orchestra. From 1978 to 1991 he served as director of the New York Philharmonic, in 1981 he was named musical director for life of the Israel Philharmonic Orchestra, and in 1998 he became the director of the Bavarian State Opera in Munich.
Haing S. Ngor (1947–1996)	Cambodian	A survivor of the Khmer Rouge regime, Ngor escaped to Thailand and came to the United States in 1979. He won an Academy Award for best supporting actor for *The Killing Fields* in 1985, portraying Dith Pran, a renowned photographer who also survived the Khmer Rouge labor camps.
Maniya Barredo (1951–)	Filipina	Barredo is a prima ballerina with the Atlanta ballet, one of the most prestigious dance companies in the United States.
Yo-Yo Ma (1955–)	Chinese	Regarded as one of the world's best musicians, Ma plays the cello with extraordinary technique and interpretation.
Maya Lin (1959–)	Chinese	Lin is the architect and designer of the Vietnam War Memorial in Washington, D.C., the Civil Rights Memorial in Atlanta, and the Musum of African Art in New York City.

Zubin Mehta (courtesy of Los Angeles Philharmonic Symphony)

The Eight Stages of Yoga

Yoga is an eight-stage discipline involving integration of the body, mind, and spirit. Each stage is designed to bring the individual closer to Brahman, the universal soul, and to rectify imbalance of the body, spirit, and mind. The states are as follows:

1. Ethical training, involving the renunciation of lying, stealing, or violence
2. Mental restraint, involving the acceptance of life and death
3. Discipline of the body and mind, involving practicing asanas, or postures—for example, the headstand or the cross-legged position
4. Breathing exercises
5. Liberation of the mind from the senses
6. Concentration and meditation
7. Further meditation
8. Samadhi, involving a deep state of meditation in which union with Brahman is achieved

system was once uncommon in the West, more and more Western-trained physicians are embracing some Ayurvedic techniques under the umbrella of "alternative" medicine.

Like Chinese health techniques (discussed later in this chapter), Indian health practices are sometimes referred to as "holistic." This term refers to the fact that Indian medicine espouses a concept of well-being that balances and individual's physical, mental, and spiritual aspects and aims to treat the causes of illness rather than the symptoms. The components of Ayurvedic health include practicing yoga and meditation.

Yoga means "harnessing" or "union" in the Sanskrit language. There are many different types of yoga, including hatha, kundalini, and iyengar. It is an eight-stage discipline involving integration of the body, mind, and spirit. Each stage is designed to bring the individual closer to Brahman, or the universal soul, and to rectify imbalance of the body, spirit, and mind. It has a proven therapeutic

AYURVEDIC MEDICINE

The term "Ayurvedic" comes from the Sanskrit roots *ayus,* or "life," and *veda,* or "knowledge." Ayurvedic medicine is based on three concepts: assessment of clinical symptoms, acknowledgment that behavior and environment influence health, and belief in the restorative elements of proper diet.

According to the Ayurvedic system, the body is made from earth, water, fire, air, and ether. Foods taste either sweet, sour, salty, pungent, bitter, or astringent. During the digestive process, the body's organic juices break down food, producing organ feeders and humors (wastes). Organ feeders include blood, flesh, fat, bone, marrow, and, in men, semen. Humors (waste products) include phlegm (representing water), bile (fire), and wind (air).

The Ayurvedic system holds that both food and the body contain five basic elements: earth, water, fire, air, and ether. Food, which has six tastes (sweet, sour, salt, pungent, bitter, and astringent), is digested and converted to organic juices, which then turn into blood, flesh, fat, bone, marrow, and semen.

After digestion, three important waste products (humors) emerge: water, fire, and air. Humoral balance is achieved through proper diet and thus balance of the six tastes. Foods have properties that work in contrast to humors to help restore balance. For example, oil (whose properties are hot, heavy, and smoothing) counters air (cold, light, and rough); honey (astringent, rough, sharp) counters water (sweet, smoothing, dull); and ghee (cold, dull, sweet) counters fire (hot, sharp, sour). Diseases are therefore treated by proper doses of food.

Yin and Yang

The concept of yin and yang is central to the Chinese Taoist concept of balance and harmony. Yin (black) is the passive element of life, encompassing the moon, earth, water, and female energy. Yang (white) is the active element of life, encompassing the sun, heaven, fire, and male energy. Yin and yang interact and are in balance within the circular form that represents the Tao, or the universal harmony of nature. Chinese medicine aims to restore the disrupted balance between yin and yang. Diagnosis is conducted by examining the pulse of both wrists, which reflects the condition of internal organs. Balance is restored using herbs, massage, acupuncture, and moxibustion.

Journalist Connie Chung (Corbis-Bettmann)

effect, improving blood circulation and reducing tension.

KOREAN AMERICANS

Strong networking ties between Koreans have helped all members succeed by keeping profit and employment circulating within the community. Korean Americans have created organizations to match newly arrived businesspeople with established Korean wholesalers and distributors. Perseverance in the early days of their settlement as a group has led to success, as have individual business savvy, intense commitment, hard work, and prudent decisions. Korean businesspeople, like many immigrants, open stores in run-down neighborhoods where rents are cheap. As the years go by and the stability provided by these Korean businesses help the neighborhoods thrive, property values skyrocket. Estimates hold that the property values in Los Angeles's Koreatown have increased 20 times in two decades. A high level of education is also the norm among Korean Americans—as of 2001, the majority of Korean small business owners in New York City possessed college degrees.

Among all Asian groups in the United States, Korean Americans exhibit the highest self-employment rate—twice as high as the American average and ranking second only to that of Greek Americans. When Korean professionals cannot find employment in their chosen fields upon arrival, they turn to small business ownership. It is also common nowadays for Koreans planning a move to America to save large amounts of capital before leaving Korea so that they will arrive with the means to open their businesses right away.

Korean churches provide an avenue for business networking as well as spiritual and social sustenance. As of 2000, 75 percent of U.S. citizens with Korean ancestry were of the Christian faith, mainly Presbyterian. Some churches even lend money to Korean businesspeople, asking that a share of the profit be donated to the church in payment. Joint ventures and business collaborations are deals that are sometimes worked out through church-sponsored group sessions.

Traditional Korean family life is maintained to a large degree in America. Many Koreans live in multigenerational homes, caring for their elders and other relatives. Two-thirds of Korean-American women work outside the home, but at home they are still expected to perform all domestic and child-rearing duties. A large number of Korean parents in the United States still pre-

fer arranged marriage as a route to wedlock for their children, and they expect their children to agree to the practice, as well as to care for them when they reach old age. Many younger U.S.-born Koreans are known to rebel against these expectations, but at great emotional cost to their families.

Korean cultural celebrations kept alive in the United States include Hangul Day, Children's Day, and Hwan'gap. Hangul Day commemorates the Korean alphabet (hangul) as a symbol of Korean freedom from Chinese and Japanese domination. Hwan'gap occurs when an elder Korean has passed through five 12-year cycles and is ready to be cared for by his or her children. On Children's Day, May 5, children rather than elders are honored. And every third Saturday in October, Korean Americans parade down New York City's Broadway to celebrate the autumn Korean Moon Festival.

Numerous Korean Americans have made significant contributions to American society. Among them are Nam June Paik, a musician, performance artist, and installation artist; Jae Soo Lim, an engineer who helped lead the development of high-definition television (HDTV); violinist Jennifer Koh, who won the 1994 International Tchaikovsky Competition, which honors the world's best musicians; comedienne and actress Margaret Cho; and Chan Ho Park, pitcher for the Los Angeles Dodgers, who became the first Korean or Korean American to play professional baseball in the major leagues.

CHINESE AMERICANS

Perhaps because Chinese Americans have had a longer history in the United States than Asian-Indian or Korean Americans, a higher number of Chinese Americans have achieved high profiles. The first Chinese-American woman to become mayor of a U.S. city, Lily Lee Chen, was elected to office in Monterey Park in 1984. Other prominent Chinese Americans include I. M. Pei, an architect who is internationally respected for his unique style and use of glass; Maya Ying Lin, also an architect, who designed the Vietnam Veterans and Civil Rights Memorials Washington, D.C.; An Wang, founder of Wang Laboratories; Jerry Yang, founder of the Internet search provider Yahoo; S. B. Woo, physicist and former lieutenant governor of Delaware; Connie Chung, pioneering TV anchorwoman and journalist; actor B. D. Wong, who has appeared in numerous films and plays; and David Ho, a noted researcher

SELECTED ASIAN-AMERICAN WRITERS

Name	Ethnicity	Description
Gloria Hahn (1926–1987)	Korean	Hahn's novel *Clay Walls* (1986) chronicles the life of a Korean-American woman who destroys her eyesight doing needlework to support her family while her husband runs through the family savings by gambling.
Ved Mehta (1934–)	Asian Indian	Blinded by spinal meningitis at the age of three, Mehta has written numerous books that describe the culture of India, including *Three Stories of the Raj, Delinqent Chacha,* and *Portrait of India.*
Maxine Hong Kingston (1940–)	Chinese	One of the first Asian-American writers to receive acclaim, Kingston won the National Book Critics Circle Award for *The Woman Warrior* (1976), which combined both Eastern and Western cultural influences in accounts of Chinese-American life. She also wrote *China Men* and *Tripmaster Monkey.*
Jessica Hagedorn (1949–)	Filipina	Nominated for the National Book Award for her acclaimed novel *Dogeaters,* Hagedorn writes about the Asian-American experience. The title of this work refers to the racial slur used against Filipinos.
Le Ly Hayslip (1949–)	Vietnamese	Born in Vietnam and tortured by South Vietnamese soldiers, Hayslip chronicled the experiences of her life in Vietnam and America in *When Heaven and Earth Changed Places: A Vietnamese Woman's Journey from War to Peace* (1989). She also wrote an account of her life as a refugee in *Child of War, Woman of Peace* (1993).
Amy Tan (1952–)	Chinese	A renowned novelist, Tan wrote *The Joy Luck Club, The Kitchen God's Wife,* and *One Hundred Secret Senses.*
David Henry Hwang (1956–)	Chinese	Hwang's *M. Butterfly* won a Tony for best Broadway play in 1988. Other works include awards for *F.O.B., Dance and the Railroad,* and *Golden Child.*
Mira Nair (1957–)	Asian Indian	Film director Nair's work includes *Salaam Bombay* and *Mississippi Masala,* the story of an interracial romance between an Asian-Indian American and an African American.

specializing in the fight to combat HIV, who developed life-prolonging protease inhibitor "cocktails" that attack the virus with a mixture of drug therapies.

Many Chinese cultural practices and celebrations are also well known in the United States. Chinese cuisine is one of the most popular styles of food in the United States. Because most early Chinese immigrants were Cantonese, Cantonese cooking was the first to reach the United States and remains the style most widely available in the West. However, newer arrivals that feature wide variety of flavors and spices, such as Szechwan, from western China, and Mongolian, from northern China, are becoming known among Americans. These exotic cuisines have become more popular as relations between the People's Republic of China and the United States have improved and a more diverse range of Chinese entrepreneurs have come to the United States.

Chinese New Year is also a well-known celebration in all cities that boast a Chinese community of any significant size. Festivities include folk dancing, martial arts displays, and, most famed of all, the appearance of the *gum lung* or golden dragon. The dragon, held up by numerous "dragon-bearers," symbolizes strength and long life for the Chinese. This celebration begins the lunar year and signifies the hope for happiness and prosperity in the coming year. The New Year season lasts from mid-December to mid-January and is a particularly busy time, as presents, food, and decorations are all acquired in preparation for the celebrations.

Like Ayurvedic health practices from India, a number of Chinese health care practices have also become popular in the United States. Chinese medicine is based on the concept of yin and yang, which aims for balance and harmony in the body. This aim is achieved through the use of herbs, acupuncture, and moxibustion, in which plant substances are burned on the skin after acupuncture needles are withdrawn. Many Chinese Americans, particularly more recent immigrants living in Chinatowns, prefer these Eastern remedies to Western medicine. Although some remedies are controversial among Westerners,

Internet entrepreneur Jerry Yang (courtesy of Yahoo, Inc.)

Japanese-American figure skater Kristi Yamaguchi (Corbis-Bettmann)

and some, such as rhinoceros horn, are derived from endangered species, others, such as ginseng and ginkgo, have been widely accepted by the general American public. The World Health Organization has endorsed a number of Chinese techniques, including acupuncture, which it has called an effective treatment for at least 50 common disorders. There are currently more than 5,000 acupuncturists in the United States today, most of them Chinese Americans.

FILIPINO AMERICANS

Although Filipino Americans have not tended to congregate in distinct ethnic enclaves in the same way that some Chinese, Koreans, and Southeast Asians have, recent immigrants from the Philippines have maintained close ties to home and have sought to uphold cultural traditions. For example, Filipino-American festivals are quite common, particularly in California, where a large percentage of Filipino Americans live. Traditional dances, such as the *tinikling*, which is performed among moving bamboo poles, are a common activity at such celebrations, as are meals consisting of traditional Filipino foods, such as the national dish, adobo, a dark stew made with chicken, octopus, pork, and vegetables cooked in vinegar, pepper, and garlic. An increasing number of Filipino Americans are making names for themselves in a large

number of fields. Among them are Benjamin Cayetano Jr., governor of Hawaii; actress and singer Lea Salonga, who starred in such musicals and *The King and I* and *Miss Saigon*, as well as films *Mulan* and *Aladdin*; actress Tia Carrere, who appeared in the films *Wayne's World* and *Rising Sun*; and novelist Jessica Hagedorn.

JAPANESE AMERICANS

Like Chinese Americans, Japanese Americans have had a long history in the United States, and thus are one of the most highly assimilated Asian-American populations. Much of that is by design, as early Japanese-American history was often tempered by the desire of conservative issei and nisei like Mike Masaoki of the Japanese American Citizens League (JACL) to prove their loyalty to the United States through adoption of American cultural practices. This circumstance combined with the relatively small amount of new immigration to the United States from Japan compared with immigration from other Asian nations might lead one to believe that Japanese Americans have a weaker connection to the cultural traditions of their ancestoral home.

If anything, the opposite is true. Particularly since the 1960s and 1970s, when the Yellow Power movement emphasized cultural heritage and the redress movement highlighted the injustices done to the issei and nisei generations, traditional Japanese culture is very much alive and well in the United States. Nisei Week, which began in 1934, continues to be celebrated in Los Angeles every year. The 2001 festival, like every other Nisei Week held since that first year, featured traditional dancing, Japanese floral arrangements, tea ceremonies, martial arts, fashion shows, a kimono-clad queen and attendants, calligraphy, and art shows.

Many of these traditional Japanese practices have also become popular among non-Japanese Americans. As mentioned previously, Japanese forms of martial arts such as karate and judo have been common features of American life since the 1960s. Likewise, particularly among urban and suburban dwellers along the West and East Coasts, sushi bars, which offer a choice of delicacies made of raw fish, rice, and rolled seaweed for lunch or dinner have become a standard dining option.

Noted Japanese Americans also populate the mainstream of American culture. Among the best known figures are the noted sculptor Isamu Noguchi; conductor Seiji Ozawa; actor Pat Morita, star of the television show

Happy Days and the *Karate Kid* films; astronaut Ellison Onizuko, the first Japanese American in space; veteran baseball pitcher Hideo Nomo, as well as more recently arrived stars such as teammates Ichiro Suzuki and and Kazuhiro Sasaki of the Seattle Mariners; and perhaps the best-known Japanese-American athlete, figure skater Kristi Yamaguchi.

SOUTHEAST ASIAN AMERICANS

As discussed in chapter 6, among all of the various groups of Asian Americans, those originating in the Southeast Asia have had the most difficulty in adapting to U.S. culture. All too often mired in poverty, many Southeast Asian communities remain relatively isolated from outside influence. By the same token, people from Cambodia, Laos, and Vietnam constitute the largest group of refugees ever to build new lives in the United States. In all, 1,342,532 Southeast Asian refugees entered the United States between 1975 and 1998. Southeast Asians are also the fastest growing racial group in the United States.

In discussing the present-day status of Southeast Asians, however, one must remember they are not a monolithic group. Vietnamese, Lao, Hmong, and Cambodian Americans do not share a common language other than English, which most do not speak. Despite the fact that many share a government classification as refugees, they came out of different experiences and took unique paths in getting to the United States over the quarter century since the first Vietnamese refugees began to arrive.

The diversity of experiences among Southeast Asian refugee groups has challenged social service providers attempting to assist each group. For example, Cambodians tend to have higher rates of mental illness as a result of the Khmer Rouge period. Consequently, many find it especially difficult to learn English and adapt to their new environments, particularly when they do not have access health services in their own language. Hmong also tend to live in almost exclusively non-English-speaking communities, and when they do come in contact with social service providers, fear, misunderstanding, and mistrust often result. The best-selling book *The Spirit Catches You and Then You Fall Down*, by Anne Fadiman, relates the story of a Hmong child with epilepsy, a condition believed by Hmong to signify higher spiritual wisdom. American doctors' efforts to treat the condition were therefore met with great resistance—a resistance not understood because of the language barrier.

Despite difficulties such as these, there are signs of change in both the Southeast Asian community itself and in its interaction with the larger American culture. Because of the diversity of experience and individual need in Southeast Asian–American communities, numerous ethnically based mutual assisance associations have emerged to aid Southeast Asian Americans in navigating their new lives—much in the same way that the Chinese Six Companies emerged in the early years of the Chinese-American community of the 19th century.

According to Ka Ying Yang, executive director of Southeast Asia Resource Action Center, Southeast Asian Americans have begun to think of themselves as new Americans rather than as refugees. As Southeast Asian Americans have begun to view themselves differently, they have entered mainstream political life in increasing numbers. Among these are Tony Lam, a Vietnamese American who serves as mayor pro tempore of Westminster, California; Choua Lee, a Hmong American who became the first Hmong ever voted into office when she was elected to the St. Paul, Minnesota, school district board; and John Quoc Duong, named by President George W. Bush the executive director of the White House Initiative on Asian Americans and Pacific Islanders.

Another sign that Southeast Asian Americans are making progress is the emergence of a number of Americans of Southeast Asian descent in a variety of professions. Among these is author Le Ly Hayslip, a Vietnamese refugee who survived torture by South Vietnamese soldiers. Hayslip chronicled her experiences in Vietnam and the United States in *When Heaven and Earth Changed Places: A Vietnamese Woman's Journey from War to Peace* (1989), as well as in *Child of War, Woman of Peace* (1993).

In some ways, Hayslip's ability to transform her painful experiences into a best-selling memoir mirrors not only the adaptation of other Southeast Asian refugees to U.S. living, but that of many Asian immigrants. For many Asians who immigrated over the past century and a half, the experience of coming to America has been one of transformation. Often, that experience has been difficult—whether in the gold fields of California, the plantations of Hawaii, the internment camps of the desert West, or the tenements of present-day cities. With each successive generation, however, the social fabric of the United States has undergone a reciprocal transformation, as each new piece of the multicultural American tapestry has been sewn into place.

SELECTED BIBLIOGRAPHY

Almaguer, Tomas. *Racial Fault Lines: The Historical Origins of White Supremacy in California.* Berkeley: University of California Press, 1994.

Authentic Kung-Fu. "Kung-Fu Explanations and Definitions." Authentic Kung-Fu. Available online. URL: http://www.authentickungfu.com/seven_star/explanations.html. Downloaded January 22, 1999.

Avakian, Monique. *The Meiji Restoration and the Rise of Modern Japan.* Englewood Cliffs, NJ: Silver Burdett Press, 1991.

Barringer, Herbert, et al. *Asians and Pacific Islanders in the United States.* New York: Russell Sage Foundation, 1995.

Barth, Gunther. *Bitter Strength: A History of the Chinese in the United States, 1850–1870.* Cambridge, MA: Harvard University Press, 1964.

Berkin, Carol, et al. *Land of Promise: A History of the United States.* Glenview, IL: Scott, Foresman and Company, 1983.

Buddhism Depot. "Introduction to Buddhism." Buddhism Depot. Available online. URL: http://www.edepot.com/buddha.html. Downloaded February 2, 1999.

Cao, Lan, and Himilce Novas. *Everything You Need to Know About Asian-American History.* New York: Plume, 1996.

The Centre of Indian Arts. "Introduction to Indian Classical Music." Classical Music of India. Available online. URL: http://www.aoe.vt.edu/~boppe/MUSIC/PRIMERS/icmn.html. Downloaded February 22, 1999.

Chan, Sucheng. *Asian Americans: An Interpretive History.* Boston, MA: Twayne Press, 1991.

———. *This Bittersweet Soil: The Chinese in California Agriculture, 1860–1910.* Berkeley, CA: University of California Press, 1986.

Chandrasekhar, S., ed. *From India to America: A Brief History of Immigration, Problems of Discrimination, Admission and Assimilation.* La Jolla, CA: Population Review Publications, 1982.

Chen, Jack. *The Chinese of America.* San Francisco: Harper & Row, 1980.

Daniels, Roger. *Asian America: Chinese and Japanese in the United States since 1850.* Seattle: University of Washington Press, 1988.

Fieldhouse, Paul. *Food and Nutrition: Customs and Culture.* New York: Chapman and Hall, 1995.

Gall, Susan, and Irene Natividad, eds. *The Asian American Almanac: A Reference Work on Asian Americans in the United States.* Detroit, MI: Gale Research Inc., 1995.

Gall, Susan, and Timothy Gall, eds. *Statistical Record of Asian Americans.* Detroit, MI: Gale Research Inc., 1993.

Haines, David, ed. *Refugees as Immigrants: Cambodians, Laotians, and Vietnamese in America.* Totowa, NJ: Rowman and Littlefield, 1989.

Hing, Bill Ong. *Making and Remaking Asian America Through Immigration Policy, 1850–1990.* Stanford, CA: Stanford University Press, 1993.

Hoobler, Dorothy, and Thomas Hoobler. *The Japanese American Family Album.* New York: Oxford University Press, 1996.

Hosokawa, Bill. *Nisei: The Quiet Americans.* New York: William Morrow, 1969.

Inada, Lawson Fusao. *Only What We Could Carry: The Japanese-American Internment Experience.* Berkeley, CA: Heyday Books, 2000.

Johnston, Hugh. *The Voyage of the Komagata Maru: The Sikh Challenge to Canada's Color Bar.* Seattle: University of Washington Press, 1989.

Ketkar, Ashutosh, and Krithika Ketkar. "Tabla: Information and History." Tabla: King of Percussion Instruments. Available online. URL: http://www.freeyellow.com/members2/tabla/tblaintro.html. Downloaded February 22, 1999.

Kim, Hyung-chan, ed. *Dictionary of Asian-American History.* Westport, CT: Greenwood Press, 1986.

———. *Distinguished Asian Americans: A Biographical Dictionary.* Westport, CT: Greenwood Press, 1999.

———. *The Korean Diaspora: Historical and Sociological Studies of Korean Immigration and Assimilation in North America.* Santa Barbara, CA: ABC-Clio, 1977.

Kim, Illsoo. *New Urban Immigrants: The Korean Community in New York.* Princeton, NJ: Princeton University Press, 1981.

Korean Overseas Information Service. *A Handbook of Korea.* Seoul, Korea: Seoul International Publishing House, 1988.

Lai, Him Mark. *Island: Poetry and History of Chinese Immigrants on Angel Island 1910–1940.* Seattle: University of Washington Press, 1980.

Lehrer, Brian. *The Korean Americans.* New York: Chelsea House, 1996.

Lim, Genny, ed. *The Chinese American Experience: Papers from the Second National Conference on Chinese American Studies.* San Francisco: Chinese Historical Society of America and Chinese Culture Foundation, 1984.

Mark, Diane Mei Lin, and Ginger Chih. *A Place Called Chinese America.* Dubuque, IA: Kendall Hunt, 1993.

McWilliams, Carey. *Factories in the Field: The Story of Migratory Farm Labor in California.* Boston, MA: Little, Brown & Co., 1939.

Melendy, Howard Brett. *Asians in America: Filipinos, Koreans, and East Indians.* Boston: Twayne Publishers, 1977.

Miller, E. Willard. *United States Immigration: A Reference Handbook.* Santa Barbara, CA: ABC-Clio, 1996.

Montero, Darrel. *Japanese Americans: Changing Patterns of Ethnic Affiliation over Three Generations.* Boulder, CO: Westview Press, 1980.

Niiya, Brian, ed. *Encyclopedia of Japanese American History, Updated Edition* New York: Checkmark Books, 2000.

O'Brien, David J. *The Japanese American Experience.* Bloomington: Indiana University Press, 1991.

Ohlenkamp, Neil. "What Is Judo?" The Judo Information Site. Available online. URL: http://www.rain.org/~ssa/whatis.htm. Downloaded November 21, 1998.

Palumbo-Liu, Davi. *Asian/American: Historical Crossings of a Racial Frontier.* Palo Alto, CA: Stanford University Press, 1999.

Park, Kyeyoung, and Ruby Danton. "Korean Small Businesses in New York City." The Korean American Dream: Ideology & Small Businesses in Queens. Available Online. URL: http://www.qc.edu/Asian_American_Center/aacre_23.html. Downloaded January 12, 1999.

Philippine-American War Centennial Initiative. Available online. URL: http://www.phil-am-war.org. Downloaded November 20, 1998.

Plée, Henry. "What Is Karate?" *Shotokai Encyclopedia: Karate-do & Martial Arts.* Available online. URL: http://www.shotokai.cl/ingles/karateng.html. Downloaded November 21, 1998.

Qi: The Journal of Traditional Eastern Health and Fitness. "Taijiquan." Available online. URL: http://www.qi-journal.com/AcuPoints/html. Downloaded December 5, 1998.

Quincy, Keith. *Hmong: History of a People.* Spokane: Eastern Washington University Press, 1997.

Randall, Varnellia R., ed. "Selected Laws and Policies Affecting Asian Pacific Americans." Race, Racism, and the Law. Available online. URL: http://www.udayton/~race/asianlaws.html. downloaded November 5, 1998.

Robinson, Francis, ed. *Cambridge Encyclopedia of India, Pakistan, Bangladesh, Sri Lanka, Nepal, Bhutan, and the Maldives.* New York: Cambridge University Press, 1989.

Russell, Cheryl. *The Official Guide to Racial and Ethnic Diversity.* Ithaca, NY: New Strategists Publications, 1996.

Sandmeyer, Elmer Clarence. *The Anti-Chinese Movement in California.* Urbana: University of Illinois Press, 1973.

Shinagawa, Larry, and Michael Jang. *Atlas of American Diversity.* Walnut Creek, CA: Sage Publications, 1998.

Silver Bush Music. "Stringed Instruments of India." Available online. URL: http://www.silverbushmusic.com/eastind.htm. Downloaded February 22, 1999.

Simonds, Nina. *Classic Chinese Cuisine.* Boston, MA: Houghton Mifflin Co., 1994.

Spicer, Edward, et. al. *Impounded People: Japanese Americans in the Relocation Centers.* Tucson: University of Arizona Press, 1969.

Spickard, Paul. *Japanese Americans: The Formations and Transformations of an Ethnic Group.* New York: Prentice Hall International, 1996.

Takaki, Ronald. *Democracy and Race: Asian Americans and World War II.* New York: Chelsea House, 1995.

———. *From the Land of Morning Calm: The Koreans in America.* New York: Chelsea House, 1994.

———. *In the Heart of Filipino America: Immigrants from the Pacific Isles.* New York: Chelsea House, 1994.

———. *Issei and Nisei: The Settling of Japanese America.* New York: Chelsea House, 1994.

———. *Strangers from a Different Shore.* New York: Penguin, 1998.

Thernstrom, Stephen, ed. *Harvard Encyclopedia of American Ethnic Groups.* Cambridge, MA: Belknap Press of Harvard University, 1993.

Tsai, Shih-shan Henry. *The Chinese Experience in America.* Bloomington: Indiana University Press, 1986.

Tuan, Mia. *Forever Foreigners or Honorary Whites: The Asian Ethnic Experience Today.* Piscataway, NJ: Rutgers University Press, 1999.

U.S. Census Bureau. *Historical Statistics of the United States.* Washington, DC: Government Printing Office, 1989.

U.S. Immigration and Naturalization Service. *Annual Reports.* Washington, DC: U.S. Government Printing Office, 1891–1996.

Wilson, Robert A., and Bill Hosokawa. *East to America: A History of the Japanese in the United States.* New York: Morrow, 1980.

Wyatt, David. *Five Fires: Race, Catastrophe, and the Shaping of California.* Reading, MA: Addison-Wesley Publishing Co., 1997.

Yu, Henry. *Thinking Orientals: Migration, Contact, and Exoticism in Modern America.* New York: Oxford University Press, 2001.

Yuan, Haiwang. "Chinese New Year." Chinascape. Available online. URL: http://harmonywit.com/chinascape/china/culture/holidays/hyuan/newyear.html. Downloaded November 20, 1998.

Zig, Helen. *Asian American Dreams: The Emergence of an Asian American People.* New York: Farrar, Strauss and Giroux, 2001.

A

acupuncture 204
"Address to the People of the United States upon the Evils of Chinese Immigration" 46
Ad-Hoc Japanese Americans for Peace 166
African Americans
    civil rights movement of 165, 166
    and Korean-American relations 195
Agent Orange 170, 177
agriculture. *See* farmers and farming; plantation system (Hawaii)
Aguinaldo, Emilio 79, 80–81, 82
Aiea Plantation strike 77, 78
aikido 164
Akbar (Mughal rajah) 4–5
Akibo, Kyutaro 107–9
Alaska 87, 93, 94, 122
Albuquerque, Alfonso de 19
Alexander & Baldwin 116
Alexander VI (pope) 19
Alien Act of 1790 98–99
alien land laws
    California (1913) 94, 98, 107, 110–11
    California (1920) 107, 146
    states with 112
    Supreme Court ruling on 146
All-American Overseas Chinese Anti-Communist League 148–149
Altai Mountains 9
Amaterasu (Shinto goddess) 10
Amerasian Homecoming Act of 1987, 177
America Is in the Heart (Bulosan) 123
American Council for Nationalities Services 179
American Factors 116
American Federation of Labor 112
American Land and Produce Company 109
American Legion 112, 136
American Loyalty League 119
American Party (Know-Nothings) 44
Amnesty International 189
Andersen Air Force Base 178
Angel Island immigration station 103–5, 119
Ankor period, Southeast Asia 15–16
Ankor Wat 16
anticommunism, in cold war period 150, 151–52, 153, 154, 155
Anti-Communist Committee for Free China 148
antiwar movement 165, 166, 167
Aoki, Dan 156, 157
Aoki, Suizo 89
Aquino, Benigno 189

Aquino, Corazon 189
architects 200, 202
Ariyoshi, George Ryoichi 156, 157
Ariyoshi, Koji 156, 157
Arizona
    alien land law in 112, 113
    anti-Japanese violence in 113, 114
    Korean Americans in 93, 94
armed forces
    Chinese Americans in 131
    Filipino Americans in 127–30
    Japanese Americans in 111, 140–42
artists 13, 14, 200, 204
Aryan Liberation Front 193, 195
Aryans 2, 3
Asia. *See also* Southeast Asia; *specific countries*
    as crossroads of civilization 1–2
    exploration of 8–21
Asian American Political Alliance 167
Asian Americans. *See also* *specific groups*
    and Clinton administration 197
    cultural influence of 162–65, 200–201
    and model minority stereotype 197–98
Asian Americans for Action 166, 167
Asian Americans for Peace 166
Asian Pacific American Legal Consortium 195
Asian Pacific Student Union 191
Asiatic Barred Zone 97, 98
Asiatic Exclusion League 88, 91, 98–99, 109–10
Askikaga (Muromachi) period, Japan 12
Asoka (Maurya ruler) 3
Association for the America-Bound 118
Association of Indians in America (AIA) 200
Atlantic Charter 121
Ayurvedic health practices 162, 200–201
Azuchi-Monoyama period, Japan 12–13

B

Babur (Mughal rajah) 4
Barredo, Maniya 200
Basho 13
Bataan Death March 129
Battle of Bataan 128
Battle of Sekigahara 13
Bemis, Polly 48
Black, Hugo 146
boat people, Vietnamese 175, 176
Bong Jae Jang 196

Border Patrol, U.S. 98 106
Brahma (Hindu god) 2
brahmans (caste) 2, 4
Brewer (C.) & Co. 116
Britain, in India 21-24, 94
British East India Company 21–22, 23, 24
Brown, George 57
Brown v. Board of Education 146, 147
Brunei 15
Bryan, William Jennings 110
Buddha (Siddhartha Gautama) 3
Buddhism
    in China 6
    in India 3
    in Japan 11, 12, 13
    in Korea 9
    in Southeast Asia 15, 16
Bull, E. K. 78
Bulosan, Carlos 122, 123
Bun H. Tao 182
Bun Tek Ngoy 182
Burlingame, Anson 41
Burlingame Treaty of 1868 41–42, 50
Burma (Myanmar) 15, 17
Burns, John Anthony 156, 157
Bush, George W. 195, 205
Bushido ("way of the warrior") 11
businesses
    Chinese-American 34–35, 37–38
    Asian Indian–American 185
    Japanese-American 85–86, 116
    Korean-American 92, 93–94, 186–87, 196, 202

C

Cable Act of 1922 98, 105–6
California. *See also* Los Angeles; San Francisco
    alien land laws 94, 98, 107, 110–13, 146, 147
    Angel Island immigration station 103–5
    anti-Chinese discrimination in 33, 43–44, 50
    anti–Asian Indian discrimination in 98, 101
    anti-Japanese discrimination in 87–88, 107, 109–13
    anti-Japanese violence in 113, 114
    anti-Korean discrimination in 91–92
    Chinese Americans in 27, 31–32, 36, 42–43
    Filipino Americans in 122–24
    gold rush 27, 31–32
    hate crime increase in 195

Asian-Indian Americans in 96, 99, 100, 185- 86
Japanese Americans in 85–89, 103, 107–14
Korean Americans in 91–94
Korean independence movement in 90, 91
legal challenges to land laws 113–15, 146, 147
Vietnamese Americans in 180
Workingman's Party in 43, 44, 51
Yamoto Colonies in 107–109
Yellow Power movement in 166, 167
Cambodia 15
    Vietnam War in 171–73
Cambodian refugees 176–77, 181–82, 205
Cameron, Donaldina 48
Camp Pendleton resettlement center 178
Canada, Asian Indians in 94–95, 96
cannery industry
    Filipino Americans in 122
    Japanese Americans in 87
    Korean Americans in 93, 94
Cape of Good Hope 18–19
caravel 18
Carrere, Tia 204
Carter, Jimmy 175
caste system 2, 3, 4
Castle & Cooke 60, 116
Caucasian, defined by Alien Act of 1790 98–99
Cayetano, Benjamin, Jr. 204
Central Intelligence Agency (CIA) 173
Central Pacific Railroad 41
Chandra, Ram 100
Chandrasekhar, Subrahmanyan 200
Chang In-hwan 90
Chan Yong 49
Chen, Lily Lee 202
Chiang Kai-shek 130, 131, 148
Chiang Kai-shek, Madame 131–32, 133
Chicago, Chinese Americans in 44, 48
children
    Amerasian refugees 177
    in plantation system 62, 69
    of Southeast Asian refugees 180, 183
Child of War, Woman of Peace (Hayslip) 205
Chin, Vincent 193–94
China
    ancient 5–6
    civil war in 130–31, 148
    Communist Revolution 148, 149
    foot binding in 28
    and Korea 73, 74

Manchu period (Qing dynasty) 8–9, 24–25, 28
Ming dynasty 6–8, 17, 21
Mongol Empire 6, 7, 17
Nationalist (Kuomintang) Party 119, 130, 148
Opium Wars 24–25, 28
Sino-Japanese War of 1894 73, 74
and Southeast Asia 17
Taiping Rebellion 25, 28
trade with Europe 21, 24
in World War II 131
Chinese American Citizens Alliance 119, 120, 148
Chinese Americans
    in armed forces 131
    assimilation of 119–120
    business associations of 38–39
    businesses of 34–35, 37–38
    in California gold rush 27, 31–32
    civil rights movement of 41–42, 49–50, 120, 132, 167
    Communist Revolution, attitude toward 148–49
    communities of 34–39, 44, 159–60, 187–88
    and contract labor system 30, 60–61
    crime among 38, 45, 46–47, 48
    cultural practices of 203
    discrimination and prejudice toward 38, 43–47, 49–52, 62–63, 154
    displaced persons 149–50
    educational attainment of 150, 162
    farmers 42–43, 62
    in fishing industry 62
    in Hawaii 61, 62–63, 68, 69–73
    from Hong Kong and Taiwan 188
    illegal immigration by 101–2, 154
    immigration of 27–32, 41–42, 104–5, 159, 176, 187, 188
    and immigration restriction 33, 51–52, 63, 65, 68, 88
    and INS Communist investigations 152, 154
    martial arts of 162, 164
    medicine of 203–4
    miners 31–32
    places of origin 28, 29, 61
    in plantation system 61, 62, 69–73
    political participation of 120
    population of 35, 36, 44, 49, 187
    prominent persons 202–3
    in railroad construction 39–41

refugees 149–50, 174, 176
in tongs 46–47
violence against 33, 45, 50, 192–94
in war effort 131–32
women 159–60
Chinese Communist Party (CCP) 130
Chinese Consolidated Benevolent Association (CCBA) 39
Chinese Exclusion Act of 1882 51–52, 63, 65, 68, 101, 159
Chinese Six Companies 38–39, 41, 47, 48
Chinese Times 120
Chiu, Kenneth 193
Cho, Margaret 202
Chopra, Deepak 200
Chorus from America (Bulosan) 123
Chosun (Korea) 9
Christianity. *See also* missionaries
in Hawaii 58
in Japan 13–14, 21
among Korean Americans 76, 202
Christopher, Dominic 193
Chung, Connie 202
Chung, Margaret 131
Churchill, Winston 121
cigar workers, Chinese-American 38
citizenship rights
under Alien Act of 1790 98–99
under Cable Act of 1922 98, 105–6
congressional bill for 120–21
for Filipinos 159
under McCarran-Walter Act 153
Supreme Court rulings on 98, 99, 111, 114–15, 121
for veterans 111, 113, 129–30
City College of New York 166, 167
Civilian Exclusion Order No. 41 135
Civil Rights Act of 1988 190, 191
civil rights movement
Chinese-American 41–42, 49–50, 120, 132, 167
court cases 146–48. *See also* Supreme Court decisions
Asian Indian–American 120–21
influenced by protest movements 162, 165–66
Japanese-American 117, 118, 119, 146, 148, 166, 167
and Japanese redress 189–91
and Yellow Power movement 162, 166–67
Cleveland, Grover 67
Clinton, Bill 194, 197
Clive, Robert 22
clothing
Chinese miners 32
Manchu 8
Mughal 21, 23
samurai 12
Sikh 96

cold war 150–54
colleges and universities
graduates 161, 162
Yellow Power movement in 166, 167
Colorado 93, 94
Columbus, Christopher 19
Commission on Wartime Relocation and Internment of Civilians (CWRIC) 190, 191
Communist Control Act of 1955 154
Communist Revolution, in China 148
Comrade Society 90, 91
Confession Program 154
Confucianism
in Japan 11, 13
in Southeast Asia 16
teachings of Confucius 5–6
contract labor system
and credit tickets for immigration 30
farmworkers in 97–98
and plantation system 60–61, 62, 63–66, 75–76, 83–84
railroad workers in 87
Cook, James 54–56
Coolidge, Calvin 115
coolies 28, 29
court decisions 146, 147. *See also* Supreme Court decisions
credit rotating system, Korean-American 187, 195, 196–97
credit-ticket system 30
crime
in Chinatowns 38, 45, 46–47, 48
hate crimes 192–95
Crocker, Charles 41
cropping contracts 113
cultural influences, Asian 162–65, 200–201

D

daimyo 12, 26
Daiyho Sha Kai 140
Das, Tarak Nath 98
Dayal, Har 100
Declaration of the All-Korean Convention 133
deep shaft mining 31
Delta Agricultural Association 117
DeWitt, John L. 135–36, 138
Dias, Bartholomeu 18, 19
Diem, Ngo Dinh 165, 170, 171
discrimination and prejudice. *See also* legislation, discriminatory; violence
anti-Chinese 32–34, 42, 43–47, 49–52, 62–63
anti-Filipino 121
anti–Asian Indian 96, 98
anti-Japanese 64, 87–88, 109–13, 145–146
anti-Korean 91–92
during cold war 154
growth of 107
in media 110
Displaced Persons Act of 1948 149–150, 159
Disraeli, Benjamin 23

DMZ (Demilitarized Zone) 151
docking system, in sugar plantations 70
Dole, Sanford B. 67, 154
Dole Corporation 60
Dotbusters 193, 194
Dravidians 2
Drummond, Everett F. 154
DuBois, W. E. B. 123
Duong, John Quoc 205
Dutch 14, 21
Dutch East India Company 21

E

Ebens, Ronald 193, 194
education
literacy rates 94
pensionados program 82, 121
in segregated school system 50, 89–90
of women 162
and Yellow Power movement 167
educational attainment 161–62, 197
Chinese-American 150, 162, 180
Asian Indian–American 200
Japanese-American 162, 180
Vietnamese-American 180
Eglin Air Force Base resettlement center 178
Eightfold Path 3
Eisenhower, Dwight D. 153
Eisenhower, Milton 144
Ellis Island 104
Emergency Quota Act of 1921 98, 105
Emmons, Delos 135, 141
Endo, Mitsuye 144
"Era of Warring States" 12
Evacuation Claims Act of 1948 146, 148
Exclusion Decrees 13–14
Executive Order 9066 134–35, 146
Ex Parte Endo 142, 142–44, 145
explorers, European 18–21

F

Fadiman, Anne 205
fan-tan 47
farmers and farming
Chinese-American 42–43, 62
Filipino-American 122–24
fruit cultivation 43, 93
Asian Indian–American 97–98
irrigation techniques 43
Japanese-American 86, 87, 107–9, 144
Korean-American 92–94
labor union of 117
rice cultivation 61, 86, 93–94
sugar plantations. *See* plantation system (Hawaii)
Yamato Colonies 107–9, 144
Farrington, Elizabeth P. 156

Farrington, Joseph R. 134
Fast, Howard 123
Federal Bureau of Investigation (FBI) 194
Felissaint, Ghislaine 196
Fiji 53
Filipino Americans
citizenship for 159
cultural practices of 204
discrimination and prejudice against 121, 124–25
educational attainment of 162
in farming 122–24
immigration of 83–84, 121, 159, 188–89
labor movement of 77, 78, 84–85, 116, 123–24
occupations of 122
in plantation system 64, 69, 72, 77, 83–84
remigration of 121, 125
in World War II 127–30
violence against 124
Filipino Federation of Labor 84–85
Filipino Laborers' Association 77, 116
Filipino Labor Union (FLU) 123
fishing
Chinese-American 62
Japanese-American 86–87, 147
Florida, Yamato Colony in 107
Fong, Hiram L. 158
foot binding 28
Ford, Gerald R. 189, 190
foreign miners' license tax 32–33
Fort Chaffee resettlement center 178
Fort Indiantown Gap resettlement center 178
442nd Regimental Combat Team 140–42, 143
Four Noble Truths 3
14th Amendment 45, 147
France
in Asian trade 21
in Vietnam 168, 169, 171
Francis Xavier, St. 12
Free Hindustan 98
Freeman, Dwight James 156
Fresno Labor League 117
Frick v. Webb 114, 115
fruit cultivation 43, 93
Fujian province, immigrants from 28, 29, 61
Fujii Sei v. State of California 146, 147
Fujimoto, Charles 156
Fujimoto, Eileen 156–57
Fujiwara family 11
Fulbright, James W. 171

G

Gage, Henry 88
Gama, Vasco da 19
gambling of Chinese Americans 47
Gandhi, Mohandas K. 99–100
gangs
anti-Asian 193, 194
Vietnamese 180
Gannen Mono ("first year men") 64–65
Geary Act of 1892 52
Gemmyo (Japanese empress) 11
Geneva Accords 169, 170, 171
Genghis Khan 4, 6, 7

Genroku period, Japan 13, 14
Gentlemen's Agreement of 1908 83, 89–90, 105
Ghadr 100
Ghadr (Mutiny) Party 100
Gidra 166, 167
G.I. Fiancées Act of 1946 158
gods
Chinese 35
Hindu 2
Japanese 10
Polynesian 57
gold rush, Chinese miners in 27, 31–32
Grant, Ulysses S. 46, 66
Great Mahele program, Hawaii 59–60
Great Northern Railway 87
Guangdong province, immigrants from 28, 29
Gulf of Tonkin Resolution 171
Gupta Empire, India 3–4
guru 2

H

Haan, Kilsoo 134
Hagedorn, Jessica 203, 204
Hahn, Gloria 203
haiku 13
Hakkas ("guest people") 61
Hall, George W. 33
Hall, Jack 155, 156, 157
Han dynasty, China 6, 9, 17
Hangul Day 202
Hanihara, Masanao 115
hara-kiri 11
Harappa 2
Harrison, Benjamin 67
Hart-Cellar Act (Immigration Act of 1965) 174, 183–84, 187
Harte, Bret 46
hate crimes 192–95. *See also* violence
Hate Crimes Statistics Act of 1990 193, 194
Hawaii
annexation to United States 65, 67–68, 85, 154
Chinese Americans in 61, 62–63, 68, 69–73
Cook's expedition to 54–56
disease epidemics in 4, 57, 60, 63, 84
ethnic makeup of 67
and European contact 57–58
Filipino Americans in 69, 72, 77, 83–84
Japanese Americans in 63–66, 68, 69–73, 103,116, 140, 156–57, 158
Japanese internment in 135
Kingdom of 56–67
Korean Americans in 63–64, 72, 75–76, 93, 103
Korean independence movement in 90
labor unions in 64, 68, 72, 77, 78, 116–17, 154–57
land ownership in 59–60
politics in 116, 155, 156, 157–58
Polynesian settlement of 53, 54
sandalwood industry in 56, 59

statehood for 158
sugar plantations in. *See*
  plantation system
whaling industry in 59
Hawaiian Fruit Packers
  Company 116
Hawaiian Sugar Planters
  Association (HSPA) 68, 75,
  83, 84, 116, 155
Hawaii Employment Relations
  Act of 1945 155
Hawaii Laborers' Association
  85
Hawaii Seven 155–57
Hayakawa, Samuel Ichiye 166,
  167, 190
Hayes, Rutherford 81
Hayslip, Le Ly 203, 205
Hearn, Christopher Charles
  193
Hearst, William Randolph
  110
"Heathen Chinee, The" (Harte)
  46
Heian period, Japan 11
Henry the Navigator (Portu-
  guese prince) 18
Hideyoshi Toyotomi 13
Hien Nguyen 193
Higher Wage Association 78
Hilo Massacre of 1938 116
Himalaya Mountains 2
Hinduism
  caste system of 2, 4
  Muslims and 4
  reincarnation under 2–3
  Sepoy Rebellion and 22–23
  in Southeast Asia 15, 16
Hindu Kush Mountains 2
Hirabayashi, Gordon 143, 190,
  191
Hirabayashi v. United States
  142–43
Hirohito (Japanese emperor)
  127
Hiss, Alger 153
Hmong
  refugees 177, 178, 182–83,
  205
  in Vietnam War 173
Ho, David 202–3
Ho Chi Minh 165, 168–70, 171,
  172
Ho Chi Minh Trail 173
Hohri, William 191
Hokkaido 10
Hong Kong 25, 188
Honolulu Longshoremen's
  Association 116
Honolulu Record 157
Honolulu Waterfront Workers'
  Association 116
Honshu 10
Hooper, William 57, 60
House Un-American Activities
  Committee (HUAC) 153
housing discrimination
  147
Humphrey, Hubert 165
Hung Hsiu-chuan 25
Hung Wu 6
Hwang, David Henry 203
Hwan'gap 202
Hwui Shan 27

I

Idaho 112
ideograms 5
Ignacio, Amos 155
Ileto, Joseph 193

immigration
Amerasian Homecoming
  Act of 1987 177
Angel Island station 103–5
Chinese 27–31, 41–42,
  104–5, 159, 176, 187, 188
contract labor system 30,
  60–61, 63–66, 75–76,
  83–84
Displaced Persons Act of
  1948 149–150
Ellis Island station 104
Filipino 83–84, 121, 159,
  188–89
G.I. Fiancées Act of 1946
  158
illegal 101–2, 106, 154, 197
Immigration Act of 1965
  (Hart-Cellar Act) 174,
  183–84, 187
Asian-Indian 94–96,
  184–86
Japanese 63, 64–65, 102–3
Korean 75–76, 94, 159, 186
McCarran-Walter Act of
  1952 153, 174,
1900–1925 106
1925–1945 108
Pacific crossing 29–31
postwar 158–59
of refugees. *See*
  immigration restriction
  of refugees from
  Southeast Asia 168,
  174–77, 180
War Brides Act of 1945
  158–159
and welfare reform 197
of women 28, 48, 49, 51, 63,
  76, 102–3
Immigration Act
  of 1907 90, 106, 107, 112
  of 1924 115, 121
  of 1965 174, 183–84, 187
Immigration and Naturalization
  Act of 1952 (McCarran-Walter
  Act) 153, 174
Immigration and Naturalization
  Service (INS) 154
immigration restriction
  Asiatic Barred Zone 97, 98
  Chinese Exclusion Act of
  1882 51–52, 63, 65, 68,
  101
  in Clinton administration
  197
  Emergency Quota Act of
  1921 98, 105
  Gentlemen's Agreement of
  1908 83, 89–90, 105
  Immigration Act of 1907
  90, 106, 107, 112
  Immigration Act of 1924
  115, 121
  Japanese government
  reaction to 115
  labor union campaign for
  51, 88
  Repatriation Act of 1935
  125
  repeal of exclusion laws
  132–33
income
  Asian/Caucasian
  differentials 160, 161
  of Asian-Indian Americans
  185
  of Southeast Asian refugees
  179, 180
India
  ancient 2–4
  "brain drain" from 185

Britain and 21–24, 94, 95
Buddhism in 3
Hinduism in 2–3, 4
independence movement
  in 99–100
Indus valley civilization 2
Islam in 4, 5
Mughal Empire 4–5, 21
Portuguese traders in 19
and Southeast Asia 15–16
India League of America 121
Asian-Indian Americans
  businesses of 185
  civil rights movement of
  120–21
  cultural practices of
  199–201
  discrimination and prejudice against 96, 98–99
  educational attainment of
  200
  immigration of 94–96,
  184–85
  and Indian independence
  movement 100
  and land ownership 99, 110
  with Mexican-American
  wives 99, 101
  migrant workers 96–98
  music of 162, 163
  population distribution for
  185–86
  violence against 96, 193,
  194, 195
Indian Home Rule League 98
India Welfare League 120
Indochinese Parole Programs
  178–79
Indonesia 15, 53
Industrial Revolution 24
Indus valley civilization 2
Inland Boatmen's Union 116
Inouye, Daniel K. 145–46, 156,
  157, 158
Inter-Island Steamship
  Company 116
Internal Security Act of 1950
  (McCarran Act) 148, 150,
  151–152
International Longshore and
  Warehouse Union (ILWU)
  116, 117, 123, 142, 154–55, 157
International Rescue Committee
  179
internment. *See* Japanese
  internment
interracial marriage 98, 105–6,
  110, 147
Irons, Peter 190, 191
irrigation techniques, Chinese 43
Irwin, Wallace 112
Islam
  in India 4, 5
  Sepoy Rebellion and 22–23
  in Southeast Asia 17
  and World Trade
  Center/Pentagon attacks
  195
Ivan IV (Ivan the Terrible) (Russian czar) 9
Izanagi (Shinto god) 10
Izanami (Shinto goddess) 10
Izuka, Ichiro 155

J

JACL. *See* Japanese American
  Citizens League
Jahan (Mughal shah) 4, 5
Japan
  arts in 13, 14

Askikaga (Muromachi)
  period 12
Azuchi-Monoyama period
  12–13
Buddhism in 11, 12, 13
Chinese influence on 11
Christianity in 13–14, 21
Confucianism in 11, 13
Dutch in 14
European trade with 21
founding of 10
Gentlemen's Agreement of
  1908 83, 89–90
isolationism of 14
and Japanese emigration
  64, 65, 66, 115
Kamakura period 11–12
and Korea 9–10, 13, 73,
  74–75, 76, 133
and Korean independence
  movement 90
in Manchuria 130–31
Meiji Restoration 14, 26, 64
Pearl Harbor attack of
  126–27
Russo-Japanese War of
  1904–1905 73, 74, 89
Shintoism in 10–11
Sino-Japanese War of 1894
  73, 74
Tokugawa shogunate 11,
  13–15
in Vietnam 168
in World War II 128–29
Yamato dynasty 11
Japanese American Citizens
  League (JACL)
  court cases of 143–44
  hate crime against 193, 195
  and internment 135, 146
  origin and goals of 118,
  119, 15
  and redress movement
  189–90
Japanese American Evacuation
  Claims Act 190
Japanese Americans
  in armed forces 111, 140–42
  businesses of 85–86, 116
  in California 85–89, 103,
  107–14
  citizenship for 114–15, 153
  civil rights groups of 117,
  118, 119, 135, 166, 167
  communities of 85
  contract laborers 63–66, 87
  culture of 164, 204
  discrimination and prejudice against 64, 87–88,
  107, 112, 127, 145–146
  educational attainment of
  162, 180
  farm colonies of (Yamato
  Colonies) 107–9, 144
  farmworkers 86, 87
  in Hawaii 63, 64–66, 68,
  69–73, 103, 135, 140,
  156–57, 158
  immigration of 63, 64–65,
  102–3
  and immigration restriction
  88, 90
  internment of. *See* Japanese
  internment
  labor unions of 68, 76, 77,
  84–85, 117–19
  land ownership appeals by
  113–14, 146
  occupations of 86–87
  picture brides 102–3
  in plantation system 63,
  64–66, 69–73, 77, 84

in politics 116, 156,
  157–158
prominent persons 204–5
redress movement of 144,
  189–91
remigration of 85
violence against 113, 114
in Yellow Power movement
  166, 167
Japanese Americans for Peace
  167
Japanese-American Yearbook 108
Japanese Association of America
  (JAA) 117–18
Japanese Deliberative Council of
  America 117
Japanese Exclusion League of
  California 112
Japanese Federation of Labor
  77, 84–85, 118
Japanese internment
  camps 136, 137
  and compensation claims
  146, 148, 190
  daily life during 138–39
  early release program 145
  end of 145–46
  evacuation and relocation
  135–36, 138
  Executive Order 9066
  134–35
  in Hawaii 135
  loyalty questions during
  139
  Manzanar Pilgrimage 166,
  167
  Supreme Court rulings on
  142–44, 145
  Tule Lake camp 139–40
Japanese and Korean Exclusion
  League 91–92
Japanese Labor League of
  America 118
Japanese-Mexican Labor
  Association 117
Japanese Pioneer Community
  Center 166, 167
Jayavarman II (Khmer king) 16
Jennings, William 107
Jersey Journal 194
Jessup, Roger W. 125
Jhamandas, Gobindram 200
Jhamandas, Watumull 200
Jia Qing (Chinese emperor)
  24–25
Jimmu (Shinto god) 10
jobs. *See* labor force
John II (Portuguese king) 18–19
Johnson, C. D. 113
Johnson, Hiram 110, 112
Johnson, Lyndon B. 170, 171,
  183
Joint Resolution of Annexation
  67
Jomon 10
judo 164, 204
Justice for Vincent Chin
  Committee 194

K

Kaahumanu (Hawaiian queen)
  57
Kabuki theater 13
Kaholokula, Joseph, Jr. 155
Kalakaua (Hawaiian king) 66–67
Kamakura period, Japan 11–12
Kamehameha I (Hawaiian king)
  56, 57
Kamehameha II (Hawaiian king)
  57

Kamehameha III (Hawaiian king) 58, 59
Kamehameha IV (Hawaiian king) 63
Kamehameha V (Hawaiian king) 63
kami 11
Kanaloa (Polynesian god) 57
Kanda, Shigefusa 111
Kansas 112
karate 164, 204
Kauai 54, 57
Kaufman, Charles 193
Kawano, Jack 116, 155, 157
Kealoha, James K. 158
Kearny, Dennis 51
kenjinkai (social/cultural groups) 85
Kennedy, John F. 165, 170
Kennedy, Robert F. 165, 171
Khan, Mubarak Aki 120
Kharaiti Ram Samras v. United States 121
Khmer Empire, Southeast Asia 16–17
Khmer Rouge 171, 172, 173
Kidwell, John 60
Kim Brothers Company 93–94
Kim Chong-nim 90, 93
Kim Ho 93
Kim Hyung-soon 93
Kimoto, Jack 156
King, Martin Luther, Jr. 165
King, Rodney 196
Kingston, Maxine Hong 203
Know-Nothings (American Party) 44
Knox, Frank 127
Koguryo, Kingdom of, Korea 9
Koh, Jennifer 202
kokugaku movement, Japan 15
Korea
 ancient 9–10
 Buddhism in 9
 China and 73, 74
 division of 134, 150, 151, 152
 Japan and 9–10, 13, 73, 74–75, 76, 133
Korean Americans
 and African-American relations 195–96
 Brooklyn greengrocer boycott of 1990 196
 businesses of 92, 93–94, 186–87, 195, 196, 202
 Christianity of 76, 202
 credit system of 187, 195, 196–97
 culture and values of 202
 discrimination and prejudice against 91–92
 farmers 92–93
 immigration of 75–76, 94, 159, 186
 in Korean independence movement 90, 91
 literacy rate for 94
 nationalism of 73, 76, 78
 picture brides of 102–3
 in plantation system 63–64, 72, 75–76, 84
 population of 76, 186
 remigration of 76, 93, 94
 war brides 159
 in war effort 133–34
Korean Consolidated Association 90, 91
Korean Mutual Assistance Association 91
Korean National Association of Los Angeles 133

Korean National Association of North America 84, 90, 91
Korean National Brigade 90, 91
Korean National Independence League 90, 91
Korean Restorative Association 91
Korean Student Federation of North America 90, 91
Korean War 150–151, 159
Korematsu, Fred Toysaburo 143, 190, 191
Korematsu v. United States 143
Koroyo dynasty, Korea 9
kshatria 2
Ku (Polynesian god) 57
Kublai Khan 6, 11, 17
Ku Klux Klan 193, 194
kuleana lands, in Hawaii 60
kung fu 162, 164
Kuomintang (Nationalist) Party 119, 130, 148
Kurusu, Saburu 126
Kwan Kung (Chinese god) 35
Kwan Yin (Chinese goddess) 35
Kyne, Peter B. 112
Kyoto, Japan 11, 12
Kyushu 10

L

Laamaomao (Polynesian god) 57
labor force. See also businesses; contract labor system; plantation system (Hawaii)
 in defense industries 145
 farmers 42–43, 62, 86
 in fishing industry 62, 86–87
 miners 31–32
 professional and managerial 185, 198
 in railroad construction 39–41, 86, 87, 96
 second generation in 161
 Southeast Asian refugees in 180, 181–82
 wage/income differentials 37, 38, 43, 161
 women in 145, 160, 161
labor unions. See also strikes
 anti-Asian campaigns of 51, 88, 107, 109
 Filipino-American 77, 78, 84–85, 116, 123–24
 in Hawaii 116–17, 154–57
 Hawaiian plantation workers in 64, 68, 71–72, 76, 77, 78, 84–85, 116, 154–155
 Japanese-American 68, 76, 77, 84–85, 117
Lam, David 198
Lam, Tony 205
land ownership
 and alien land laws 94, 98, 110–13, 146
 and Hawaiian plantation system 59–60, 84–85
 Supreme Court rulings on 98, 113–14, 115, 120, 146
language
 pidgin 72–73
 Sanskrit 2, 3
Laos 15, 173
Laotian refugees 177, 182–83
Lapita colonists, in Melanesia 53
lateen 18
laundries, Chinese-American 34–35

Lea, Homer 110
Lee, Bruce 162
Lee, Choua 205
Legalism 6
legislation, discriminatory 32–33
 Alien Act of 1790 98–99
 alien land laws 94, 98, 107, 110–13, 146
 Cable Act of 1922 98, 105–6
 Chinese Exclusion Act of 1882 51–52, 63
 foreign miners' license tax 32–33
 Geary Act of 1892 52
 in Hawaii 63
 Nationality Act of 1870 43, 50
 Page Act of 1875 43, 49
 Queue Ordinance of 1873 45
 Scott Act of 1888 52
 Tydings-McDuffie Independence Act of 1934 124–25
Letter from America (Bulosan) 123
Liga Filipina 79
Liliuokalani (Hawaiian queen) 67, 68
Lim, Jae Soo 202
Lindberg, Gunner 193
Ling Sing v. Washburn 50
Lin, Maya Ying 200, 202
Lin Tse-hsu 25
literacy rate 94
Livingston Farmers Association 144
Lodge, Henry Cabot 115
Lon Nol 172, 173
Los Angeles
 Korean Americans in 92, 186, 196–97
 Riots of 1992 196
 Yellow Power movement in 166, 167
Los Angeles Community Coalition for Redress/ Reparations (LACCRR) 191
Louisiana 112
Loving v. Virginia 147
Lowell, Massachusetts, Cambodian Americans in 181
Lowry, Mike 190, 191
loyalty questions, Japanese-American internees and 139
luna (plantation overseer) 70, 71, 72, 77
Lutheran Immigration and Refugee Service 179
Luyen Phan Nguyen 193

M

Ma, Yo Yo 200
MacArthur, Douglas 128, 130
McCarran, Pat 154
McCarran Act (Internal Security Act of 1950) 150, 151–152
McCarran-Walter Act (Immigration and Naturalization Act of 1952) 121, 153–54, 174
McCarthy, Joseph 151, 153
McClatchy, Valentine Stuart 110
McCreary, James Bennet 52
McGovern, George 171
McKinley, William 67, 80, 81, 82
McVeigh, Timothy 195
Magellan, Ferdinand 19–20
mahjong 47
Maine, USS 80

Malaysia 15
Manchu period (Qing dynasty), China 8–9, 24–25, 28
"Mandate of Heaven" 5
"manifest destiny" 40, 72
Manlapit, Pablo 84
Manzanar Pilgrimage 166, 167
Mao Zedong 130, 148, 154
Marcos, Ferdinand 189
Marcos, Imelda 189
marriage
 interethnic 99, 101, 122
 interracial 98, 105–6, 110, 147
 with picture brides 102–3
Marshall, James 27, 32
martial arts 162, 164, 204
Masaoka, Mike 119, 190, 191, 204
Masaoka v. State of California 146
Matson Navigation Company 116
Matsunaga, Masayuki "Spark" 156, 157
Maurya Empire, India 3
media
 anti-Japanese propaganda in 110, 134, 136
 Chinese-American 120
 Japanese-American 108
medicine
 Ayurvedic 162, 200–201
 Chinese 203–4
Mehta, Ved 203
Mehta, Zubin 200
Meiji Restoration 14, 26, 64
Melanesia 53
merchants' associations, Chinese 38–39
Metal Trades Council 116
Metcalf, Victor H. 89
Michigan, anti-Chinese violence in 192–94
Mien Laotian refugees 182, 183
mikado 11
Militia Task Force 195
miners, Chinese-American 27, 31–32
Ming dynasty, China 6–7, 17, 21
mining
 camps 31, 48
 deep shaft 31
 and foreign miners' license tax 32–33
 placer method 31
 preemptive claims for 32
Mink, Patsy 156, 157
Minnesota 112
missionaries
 in Hawaii 58
 in Japan 13, 21
 in Korea 75, 76
 in Southeast Asia 16
Missouri 112
model minority stereotype 197–98
Mody, Navrose 193, 194
Mohenjo-Daro 2
Moluccas islands 53
Mongol Empire, China 6–8, 17
Mongols
 in China 6
 in India 4
 in Japan 11
 in Southeast Asia 17
Moon, Hung June 94
Morita, Pat 204
mridanga (drums) 163
Mughal Empire, India 4–5, 21
Murasaki, Shikubu 11
Muromachi (Askikaga) period, Japan 12

music and musicians 162, 163, 200, 202
Mutual Aid Associations (MAAs) 179
Myanmar (Burma) 15, 17
My Lai massacre 171

N

Nagasaki, Japan 12
Nair, Mira 203
napalm 170
National Coalition for Redress/Reparations (NCRR) 189, 191
National Committee for Redress (NCR) 189, 190–91
National Council for Japanese American Redress (NCJAR) 189, 190, 191
Nationality Act of 1870 43, 50
National Liberation Front (NLF) 170
Native Sons of the Golden State 120
Native Sons of the Golden West 88, 112, 136, 148
Naturalization Law of 1798 49
navigation
 Chinese 7
 Polynesian 53–54
 Portuguese 18
Nebraska 112
Nehru, Jawaharlal 165
New Hindu Association 100
New Mexico 112
New People's Association 91
New York City
 Chinese Americans in 37, 44, 47, 48, 150
 Asian-Indian Americans in 185
 Korean Americans in 186–87, 196
 Korean greengrocer boycott of 1990 196
 Yellow Power movement in 166, 167
Ngo Dinh Diem 165, 170, 171
Ngor, Haing S. 200
Nhem, Sam 193
Nichibei Shimbun 108
nirvana 3
Nisei Week 204
Nitz, Michael 193, 194
Nixon, Richard M. 171, 172
Nobunaga, Oda 12–13
No drama 12
Noguchi, Isamu 200, 204
Noguchi, Thomas 166
Nomura, Kichasaburo 126
Northern Pacific Railway 87
Northwest Passage 54

O

Oahu strike
 of 1909 77, 78
 of 1920 84, 116
Oahu Sugar Company strike 77
Office of Redress Administration (ORA) 190, 191
Office of Refugee Resettlement 179
Office of Strategic Services (OSS) 168–69
Oka, Tasaku 116
Onin War of 1457–1477 12
Onizuko, Ellison 205
opium dens 47, 48

opium trade, in China 24–25, 47–48
Opium Wars 24, 25, 28
Orderly Departure Program 180
Oregon 85, 87, 113, 114
Organic Act of 1900 67, 68, 71, 85
Oriental Concern 166
O'Sullivan, John L. 40, 72
Oyama, Fred 146
Oyama, Kajiro 146, 147
Oyama v. State of California 146, 147
Ozawa, Seiji 200, 204
Ozawa, Takao 114–15
Ozawa v. United States 114–15

P

Pacific Spruce Company 113
Paekche, Kingdom of, Korea 9
Page Act of 1875 43, 48–49
Page, Robert 193
pai gow 47
Paik, Nam June 200, 202
pakhawaj (drums) 163
Palmer, Aaron H. 39, 40
"paper sons" 102, 154
Paris Peace Agreement 171
Park, Chan Ho 202
Patek, Mukesh 193
Patel, Kanu 193
Pathet Lao 173
Pearl Harbor 56, 67
    Japanese attack on 126–27
Pei, I. M. 200, 202
Pele (Polynesian god) 57
pensionados program 82, 121
People v. Hall 33–34, 43
Perry, Matthew 64
Personal Justice Denied 191
Phelan, James Duval 88, 112–13, 115
Philippines 15. *See also* Filipino Americans
    commonwealth status for 124
    independence of 130, 159
    liberation movement of 79–81
    pensionados program 82, 121
    politics in 189
    under Spain 20–21, 78–79
    and U.S.-Philippine War of 1899–1902 80, 81–82
pictograms 5
picture brides 93, 102–3
pidgin 72–73
Pioneer Project 166, 167
placer method of mining 31
plantation system (Hawaii) 58–59
    Chinese laborers 61, 62, 69–73
    contract labor system 60–61, 62, 63–66, 71, 75–76
    daily life in 69–73
    "divide and rule" strategy 72, 76, 78
    docking system 70
    Filipino laborers 64, 69, 72, 83–84
    Japanese laborers 63, 64–66, 69–73, 77, 84
    Korean laborers 63–64, 72, 75–76, 84
    and labor movement 68, 72, 77, 78, 116, 154–155
    and labor shortage 60, 65
    and land ownership 59–60, 84–85
    Portuguese laborers 63, 72, 78
    in U.S. trade agreement 61–62, 66–67
    women and children in 62, 69, 84
political action committee (PAC), in Hawaii 155
Polo, Marco 6, 8, 17, 18
Pol Pot 171, 172, 173, 176
Polynesians
    European contact with 54–58
    origins of 53
    religion of 57, 58
    settlement of Hawaii 53, 54
    voyages of 54
Porterfield v. Webb 113–14, 115
Portugal
    exploration of 18–20
    slave trade and 18
    trade of 19, 21
Portuguese, in plantation system 63, 72, 78
post-traumatic stress disorder, among Southeast Asian refugees 181
prejudice. *See* discrimination and prejudice
Pride of Palomar (Kyne) 112
Proclamation Number 1 136–37
Proclamation Number 3 138
Promontory Summit, Utah 41
prostitution 48–49
Punjab, immigration from 94–96, 98
Punti ("local people") 61
Purdy, Patrick 193

Q

Qin Empire, China 6
Qing dynasty (Manchu period), China 8–9, 24–25, 28
Qing Ming festival 35
Quarryworkers Internaional Union of North America 116
Queue Ordinance of 1873 45
Quinn, William F. 158

R

racism. *See* discrimination and prejudice; legislation, discriminatory; violence
railroad workers
    Chinese-American 39–42
    Asian Indian–American 96
    Japanese-American 86, 87
Read, R. D. 84
Reagan, Ronald 190, 191
Reciprocity Treaty of 1875 61–62, 66–67
redress movement, Japanese-American 144, 189–91
Refugee Act of 1980 175
Refugee-Escape Act of 1957 150, 159
Refugee Relief Act of 1953 150, 159, 174
refugees
    Amerasian children 177
    Cambodian 176–77, 178, 181–83
    in camps 176
    Chinese 149–50, 174, 176
    in first-asylum countries 175
    Indochina Migration and Refugee Assistance Act of 1975 178
    Laotian 177, 178, 182–83
    organizations for 179
    Refugee Act of 1980 175
    Refugee-Escape Act of 1957 150
    Refugee Relief Act of 1953 150, 174
    resettlement in United States 178–83
    Vietnamese 174–76, 178, 179–81
reincarnation 2–3
Reinecke, John 156
religion. *See also* Buddhism; Christianity; Hinduism; Islam; missionaries
    in plantation system 76
    Polynesian 57
    Shintoism 10–11
    Sikhism 96
    of Southeast Asian refugees 181
    Taoism 6
    transcendental meditation (TM) 163, 165
Repatriation Act of 1935 125
Resolution 55
Rhee, Syngman 90, 92, 150
rice cultivation 61, 86, 93–94
riots
    anti-Chinese 50
    of plantation workers 72
Rizal, José Protasio 79
Rock Springs, Wyoming, anti-Chinese riot in 50
Roman Catholicism
    in Hawaii 58
    in Japan 12, 21
Roosevelt, Eleanor 129
Roosevelt, Franklin Delano 120, 121, 125, 131, 134, 138, 168, 169
Roosevelt, Theodore 88, 89
Root, Elihu 89
"Roughing It" (Twain) 50
Russia
    eastern expansion of 9
    and Russo-Japanese War of 1904–1905 73, 74, 89

S

Sacramento Bee 110
Sakai, Jo 107
Salinas Valley Japanese Agricultural Contractors' Association 117
Salonga, Lea 204
Samoa 53, 54
Samras, Khairata Ram 121
samurai 11, 12, 14
sandalwood industry, in Hawaii 56, 59
Sandwich Islands (Hawaii) 54–55
San Francisco
    Angel Island immigrant station 103–5
    anti-Chinese riot in 50
    anti-Japanese movement in 88
    Chinese community in 36
    Chinese prostitutes in 48
    Chinese Six Companies in 38–39, 41, 47, 48
    earthquake of 1906 101–2
    Japanese community in 85
    School Board Crisis 89–90, 110
    Workingman's Party in 44
    Yellow Power movement in 166, 167
San Francisco Chronicle 88, 110
San Francisco Examiner 110
San Francisco Labor Council 88
San Francisco State College 166, 167
Sansei Concern 166
Sanskrit 2, 3
Sasaki, Kazuhiro 205
Saund, Dalip Singh 200
Scharrenberg, Paul 120–21
Schmitz, Eugene E. 88
Scholastic Aptitude Test (SAT) 197
school segregation 50, 89–90
Scott Act of 1888 52
Seattle & International Railway 87
Seattle Central Community College 166
Seattle Plan, for Japanese American redress 189, 190
Seed of the Sun (Irwin) 112
segregation, school 50, 89–90
"separate but equal" doctrine 147
Sepoy Rebellion 22–23
77 Cents Parade 77
Shang dynasty, China 5
Sharan, Kaushal 193, 194
Shelly v. Kraemer 147
Shih Huang Ti 6
Shintoism 10–11
shipbuilding 7, 18
Shiva (Hindu god) 2, 15
shoguns 11, 12, 13
Shotuku (Japanese prince) 11
Siddhartha Guatama (Buddha) 3
Sihanouk, Norodom 171, 172
Sikh immigrants 96–99, 101, 186, 195
Sikhism 96
Silk Road 8
Silla, Kingdom of, Korea 9
Singapore 15
Singh, Jane 200
Singh, Moola 98
Singh, Nand Kaur 100–101
Singh, Sirdar Jagit 121
Sino-Japanese War of 1894 73, 74
Sino-Korean People's League 133–34
sitar music 162, 163
slave trade 18
Slocum, Tokutaro 111
Smith Act of 1940 156
Smith, Robert R. 166, 167
Social Revolutionary Party 117
Soeung, Sophy 193
Southeast Asia
    Chinese influence on 17
    early civilizations of 15
    Indian influence on 15–16
    Khmer Empire 16–17
    Polynesian origins in 53
    Vietnam War 168–73
Southeast Asian refugees
    boat people 175, 176
    in camps 175, 176
    cultural adaptation of 205
    evacuation of 168, 174–77
    resettlement in United States 178–183
    violence against 193
Southern California Farm Federation 118, 119
Southern California Gardeners Federation (SCGF) 118, 119
Southern Poverty Law Center (SPLC) 194–95
South Korea, in Korean War 150, 151
Spain
    exploration of 19–21
    in Philippines 20–21, 78–79
    Spanish-American War 79–81
spice trade 19, 21
Spirit Catches You and Then You Fall Down, The (Fadiman) 205
steamships 29
Stevens, Durham 90
Stimson, Henry 128
Strait of Magellan 20
Strait of Malacca 19
strikes
    dock workers 155
    Hilo Massacre of 1938 116
    plantation workers 72, 77, 78, 84, 116
    railroad workers 41
    student 166, 167
student protests 166
sudden unexplained nocturnal death syndrome (SUND) 183
Suez Canal 24
sugar plantations
    in Hawaii. *See* plantation system (Hawaii)
    Yamato Colony, Texas 109
sultans 4
sundra 2
Sun Yat-sen 119, 130
Supreme Court decisions
    on citizenship rights 98, 99, 111, 114–15, 121
    on Japanese internment 142–44, 145
    on land ownership 98, 113–14, 115, 120, 146, 147
    on school segregation 146, 147
Sutter, John 32
Suzuki, Bunji 118
Suzuki, Ichiro 205

T

tabla music 163
Taft, William Howard 82
Tahiti 54
t'ai chi ch'uan 164
Taiping Rebellion 25, 28, 29
Taiwan, immigration from 188
Taj Mahal 4, 5
Takahashi v. California Fish and Game Commission 147
Takaki, Ronald 182–83
Tale of the Genji, The (Murasaki) 11
Tan, Amy 203
Tang dynasty, China 6, 17
Tangun 9
Tang, Winnie 167
Taoism 6
Taruc, Luis 123
Terrace v. Thompson 115
Tet Offensive 171, 172
Texas
    alien land law in 112
    Vietnamese Americans in 180
    Yamato Colony in 107, 109
Thai Binh Brigade 166
Thailand 15, 175, 176

Theo. H. Davies & Co. 116
Thien Minh Ly 193
Thieu, Nguyen Van 175
Third World Liberation Front 167
Thong Hy Huynh 193
Tiger Brigade 134
Tokugawa Iemitsu 13
Tokugawa Iyeyasu 13, 14
Tokugawa shogunate, Japan 11, 13–15, 26
Tokyo, Japan 13, 14
Tonga 53, 54
tongs 46–47
Touch Me Not (Rizal) 79
Toyota, Hidemitsu 111
Toyota v. United States 111, 113
trade
    Hawaii-U.S. sugar 61–62, 66–67
    with Mongol Empire 6
    opium 24–25
    Portuguese 19, 21
trade routes, in Asia 8, 20
transcendental meditation (TM) 163, 165
transcontinental railroad, Chinese laborers in 39–42
Travelers' Aid International Social Services 179
treaties
    Burlingame (1868) 41–42, 50
    Reciprocity (1875) 61–62, 66–67
Triad Society 47
tribute system, in China 6–8
"truck" gardens 43
Truman, Harry S 142, 151–152, 153, 168, 181
Truth About Communism in Hawaii, The 155
Tule Lake Relocation Center 139–40, 152
Turks 4
Twain, Mark 50, 54
Tydings-McDuffie Independence Act of 1934 124–25, 159

U

ukiyo-e art 13
Union Pacific Railroad 41, 87
United Chinese Society 63
United Hebrew Immigrant Aid Society 179
United Japanese Deliberative Council of America 117
United Korean Committee 133

United Nations High Commissioners for Refugees (UNHCR) 179
United States. *See also* immigration; legislation, discriminatory; *specific immigrant groups (e.g., Chinese Americans)*
    annexation of Hawaii 65, 67–68, 85
    Asian culture in 162–65
    during cold war 150–54
    Gentlemen's Agreement of 1908 83, 89–90
    and manifest destiny 40, 72
    in Philippines 81, 82–83
    protest movements in 165–67
    in Spanish-American War 80–81
    and U.S.-Hawaii Reciprocity Treaty of 1875 61–62, 66–67
    in U.S.-Philippine War of 1899–1902 80, 81–82
    in Vietnam War 168–71, 172, 173
    and World Trade Center/Pentagon attacks 195
    in World War I 111
    in World War II. *See* World War II
United States Catholic Conference 179
United States v. Balsara 115
United States v. Bhagat Singh Thind 98, 99, 115, 120
United States v. Mazumdar 115
U.S.-Philippine War of 1899–1902 80, 81–82
University of California at Berkeley 167, 193
University of California at Los Angeles (UCLA) 167, 168
Uno, Edison Tomimaro 189, 190
untouchables 2
Upanishads 2
Utah 85, 93, 94, 101

V

vaisia 2
Valor of Ignorance, The (Lea) 110
Van Reed, Eugene M. 64
Van Troi Anti-Imperialist Youth Brigade 166
varna 2
Vedas 2

Victoria (British queen) 23
Vietcong 170, 171
Vietminh 168, 170, 173
Vietnam 15, 17 division of 169–70
    French colony 168
    human rights in 180–81
    reunification of 171
Vietnamese refugees
    Amerasian children 177
    boat people 175–76
    evacuation of 174–76
    resettlement in United States 179–81
    violence against 193
Vietnam War
    in Cambodia 171–73
    fall of Saigon 174
    in Laos 173
    protests against 165, 166, 167
    U.S. involvement in 168–71, 172
vina music 163
violence
    anti-Chinese 33, 45, 50, 192–94
    anti-Filipino 124
    anti–Asian Indian 96, 193, 194
    anti-Japanese 113, 114
    anti-Korean 91–92
    hate crimes 192–95
    labor 116
    and World Trade Center attack 195
Vishnu (Hindu god) 2, 15, 16
VOLAG system 179
Voting Rights Act of 1965 183

W

wages
    Asian/Caucasian differentials 37, 38, 43
    in plantation system 69, 78
Waipahu Plantation strike 77, 78
Wang, An 202
Wang Laboratories 181
War Brides Act of 1945 158–59
War Relocation Authority (WRA) 135, 136, 139, 144, 145, 146
Washington State
    alien land law in 112
    anti-Asian violence in 96, 124

Asian-Indian Americans in 96, 98
    Japanese Americans in 85, 87
WAVES (Women Accepted for Voluntary Emergency Service) 131
Webb, U. S. 99
Webb v. O'Brien 114, 115
welfare reform 197
whaling industry, in Hawaii 59
When Heaven and Earth Changed Places (Hayslip) 205
White House Conference on Hate Crimes 194
Wilson, Woodrow 110
women
    educational attainment of 161
    education of 162
    foot binding of 28
    immigration of 28, 48, 49, 51, 63, 76, 122, 158–59, 160
    in Khmer society 16
    in labor force 145, 160, 161
    in Mexican-Sikh marriages 99, 101
    as picture brides 93, 102–3
    in plantation system 62, 69, 84
    Polynesian 57, 58
    and prostitution 48–49
    Sikh 100–101
    Southeast Asian refugees 181
    war brides and fiancées 158–59
Wong, George 194
Won-Joon Yoon 193
Woo, S. B. 202
Woods, Cyrus E. 115
workforce. *See* labor force
Workingman's Party of California (WPC) 43, 44, 51
Workingmen's Union 62
World Trade Center/Pentagon attacks, anti-Asian violence following 195
World War I, Japanese-American troops in 111
World War II
    China-U.S. alliance in 131, 132
    Chinese-American civil rights during 132–33

Chinese-American troops in 131
    Filipino-American troops in 127–30
    Asian Indian–American civil rights during 121
    Japanese-American troops in 140–42
    Japanese internment during. *See* Japanese internment
    Korean-American civil rights during 133–34
    Pearl Harbor attack 126–27
writers 11, 13, 14, 123, 203, 205
writing, Chinese 5, 11
Wu, Eddy 193
Wyoming 50, 93, 94

Y

Yalta Conference 134
Yamaguchi, Kristi 204, 205
Yamashiro, Masayoshi 116
Yamato Colonies 107–9, 144
Yamato dynasty, Japan 11
Yang, Ka Ying 205
Yano Guardianship case 113–14
Yan Than Ly 193
Yasui, Minoru 142, 190, 191
Yasui v. United States 142
"yellow peril" 45–46, 50–51, 88, 110
Yellow Power movement 162–67
Yellow River valley 5
Yi dynasty, Korea 9
yoga 2, 201–2
Yogi, Maharishi Mahesh 163
Yoritomo, Minamoto 11
Young Koreans' Academy 91
youth culture 162–65
Yuan Shih-k'ai 130
Yung Lo 6–7

Z

Zen Buddhism 12, 13
Zheng He 7, 8, 17
Zhou dynasty, China 5